THE END OF EMPIRE

THE END OF EMPIRE

by

JOHN STRACHEY

"In a great pool, a swan's nest."
(*Cymbeline, Act III, Scene 4*)

FREDERICK A. PRAEGER, *Publisher*
New York

BOOKS THAT MATTER

Published in the United States of America in 1964 by
Frederick A. Praeger, Inc., Publisher
111 Fourth Ave., New York 3, N.Y.

The original clothbound edition of this book
was published in 1960 by Random House, Inc., New York.

Library of Congress Catalog Card Number: 64-22498

Manufactured in the United States of America

CONTENTS

PREFACE

THE PRIMARY PURPOSE of this book is to consider Britain's relationship to the world now that her empire is being dissolved.

Part I attempts to convey an adequate impression of what empire has meant to Britain and to the other imperial nations, on the one hand, and to the colonised peoples on the other, during the past 500 years. It attempts to do so by giving, as examples, the story of the British conquest of India, and some episodes in the acquisition of the later British Empire of the last 80 years.

Part II discusses the economic, political and psychological consequences for Britain of the dissolution of her empire in its old form and of the development of the Commonwealth. The possibilities and prospects open to a post-imperial society such as Britain has suddenly become are considered. This is the book's main theme. Next, the possibility of the British, and generally European, imperialist epoch being followed by (a) an American (b) a Russian, or Sino-Russian, or (c) a non-imperialist, epoch, is canvassed. Finally, the question of how the under-developed world can develop on a non-imperial basis is raised.

Part III contains observations upon the practicability of evolving an adequate theory of imperialism.

A note on the way in which the words empire and imperialism are used throughout these pages may be useful. Such definitions should arise out of the argument rather than be laid down in advance. And in fact the justification of my usage is only attempted in Part III, in which different kinds of empires and different periods and motivations of imperialism are distinguished. Because of that postponement it may avoid confusion if I say that I have chosen to mean the following by these two variously used terms. By imperialism I mean the process by which peoples or nations conquer, subdue and then permanently dominate (either *de jure* or *de facto*) other peoples or nations. By empire I mean the state of things in this way established.

This is, after all, the most natural way of using the words. We all speak of the Assyrian, the Roman, the Spanish, the British or the Japanese empires. (And we may or may not come in the future to speak of the American, Russian or Chinese empires.) This shows that usage leaves aside the social structure of the dominating nations and calls imperialist alike the conquests of a relatively simple people of slave owners, such as the Assyrians, and the territorial acquisitions of a highly sophisticated democratic capitalist society such as late nineteenth-century Britain. The question of whether the primary object of such domination is always the economic exploitation, by one means or another, of the subjugated peoples is discussed in several chapters. But again a statement of conclusions is postponed to Part III. Thus my usage only limits the meaning of the words empire and imperialism sufficiently to prevent their being made synonymous with any act of aggression, *i.e.* with war itself. For acts of aggressive war were undertaken freely in pre-civilized periods when, for reasons to be discussed in Part III, the foundation of empires was impracticable. The words imperialism and empire should, therefore, always carry with them the connotation not only of conquest but also of an attempt at continuing domination of one people by another. That minority of readers who, like me, is attracted by questions of theory might read Part III first.

This is the second volume of a study which, taken as a whole, is intended to illustrate the democratic socialist approach to the world's problems in the mid-twentieth century. Readers of this volume will not find that it is directly dependent upon the arguments of the first. Indeed those who have read the first may well, at the outset, wonder what connection the present volume has with it. If they persevere, however, they will find that while the two volumes do not follow each other in linear order, they are joined, like Siamese twins, about the middle. In fact the whole approach here made to the dissolution of imperialism, and to the question of what relationship can be put in its place, is dependent upon the economics set out in the first volume, entitled *Contemporary Capitalism.* Similarly the economics set out in the first volume would remain partial and parochial, confined as they are in the main to considerations which apply only to advanced economies, unless they were supplemented by the world outlook which, in this volume, I strive to set forth.

I may be asked what is the purpose of the expenditure of ink involved in this study. I cannot give a better answer than to quote Mr R. H. S. Crossman's demand for books as nourishment for the democratic socialist movement:

"If I were challenged to say in a single sentence what is wrong with British Socialism, I should reply that it is bookless. The electorate can make do with the kind of popularization possible in an article or a broadcast; those who presume to form public opinion cannot.

Since most Labour politicians and trade union leaders are unable themselves to study the changes in modern society, they need books to keep them in touch with reality. If the books are not there, their 'new thinking' will consist of picking up some new facts and arguments to confirm their old prejudices. There cannot be a vital Socialist Party without a vital Socialist literature." (*The Charm of Politics*, 1958.)

Whether the books of such a literature will in fact succeed in helping their readers to keep in touch with reality is of course another matter. But of the need for someone to try there can be no doubt.

Once again I am deep in debt to my friends and colleagues for their help by way of reading and criticising various drafts of this book. They are: Dr Thomas Balogh, Mr James Callaghan, Mr R. H. S. Crossman, Mr Hugh Gaitskell, Professor John Kenneth Galbraith, Mr Victor Gollancz, Professor Gunnar Myrdal, Mr Reginald Paget, Mr K. M. Panikkar, Mr Paul Sweezy, Professor Arnold Toynbee, my wife and my son. My ex-secretary, the late Miss C. K. Edgley, and my present secretary, Mrs Ruth Sharpe, have not only typed and re-typed but also spotted numerous errors. As in the case of the first volume it is perhaps only necessary to point out that so diverse a list of critics could not possibly be held responsible for anything written here.

JOHN STRACHEY.

PART I

EMPIRE

CHAPTER I

HOW AN EMPIRE IS BUILT

IT IS INDISPENSABLE to grasp the nature of the events by which the nations of Western Europe established their rule over the greater part of the habitable globe. For if we suppose that the European conquests of the last four and a half centuries are now merely of historical interest, we deceive ourselves. The whole climate of opinion of that large majority of the human race which passed in varying degree under imperial rule has been largely formed by the experience. We shall never understand the springs of their present-day actions unless we understand this fact. And unless we come to understand the actions, the passions, the prejudices, the hopes and the ideals of what were so recently the subject peoples, we shall understand very little of the contemporary world.

We shall hardly succeed, however, in getting the feel of modern imperialism if we attempt to retell the story of each conquest. For the result would be a mere catalogue of events giving no sense of what the actual process of empire building was like. A more hopeful method will be to consider one such conquest in some detail. Which empire, however, are we to choose as our illustration? We might choose the Spanish conquests in the Americas. The story of the Conquistadors is the most improbable and perhaps the most bloody. A ship load or two of Europeans totally destroyed several Central and South American civilisations, which were technically primitive, without horse or wheel, but which were yet highly organised into considerable local empires. This is, surely, the most fantastic of all collisions between civilisations at different stages of development.

Nevertheless, this Spanish-American encounter is not particularly significant for the purposes of a study such as this, the main subject of which is the contemporary capitalist empires and their successor societies. The Mexican and Andean societies were swept away by the Spaniards. Several million full-blooded Incas continue, it is true, to inhabit the uplands of Peru. But their elaborate political organisation was quite destroyed, and the new Central and South American bi-racial societies which are at length developing have only a tenuous connection with the societies which existed before the European conquests. Again, before the epoch of the fully capitalist empires began in the second half of the nineteenth century, the Spanish empire of the Indies had itself been dissolved. The Spanish conquests have thus only an indirect and interrupted connection with our main subject.

It will be more fruitful to choose as our example the conquest of India by the British in the second half of the eighteenth century. Indian society of that period was far more highly developed than the local American empires encountered by the Spaniards: indeed, in some respects it was more rather than less developed than the contemporary European states with which it collided. It is true that India was relatively backward in certain respects which turned out to be decisive. On the other hand Indian industrial and commercial techniques in, for example, the production of textiles and in some respects in banking and public finance, were ahead of Europe. In any case, and however we may evaluate the relative development of the two contemporary civilisations, the Indian and the European, when they collided in the sixteenth, seventeenth and eighteenth centuries, there was certainly no yawning gap between them, such as existed in the American and Spanish examples.

Second, Indian society was by no means swept away by the British conquest. It was initially ravaged and deformed but it was also, in the end, unified and developed. Third, the British eighteenth- and early nineteenth-century conquest of India, although a prime example of the establishment of what might be called a mercantile pre-capitalist empire, was transformed without interruption into the core of the late nineteenth- and early twentieth-century British Empire of capitalism proper. Fourth, the independent, post-imperialist Indian society which is developing in the second half of the present century is closely connected both with these eighteenth- and nineteenth-century events and with the ancient and rich history of India before the British conquest. Indeed, the British conquest will be increasingly seen as an important but brief incident in Indian history.

We do not, however, choose the British conquest of India to illustrate modern European imperialism, because this was a particularly outrageous event. On the contrary a British writer may be pardoned for adhering to the view that of all the great imperialisms the British contained the greatest proportion of constructive elements. So if we recall here the story of the initial British acquisition of Bengal, we may depend upon it that most of the other great acts of imperialist conquest were more destructive in their commission and less regenerative in their consequences. For that matter the reader will find, perhaps to his distaste, that it is not the purpose of these pages to blame or to praise British imperialism, or any other. They attempt rather to elucidate its nature and to consider the consequence, for Britain in particular, of its passing. It would indeed be easy to moralise over the history of imperialism, since that history includes some of the most ferocious events in the whole of human development: but it would not be useful. For example, the British empire in India was both iniquitous and beneficent: it was founded by violence, treachery and insatiable avarice, but also by incomparable daring and sustained resolution; it united India: it partitioned India: it industrialised India: it stunted India: it degraded India: it served India: it ravaged India: it created modern India: it was selfish and selfless, ruinous and constructive, glorious and monstrous. Such events cannot usefully be either celebrated or arraigned, but perhaps they can be understood.

Again, there are simpler reasons why it seems to me appropriate to begin a book dealing with imperialism with an account of the conquest of Bengal. For us in Britain this eighteenth-century event lives in a way that none of the other conquests of world imperialism can do. The Black Hole of Calcutta, Clive's feats of arms, Hastings' trial and all the rest, are part of our national folk-lore. Countless British families, exalted and obscure, have served—as mine did—generation by generation in India; their children still see hanging on the walls of their homes this or that memento of the conquest. Thus it is especially desirable for us in Britain to reconsider this historic event. For if we have preserved the story in our folk-lore we have done so in a decidedly one-sided way, to say the least of it. For our own mental health we need to try to get the record straight.

The necessary impulse to write this book arose out of a visit to the independent India of to-day. The book was begun at Calcutta, on the verge of sparse grass which now separates the low brick wall of Fort William, the original trading post of the East India Company in Bengal, from the river Hooghly, or lesser Ganges. It is a place in which a mid-twentieth-century Englishman can hardly refrain from reflecting on the rise and fall of empires. The Hooghly rolls before him; contemporary Calcutta seethes behind his back and upon either hand. It was here that the corner-stone of what became a world-wide empire was laid down. Here, only two hundred years ago there occurred those obscure scuffles between the incompetent Viceroy of a previous empire in India and the forces, not indeed directly of Britain, but of the East India Company. That Company became a robber band. More surprisingly, that robber band evolved into what was probably the most successful of all colonial governments. Finally, in the twentieth century, as the unintended result of these events, Calcutta, and India, have been transformed. Two hundred years ago Calcutta was a settlement of Indian weavers and merchants clustered round a foreign fort. Now it is one of the great cities of the world, a city of four and a half million inhabitants; a city, moreover, exhibiting all the more typical, and least attractive, characteristics of industrialism in its earlier phases. In these vast cities of present-day India, and in her still vaster countryside, the character of the next phase of human history may be to a considerable extent decided. For India may prove to be the balancing factor in an uneasily poised world. Whether democratic institutions and empirical methods of organising social life survive and flourish in the world may depend, as much as upon any other single factor, on whether they survive and flourish in India.

And then finally the story of the conquest of Bengal can be retold for its own sake—simply as one of the supreme stories of history.

For all these reasons, historical, national, personal, political, I turn to Orme, the historian of the first decisive stage of the British conquest of India, rather than to Prescott, the historian of the conquest of the Americas, or to any other of the chroniclers of imperial conquests, as the source of my narrative.[1]

The British conquest of India was originally set in train, it has always seemed to me, by a decision of King James II taken in 1685, three years before his deposition. This decision approved of the East India Company attempting to carry out maritime reprisals for the harrying

[1] An advantage of selecting the British conquest of India as our example is the existence of a first rate contemporary account in Orme's *History of the Military Transactions of the British Nation in Indostan.* Orme was a participant and colleague of Clive's in the process of conquest. He admired Clive passionately and then grew to dislike him, shared in Clive's early adventures, and went home with a pleasant share in the spoils of what he so aptly called Clive's "military transactions". But from first to last Orme was determined to be the Thucydides of the business. In fact he was neither a Thucydides nor even a Prescott. Orme threw up the job after the publication of his account of the clashes in 1756-7. He had quarrelled with Clive and no doubt the whole subject of the conquest was becoming too hot to be handled by "a Nawob" who had come home to England with his share. For our particular purpose, however, all this is more than compensated for by Orme having been an actual eye-witness and participant in many of the events which he describes; from him we know what they really looked and felt like at the time.

of its tiny trading posts on the East and West coasts of India. These posts were at the time suffering at the hands, not so much of the central Indian government of the Great Mogul, as of the provincial representatives of that imperial government. As Orme characteristically puts it, "the Company determined to try what condescensions the effect of arms might produce; and with the approbation of King James the Second, fitted out two fleets, one of which was ordered to cruise at the bar of Surat, on all vessels belonging to the Mogul's subjects". By "cruising on", it should be explained, Orme means attacking, taking, pillaging, blowing out of the water, and generally destroying, every Indian vessel encountered. And this the Company's fleet at the bar of Surat duly did.

This effect of arms duly produced some "condescensions" both from the Mogul's government and from the various Indian provincial authorities. But for a long time it had no other apparent consequences. For the next thirty years the East India Company carried on its commerce in India, sometimes in tolerably good, sometimes in pretty bad, relations with the Indian authorities in the territories in which it had its trading posts or "factories". If anyone had told the British merchants of that day that events had already occurred which would lead their company into making a successful attempt to subvert, and ultimately occupy, the Mogul Empire itself, he would have been deemed demented. For this, it must be recalled, was still the India of a functioning empire. Until 1707 Aurungzeeb, a fully effective Mogul emperor of a largely unified India, still reigned at Delhi. And for some thirty years after his death in that year the fabric of the empire, which had been established by Babar's conquests about the turn of the fifteenth and sixteenth centuries, was still in existence.

Nevertheless, during the first half of the eighteenth century there occurred a progressive loosening of the Mogul imperial structure. One by one the major provinces of India, and Bengal in particular, were becoming more like independent states, their viceroys, or "Nawobs", approximating to kings by right of conquest or succession, a right which the Mogul Emperor at Delhi confirmed rather than bestowed. And in Bengal, in the second decade of the eighteenth century, the East India Company as a consequence of this disintegration began to run into growing trouble. The reigning Nawob of Bengal, Jaffier Khan, began the familiar process of making exactions on the Company, since he saw in the Company's wealth a source of revenue. On this occasion the Company sought redress, not, as previously, from an "effect of arms", but by despatching what Orme calls "an embassy of complaint" to the Nawob of Bengal's overlord, the reigning Mogul, Furrakshir[1] at Delhi. The Company chose two of its ablest factors, by name John Surman and Edward Stephenson, to lead this important mission. And on July 8th, 1715, after a march of three months, the two Englishmen and their party reached Delhi from Calcutta.

We must recollect that in 1715 it cannot have seemed certain or even probable that the dissolution of the Mogul Empire was at hand. There had often previously been rebellious provinces, civil wars, disputed successions, Afghan invasions and general disorders. But these disturbances had always hitherto been overcome by the accession of a vigorous emperor. Who could say that there would be no recovery this time? In 1715 an emperor still sat upon the peacock throne in the great audience chamber in the Red Fort at Delhi. This was the chamber on the jewelled walls of which was—and still is—inscribed that most vehement of the inscriptions of hedonism—"if there is a paradise on earth, it is here! it is here! it is here!" Within the enclosure of the Red Fort, itself a kind of Kremlin or inner city, the fountains still ran with rose water, the shrubs were still nourished with milk and honey, and across the vast quadrangles the Vizier, the reigning favourites, the generals, the courtiers, the eunuchs, the seraglio, the household slaves, all paced or scurried throughout their intricate lives. Without the walls of the Red Fort the vast capital city of Delhi, sustained by the revenues of the sub-continent, and containing bankers, merchants, zemindars, nobles, priests, incomparable weavers and highly skilled artisans of all sorts, presented the spectacle of a highly developed society. Besides the Delhi of the Moguls the London of 1715 must have seemed in many respects a country town.

Nevertheless Messrs. Surman and Stephenson were by no means overawed. On the contrary, they set themselves down to the task of pestering (since they had few other means) the Mogul and his ministers into giving the East India Company what we should now call "extra-territorial rights" for their commerce and their establishment in Bengal. But why, we may well ask, should the Emperor have even considered granting them such precious, and perilous, privileges? Why should he have dreamt of exempting this foreign company from the taxation, and in effect from the jurisdiction, of his own viceroy, the Nawob of Bengal? What were Mr Surman and Mr Stephenson but insignificant foreign merchants backed by neither a finance nor a

[1] Unless there is some special reason to the contrary, I retain Orme's spelling of Indian names. It is often very different from what we now adopt. For example, we call this Mogul Farakhsiyar.

force which could conceivably threaten the position of the great Mogul if he simply sent them about their business?

And yet the Emperor did not do so. The two "ambassadors of complaint" had come supplied with considerable presents, not only for the Mogul himself, but for any member of his court who seemed worth bribing. In the event our two pertinacious fellow countrymen stayed in Delhi, working on the Mogul's court with a relentless persistence of corruption for two whole years. They bribed the Vizier to overrule the favourite; then they bribed the favourite to overrule the Vizier; at one moment they received a *firman*, or ukase, granting the whole of their demands, only to find on examination that it was issued under the seal of the Vizier and not under that of the Emperor. As such it would have been worthless in Bengal. They returned the firman and demanded the Emperor's seal. They waited for six months while the Emperor's son was getting married and no business could be transacted. They waited while the Emperor went campaigning against the Sikhs. They bribed the court eunuch, only to find that he was the wrong eunuch. They used the very last of their money to bribe what they hoped would prove to be the right eunuch. And then suddenly, they did not know why, they got all they were asking for, and got it under the Emperor's own seal.

According to Orme it was not that they had at last found the right eunuch to bribe. What had happened was that the Indian provincial authorities on the West coast had suddenly sent word to Delhi that the Company's merchants at Surat had withdrawn to Bombay and shut up their "factory".[1] Now this was what they had done—for safety—nearly thirty years before when the Company's fleet had "cruised on" the Mogul's commerce. The effect of this naval reprisal had been so devastating that it was still remembered and dreaded. Both the provincial and the imperial authorities thought that the Englishmen's new withdrawal from Surat meant that another fleet was on its way from Britain to ravage their commerce in the Indian Ocean. Rather than face that, they gave the "ambassadors of complaint" what they asked for. But it was all a mistake. There was no fleet on its way from Britain. The Company's representatives at Surat had withdrawn to Bombay merely because business was so bad at Surat that it was not worth keeping the place open. Thus in muddle and misapprehension the fatal *firman* was issued, and the Company obtained its

[1] All that "the right eunuch" had done was to get advance news of this and so put himself into a position of being able to foretell that the embassy's petition would be granted. He got his money, as many another has done, by means of being well informed "before the market opened".

extra-territorial rights in Bengal: those rights which were to prove nothing less than the beginning of the end of the independence of India.[1]

The story of "the embassy of complaint" is worth telling for a number of reasons, but above all because it illustrates the interlocking strands of daring, corruption, resolution, violence and chicanery used by the British; and equally, it must be said, it illustrates the folly, pusillanimity, panic, and, above all, administrative incompetence manifested by the contemporary Indian authorities.[2] It was to be the combination of these factors which led to the otherwise inconceivable event of the conquest. Moreover the story of "the embassy of complaint" illustrates the respective positions of the Company and the Mogul Empire immediately before their decisive encounter. The Company was able to harry the empire's sea-borne commerce, if its own commerce was too much harried on land. But so far as the sub-continent itself was concerned, the Company was still not dreaming of doing more than sending what was, formally at least, a humble embassy to Delhi.

Then again it must be remembered that the Mogul's imperial government, ever since it had been established two hundred and fifty years before, had been dealing, largely through its provincial authorities, with the Europeans. As K. M. Panikkar reminds us, in his major work,[3] the Portuguese in particular had been all this time in far closer commercial and political contact with India than had been the British. And no harm had come of trading with the Portuguese, or even of allowing them to acquire an appreciable bit of Indian territory at Goa (a far larger settlement than anything which seemed in question at Calcutta). The Mogul authorities cannot have had the slightest inkling that the British traders intended to subvert them, for indeed they did not so intend, any more than had done the Portuguese. But history was to take its own course. And that course led to the still

---

[1] Here I am simply following Orme. K. M. Panikkar, one of the highest authorities on Indian history, is completely sceptical of Orme's assertion that it was the memory of the Surat naval attack which influenced the Mogul. He considers it far more likely that it was simple bribery that did the trick. At any rate, for whatever reason, the grant of "extra-territoriality" was made.

[2] See below, as to the need for British and Indian students to write of each others' pasts without circumlocution and false tact.

[3] *Asia and Western Dominance*, by K. M. Panikkar, successively Indian Ambassador to China, Egypt and France, Allen and Unwin, 30s. (1953). This is one of those rare books the appearance of which is itself an historical event. For, to quote the concluding words of Panikkar's own Introduction, "this is perhaps the first attempt by an Asian student to see and understand European activities in Asia for 450 years".

mysterious event of the conquest of a vast empire by an only moder-
ately successful trading company, intermittently supported by the
government of a European state of the second rank, itself inhabited by
less than six million people.[1]

All this, however, lay in the future. For the years immediately ahead
the grant of extra-territoriality in Bengal, as a result of the embassy of
complaint, did not seem to be having any fatal consequences. Just as
"cruising on" the Mogul's commerce in the sixteen eighties had had
no far-reaching consequences till thirty years later, so the grant to the
embassy of complaint in 1715 of "extra-territoriality" for the Company
in Bengal, did not produce any dramatic developments for a further
period of forty years. The explanation of this delayed action effect is
that it so happened that during most of that time Bengal was governed
by a competent Nawob (nominally as viceroy of the Mogul, but by
now as half independent prince) named Alleverdi Khan. Alleverdi
appointed his own successor, his nephew Surajah Dowlah, and this
act proved to be the next link in the chain of causation which led to
the conquest. For the young man was notoriously so incompetent and
unpleasant that important factions of the Indian ruling classes of Bengal
immediately felt compelled to back rival pretenders. There was nothing
unusual in such a disputed succession. But on this occasion a new and
extraneous element was introduced into the struggle. The foreigners
established, albeit still precariously, on their extra-territorial strip of
land beside the Hooghly decided to take a hand. No doubt they felt
that they had to; an impossible nawob was as great a menace to them as
to the other important interest in the province. At any rate, Mr Drake,
the Governor of the Company's establishments in Bengal, became
involved in this initially purely Indian conspiracy. He backed one of
the pretenders and used his extra-territorial rights to give that pretender
sanctuary in the Company's fortified area in and around Fort William
at Calcutta.[2]

[1] Surajah Dowlah, the Nawob of Bengal whom Clive overthrew, was to say that he
did not believe that there were 10,000 people in all Europe. He was a long way out;
nevertheless he was right in supposing that the British themselves were so small a people
that he *should* have been able to brush them off with the greatest of ease.
[2] I am following Orme's account. Mr A. Mervyn Davies, Clive's most recent biographer (see *Clive of Plassey*, by A. Mervyn Davies, Nicholson and Watson, 1939) does not
mention this surely decisive *casus belli*. Nor does Macaulay in his famous essay on Clive,
in which he otherwise follows Orme closely. Apparently British writers have been
reluctant to admit that the Company was a party to the conspiracy, so that Surajah Dowlah
had an adequate reason for attacking Calcutta. There seems no reason for doubting Orme's
story: after all, he and he alone was there in India at the time. Thompson and Garrett in

It fell out, however, that the Surajah Dowlah was initially successful. None of the pretenders showed any fight and he was able to establish himself upon the *musnud*, or vice-regal throne, of Bengal. He immediately and not unnaturally determined to deal with the one pretender who was still in the field, since he had taken shelter in Calcutta. This determination led to Surajah Dowlah's attack upon Fort William in June 1756, to the fall of the Fort, to the Black Hole of Calcutta and thus to what seemed to the British in Bengal their total ruin.

The story of the Black Hole of Calcutta is of high interest to the student of political psychology. The British prisoners who were captured when Fort William fell to the Nawob's army were crowded into the Fort's own guard-room or jail and during one night most of them perished miserably. Several considerations should be taken into account in any discussion of this celebrated event. First, the atrocity could not have happened but for the conduct of half the garrison of Fort William which fled, led by the Governor, in the middle of the siege, leaving the other half at the mercy of the besiegers. This does nothing to condone Surajah Dowlah. But it is not a factor which is given much emphasis in the British tradition. Second, Surajah Dowlah had no intention of murdering or torturing his captives. He couldn't have cared less what happened to them. They were shut up in the Fort's prison, simply because no one had any idea of what to do with them. The fact that only 20 out of 146 survived the night in their own horribly overcrowded prison was a result of contemporary Bengali inefficiency and indifference rather than malice. Third, the casual and accidental slaughter of 126 Europeans, or of 126 Indians either, in the Bengal of the seventeen-fifties was in itself an event of minute importance to contemporary Indian opinion. Fourth, the slaughter of 126 British, whether accidental or deliberate, might well have made no particular impression in Britain. It might just as easily have been regarded as the sort of thing that happened in that sort of trading enterprise in the East.

Why, then, has every British schoolboy heard of the Black Hole of

their *Rise and Fulfilment of British Rule in India* (Macmillan, 1934) agree that the Company was in the conspiracy to dethrone Surajah Dowlah almost from the start. No doubt it had to be. This was just after the "Mahratta Ditch" was dug. The Mahratta ditch was a considerable defensive moat which the Company began to dig (but failed to complete) round its whole extra-territorial area at Calcutta, on the excuse (quite a good one) of self-protection against the Mahratta raids which, in the growing chaos of the times, were becoming a menace. But equally its digging marked the next step: the step from extra-territoriality to the fortification, not just of a trading post but of a piece of territory. The twentieth-century visitor to Calcutta will have the Mahratta ditch pointed out to him by historically-minded Bengali hosts, as it winds its way through industrial Calcutta, looking like a disused canal.

Calcutta? The answer is that this incident was made into the centre-piece of one of the first great atrocity campaigns of modern times. With a virtuosity which could teach our contemporary exponents of political warfare many a lesson, the spokesmen of the East India Company made the need to avenge the Black Hole the psychological mainspring of their campaign to gather public support for a forward policy in India. And so this queer little, although quite genuine, atrocity has found its way into British folk-lore. The twentieth-century student, gorged with horrors which make the Black Hole sound like a tea party, can only wonder how it was ever possible to make the deaths, however tragic and undeserved, of 126 men and women—not half an hour's input for the ovens of Auschwitz—the excuse for the conquest of a sub-continent. In fact, of course, that conquest either needed no excuse or was inexcusable. It is a curious reflection on the workings of the British mind that successive genera-tions of us have always clung to the idea that somehow or other "we had to do it" because of the Black Hole. All this, of course, is not to overlook the degenerate character of much of eighteenth-century Bengali society. It is one of the worst effects of foreign conquest that it causes the subject people to idealise even the worst periods of their own independent pasts. Thus many Indian readers may feel that these pages make intolerably outspoken comments on the eighteenth-century Indian governments with which the Europeans collided. But they should note that comments at least as outspoken are made on my fellow countrymen. Is it not now time, ten years after the achievement of Indian independence, for British and Indian writers alike to treat our respective pasts without diplomacy?

It is interesting to contrast the reaction of the Company to the fall of Calcutta in 1756 with the reaction of the Mogul Empire to the Company's reprisal on the Imperial shipping off Surat half a century earlier. Few catastrophies could have been greater for the Company than the fall of Calcutta. The Nawob had taken the Company's establishment in Bengal with an army of 50,000 men: much of the garrison had fled shamefully. Nevertheless "the gentlemen at Madras", as Orme calls them, i.e., the Company's servants at Fort St George at Madras in Southern India, the nearest point from which help could come to Calcutta, did not hesitate for a moment before launching their counter-blow. They did not hesitate in spite of the fact that the forces at their disposal must have seemed preposterously inadequate for waging war against the government of Bengal. They had, it is true, more or less at their disposal, a considerable naval force of five of His

Majesty's ships of the line. These, however, had been provided by the Crown to fight, not the Bengal government, which in any case could not be effectively got at from the sea, but the French. For the British were by no means the only European people attempting to increase their power and wealth in India in the mid-eighteenth century. On the contrary, the French in 1756 appeared to be well ahead of them. In Bengal the French were firmly established at Chandanagore, a few miles up the river from Calcutta, and had not quarrelled with the Bengal government. In Southern India they possessed in Pondicherry a better factory than Madras, and had been conducting, partly directly and partly by proxy, a series of, on the whole, successful little wars against the British. As it happened, the gentlemen at Madras were just expecting another bout of war with the French when they received the appeal of the fugitives from Calcutta. It is all the more remarkable that they decided to send off almost all of both their land and sea forces to Bengal. On this counterstroke they staked everything with really breath-taking temerity: and in the event they won everything.

Their land forces were minute. There was one regular battalion of infantry (Aldercron's), plus a few guns and an extremely scratch force, part European, part Indian—in all less than 1,000 men. The prospect of taking on the government of Bengal in full-scale war with such forces as these did not dismay these remarkable adventurers. And yet that government was, at least on paper, one of the most powerful of the contemporary world, with financial and military resources equal to those of a first-rate European power of the time. All this, however, merely steeled the purpose of the gentlemen at Madras. As well as fitting out their Bengal expedition, they sent off despatches to London, in which, far from minimising the Bengal disaster, they began the process of erecting the Black Hole atrocity into a great propaganda set-piece. It must be recalled that public opinion in Britain was anti-imperialist on the whole, and was unlikely to take kindly to the idea of a British chartered company waging war on a major foreign government. It is very doubtful whether, without the propaganda which the Black Hole atrocity made possible, the Company could have got the sanction, let alone the minimum necessary measure of support, for the wars of aggression which it was to wage almost uninterruptedly for the next seven or eight decades.

How are we to account for such ferocious resolution on the part of the gentlemen at Madras in face of the catastrophe which had befallen their colleagues in Bengal? This is a crucial question, for it was above

all, in my view, because the British traders reacted in that summer of
1756 to the Calcutta disaster in this astonishing way that the otherwise
inexplicable event of the conquest of India took place.

What was it which drove these men to take their extraordinary
decision? Their motives were, as usual, indescribably mixed: but we
must not forget the immense direct personal and pecuniary stake which
each one of them had in the issue. For example, in rather disputed
command of their little expeditionary force was Robert Clive, who a
few years before had been a young civilian clerk in the Company's
Madras factory, but who had turned amateur soldier and had performed dazzling feats of arms in the little wars of Southern India.
He really had been, as we all learnt at school, a boys' story sort of
hero if ever there was one. But Clive had also, as every British schoolboy is less emphatically informed, made £40,000[1] out of the contract
which the Company had given him for providing the commissariat of
their army of Madras. Think what that amount of money meant to
Clive, who was still only 31, and who ten years before had arrived at
Madras as an unpromising clerk in the Company's employment, with
only his mortgaged Shropshire manor, his spendthrift father, his un-
marriageable sisters, and his own dark passions, to his name. He and
every one of the other gentlemen at Madras knew that for them
personally everything was at stake. Seldom in human history has a
small, chance-picked body of men had so much actual cash to gain and
to lose.

However, when all this is realised there still remains something unaccountable about their decision. We may think of the decision to
attack Bengal on the part of that group of British traders and military
and naval officers at Madras as marking the moment in history when a
dæmonic will to conquer and to rule seized the British, an imperial
will which possessed them for the next two centuries. After all, until the
middle of the eighteenth century the British had been, in Asia and
Africa, mere adventurous traders, and in North America peasant
settlers. The true empire-builders had been the Spanish and the
Portuguese. This extraordinary expedition to Bengal was something
relatively new in British history. It is a main theme of these pages that
this will to empire is now leaving us, and that it is most fortunate that

---

[1] It will be important, in order to grasp the realities of the situation, to be able to
translate the purchasing power of the pound in the seventeen-fifties into contemporary
nineteen-fifties values. Economic historians whom I have consulted point out that objects
of expenditure have varied so widely during the period that it is difficult to make a
comparison. But taking such things as a nawob would buy—food, clothing, houses,
personal service—I am informed that a multiplier of at least 10 is appropriate. So Clive,
before ever he went to Bengal, had made some £400,000 in our money.

this is so: for in the changed relation of world forces the assertion of such an imperial will could now lead us only to national disaster.[1]

The story of Clive's conquest of Bengal is wonderful. But we are often given a very bowdlerised version of it. Clive's own characterisation of it, when he sent his papers to Orme for immortalisation, cannot be bettered. Here, he wrote, Orme would find the record of "Fighting, tricks, chicanery, intrigues, politics and the Lord knows what; in short, there will be a fine Field for you to display your genius in".

As a matter of fact, there were more tricks, chicanery, intrigues and politics than fighting. At the outset of the expedition in the autumn of 1756 Fort William at Calcutta was easily recaptured. For the men-of-war under Admiral Watson of the Royal Navy could get up the river, and the ill-manned, ill-furnished mud forts of the Bengal government on the banks of the river could not withstand their guns. But no sooner had Calcutta been recaptured than Surajah Dowlah came back with his army of 50,000 men. There must have seemed to be very little reason why he should not again succeed in capturing the city and Fort William itself. True, the British land and sea forces were now a little more considerable. But the difference ought not to have been nearly enough to turn the issue. The event was decided however on the reactions of the British and Indian leaders respectively to the actual clash of arms. As soon as the Nawob's army marched in, Clive, with his few hundred men, one early morning of fog, raided and beat up the great camp which the Nawob and his generals had formed outside Fort William. Neither Clive nor his men thought that the action had been a success. They incurred serious casualties to their little force, and seemed to have effected very little. Yet in fact they had effected everything. For, according to Orme, they got physically near enough to the tent and person of Surajah Dowlah, who was one of those rather rare human beings who have been extreme physical cowards, to scare the

[1] It is one of the commonest distortions of the materialist conception of history to allege that this theory holds that men always act in their own personal pecuniary interests. What this view of history does assert as to human motivation is that men have, on the whole, acted in the interests of the social class or group to which they have belonged; that they have acted as slave-owners or slaves: as landlords or as peasants: as employers or as wage earners, rather than as individuals happening to hold this or that set of opinions arrived at by a process of intellection. They have usually (though not invariably) acted, that is to say, in their group or class, rather than in their individual, interests. Thus the theory fully recognises that class or national motivations (or the two intertwined) have often led men to sacrifice their own personal interests, even to the point of giving up their fortunes or their lives. There have, however, been a few exceptional moments in history in which the motive of direct personal enrichment, acting powerfully upon a few key figures, has been important: and this was pre-eminently one of these moments.

wits out of him. Apparently, the Nawob was so frightened that he withdrew with his whole army, leaving the Company in undisputed possession of Calcutta.[1]

This, however, was only the very beginning of the struggle. Few, if any, of the Company's officers as yet envisaged the conquest and annexation of Bengal—let alone, of course, of India. On the other hand, they did consider that they could and must remove Surajah Dowlah from the *musnud*. For what made him vulnerable was not their still tiny force but the fact that he had never been an acceptable Nawob to Bengal society. Not only had his succession been disputed from the outset but he was still opposed in secret by an important faction of his Moslem nobles, by almost all of his Hindu ministers and administrators, and, in particular, by the Seats, the great Hindu merchants and bankers of his capital, Murishidabad. Accordingly what Clive and his gentlemen did was to take up again the threads of the conspiracy to dethrone him, and put any suitable pretender in his place.

The details of the conspiracy (Orme always uses this word) must not be our concern, although they are incomparably fascinating and lurid. It was a four-cornered affair in which were pitted, in shifting alliances and deadly antagonisms (1) Clive and the British, (2) Surajah Dowlah, (3) The Indian (both Moslem and Hindu) conspirators against him, and (4) the French. For the French, as we have noted, had a large fortified factory of their own in Bengal, a little way further up the Hooghly at Chandernagore. The first essential for Clive was to prevent Surajah Dowlah and the French from combining against him, for together they could certainly have crushed him. This he succeeded in doing, thanks to his own consummate chicanery, the irresolution of the Nawob, which bordered on feeble-mindedness, and the over-caution and passivity of the French. Here again, as in the case of Surman's and Stephenson's embassy of complaint the Indians seem to have been simply pestered— as well as bribed—into doing something that was obviously fatal to their own vital interests. Clive somehow succeeded in making the Nawob allow the British to attack the French without interference,

---

[1] We must dismiss, however, any suggestion that the British conquest can be accounted for by superior courage. For the simple fact is that the conquest was largely carried out by Indian troops. Indians, both at Plassey and Buxar and at every other major engagement, formed the bulk of the victorious as well as the defeated armies. Superior resolution on the part of the European leaders, on the other hand, was a factor of great importance. True, Governor Drake ran away at Calcutta almost as disgracefully as Surajah Dowlah ran away at Plassey. Still, the Indian leaders were by and large far the less resolute. This applied above all to the supreme leaders on each side, and also no doubt to the subordinate commanders at what we should now call "general officer" level, but hardly to the regimental and company officers, for it will be recalled that in Clive's victorious Sepoy army many of these were themselves Bengalis.

the Nawob was cajoled, as much, it almost seems, by the sheer will-power of Clive, as by the wholesale bribing of his generals and agents, which, of course, Clive did not neglect to undertake.

On March 23rd (1757) Chandernagore, which could just be reached by the British ships of the line under Admiral Watson, was duly blown to bits by them, although not without a furious and bloody action. With the French thus eliminated, Clive was free to pursue the conspiracy. But he could not get very far with it until suddenly he heard that a certain Mir Jaffier, one of the Nawob's generals and the greatest Moslem nobleman in Bengal, was willing to betray the Nawob and join forces with the Company in return for being made Nawob if the conspiracy succeeded. Now all the pieces began to fall into place. In addition to the Seat brothers, most of the Hindu administrators who ran the province for its Moslem rulers had been contacted, bribed and were favourable in various degrees.

Clive was here beginning to undo the, on the whole, successful symbiosis of contemporary Indian society. That society was a sort of partnership between the Moslem conquerors, who had taken the country two hundred years before, and the previously existing Hindu governing class. The Moslems almost monopolised the possessions of actual physical power: they held the Nawobship and most of the high posts in the army. But the Hindus ran the country for them. For the Hindus alone had the secrets of Indian high finance at their fingertips. To what extent the Hindus still felt the Moslems to be foreign conquerors, not necessarily nor particularly to be preferred to the Europeans, it is difficult to say. The answer seems to be that they felt this by no means completely, but yet sufficiently for Clive (and his successors) to be able usually to support the Hindu interest against the Moslems. The Hindu administrators, to some extent at least, seem to have felt that in co-operating with the British they risked merely a change of masters.

Clive had been using one of the most picturesque of these Hindu notables, a millionaire merchant named Omichund, as his chief agent in the conspiracy. Mir Jaffier himself was on the point of signing an elaborate treaty with the Company, promising to pay it vast sums and to give equally vast "presents" to individuals (nominally by way of reparations for the damage done by Surajah Dowlah at Calcutta) if and when their combined efforts to make him Nawob succeeded. Things had got to this point and then they stalled. Neither Mir Jaffier nor anyone else dared actually to start the revolt. Clive and his small forces were lying in an exposed position near Chandernagore, about a third of the way up the Hooghly from Calcutta, their base, to Murishidabad, the Nawob's capital and their objective. Sooner rather than later the British would have either to attack or to retreat. But even Clive had never contemplated plunging into the interior of Bengal with under 3,000 men (he had by this time added some 2,000 predominantly native Bengali troops to the 1,000 men he had brought from Madras) to pit against 50,000, until and unless some considerable Indian rebel had openly raised his standard against the Nawob.

The stifling weeks of the early summer of 1757 went by. For this was still less than a year after Surajah Dowlah had taken Calcutta. The rainy season, when it was thought that it would be impossible to move, came nearer and nearer. At this moment of extreme suspense Clive's principal agent, Omichund, resorted to blackmail. Unless, he calmly intimated, he was given a 5% rake-off on the total spoils (he would have got 2 million rupees) he would divulge the conspiracy to the Nawob. But if Omichund supposed that in Clive he was faced by a simple soldier, he was horribly mistaken. Clive met his move rather easily. The basic document of the conspiracy was a treaty in which was recorded what each party was to get in cash in the event of success. Clive had two copies made of this treaty, one on white paper, one on red. The white paper was the genuine agreement and it said nothing about any 5% rake-off for Omichund. The red paper treaty alone mentioned the rake-off. Clive and his immediate colleagues (except Admiral Watson, who had scruples and whose signature was accordingly forged on the red treaty) and Mir Jaffier signed both treaties, but had a tacit agreement that the red treaty was null and void. This dealt with the Omichund situation.

The position of the conspirators was nevertheless becoming more and more desperate. Inevitably news of the conspiracy was beginning to spread. Everyone in Murishidabad seemed to know about it except the Nawob, and even he was becoming suspicious. Yet neither Mir Jaffier nor any of the other Indian conspirators would come out into open revolt. It was in this situation that Clive took the decision to advance on his own towards Murishidabad. Even now, however, he moved essentially in the hope that his indispensable but timid allies, the potential rebels, would be stirred to action. Still nothing happened, except that Mir Jaffier, who himself commanded a large part of the Nawob's army, sent Clive continual secret letters, sewn up in the heels of slippers and so on, in the best conspiratorial style, but entirely equivocal in content.

Finally, Clive's force reached the point of no return. They had either to cross the river, the lesser Ganges, after which they could not go back, or to retreat on Calcutta. After the well-known agonies of indecision in the Mango Grove, Clive crossed. The Nawob's 50,000 men were entrenched at Plassey. There was still, on the day of battle itself (June 23rd, 1757), no indication of on which side Mir Jaffier and his part of the Nawob's army would fight. In the event they stayed neutral. The battle itself was a muddle, almost a farce. For as soon as his troops began to suffer a few casualties Surajah Dowlah again lost his head, panicked and fled. His army then fled also. His 50,000 men were pursued by Clive's 3,000. Clive advanced on Murishidabad and proclaimed Mir Jaffier Nawob. In the twelve months from June 1756 to June 1757 Clive and the Company had taken all effective power in Bengal into their hands.

CHAPTER II

". . . SUCH A PRIZE IN SOLID MONEY . . ."

THE FIRST THING that Clive did after he had got his man, Mir Jaffier, on to the throne of Bengal was to put through one of the most remarkable pay-offs in history. As an incidental part of that pay-off it was necessary to deal with his unreliable agent, Omichund. A famous page of Orme, describing the final confrontation of Clive and Omichund, still conveys an unsurpassed impression of the times.

When Clive got to Murishidabad a conference between him and the new Nawob, Mir Jaffier, took place at the great town-house of the Hindu bankers, the Seats, who had, cautiously, assisted the conspiracy. For the Hindu Minister, or Diwan, Roydoolub, whom Mir Jaffier had taken on from the Surajah Dowlah régime, had at once said that there was not enough money in the treasury to fulfil the promises to the British contained in the treaty between Clive and the new Nawob. The Seats were accordingly asked to arbitrate. Omichund came hopefully along to the conference, relying on the dummy red treaty and expecting his 5%. Orme writes:

"Omichund, who was attending, followed, thinking himself at this very time, in as high a degree of estimation with Clive, as any one who had contributed to the revolution; but, on his arrival at the *Seats*, finding that he was not invited to the carpet where the others were in conference, he sat down at a distance near the outward part of the hall.

"The treaties, as written in Persic and English, were read, explained, and acknowledged. After much conversation, Roydoolub insisting always on the scantiness of the treasury, it was agreed that one half of the money stipulations should be paid immediately; two thirds of this half in coin, and one third in jewels, plate, and effects, at a valuation; but that the other half should be discharged in three years at three equal payments; Roydoolub was allowed a commission of five in the hundred on the sums for restitution, which amounted to 17,700,000 rupees, and this was one of the gratuities which had been held out to Omichund. The conference being ended, Clive and Scrafton went towards Omichund, who was waiting in full assurance of hearing the glad tidings of his good fortune; when Clive said, 'It is now time to undeceive Omichund:' on which, Scrafton said to him in the Indostan language, 'Omichund, the red paper is a trick; you are to have nothing.' These words overpowered him like a blast of sulphur. . . . Grounded on his importance, by knowing the secret, he held out the terror of betraying it, to secure his own advantages. Whether he would have betrayed it, if refused, is uncertain: for part of his fortune was in the power of the English, and he had the utmost vengeance of Jaffier and his confederates to fear. However, the experiment was not to be tried. But, on the other hand, as his tales and artifices prevented Surajah Dowlah from believing the representations of his most trusty servants, who early suspected, and at length were convinced, that the English were confederated with Jaffier; the 2,000,000 of rupees he expected should have been paid to him, and he left to enjoy them in oblivion and contempt" (pp. 181-3, Vol. II).

We may agree with Orme's final offhand sentence. Why not have paid off the double-crosser? After all, and as it happened, he double-crossed his own prince and not Clive. But beyond that what is there to say? And yet oceans of ink have been spilt, almost from that day to this, on a controversy begun before a House of Commons Committee of Inquiry, into the morality or immorality of Clive's treatment of Omichund.

On the level of morality could any discussion be more barren? Clive and Omichund were almost perfectly amoral beings. Omichund was subtle, but Clive was both subtle and ferocious, and the subtle and ferocious man destroyed the man who was subtle only. That is all. And yet on another level there was something redeeming about the fact that eighteenth-century British public opinion was capable of being shocked by Clive's ruthless deception of Omichund, or, to take another example, by Hastings' judicial murder (if such it was) of Nuncomar, and in general by the inevitable concomitants of acquiring an empire. Of course the parliamentary proceedings, the Select Committees, the state trials and the public controversy all became, to a lesser or greater extent, moves in the British party political struggle. Nor did all the righteous indignation bear any particular fruit, immediately, for the subjugated Indians. The conquest proceeded with all its outrages. But yet the very fact that there were protests kept standards of conduct other than those of naked force or total deception alive: and in the end these other standards of conduct were to bear fruit both for Britain and for India.

We may test these assertions by comparing the British attitude, with all its hypocrisy and inconsistency, with the deadly logic of Dutch imperialism in Indonesia. For example, the sixteenth-century Dutch founder of Batavia made the following defence of his conduct: "May not a man in Europe do what he likes with his cattle? Even so, does the master here do with his men, for everywhere, these with all that belong to them, are as much property of the master, as are the brute beasts in the Netherlands. The law of this land is the will of the king and he is king who is the strongest" (quoted by Panikkar, op. cit., p. 111). It is to be feared that Dutch policy in Indonesia was founded on this view, faithfully reflected it for many decades, and never became wholly free of it right up to the loss of Indonesia in 1946. Experience shows moreover that the difference between the Dutch and British attitudes really was important for the subject peoples. To measure their respective consequences we have only to compare the degree of successful self-government achieved in present-day India and Indonesia, and in particular their respective attitudes to Britain and Holland. So Burke's outpourings, Sheridan's vapourings, Fox's posturing, Grey and Wilberforce's sanctimoniousness, even Francis' venom, and all the rest of the apparently preposterous Whig proceedings, in Westminster Hall at the trial of Warren Hastings, and elsewhere, served a vital purpose. They did not get the Whigs into office (which, no doubt was the direct object of the exercise), but they did keep alive in Britain the view that the Indians were not simply our cattle. Panikkar (op. cit., p. 118) comes to the following verdict upon Dutch and British imperialism respectively:

"The British for a short period of fifteen years in Bengal established a robber state where, without reference to the rights of others, they freely plundered and looted under cover of their 'rights', but even during that period the Indian merchants were not interfered with[1] and the public had the right even of protesting in public as we have seen. The Dutch alone of the European nations in the East carried out a policy which systematically reduced the whole population to the status of plantation labour, without recognising any moral or legal obligation to them."

The question of whether Omichund was to get his 5% or not, on

[1] Panikkar is in one sense being rather generous here. It is quite true that even during the 15 years of the "robber state" the Indian merchants were not interfered with physically: but they were systematically driven out of business (as we shall see immediately) by British merchants and their agents who traded free of all taxation.

that June day of 1757, was, however, a mere detail, both materially and morally, in that gigantic "military transaction" which Clive was conducting in Bengal. Only twelve months, from June 1756 to June 1757, had elapsed, and yet the British in Bengal had been transformed from helpless fugitives to the effective rulers of the country. Another page of Orme's (which confirms the impression that he might have stood in the very first rank of historians if he had finished his work) gives an account of the reactions of the gentlemen at Calcutta to this portentous fact.

"The news of the battle of Plassey was brought to Calcutta on the 25th of June in a letter from Colonel Clive to Mr Drake, the governor, who immediately communicated it to the council. The victory was deemed decisive; and all restraints of secrecy being now removed, the purport of the treaties were immediately revealed by the members of the council to all they met. In a few minutes all the inhabitants of the town, impatient to hear or tell, were in the streets. The restitution of public and private property; the donations to the squadron, the army, and individuals; the grants to the company; the privileges to the English commerce; the comparison of the prosperity of this day with the calamities in which the colony was overwhelmed at this very season in the preceding year: in a word, this sudden reverse and profusion of good fortune intoxicated the steadiest minds, and hurried everyone into the excesses of intemperate joy, even envy and hatred forgot their energies, and were reconciled, at least for a while, to familiarity and good-will; for every one saw that his own portion of advantages was intimately and inseparably blended with that of every other person in the settlement."

"The first care", Orme continues, of the British "... was to get the money stipulated by the treaties. ... This treasure was packed up in 700 chests, and laden in 100 boats, which proceeded under the care of soldiers to Nudiah; from whence they were escorted by all the boats of the squadron, and many others, proceeding with banners displayed and musik sounding, as a triumphal procession, to contrast that in which the inhabitants of the Ganges had seen Surajah Dowlah returning the year before from the destruction of Calcutta. Never before did the English nation at one time obtain such a prize in solid money; for it amounted (in the mint) to 800,000 pounds sterling. From real or pretended difficulties, no more money was received until the 9th of August, when Roydoolub paid 1,655,358 rupees; and on the 30th of the same month he delivered gold, jewels, and cash, amounting to 1,599,737 rupees: the three payments amounted to 10,765,737 rupees" (Orme, Vol. II, pp. 187-8).

The "prize in solid money" went partly to the Company and partly to individuals, starting with Clive who, on this occasion, took £234,000 for himself.[1] In all, Clive asserted in later years, this initial settlement resulted in some £4 m. (£40 m. in our money?) being "moved across the exchanges", as we should say, between India and Britain, by way of both public and private payments, as the direct and immediate result of Plassey. This £4 m. was, however, merely the first freshet of the tribute which was to flow for many years to come, first from Bengal, and then from all India, to Britain.

So long as Clive remained in India Mir Jaffier proved to be a fairly satisfactory puppet Nawob. Clive was to say years later in the House of Commons, somewhat rhetorically, "If ever a Mussulman loved a Christian, Mir Jaffier loved me." That is as it may be, but the men were certainly bound together by the parts which they had respectively played in the conspiracy. However, three years after Plassey, in 1760, Clive left for England with his vast fortune. Immediately the British at Calcutta found Mir Jaffier unsatisfactory. In reality they found him unsatisfactory in his capacity as a bottomless well out of which they could draw money; in theory his offence was that his criminally in-clined son Miran murdered some of the court ladies. He was deposed and his son-in-law, Mir Qasim, put in his place. Warren Hastings, then the junior Member of Council in Bengal, with his stormy Governor-Generalship still a decade ahead of him, described in some detail the reasons why the British made this choice. Mir Qasim was, Hastings wrote, "a man of understanding, of an uncommon talent for business and great application and perseverance. . . . His timidity, the little inclination he had ever shown for war . . . effectively secured us from any designs that he might form against our government . . . since a spirit superior to that of a worm when trodden upon could not have brooked the many daily affronts which he was exposed to . . ." (*The Rise and Fulfilment of British Rule in India*, p. 100).

[1] This was one half of the foundation of Clive's fortune. The other was his famous "Jaghir", or estate, extracted from the Mogul himself, which brought him in £27,000 a year. If we apply a ten-fold multiplier to allow for the depreciation of the pound over two hundred years, we get a capital gain of £2 m. 300 thousand + an income of £270,000 a year in terms of "1959 pounds".

No wonder that the British thought that they had found the ideal man to make their puppet Nawob. Intelligent, industrious, timid, abject—it must have seemed a perfect combination of qualities. It is difficult, however, to find such qualities in combination, and Mir Qasim turned out to be by no means so abject as he seemed even to the perspicacious Hastings. Indeed, there had been cautious voices raised against the proposal to get rid of Mir Jaffier, precisely on the grounds that his successor might *not* be sufficiently wretched. A Col. Calliaud had remonstrated with soldierly frankness, ". . . we may raise a man to the dignity" (of the Nawobship) "just as unfit to govern and as little to be depended upon, and in short as great a rogue as our Nabob, but perhaps not so great a coward, nor so great a fool, and of consequence much more difficult to manage" (Thornton's *History of British India*, Vol. I, p. 413).

The worthy Colonel's words sum up an abiding dilemma of imperialism. One of the system's favourite devices is what is called "indirect rule", *i.e.*, rule through puppets. But, then, what sort of puppet are you to choose? If you choose rogues, cowards and fools, everything is apt to go to pot in your semi-colony. If you choose better puppets, may they not prove "much more difficult to manage"? Imperialism, let us assure potential aspirants, is a most worrying business.

For a time Mir Qasim seemed to be proving satisfactory. He made a heroic effort to pull the finances of the province together and yet to provide the tribute demanded by the British. Perhaps he might have succeeded had it not been for the monopolisation of the internal trade of his province by individual Englishmen and their agents, which we shall describe below. It was this which destroyed the Nawob's revenues and made his position, and that of his wretched subjects, hopeless. After three years of struggling to fulfil his obligations to his relentless masters, and yet to save his people from ruin, the unhappy Nawob took a step which he knew meant a renewal of war with the British. In 1763 he retreated up river from his capital of Murishidabad and began to collect an army. At the same time he suddenly declared *all* internal trade, whether conducted by the British or their agents or by the ordinary Bengali merchants, to be duty free. This, no doubt, was an act of desperation, since it would have destroyed his own revenues; but at least it destroyed also the vast differential advantage of the British and the monopoly which they had built on it.

Hastings and the Governor of the East India Company's Council at Calcutta, Vansittart, actually wished to acquiesce in this act of Bengali defiance, and so voted in Council. Hastings wrote, "The Nawob has granted a boon to his subjects and there are no grounds for demanding that a sovereign prince should withdraw such a boon, or for threatening him with war in the event of refusal." It is fascinating to speculate as to what would have happened if Hastings and Vansittart had had their way and a decent and equitable settlement had been come to with a responsible Bengali government such as Mir Qasim was evidently attempting to establish.[1] Perhaps it would have altered the whole of subsequent history. But it was not to be. Such a settlement would have involved the suppression of the British monopoly in the inland trade, out of which the individual Company's servants were making their fortunes. And that was what they were there for.

Hastings and Vansittart were outvoted in Council. War was declared upon Mir Qasim. At this Mir Qasim's timidity turned into fury and he slaughtered all the Europeans, and all the Indian "collaborators" whom he could lay his hands on, to the number of some two hundred. Mir Qasim then fell back, after some hard fighting, further and further up the Ganges, on to the support of what was left of the central Indian government of the Great Mogul. Between them they raised what must have been the most considerable and best organised Indian army to challenge the British in this period. But the British now commanded more considerable forces than they had done six years before at Plassey. The Company put a force of 7,000 into the field, of which over 6,000 were Bengali sepoys in their employ.

This force slowly, and with some difficulty, drove Mir Qasim out of Bengal and pursued him into the heart of India, to Patna. There Mir Qasim rallied and was joined by the imperial army under the Emperor and his Vizier. I do not pretend to know how great was the effect of this first direct involvement of the imperial forces with the British invaders upon Indian opinion. British historians have tended to take it for granted that the Mogul's imperial authority was by this time a negligible factor. And there is no doubt that as a result of a series of catastrophes, culminating in the battle of Paniput, the material power of the Mogul was at a much lower ebb than ever before.[2] The young

[1] In this favourable estimate of Mir Qasim, I am following Thompson and Garret. Most other British authorities are hostile to him. But then to look for a favourable estimate of Mir Qasim in them would be rather like expecting a Roman historian of the first or second centuries to take a good view of Boadicea.

[2] In considering the almost inexplicable fact of the British conquest it must not be forgotten that during the decades of the eighteenth century during which the British were securing first a foothold in, and then an increasing hold over, India, the Indian military powers which might have effectively resisted them were engaged in a process of self-elimination. First there was a new wave of invasion from Afghanistan which in 1739

Emperor who now met the British in battle had, as the Crown Prince, long been a fugitive from his father's court. And even now he was in an uneasy alliance with his own Grand Vizier, as well as with his Viceroy, Mir Qasim, rather than in true command of the Indian forces. So disordered had become the heritage of Aurungzeb.

Present-day Indian opinion does not concur in this estimate of the situation, however. The disorders of the dynasty, it is pointed out, were little greater than others from which it had previously recovered. And its lack of material power was beginning, it is suggested, to be compensated for by a dawning sense that this was after all the national dynasty. An increasing Hindu loyalty to the Mogul Raj was actually beginning to appear not only in spite of, but actually because of, the terrible buffetings to which the imperial dynasty was being subjected. Up till now, it is pointed out, the British had not, to Indian minds, even challenged the Mogul power. In defeating Surajah Dowlah they had actively intervened in the politics of the Province of Bengal. But there was nothing necessarily outrageous in that. After all much of the governing class of Bengal itself had been determined to get rid of Surajah Dowlah. It is true that these Bengali notables had found that they had been appallingly rash to league themselves with the British: the result of the conspiracy had been to put all power in Bengal into British hands, and these hands were exacting money from them far more systematically than had any previous rulers. All this, however, it is suggested, had not yet made a marked impression outside Bengal. Or rather it was only when the imperial authority, in spite of all its disarray, rallied to Mir Qasim in revolt, that Indian opinion began to grope towards a realisation that the sub-continent was at grips with ruthless invaders.[1]

took and sacked Delhi itself. This opened the way, not for the assertion of the still quite minor British power, but for an almost successful Hindu reconquest of India from the Moslems, led by the Mahrattas, the ferociously courageous Hindu fighting race of Central India. Yet when the Mahrattas swept up almost to the walls of Delhi, and seemed for a moment to be about to unite India again under a Hindu Raj, they were defeated by still another wave of invasion from the Moslem lands in the West, in the great battle of Paniput (in which 200,000 men are said to have been killed). This was in 1761 *after*, be it noted, the British conquest of the whole of Bengal. India was so big and so decentralised that Indian history could go on working itself out, as it were, for several years after the whole great province of Bengal had fallen to the Europeans. To contemporary Hindu and Moslem consciousness their internecine struggle, culminating at Paniput, must have seemed far more important than the British intrusion in Bengal. In this they were mistaken.

[1] The more or less unified India of *circa* 1550 to 1750 was a marvellous achievement. When we think of the extreme slowness of communication, of the vast territory involved and the clumsiness of contemporary administrative and military methods, it was remarkable that most of the sub-continent was fairly effectively held together as one unified state for those two hundred years. But this unification had evidently been bought at a high price. It was not a natural or indigenous unification, as Asoka's India of some

There is evidence for this present-day Indian interpretation of history in the strange, savage story of the battle of Buxar, which now ensued. An intensely critical situation arose for the British before Patna. Not only did Bengali sepoys begin to desert individually from the British army, but "the mutineers soon went to the extent of threatening to carry off their officers and deliver them up to the enemy" (Thornton, op. cit., p. 453). And in fact a whole battalion of sepoys actually marched off with their arms and accoutrements to join their own compatriots, as they seem to have suddenly half recognised them to be. For while individual desertions are nearly always individually motivated and usually have little to do with patriotism or the reverse, when it comes to organised formations, such as whole battalions, attempting to change sides, we may agree that there is distinct evidence that some general motive, such as a stir of national consciousness is at work. The process of desertion went so far that, as Thornton writes, "the entire force of the British which had been assembled in the neighbourhood of Patna seemed to be breaking up". Either the intervention of the imperial authority, or Mir Qasim's defiance, or both, do indeed seem to have stirred a spark of national, specifically Indian, consciousness in the Bengali peasant-mercenaries of the British.

If once such a national consciousness had really awakened, the few hundred British would no doubt have been easily destroyed. But in the event, the awakening did not take place. On the contrary, Munro, the British commander, marched off after the battalion of mutineers with another sepoy battalion which had not yet mutinied, overtook them, made them prisoners, and marched them back to camp. Twenty-four of the leading mutineers were "forthwith bound to the guns and blown away".

After this preliminary, Munro (he was still only a Major) considered that his army was now "in a state in which it might be trusted to meet the enemy". And so complex a thing is human nature that so it proved. For at Buxar, nearby, they encountered (October 23rd, 1764) the huge

---

1500 years before had been, but a unification brought about by foreign conquest. The rulers of India (except in the extreme south) were what we should call Mongols or Turks, speaking Persian or Urdu (which simply means "camp-Persian") and with a typically Moslem culture. In origin they were no more Indian than the British, and it is sometimes suggested that all that happened in the eighteenth century was that India exchanged one set of foreign rulers for another. But this is an unreal view. The Moslem conquerors had long before 1756 become in some respects thoroughly Indianised. They had severed all connection with their original homes to the westwards and had been born and had died in the sub-continent for several generations. To say that the British conquest meant merely a change of foreign rulers would be rather like saying that if England, say in 1266, two hundred years after the Norman Conquest, had been conquered and occupied by the Arabs, she would have had no sense of anything but a change of alien rulers.

army of Mir Qasim and the Emperor, numbering between 40,000 and 60,000 (to their 7,000). Nor was the Indian army by any means a mere rabble. Mir Qasim was an ardent "moderniser" and had made serious efforts to introduce European standards of drill and discipline.[1] The battle was accordingly far more severe than Plassey had been (the British side lost over 800 men). Nevertheless, the 7,000 semi-mutinous mercenaries in the end outfought and drove off the 40,000 men of the imperial army. Perhaps a key to this otherwise inexplicable event is, after all, provided by the story of the last request of the mutineers amongst the sepoy mercenaries of the British, who were, as we noted, blown away from the guns. (This story is all that the English reader is often told about the battle of Buxar.) Munro, in his despatch, described what happened: "Three of the grenadiers entreated to be fastened to the guns on the right, declaring that as they always fought on the right they hoped their last request would be complied with, by being suffered to die in the post of honour. Their petition was granted, and they were first executed."

Can we not here obtain a glimpse of the conflicts going on in the minds of the Bengali mercenaries of the British? The stir of national consciousness which may have made them try to desert to "their" side—which was in some respects only the side of their *previous* Moslem conquerors—was, after all, fitful. It came into conflict with their

[1] It is often thought that the British enjoyed an overwhelming technical superiority in their armaments. But in land warfare this does not seem to have been so. We must not think of the Indian armies of the period as primitive forces armed with nothing better than spears and bows. On the contrary, they had plentiful firearms. In artillery Surajah Dowlah's force at Plassey was, for example, immensely superior to Clive's. It is true that the Indian infantry's flintlocks were out of date in comparison with the contemporary British musket. We may think of the Indian firearms as the equivalent of early seventeenth- rather than eighteenth-century European arms: but the gap was not wider than that. And in one important arm, the cavalry, the Indians had what should have been overwhelming superiority. We cannot then account for the conquest as a result of any invincible superiority in armaments.

Of the strictly military factors the least considered may have been the most important: namely, drill. The Indians had not acquired the fairly recently developed European technique of "conditioning" their troops (in the modern psychological sense) to stand up to fire, by means of drilling them beforehand. It is a remarkable but unquestionable psychological fact that bodies of men will let quite a considerable proportion of their number be killed and wounded without running away, if they have been "trained" in the sense of having had sufficiently loud and hortatory commands shouted at them sufficiently frequently. In order to produce this extraordinary modification of normal human conduct, they must have been conditioned to obey these shouted commands instantly and on pain of certain punishment. But, if this is done, it has proved possible largely to overcome men's fear even of death itself by implanting in them, by repetition and by punishment for disobedience, a reflex obedience to words of command given to them by their officers. Part of this conditioning process, in the eighteenth century, was to draw the troops up shoulder to shoulder in a close-packed line, giving them a sense of solidarity, and to teach them to fire their muskets in fairly effective volleys. This technique of conditioning by drill may have been the most important military advantage enjoyed by the British.

experience that the British, trained, led, drilled and paid army, in which they served, was what a British service man of to-day would call "a better show" than any Indian army of the period. They had found that the British-run army always won, even against extreme odds. They had fought in it with courage and had obtained the enormous satisfaction which men do obtain from triumph in battle, even if that triumph brings them personally no particular reward. Their pride as men had found, in a word, successful vent in the British-organised forces. In their last moments this feeling seems to have overwhelmed the stir of national consciousness which had apparently moved the mutinous grenadiers. In the case of the rest of the mercenary army it was enough to make them fight like heroes for their British employers the next day at Buxar. The immense power of the satisfaction which men get merely from belonging, without much personal advantage, to a successful "show" should never be forgotten by the student of history and politics who is searching for the reasons which have made things happen in the otherwise inexplicable way in which they *have* happened.

Thus ended Mir Qasim's revolt. Total British power in Bengal was reaffirmed; the Mogul authority was still further shattered and the Emperor became as much a dependant as an overlord of the British provincial authority in Bengal. But no immediate British territorial expansion beyond Bengal was attempted. Within the province Mir Qasim was duly deposed and Mir Jaffier, now old, decrepit and indifferent, was trotted out again and replaced upon the *musnud* by "the merchant-strangers into whose hands had passed, as though by enchantment, the balance in which was poised the destinies of India" (Thornton). The indirect form of the puppet Nawobship was now wearing thin. Clive, who came back to Bengal at this moment (1765), preserved it for a time, but in the end the Company was forced to take the sovereignty of the province into its own hands in name as well as in fact. As Clive wrote to the Court of the Company in Leadenhall Street: "With regard to the magnitude of our possessions be not staggered. Assure yourself that the Company must either be what they are or be annihilated. . . . We must go forward—to retract is impossible."

The immediate economic consequences for Bengal of its conquest by the British, which was thus completed, must now be noted. These are perhaps best illustrated in the change which almost at once occurred in the trading practices of the East India Company. Ever since its foundation 150 years earlier, the Company had found that it had had to trade with India by sending out means of payment, which it called "the investment", with which not only to purchase but also to finance the production of cottons and silks by the Indian weavers. For, as Orme explains, the Indian weavers were too destitute to produce unless they were financed by some factor or merchant during the period of production. This "investment" had always consisted, for the most part, of the precious metals, for there were few European goods for which there was a market in India. It was this export of gold and silver in its annual "investment" which had made the Company vulnerable to the merchantilist criticism that it was draining Britain of its reserve of precious metals for the sake of importing luxuries. The charge was probably ill-founded, for the Company re-sold a considerable part of its Indian-produced goods all over Europe, and at a very high rate of profit. So that it is by no means clear that Britain came out of the transaction, even before the conquest, with what we should now call an adverse balance of payments. But, in any case, soon after the conquest of Bengal the charge became wholly ill-founded, and for the following reason.

The Company ceased (or at least attempted to cease) to send out "an investment" at all.[1] In other words, Bengal as a whole got nothing at all in exchange for its goods. Of course the individual weavers, working in their huts at their handlooms on cottons or silks for the Company, had still to be paid, or else they would have starved before they could complete their tasks. But the money to pay them, instead of being sent out from Britain, was now raised by taxation in Bengal. In a word, Bengal as a whole was made to pay for its own exports to Britain. When (a few years after Clive's conquest) the Company had itself assumed the "Dewanee", i.e., the direct management of the province (though still for a few years longer nominally on behalf of a function-less "Nawob") all political obstacles to this extreme form of exploitation were removed.[2]

[1] *Rise and Fulfilment of British Rule in India,* Thompson and Garrett (Macmillan, 1934), p. 99.

[2] It is true that the servants of the Company went on talking about "the investment" long after this. But now they appear to have meant the working capital of the Company, whether raised, as whenever possible it was, by taxation in India (or borrowed from individuals in the Company's own employment), and not a sum sent out from Britain. On the other hand, as we shall notice in the next chapter, the complete abolition of any actual payment by Britain for the goods she bought in India was an ideal towards which the Company ardently aspired rather than something which they completely and securely achieved. Even at the end of the eighteenth century some money or goods had often to be sent to India as a means of payment, but to a much lower value than the goods received from India.

Logically the value of the whole shipments from India, minus only the cost of their transport and sale, should have become pure profit to the Company. And in principle they did. Nevertheless it is an ironic fact that it was just in this period that the Company, in effect, went bankrupt! But this was only because it was so pillaged by its own agents, by the British government, and in general by everyone who could possibly get their feet into the trough, that it could not meet its obligations. The flow of almost unrequited wealth from Bengal to Britain went on uninterruptedly; it was merely diverted to private pockets and away from the pockets of the stockholders of the Company. The line between the trader and the simple robber, which had disappeared altogether in the case of the Spanish conquistadors, had worn thin.

But, it may be asked, did not Bengal at least receive some recompense by way of good government and law and order for the tribute that it thus paid to its conquerors? No doubt it did, and in the fullness of time regular government and law and order were to be of value. But for some 15 years after the conquest the fact that Bengal was now protected from being ravaged by its neighbours was of no advantage to the unhappy province. For it was now ravaged far more systematically by its new rulers. No Mahratta raid ever devastated a countryside with the thoroughness with which both the Company and, above all, the Company's servants in their individual capacities, sucked dry the plain of Bengal. In fact in their blind rage for enrichment they took more from the Bengali peasants than those peasants could furnish and live. And the peasants duly died.

It was not principally the exaction of the goods exported to Britain on the Company's account as an unrequited tribute, that caused this frightful result. The natural riches of the province could probably have supported that. It was the fact that the Company's servants, civilian and military alike, with one accord turned to their personal enrichment, not mainly by an overseas trade with Europe, but by engaging in the internal trade of the province. They did so by arbitrarily declaring that the original firman of the Great Mogul (see the previous chapter), which had given the Company extra-territorial rights and exemption from taxes for its export and import trade, which was bad enough, applied to internal trade as well.[1] This was

[1] Orme relates how 40 years earlier when Surman and Stephenson, during "the embassy of complaint", stretched their demands to cover exemptions from taxation for the internal as well as the overseas trade, the Mogul exclaimed oracularly, "The Sea"! Orme writes that this undoubtedly meant that the firman of exemption was to apply only to the overseas trade. But of course by the seventeen-sixties such questions had become a matter of brute force; no one really cared what had been written into the original concession.

completely ruinous. Since the taxes and internal custom dues had to be high, in order to enable the Nawob's government to pay its tribute to the Company, any Briton, or in practice his Indian agent to whom he sold his *dustuck*, or *laisser passer*, could undersell and ruin all native competitors. For he traded without paying any taxes or dues. Soon the British and their agents had achieved a virtual monopoly of the trade of the province: but by then it was a dying province. Only 12 years after the conquest in 1769 Mr Becher, the Company's agent at Murishidabad, was reporting: "I well remember this country when trade was free and the flourishing state it was then in; with concern I now see its present ruinous condition." Still earlier Hastings, then a young servant of the Company, on a visit up-country reported that the approach of his party of British was regarded by the inhabitants rather like that of tigers. "Most of the petty towns and sarais (markets) were deserted on our approach, and the shops shut up from the apprehensions of the same treatment from us", *i.e.*, of the same treatment as they were receiving from the other British or their agents.

True there was nothing new in devastation and famine, either in Bengal or in India generally. Civil disorders, the exactions of native princes, or of previous conquerors, had always periodically thrust the peasantry over the edge of subsistence. But there seems no doubt that there was something particularly thorough and systematic about the early British-made famines, particularly that of 1770.[1] The truth is that law and order, if it is someone else's law and order, may be a still more terrible calamity to the ruled even than anarchy and civil strife. It is precisely when all resistance, all possibility of any alternative or rival authority, has disappeared that an alien authority can extract the whole, and, if it is foolish, temporarily even more than the whole, of the surplus of men's produce above subsistence. Nor is it anything but the bitterest irony for the governed if such alien authority does its work in the most correct, orderly and, as in this case, legalistic, way imaginable.[2]

We get an illuminating glimpse of what a cultivated Indian observer thought of us in the seventeen-sixties from the following passage which

[1] And this fact was realised by some contemporary opinion in Britain. Horace Walpole wrote: "We have outdone the Spaniards in Peru. They were at least butchers on a religious principle, however diabolical their zeal. We have murdered, deposed, plundered, usurped—nay what think you of the famine in Bengal, in which three millions perished, being caused by a monopoly of the provisions by the servants of the East India Company?"

[2] Almost the most terrible thing which the British did was to import and impose the whole system and apparatus of British eighteenth-century Law, complete with barristers, judges, High Courts, etc. Such a system proved of course utterly unsuitable, and indeed incomprehensible, in Bengal.

James Mill quotes from the Seer Mutakhareen, the anonymous Moslem historian of the period. In the course of the fighting in 1760 some English got into a tight corner near Patna. They made a resolute retreat watched by the eyes of a Mogul nobleman, who, the Indian historian writes, commented as follows:

"it must be acknowledged that this nation's presence of mind, firmness of temper and undaunted bravery are beyond all question. They join the most resolute courage to the most cautious prudence; nor have they equals in the art of ranging themselves in battle array, and fighting in order. If to so many military qualifications they knew how to join the arts of government; if they showed a concern for the circumstances of the husbandman and the gentleman, and exerted as much ingenuity and solicitude in relieving and easing the people of God, as they do in whatever concerns their military affairs, no nation in the world would be preferable to them, or prove worthier of command. But such is the little regard that they show to the people of their kingdoms, and such their apathy and indifference for their welfare, that the people under their dominion groan everywhere and are reduced to poverty and distress. Oh God! Come to the assistance of thine afflicted Servants, and deliver them from the oppression they suffer" (James Mill, *The History of British India*, Vol. III, p. 262).

What a tragedy it was, the Mogul nobleman evidently felt, that such heroic savages as the British were incapable of civilised statesmanship!

British rule in the seventeen-sixties and seventies invested the extraction from the Bengali peasant of everything that could conceivably be extracted from him with many of the forms and methods of "good government". For instance, Clive, on his third and last visit to India, made it his main task, not indeed to abolish plundering by the Company or even by individual Company's servants (which he considered impossible), but to regulate and regularise it. He formed a body which he called "The Society for Trade". This fascinating institution was nothing else but a sort of well-organised Co-operative Society by means of which even the private plundering of the Company's servants was put upon a collective instead of an individual basis. For by means of this "Co-op" a trade which was so one-sided as to be very little different from robbery, was in future conducted collectively on behalf of both the British civilians and the British soldiers of the

Company's establishments in Bengal. Each gentleman now got his "proper" share in an orderly way, strictly according to seniority (for instance, a colonel got £7,000 a year—[£70,000 in our money], a Major £2,000 [£20,000 a year]). The bulk of this money came out of the salt trade. This was because a salt tax or *gabel* or still more monopoly rights to trade in salt, as the French *ancien régime* recognised, is one of the very best ways of extracting the last possible ounce of surplus value from a primitive and apparently already destitute peasantry. For salt is the one absolute necessity of life which every peasant household, however otherwise self-supporting, has to buy from the outside world, no matter what the price.

In a way the institution of "The Society of Trade" was even well intentioned. Clive (now that he had secured a vast fortune for himself) was genuinely shocked by the "Augean stables" (as he called them) of individualistic looting which he discovered when he returned to Bengal on this last visit. Yet his very achievement in regularising and organising such a trade as this drove the wretched province all the more remorselessly into ruin. By the late eighteenth century Bengal, which Orme begins his history by describing (with some hyperbole) as "a paradise", had been reduced in spite of, or even precisely because of, her conquerors having suppressed civil conflict and introduced *their* form of "law and order", to the most pitiable conditions. Large tracts of its countryside had been depopulated and had reverted to jungle, its cities were in decay, its people starving. The best summary of the results of this initial and terrible period of British rule was given at its close by one of the first great reforming Governor-Generals, Lord Cornwallis:

"I may safely assert that one-third of the Company's territory in Hindostan is now a jungle inhabited only by wild beasts" (Minute of September 18th, 1789).

These were not to be the ultimate or the only results of the conquest. But they were its immediate effects.

Clive's temperament was what modern medical science would probably call mildly manic-depressive. His moods swung, that is to say, between periods of exaltation, when he was capable of violent and heroic achievements, to periods of black despair. As a young man at Madras he had twice tried to commit suicide; and he succeeded in doing so in the end.[1] All through his life he had a series of what we should call "nervous breakdowns". For example, when he got back to Calcutta after his last tour of the conquered province he was, his biographer says, prostrated for several days on end with uncontrollable weeping. For what did Clive weep? He could not have said. Yet, though he seemed to care nothing for the people whom he had subjugated, is it not possible that somewhere in his innermost being he wept for Bengal?

[1] His recent biographer, Mr Mervyn Davies (*Clive of Plassey*, 1939) accepts the view that Clive did end his own life. But he thinks that he did so while preparing for a journey to Bath. An oral family tradition, handed down from the first Sir Henry Strachey, the present writer's ancestor, who was Clive's secretary, gives another account. Strachey had gone to spend an evening playing whist at Clive's house in Berkeley Square (now, curiously, the London headquarters of the Moral Rearmament movement). In the middle of the game Clive put down his cards and left the room. The other three players waited for him to return, until Strachey's eyes lifted from the whist table to the crack under the door. A slow, red stream was oozing into the room. They found Clive's body with its throat cut lying in the passage.

CHAPTER III

WHAT HAPPENED TO INDIA

THE BENGAL FAMINE of 1770 was the first, but also the worst, of the consequences of the British conquest. For it would be totally wrong to suggest that those first fifteen terrible years, from 1757 to 1772, in Bengal, were representative of what British rule in India as a whole was to become. In 1772, the process of the improvement and reform of the British régime may be said to have begun. In that year Warren Hastings returned to Bengal as the first Governor-General of what was in fact, although not yet in name, this vast new British colony. And he at once set in hand, as he had to do in mere self-preservation, an attempt to rescue the province by reforming the British administration.

Hastings was a far more interesting figure than Clive. It is characteristic of the man that controversy still echoes, if now only amongst the historians, over his reputation and his record. Brilliant, scholarly, brave, arbitrary, financially lax (sometimes even to his own disadvantage), loving India, conquering India, enriching India, despoiling India, this strange man stands out as the first, and perhaps the only, fascinating figure amongst the long, stiff line of Governor-Generals who came and went over the next hundred and seventy-five years. Nor has his memory faded even yet from Bengal. In 1956 one of the most distinguished of her present-day citizens, a principal author of India's Second Five Year Plan, introduced me to another distinguished public servant of Bengal, who, I was informed, was a direct descendant of Hastings' *Diwan*, or principal Indian executive officer. Talking with these twentieth-century Indian citizens of a once more independent India, I sensed a warmth in their attitude to Hastings as compared with almost any other public figure of the British period.[1] This was not indeed because Hastings abstained in any degree from imperialist policies: on the contrary, he was one of the greatest and one of the most aggressive of empire builders.

Hastings was arraigned at his seven years' trial in Westminster Hall

---

[1] Perhaps Ripon in the last century and Halifax in this, amongst the Viceroys, may also to some extent be warmly remembered. And at the end Mountbatten certainly earned and received true Indian affection. How curious that it should be the very first and the very last of the Viceroys who succeeded in appealing to Indian hearts.

for all the wrong reasons. It is impossible, and also fundamentally unimportant, even to-day to decide on just how badly or how well he treated "the Begums of Oude", or to prove whether the hanging of Nunkomar was an astonishingly lucky accident or (far more probably) a cold and resolute counter-thrust in his desperate struggle with his colleagues, or whether his Rohilla War was more or less justified than the dozens of other such wars which the British régime indulged in during the whole two-hundred-year period of its existence. At that time and place Hastings could not conceivably have been anything else but an imperialist. Burke and Fox and Francis, and all the rest of his accusers, could only logically have condemned him if they had condemned the British conquest also. Granted the imperialist premise, Hastings was probably one of the most enlightened (if by no means the most scrupulous) of imperial rulers. He was far more genuinely concerned with the welfare of the conquered people than any other of his contemporaries: indeed, he was the first of the conquerors to feel any such concern. The evolution of British rule in India into something which was not wholly rapacious and destructive begins with his Governor-Generalship.

In this work of reformation, however, Hastings was only the first of a long series of able men, including his immediate successors, Cornwallis, Shore, Wellesley, and Lord Hastings. Moreover, they were in a position to accomplish much more than he. And yet it is he who is remembered in Bengal. Nor, I think, is the reason far to seek. What was unique in Hastings amongst Governor-Generals was not that he was a reformer, but that he was an intellectual. He was that rare and usually uncomfortable being, an intellectual functioning as a man of action. But it was just this which made him revered in India. He was revered and is remembered because he was one of the first Englishmen to appreciate Indian culture, to learn Hindustani and Persian, and to promote the first Sanskrit translations. (He wrote, for example, an introduction to the first translation of the Gita.) His repute rests, I think, above all, on what he was *not*: on the fact that he was not an ordinary, straightforward, normal, hearty Englishman. With his adored German divorcée wife, his personal frugality and physical ascetism, his endless entertaining, his financial lavishness, his learning, and above all his utter lack of racial intolerance, he was far more sympathetic to his Indian contemporaries than the virtuous but frigid noblemen who succeeded him. In old age Hastings said that he had loved India a little better than his own country. It may well have been true. A man may stay to love what he comes to rape. Above all, he loved not only India, as many a stolid nineteenth- and twentieth-century sahib was to do; he loved Indians.

With the Governor-Generalship of Hastings the possibility at least of a constructive and beneficial, as well as a plundering and devastating, side to British rule became apparent. And in a few decades more this possibility began to become a reality. In the nineteenth century the British role in India continued indeed to be destructive of the pre-existing Asiatic economy and society which it had encountered; but it also began to lay down the basis of a new economy and society such as had never existed before in Asia. It may be well to cite a witness for this positive aspect of British rule who will hardly be accused of partiality for the occupying power. The first analyst of what he called the "at once destructive and regenerative" role of the British in India was Marx.

Marx, in his capacity as world historian and world theorist, could not help being engrossed by that major phenomenon of his times, the British empire in India. He was at pains to emphasise that, even on its destructive side, the British conquest of India had performed a function, however brutally, which had somehow to be performed. He had given in *Capital* (Vol. I, Chap. XIV) an attractive characterisation of the self-sufficient Indian village communities which the coming of, first, British pillaging commerce and, later, British machine-made products, were destroying. Nevertheless he could not regret the destruction of these communities, agonising as the process might be. For he saw that India could never grow till *something* broke through her age-old, static, social basis. He wrote a series of articles for the *New York Daily Tribune* entitled "The Future Results of British Rule in India". In a characteristically formidable passage he gave a balance-sheet of the loss and gain involved in the destruction of the village communities under the British sledgehammer.

"Sickening as it must be to human feeling to witness those myriads of industrious, patriarchal and inoffensive social organisations dis-organised and dissolved into their units, thrown into a sea of woes, and their individual members losing at the same time their ancient form of civilisation and their hereditary means of subsistence, we must not forget that these idyllic village communities, inoffensive though they may appear, had always been the solid foundation of Oriental despotism, that they restrained the human mind within the smallest possible compass, making it the unresisting tool of superstition, enslaving it beneath traditional rules, depriving it of all grandeur and historical energies.

"We must not forget the barbarian egoism which, concentrating on some miserable patch of land, had quietly witnessed the ruin of empires, the perpetration of unspeakable cruelties, the massacre of the population of large towns, with no other consideration bestowed upon them than on natural events, itself the helpless prey of any aggressor who deigned to notice it at all.

"We must not forget that this stagnatory, undignified and vegetative life, that this passive sort of existence evoked on the other hand, in contradistinction, wild, aimless, unbounded forces of destruction and rendered murder itself a religious rite in Hindostan.

"We must not forget that these little communities were contaminated by distinctions of caste and by slavery, that they subjugated man to external circumstances instead of elevating man the sovereign of circumstances, that they transformed a self-developing social state into never-changing natural destiny, and thus brought about a brutalising worship of nature, exhibiting its degradation in the fact that man, the sovereign of nature, fell down on his knees in adoration of Hanuman, the monkey, and Sabbala, the cow.

"England, it is true, in causing a social revolution in Hindostan, was actuated only by the vilest interests, and was stupid in her manner of enforcing them. But this is not the question. The question is: can mankind fulfil its destiny without a fundamental revolution in the social state of Asia? If not, whatever may have been the crimes of England, she was the unconscious tool of history in bringing about that revolution.

"The British were the first conquerors superior, and therefore inaccessible, to Hindoo civilisation. They destroyed it by breaking up the native communities, by uprooting the native industry, and by levelling all that was great and elevated in the native society. The historic pages of their rule in India report hardly anything beyond that destruction. The work of regeneration hardly transpires through a heap of ruins. Nevertheless it has begun."

Such was the severity of Marx's judgment on Indian society as it existed before the conquest; such his recognition of the necessity of it being, somehow, revolutionised. Moreover, Marx went on to list particular respects in which British rule in India would prove "regenerative". These were as follows:

(1) "political unity . . . more consolidated and extending further than ever it did under the Great Moguls", and destined to be "strengthened and perpetuated by the electric telegraph";

(2) the "native army";

(3) "the free press, introduced for the first time into Asiatic society";

(4) "private property in land—the great desideratum of Asiatic society";

(5) an educated Indian class "endowed with the requirements for government and imbued with European science";

(6) "regular and rapid communication with Europe" through steam transport.

Marx foretold that the basis of industrialisation which, from whatever motives, the British were beginning to lay down in India would in due course transform her.

"I know that the English millocracy intend to endow India with railways with the exclusive view of extracting at diminished expenses the cotton and other raw materials for their manufactures. But when you have once introduced machinery into the locomotion of a country, which possesses iron and coals, you are unable to withhold it from its fabrication. You cannot maintain a net of railways over an immense country without introducing all those industrial processes necessary to meet the immediate and current wants of railway locomotion, and out of which there must grow the application of machinery to those branches of industry not immediately connected with the railways. The railway system will therefore become in India truly the forerunner of modern industry. . . . Modern industry, resulting from the railway system, will dissolve the hereditary divisions of labour, upon which rest the Indian castes, those decisive impediments to Indian progress and Indian power."[1]

Finally Marx sums up both the extent and the limitations of the regenerative aspect of British rule.

"All the English bourgeoisie may be forced to do will neither

[1] Mr R. Palme Dutt has done much to rescue these and other pronouncements of Marx on India from unmerited neglect (see Chapter V of his *India Today*, Gollancz, 1940). Though his book is written from the most rigidly Communist standpoint, it contains both information and insights into the history of India under British rule which are nowhere else available. It remains, in my view, Mr Dutt's major work.

emancipate nor materially mend the social condition of the mass of the people, depending not only on the development of the productive power, but on their appropriation by the people. But what they will not fail to do is to lay down the material premises for both. Has the bourgeoisie ever done more? Has it ever effected a progress without dragging individuals and people through blood and dirt, through misery and degradation?

"The Indians will not reap the fruits of the new elements of society scattered among them by the British bourgeoisie till in Great Britain itself the now ruling classes shall have been supplanted by the industrial proletariat, or till the Hindoos themselves shall have grown strong enough to throw off the English yoke altogether."

Now that we have the whole story of the British period in India before us, we can see that, curiously enough, Marx exaggerated not only the destructive side (the mid-nineteenth-century British in India were by no means so wholly self-seeking as he alleges) but *also* the regeneration side of British rule. The real criticism which must be made of the British record in India is that it did *not* effectively break up the stagnation of Asiatic society: that rural India remains to this day largely untouched: that it did *not*, sufficiently rapidly, industrialise the country: that even what Marx here calls "the material premises" for development were not laid down on a sufficient scale.

To follow, even in outline, this double role of British rule in India, at once "destructive and regenerative", through the nineteenth century would necessitate attempting to write a history devoted to that subject alone. Suffice it to say that in the first half of the century the conquest was step by step completed until the last genuinely independent state, the kingdom of the Punjab, was annexed in 1849. Panikkar regards the decisive battle of the conquest as neither Plassey nor Buxar, but Assaye in 1803, in which the future Duke of Wellington broke the Mahratha power. In fact, at what particular date or battle we choose to say that the conquest of India occurred must always be an arbitrary matter. It would be quite logical indeed to say that the conquest was not really complete until the widespread Indian rebellion of the Mutiny (1857-8) had been overcome.

The best Indian and British opinion on the Mutiny seems to have reached the conclusion that it was "the last gasp of an old and dying order, and though it evoked the loyalties of the past and called forth the enthusiasm of the masses over wide areas, it had not the idealism, organisation or strength to build up and sustain a state which could at that time have taken over from the British" (Panikkar, op. cit., p. 143). This verdict is actually sustained by the fact that militarily the revolution was a success. Delhi after all was taken, the Mogul restored, and the capital held for months. But then, on the Indian side, nothing happened. Fighting is a far easier and simpler business than ruling. Neither a State administrative machine nor a national consciousness were created. And the British were able to re-conquer the capital, freely using troops levied in the newly annexed Punjab. India was not yet a nation, so she could not yet be an independent nation. Almost another century of British rule was indispensable, for the simple reason that no indigenous rule was available. Our concern is merely to note that the British empire in India did in fact perform a role of regeneration as well as destruction, and that it did so precisely because, unlike some of the other mercantile empires, such as the Portuguese or the Spanish, it persisted into the epoch of industrial capitalism. It became indeed the main element in one of the great capitalist empires, the British, and was only dissolved in the middle of the twentieth century.

And yet how slowly and with what anguish did the regenerative element in British rule in India begin to emerge out of the purely destructive. The destructive element persisted and predominated far into the nineteenth century. For example, nearly eighty years after the conquest of Bengal a reforming Governor-General, Lord William Cavendish-Bentinck, reported that "the bones of the cotton-weavers are bleaching the plains of India". There was, however, this difference between the eighteenth- and the nineteenth-century devastations. The earlier ruin was caused by what was virtually direct plunder thinly disguised as commerce. But what, in the fourth decade of the nine-teenth century, was strewing the Indian plains with the bones of her starved cotton weavers was not bad government, corruption or plundering traders. On the contrary, the methods of the British govern-ment in India had by then vastly improved. What was having this deadly effect was simply the impact of machine-made Lancashire cotton cloth which could undercut the Indian handloom weavers.

Nevertheless this new, and still destructive result of the conquest had, as Marx saw, within it at least the possibility of regeneration. For what was happening to the Indian handloom weavers was in one sense the same process that had just happened to the English handloom weavers themselves, namely extirpation by the Lancashire power looms. And yet the Indian case was far worse. The British handloom

WHAT HAPPENED TO INDIA 53

weavers were fairly quickly (although extremely painfully) reabsorbed into the new, mushrooming machine textile industry, or into the general process of industrialisation which was going on in Britain. But in India the positive side of the transformation, namely the creation of mechanised industry, was delayed for many decades. In those decades the process of industrialisation which was destroying the handloom weavers was happening indeed: but it was happening externally, in Britain. In India, therefore, the process was fatally one-sided. The hand textile industry was destroyed and for decades no other grew to take its place.

A colonial country is almost inevitably subject to these terrible dis-tortions in its development. Since its development comes from outside, and is imposed on it by alien rulers over whom its people have not even indirect control, a colonial country is apt to suffer the horrors of the industrial revolution while reaping its fruits but slowly and meagrely. This was to be the fate of India. It was not until almost the beginning of the twentieth century that a great machine textile industry (usually the first comer in industrial development) was established by both Indian and British entrepreneurs in India. (For it was not till then that India was allowed to foster it with a tariff.) It was not till then that that network of railways, of which Marx had written fifty years earlier, was completed. And even then, it is doubtful if the Indian people as a whole experienced (or have experienced even yet for that matter) any direct benefit by way of a rising standard of life, from the process of industrialisation. This was, above all, because of the most fatal, though for long the least noticed, feature of the distorted deve-lopment which is habitually suffered by subject peoples. It is not that their countries remain altogether untouched. On the contrary law and order may be established, railways built, pestilence conquered or abated, the peasants protected. But if all this is not accompanied by rapid industrial development the last state of the colony may actually become in some respects worse than the first. For the main effect of the positive features of imperial rule is to produce a continuous and rapid rise in the population. And unless that rise is matched by all-round industrial development every potential benefit is swallowed up in mere numbers. We shall find as the narrative proceeds, moreover, that imperial governments can never achieve, and seldom even allow, such all-round development. The contrast between the history of Japan, the main Asiatic society to remain genuinely independent, and that of peoples which were colonised, is striking in this connection. Thus right up to its term in 1947 what could be claimed for British rule was no more and no less than a profound disturbance of a stagnant Asiatic society and the creation of the pre-requisites for development.

The second half of the nineteenth century in India was, however, a period very different from Clive's eighteenth-century "Augean stables" of plunder. By 1860 a vast Victorian decorum had settled upon the sub-continent. In some respects this was the best and most fruitful period of British rule. The military success, and the political failure, of the Mutiny had alike demonstrated that, even when physical power had largely passed into Indian hands, India was not yet capable of organising herself into an independent society. Indian nationalists of to-day (and by no means "men of the right") have told me how much of responsible Indian opinion in the second half of the nineteenth century genuinely concurred in the view that British rule was inevitable for the time being and was conferring substantial benefits upon their country. (Gokhale, an outstanding Indian leader of the period, called it "an act of providence", for example.)

Nothing could be more opposite to its previous phase than the mood and methods of British rule in the forty-three years from the Mutiny till 1900. Gone were all the worst abuses of the eighteenth and early nineteenth centuries. India was no longer ruled by a gang of passionate adventurers, frantic to enrich themselves. She was ruled on the contrary by what was becoming the least corruptible, that ablest and the most respectable of all the great bureaucracies of the world. Carefully recruited from the ordinary "firsts" and "good seconds" of British education, the Civil Service was becoming an intensely conscientious body. There is not the slightest doubt that its members put the interests of India, as *they* saw them, far above their own fortunes, and often above the supposed interests of Britain. They were willing, on occasions, to fight the interests of British businessmen and of the British Government on behalf of "the dumb Indian masses", which they genuinely conceived of as their wards.

But this feeling of guardianship for the Indian peasant masses was associated with a growing hostility to the educated Indian middle class which was emerging. The austere I.C.S. official in his bungalow was sure that the new Indian merchants, businessmen and lawyers were going to exploit "their" peasants. And so, no doubt, they were: the Indian middle class exploited the classes below it in just the same ways as do middle classes everywhere else at comparable stages of social development. But what the I.C.S. officials forgot was that, certainly at that time, no way forward for a people had been found, other than to grow out of itself such an exploiting, but also innovating and progressive, middle class as this.

Thus there were losses as well as gains in this transformation of the nature of British rule in India. Decency and distance had succeeded pillage and intimacy. If the new rulers of India were incomparably more disinterested than the old, they also had far less to do with the Indians themselves. Especially after the Mutiny, the fatal doctrine of racial superiority came more and more to dominate the imaginations of the British in India. Perhaps the deterioration in this respect can be made concrete from the records of my own family. During the eighteenth and early nineteenth centuries two of my collateral ancestors, Colonel Kirkpatrick and Edward Strachey, had married what the late-nineteenth-century British would, so offensively, have called native women. Kirkpatrick had married a Bengali lady of a distinguished family and Strachey a Persian princess, in each case, so far as the family records go, without exciting the least adverse comment or injuring their careers in any way. How unthinkable such alliances would have been to my great-uncles, Sir John and Sir Richard Strachey, who were members of the Governor-General's Council in the eighteen-seventies. This terrible withdrawal of genuine human community went far to undo—in some respects it more than undid—the good which the immense improvement in British conduct might have done for the relations of the two great peoples.[1] Moreover another curse had descended upon the late-nineteenth-century British administrators; the curse of the doctrinaire. *Laisser faire* in general and free trade in particular had become the secular religion of the British middle class. The application of its dogmas to India had frightful consequences. Mr Philip Woodruff in the second volume of his well-known work, *The Men Who Ruled India*, entitled *The Guardians* (a work specially, and worthily, devoted to celebrating the achievements of the I.C.S.), describes what happened in the matter of famine relief. In 1866 the crops failed in the province of Orissa. The members of the Board of Revenue who advised the Lieutenant-Governor, Sir Cecil Beadon, were—

" '. . . held by the most rigid rules of the direct political economy'. They rejected 'almost with horror' the idea of importing grain.

[1] Professor Myrdal (in a letter to the writer) points out that these anti-social developments into racial segregation had deplorable economic consequences also. They tended, by segregating the races, to segregate economic enterprises also. They helped to make the British enterprises in India into mere *enclaves*, employing only unskilled Indian labour, with little tendency to spread higher techniques through the Indian economy.

They would not even allow the authorities in Orissa to take the grain from a ship which ran ashore on their coast in March. It was bound for Calcutta and to Calcutta the grain must go. In fact, it rotted in the holds while plans were made to move it.

"At Haileybury, everyone had learnt that political economy was a matter of laws, that money and goods would move by themselves in ways beneficial to mankind. The less any government interfered with natural movements, the better. If there was real scarcity in Orissa, prices would rise, grain-dealers from elsewhere would be attracted and would hurry grain to where it was needed. If the government tried to anticipate this process, they would cause waste and incur loss. . . . By the time relief came a quarter of the population were dead."

It is true that as a result of the famines of 1866, 1868 and 1874, this insane doctrine was revised and a "Famine Code" which suspended the "laws" of political economy was drawn up in 1880 by Sir Richard Strachey. But allowing men to starve to death lest feeding them interfere with doctrine was only the most extreme example of something which will concern us throughout this narrative. For if, after 1880, it was possible to interfere with "economic laws" when actual famine had broken out, this was by no means the case at any other time. On the contrary, *laisser faire* in its most rigid interpretation remained the creed of the men who conducted the economic policy of the government of India to the very end of the British period. (It is true that in the latter years they had to yield to some extent to Indian pressure in the matter of tariffs, but unwillingly.)

We here catch a first glimpse of what will be a major theme of these pages. Whatever may be our view of the advantages or disadvantages of *laisser faire*, free trade economics for a highly developed society such as Britain, it is now clear that an undeveloped society simply cannot develop if it is subjected to such a policy. The ancient hand-technique industries of a country such as India will be crushed, and the establishment of machine-technique industries prevented. The undeveloped country will remain at a peasant level, with a few large scale enterprises in the extractive industries, working for export. Under *laisser faire* and free trade between countries at unequal stages of development there is an overriding tendency for the gap between a developed and an undeveloped country to grow wider *indefinitely*. It was this tyranny of the unbridled market which the British imposed upon India: and this subtle tyranny almost undid all the truly noble and selfless work which

"The Guardians" were doing in other respects. Why did these virtuous men do such terrible things? Was it because they were, as Keynes wrote, "the slaves of some defunct economist"; was it, in other words, mere intellectual error on their part? Or was *laisser faire*, free trade dogma a cloak for imposing the (supposed) interests of Britain upon the subject people? The question is still a burning one. For we shall find that even to-day, when most of the subject peoples are politically free, the attempt is still being made to catch, or hold, them in an intellectual net which will prevent them making those drastic and continuous interferences with the laws of international trade, which they must make if they are to have any hope of developing their countries.

Leading Indians are to-day ready to pay generous tribute to the work of the British administrators in the second half of the nineteenth century. Considering both the ever increasing distance at which they were held by those administrators and the failure to initiate economic development, the extent to which the British achievement of the period is understood and appreciated in India to-day is remarkable.[1]

---

[1] Family *pietas* prompts me to instance a splendidly compiled present-day Indian State paper, *Memorandum on the Introduction of Metric System in India*, by Pitambar Pant, with Foreword by Jawaharlal Nehru (Planning Commission Government of India, 1955). Mr Pant, an extremely able young Indian Civil Servant, in assembling the evidence in favour of the adoption of the Metric System by India to-day, has reprinted in extenso as his appendices B.1, B.2, and B.3 the memorandum advocating the same system written by my great-uncle, General (then Colonel) Sir Richard Strachey and dated Simla, October 1st, 1867, the latter's Minute of Dissent from the Report of the Committee on Indian Weights and Measures, which advocates the adoption of a version of the British system, and the minute of Sir John Strachey, member of the Governor-General's Council, supporting his brother. The views of the brothers were summed up by Sir John as follows:

"3. In enquiring what measures ought to be taken to remedy the manifest evils of the existing state of things, it must be first laid down that our conclusions must not be influenced by anything but the advantage of the people of India. Questions of the present or future convenience of Englishmen must be left out of consideration. Mr Minchin's Committee seems to have been of the opinion that India, being politically dependent on England, public policy requires that she should be compelled to assimilate her weights and measures to those of the ruling power, irrespectively of her own advantage or convenience. For my part I reject entirely all such suggestions. It is our duty in this matter to think of the interests of India alone, and to do nothing without a reasonable conviction that the measures which we adopt will never be undone. It would, as Colonel Strachey has said, be utterly unjustifiable to make any organic change in the weights and measures of India, unless we are satisfied that it will be a lasting one. Whatever we do now must be done with a view to the establishment of that system which we consider will be ultimately and permanently the best for the people of India."

The Strachey brothers succeeded in getting an Act (Metric Act of 1871) on to the statute book providing for a phased introduction of the Metric System into India. Mr Pant comments on Sir Richard's work for this enactment as follows:

"The moving spirit behind this measure was that of Colonel R. Strachey, F.R.S., R.E. His brilliant notes and memoranda (Appendices B.1, B.2, B.5), in particular his Minute of Dissent (B.2), are classic in their quality, imbued with scholarship, practical wisdom

Many devoted British administrators were building the railways, the canals, the roads—the whole "infrastructure", to use a convenient present-day military term—of modern industrial development. Together with the splendid administrative and fiscal structure of the I.C.S. and the development of perhaps unsuitable, but yet considerable, educational and judicial systems, these were massive achievements. Nor is it true to say with Marx that this work was done simply and solely in the interests of Britain and in order to enable her capitalists to make more money out of India. That this was one motive, no one who represents the jute constituency of Dundee in the British Parliament (as I do at the present time), or visits Calcutta with its immense jute and cotton mills (still sometimes Scottish, or English, managed), can avoid becoming aware of. But yet the real development was immensely more complicated than that.

The British visitor to present-day India would be more, or perhaps less, than human if he did not take a pride in the mighty legacies to India which his countrymen have left. In the physical sphere the trunk railways, with their huge steel or masonry bridges over the great rivers, will surely remain the memorial of our empire in India, as do the Roman roads of Europe to the Romans, or as do the Taj Mahal and the forts and palaces of the Moguls to the former conquerors of India. At the ancient city of Agra the monuments of the Moslem Raj and the British Raj can be conveniently compared. If one stands on the battlements of the Red Fort of Akbar, one may see at one and the same time the vast aery, dream of the Taj, and the two great railway bridges spanning the Jumna. The Taj reflects the sensibility of Shah Jehan, the artist-emperor of the seventeenth century.[1] The two bridges, on the other hand, are worthy monuments of the workaday, sturdy, unlovely energy of the nineteenth-century British. Both are the heritages of present-day India.

and above all a noble earnestness which not only evokes admiration but also inspires. No aspect of this complex subject has escaped his notice and none has received but the most patient and careful treatment. With 90 years separating his writings from now, it is remarkable they are as much relevant and enlightening to-day, during our present consideration of the problem, as they were then when the subject was in his care."

The result, however, was unfortunately typical of even the most enlightened imperialist rule. Owing to the obstruction of British commercial interests, the Metric Act remained a dead letter, and the work of introducing a rational and uniform system of weights and measures to India remains to be done by an Independent Indian Government. (The introduction of the new system was actually begun in 1958.)

[1] To my taste, although not, curiously enough, to the taste of many present-day Hindus, neither the Taj nor the other great Moslem monuments have anything approaching the aesthetic importance of the indigenous Hindu monuments such as Ajunta, Ellora, Elephanta or Konarak.

The second legacy of the British, the human network of an efficient administrative Civil Service covering the face of the sub-continent, also stands to-day as firmly as do the railways. It has been completely Indianised, but its traditions, its methods of work, its whole way of life, are almost absurdly familiar to anyone who knows Whitehall. And, with all its faults, the existence of such a service, when compared with the administrative vacuum which confronts many another of the major undeveloped countries to-day, is a priceless asset.[1]

The third major British legacy to India, namely Parliamentary democracy, does not date from the period which we are considering. On the contrary, the nineteenth-century British administrators would almost all have denied the possibility of introducing such a system into India in any foreseeable future. (See, for example, the opinions expressed in Sir John and Sir Richard Strachey's joint book on India. *The Finances and Public Works of India, 1869-1881*, Sir John Strachey G.C.S.I. and Lt.-Gen. Richard Strachey F.R.S., Kegan Paul and Trench, London, 1882.) As we shall note, the tardiness with which democracy was brought to India had grave consequences. Still, in the nick of time, though unwillingly and as a result of Indian pressure, a Parliamentary system was established, so that here, too, India inherited both the Lok Sabba, or Central, Federal Parliament, and the Parliaments of the Constituent States. She possessed a workable machine of government which could hold the vast nation together.

Nevertheless in my view the mid-Victorian period was the real heyday of British rule in India. The succeeding Edwardian viceroyalties of Curzon and of Hardinge were more magnificent. But by then the justification of arbitrary British rule was fast coming to an end.

---

[1] If, on the other hand, the revolutionary road is taken, as in China, inevitably under communist auspices, then one of the first things which it will be necessary to do is to break up the old Civil Service and substitute for it a nation-wide communist bureaucracy. Of course the revolutionary method has some advantages: the old Civil Service is sure to be conservative-minded and difficult to transform into an instrument of change: on the other hand, if you wish to avoid the revolutionary method and all it entails, then the existence of a legacy such as the Indian Civil Service is, I repeat, a priceless asset. In order to see this you have only to look at the plight of the undeveloped countries—Indonesia for instance—which have neither adopted the revolutionary, communist method nor yet possess an efficient civil service.

CHAPTER IV

WHAT HAPPENED TO BRITAIN

THE BRITISH CONQUEST of India had momentous economic and political consequences for Britain also.

In order to consider the economic consequences we shall have to return to the last decades of the eighteenth century, and trace, if we can, the effect upon the development of the British economy of the unequal trade which the East India Company was carrying on with India. For it was during these decades that the British economy went through that hitherto unprecedented transformation which we now call primary industrialisation.

Indian historians, following Romesh Chandra Dutt (*Economic History of India Under British Rule* (1902), a school of American and British historians, such as Brook Adams, in his work, *The Law of Civilisation and Decay* (New York, 1910) and William Digby in *Prosperous British India* (1901), as also Marxist analysts, such as R. P. Dutt in his *India To-day*, have taken the view that the fruits of the pillage of India in the late eighteenth century played a major part in providing the initial capital for the contemporary industrial revolution in Britain. This is one aspect of the theory of "the drain", as it is often called, which has played a major part in Indian nationalist propaganda. We must attempt to assess what really happened. For it will appear that this whole issue of whether, or to what extent, one country can get fat by battening upon another: or, conversely, of whether, or to what extent, one country can help another over the critical period in its development, is of the highest present-day political importance. It is certainly a natural assumption that a "drain" of unrequited value, extorted from India (and the West Indies) by Britain not only had dire consequences for the former but also greatly helped the latter to industrialise. The question is a quantitative one. How big a part of that precious initial store of capital, command over which alone enables a nation to begin to industrialise, was provided by the British imperial conquests?

In order to answer such a question we shall have to look at the amount of wealth transferred, unrequited, to Britain, and then attempt to analyse what that wealth really was. In some cases of conquest the amount of wealth forcibly transferred to the conqueror can be

WHAT HAPPENED TO BRITAIN 61

estimated without undue difficulty. The treasure which Spain drew from South and Central America in the sixteenth and seventeenth centuries is fairly well known, for example. This is partly because it took the direct and simple form of the importation of gold and silver. But it is partly also because the Spanish system was so highly centralised that the whole of this treasure came, officially at any rate, through the hands of the Casa da Contratacion at Seville. A recent historian of imperial Spain, Mr R. T. Davies, in his book, *The Golden Century of Spain 1501-1621* (Macmillan, 1937), is, for example, able to print as an appendix a table of the total gold and silver imports into Spain from the Americas from 1503 to 1660. At their peak these imports (1591-5) were running at some £4 m. a year, to which, we are told, must be added "from 10%-50%" for smuggled imports. Perhaps £5 m. to £6 m. a year would be the order of magnitude of the sum transferred to Spain. And, since the metals were mined by slaves who were fed and maintained out of American resources not much was probably transferred in the opposite direction, from Spain to the Americas.

No such simple calculation can be made in the case of the East India Company's trade with India. In the first place, far from importing bullion or precious metals into Britain, the Company was, even after the conquest, hard put to it to avoid exporting them both to India. What it imported from India were above all textiles. Up to the conquest these were paid for in gold and silver. After the conquest of Bengal, as we noted on p. 40 above, the Company attempted not to pay for them at all, but to raise the money for their purchase by taxation in the province, and in other provinces too as the conquest extended. This ideal of the Company's ships going out empty and returning laden with free goods was never quite achieved. But it was approached.

Professor Holden Furber in his *John Company at Work* (Harvard University Press, 1948), a leading American authority on this matter, gives us the figures. During the decade 1783-93 only £721,914 in gold were sent to India from Britain. A rate of under £100,000 a year means that the flow of gold had been reduced to a trickle. For the scale of the transactions between the two countries was quite large. For example, in this decade over £23 m. of goods from India were imported. On the face of it, it looks as if during this decade, Britain only paid for about £7¼ m. worth of the £23 m. worth of her imports from India. In fact, the discrepancy was not as extreme as that. For some actual goods, as well as gold, were exported by Britain. In order to illustrate and exemplify the sort of thing that was happening, Professor Furber has given us a detailed account of the cargoes on both the outward and the homeward voyages of the *Berrington*, the ship in which Warren Hastings returned to England in 1785. The *Berrington* had carried out to India various goods, namely lead, copper, steel, woollen clothes and naval stores, to the value of £27,300. She brought back from India cotton piece goods, cotton yarn, indigo, redwood, silk and saltpetre to the value of £119,304. If her voyage was typical, as Professor Furber implies that it was, she was evidently transferring an unrequited value to Britain, on this voyage, of about £90,000. The Indian produced goods were promptly sold at auction in London, to both British and European buyers, and the profit credited to the Company. It is not particularly relevant to our purpose that at this date little of the profit so realised found its way into the pockets of the holders of East India Company stock. For the Company, largely in order to finance Clive's "military transactions", had borrowed extensively in India, above all from its own servants.

What, typically, happened was something like this. Some Company's servant made, say, £20,000 on a contract for supplying bullocks for the baggage train of one of the Company's armies. Or still more frequently such a sum was made in "the country trade", *i.e.*, in trade, either internal or sea-borne, between different places in India, or between India and some other part of Asia, a trade in which, as we saw, the Company's servants engaged at an immense advantage over their Indian competitors. What the lucky man wanted to do was to transfer the money he had made to England for his future use and enjoyment. Accordingly he lent it to the Company in India, which gave him a promise to pay him the amount, with interest, on a certain date in England. At least this is what he did if he did not have much to conceal as to how he had made the money. If he had a good deal to conceal he lent the money, on the contrary, to one of the other East India companies, the Dutch, the Danish, the French, the Ostend, or the Trieste companies, which were still operating in India more or less on British sufferance. If he had still more to conceal he bought diamonds in India and sent them back to England either by ship or overland, through Bagdad, Constantinople and Vienna. Or, yet again, he might speculate again in another trading venture either in the East, or in a voyage back to Europe, which, if successful, would leave his money there on call.

Professor Furber makes a gallant effort to estimate what this jungle of transactions really meant in terms of a transfer of wealth to Britain from India. After complex calculations, involving much guess-work, he comes to the conclusion that during the decade 1783-93, on which he concentrates his researches, something under £2 m. a year was being transferred unrequited. This is a surprisingly modest sum. For example, William Digby, in his *Prosperous British India* (1901) calculated that "the drain", or "the tribute", as it was often called, of unrequited value exacted from India averaged £18 m. a year during the whole period from Plassey (1757) to Waterloo (1815). But it may be that Professor Furber is nearer the mark. He is a recent and American investigator with no motive for minimising the figure. At any rate, before challenging it, it would be necessary to conduct researches into the original documents, bills of lading and labyrinthine accounts of the East India Company comparable to those undertaken by the professor. Moreover, on consideration, several factors may incline us to suppose that the amount may have been of this order of magnitude. First, applying our multiplier of 10, this would be equivalent to an annual transfer of £20 m. in 1959 money. Second, we must remember that Britain was then a country of some 8 or 10 million inhabitants, say a fifth of its present population. Therefore, per capita the transfer would be equivalent to one of £100 m. a year to-day. So the amount was modest, though not insignificant.

The explanation of why the devastation of Bengal seems to have resulted in such relatively modest gains for Britain is, surely, that pillage is an almost incredibly wasteful process. Clive's salt monopoly and the virtual monopolising of trade by the Company's servants and their agents produced the famine of 1770 and reduced much of Bengal, in Cornwallis' phrase, to "a jungle inhabited only by wild beasts". But that did not mean that it enriched Britain to any remotely comparable degree. By far the greater part of the values taken from Bengal were simply lost to both countries. Only a minor part was successfully brought to England.

Nevertheless, the inflow to Britain of unrequited value on the above scale, while not very great, may still have been significant for the economy. And this brings us to the question of what it was that was being transferred from India to Britain. It is only too easy to become bewildered by the maze of transactions involved. Not only the above described elaborate transactions between the Company and its own servants are involved, but also the web of exchanges which began to be woven as soon as an Indian cargo reached London. Let us return to the example of the *Berrington*'s cargo, worth £119,000, which reached London in 1885. Let us suppose that a particular "lot" of calicoes, cambrics or silks, was sold at the Company's auctions to an Austrian buyer for, say, £10,000. Let us further suppose that this £10,000 enabled the Company to pay part of its debt to the *Berrington*'s most distinguished passenger, Warren Hastings, the Company's retiring Governor-General. During his period of office the Governor-General had made, in one way or another, considerable sums which he had then lent, in Bengal, to the Company. These debts had now to be repaid to him out of the sales of the Company's goods. Thus the £10,000 now passed to him.

Now let us consider what Hastings did with the money and with all the other sums so paid to him. One thing which he did was to buy back his ancestral manor of Daylesford in Worcestershire and re-equip the estate. And in this he was typical of many of the Nawobs. The theme of repurchasing or redeeming run-down or mortgaged family estates runs through the histories of the early "Indians". This, for example, was Clive's own first action. And this was the result of my ancestor, Sir Henry Strachey's, first voyage to India. Imprudent management had so heavily mortgaged the family estate in Somerset that it would have been lost within a few months of the time when Clive engaged the young Strachey as his Secretary for his third and last voyage to India. When Clive discovered this situation he, with characteristic magnificence, lent Strachey £10,000 to be duly repaid when Strachey got his share out of the system of better-regulated pillage which, as we noticed, Clive went out to establish in Bengal. Again Scotland contains many an estate, the land of which was originally drained or the farm improved, by returning "Indians", who owed their places and opportunities to Dundas. For in the seventeen-eighties and 'nineties Dundas, as the younger Pitt's political manager in such matters, was busily staffing India with his compatriots. The significance of this for our purpose is that many of the Nawobs appear to have used their fortunes *productively* when they came home. They invested in improving their estates or in buying new ones. They took part in the revolution in agricultural technique which was going on throughout the eighteenth century and which underlay and made possible the industrial revolution.

In order to trace the significance of this, let us return to our imaginary example of the £10,000 "lot" of textiles sold to an Austrian buyer out of the *Berrington*'s cargo. Since the textiles had been taken from Bengal without any equivalent value being sent there, the transaction meant that Britain could now import £10,000 of corn, or anything else, without having to make and export anything in return.

If, on the other hand, the silks in the cargo were sold to an English buyer[1] the transaction meant that the wealthier classes in Britain could satisfy their desire for fine textiles, again without any British labour being used up for that purpose. In general the acquisition of this amount of unrequited imports meant that the existing standards of life of the British people could be maintained with less British labour. An amount of labour which would have been needed to produce £10,000 worth of goods had been freed for other purposes. Therefore this quantity—let us say for argument 500-man years—of British labour, were now available for such purposes as improving the productivity of the Nawob's estates, or more dramatically, for building Mr Boulton's and Mr Watt's new steam engines in Birmingham.

This argument is only valid, however, upon the hypothesis that the available supply of British labour was fully employed. For if it was not then there was no need to "free" a part of it in order to improve estates or build steam engines. There are no such things as eighteenth-century employment statistics. But for the sake of simplicity let us assume full employment for the moment, and continue to trace the effect of the receipt of the unrequited value from India on that assumption. We will withdraw the assumption in due course.

Workers could now be spared for the above purposes without anyone being the poorer during the time before their work on the estates or the steam engines had resulted in any more consumers' goods being available. That is the point to be observed. If it had not been for the unrequited import of the £10,000 worth of goods, the diversion of 500 man-years of labour to investment must have reduced the supply of goods for immediate consumption correspondingly. It is only by means of the advent of some outside, adventitious, aid that a community, already fully employed on sustaining its own standard of life, can divert some of its resources to producing new capital goods, without reducing its standards. Of course, as soon as the initial job has been done the *further* production of capital goods becomes far easier. In our example, as soon as the first Nawobs' estates had been improved and were producing more food with less labour, or as soon as the new steam engines had been sent to Lancashire and were turning the spindles and driving the shuttles, so that more shirts were being made by fewer workers, the thing became self-perpetuating. More and more workers were each year freed to produce more machines which, in turn, freed more workers. It is that first agonising pull off the dead

[1] In order to protect the home cotton trade, the cottons had to be exported.

centre of an undeveloped and unchanging technique of production which is the trouble. At that juncture an import of even quite a modest amount of unrequited value can be important. The present-day importance of getting this basic economic consideration clear will emerge. For to-day the position as between not only India and Britain, but the under-developed and the highly developed worlds in general, is just the opposite to the eighteenth-century situation. Then it was Britain which was in the throes of the first critical stage of industrialisation. And she managed to lay her hands on some unrequited value from abroad to help her through it. To-day it is India and the other undeveloped nations which face that same crisis. And dire will be the consequences unless they are enabled to borrow, or are given, some unrequited value in their turn.

When we have once realised this vital fact, however, we must not exaggerate the part which the import of unrequited value from India played in the British industrial revolution. Other major influences were at work. For example, if Duplieux instead of Clive had conquered India; if the spoils had flowed to Paris, not London, would the Industrial Revolution have first taken place in France instead of Britain? Imperialist gains did not, in my view, play anything like so decisive a part as that. There were more important sources for the accumulation of the primary capital which made possible the industrial revolution in Britain. Much the largest of them, was the agricultural revolution, marked by the enclosures, which had been going on, not only since the beginning of the eighteenth century (with its great technical achievements), but since before 1500. Every decade the food necessary to sustain the British population at a given standard of life, and the wool to clothe them, were being produced by a slightly smaller number of workers. This freed a slowly but steadily expanding number of workers for making the steam engines and, still more important, for building the roads and digging the canals of eighteenth-century Britain. The process of "freeing" the former peasants from not only their food-producing labour, but also, and particularly, from their hereditary holdings, was a savage business: but this was the way in which productivity in agriculture rose and so provided the basis of all subsequent development. This internal process resulted, at certain times and places, in a terrible initial fall in the peasants' standard of life, but it provided resources which were probably many times as important as the unrequited imports of the East India Company and the other imperial spoils such as the slave-produced sugar of the West Indies.

We must now withdraw the assumption that there was full employment in Britain when the unrequited Indian imports began to arrive. On the contrary the enclosures and the associated rise in agricultural techniques had for long been continually freeing labour from food production. Thus at any given moment there already existed a pool of unemployed labour. Accordingly if we take the shortest possible view it may be suggested that neither unrequited imports nor the agricultural revolution were necessary to free labour for accumulation. For there was unemployed labour available already. And this is what certain economists, brought up in the Keynesian tradition, are in fact apt to suggest. But the suggestion only shows the superficiality of the Keynesian analysis if it is applied to long periods and to major historic developments. For, of course, the pools of unemployed labour which such commentators notice had only come into existence as a result of a *previous* change in agriculture. If mediaeval agriculture had been left untouched with its huge, under-employed but unavailable labour force, securely "bound" to its peasant holdings, there would have been nobody to use for the vast work of the Industrial Revolution. On the contrary what the unrequited imports did was to add to the stream of unemployed labour which was becoming available for capital accumulation—and by so doing no doubt helped to keep wages down to a subsistence level.

It is true that all this labour might have been freed from its previous employment and then not re-employed on capital accumulation. It might simply have rotted and perished unused. And some of it did. But in eighteenth-century Britain, almost uniquely up to that time, much at least of this freed labour (though after immense suffering) actually found new employment in capital accumulation—in what we now call development. That was the remarkable thing: that is what has to be accounted for. Naturally, the major explanation is the break through in technique (the greatest since the invention of the wheel) associated with the steam engine which was occurring at the same time and place. Nevertheless it is precisely in this respect that the receipt of unrequited value from India may have played an important role. It provided a basis for the liquid funds—capital in readily disposable form —which is so hard to accumulate and which plays a major role in the actual application of new techniques. That the "enterprisers" of the early industrial revolution were able to find banks and finance houses able and willing to finance them may have been partly due to the unrequited gains of the unequal trade of the East India Company and its imitators.

We should therefore conclude that though the notorious "drain" from India was by no means the largest factor in Britain's pioneer accomplishment of primary industrialisation, it played a very real part. That process was, in comparison with present-day developments, a slow one, stretching over more than one century. Nevertheless, at the critical moment, in the mid-eighteenth century, it received the impetus of unrequited imports. In the final chapter of Part II we shall come back to this issue but, as it were, in reverse. In the middle of the twentieth century the question is: how can the undeveloped countries of the world, which are largely the ex-colonies of the empires, be provided with an external contribution to capital accumulation? For, even though such a contribution may be quite minor in amount, in comparison to the vast sums which they must somehow raise from their own peoples, it may yet be indispensable to getting the whole process fairly under way. The thing has been aptly compared to the "assisted take-off" whereby a modern fighter aircraft may be shoved off the ground by a rocket mechanism which can be easily dispensed with once it is flying.[1] We should not forget that we in Britain benefited from "an assisted take-off" in our pioneer industrial revolution two hundred years ago. To-day not merely Britain but the whole of the West must on pain of catastrophe to themselves help forward the industrialisation of the undeveloped three-quarters of the world. We must do so both in our own interests and in the interests of the human race as a whole. But we should also remember that we are repaying a debt.

The political as distinct from the economic consequences for Britain of having acquired the empire of India were far-reaching. It was by taking power over this vast Asian sub-continent that Britain decisively launched herself upon the imperial course.

It is true that already during the seventeenth and eighteenth centuries Britain, and to a lesser extent France also, were acquiring colonies of a very different type from India. These were colonies which had been inhabited thinly and by peoples so primitive that they could be exterminated, driven into the interior, or absorbed. Thus their former territories could be actually peopled by Europeans. The main territories of this character acquired by the Europeans were North America, which was steadily peopled by the British as to what is now the Eastern United States, and by the French as to what is now Eastern Canada,

[1] Professor Blackett in his Presidential Address to the British Association, 1957.

and the Southern Mississippi Valley: and, in the early nineteenth century, Australia and New Zealand, which began to be peopled by the British.

If we add such large areas as these, in which actual European settlement was beginning, to the Spanish and Portuguese Americas and to the trading posts in Asia and Africa which had come or were coming into European possession, we get a picture of a world in which, at or about the year 1770, the European states must have seemed about to acquire, immediately, by far the larger part of the earth. Three major areas of the explored world alone remained quite independent of them, viz. the Moslem world of Western Asia plus South-Eastern Europe and North Africa, under the Turkish Empire; China, under the still vigorous rule of the Manchus, and Japan in its still untouched feudalism. But in the event an immediate European conquest of the world did not occur. If we now look at the world as it was, say, seventy years later, in 1840, the possessions of the European states are smaller, not larger. In particular, all three of the Americas, with relatively small exceptions, had become independent.

This ebb of the imperial tide began, of course, with the successful revolt of the thirteen British North American colonies in the seventeen-seventies. But that event was followed during the first half of the nine-teenth century by the equally successful revolt of the Spanish and Portuguese colonies of Central and South America. Neither of these revolts, it is to be noted, were made by the indigenous inhabitants of the Americas; for they had been exterminated, dispersed, driven away or securely subjugated. They were both undertaken by the colonists of the European states which had settled across the Atlantic. Therefore they did not prevent the Americas from being peopled by Europeans. Nevertheless, they created independent states, not empires. Moreover, during the same period the one significant part of the Americas—namely, Canada—which had not become independent by means of revolt, took the first step in the process of achieving her present independence by means of agreed constitutional development. And this same development took place a little later in Australia and New Zealand also.

Nor was this major ebb in the imperial tide counterbalanced by forward moves in Africa. The European possessions remained mere trading posts upon the periphery of the continent. In Asia alone the imperialist process still went forward. And this was above all due to the fact that the British completed their conquest of India in these eighty years. By the fall of the Sikh kingdoms of the Punjab in 1849, the original colony of Bengal had become, in all but name, the British empire in India. With the suppression of the mutiny ten years later its power was consolidated and in 1876 it received the name of empire. It was this acquisition by a European nation of sovereignty over one of the two major civilisations of Asia which determined the fact that European conquest proceeded in Asia, while it receded in the Americas and stood still in Africa. For the extension of European, and predominantly British, power further into Asia during the first two-thirds of the nineteenth century was essentially based upon the fact that the British had become a major Asiatic power. It was from India, and through the agency of the East India Company, that Europe began to knock upon the door of China herself.

The story of the earlier encounters between Europe and China, in the eighteenth and early nineteenth centuries, has been often told. The behaviour of the Europeans was so atrocious, and the attitude of the Chinese so superciliously correct, that the defects of the latter have, perhaps, tended to be overlooked, in the case of non-imperialist historians at least. Certainly nothing whatever can condone the two opium wars or the process at once arbitrary, violent, yet at the same time covert and hypocritical, by which Chinese sovereignty was slowly destroyed, first in the ports along her coast, and then gradually in extending spheres of influence into her huge interior. Still, was there not something blind and self-righteous—not to say downright silly—in the Chinese refusal, over a century, to face the facts of European physical power and do something about it? The Chinese are so consummately great a people that it must be a wonder to a European that they did not sooner (since they have done so very adequately in the end) see what they were up against: that they did not see that they were up against societies which in respect of their control over their natural environment had moved far ahead of them.

It was no doubt natural that when the Chinese first met the Europeans they should have supposed that they were unimportant "Western barbarians", to be permitted to pay tribute, but of no conceivable danger to their own age-long empire over that part of the world which they alone know. And yet the Chinese had had some direct contact with Europe ever since Marco Polo, and an appreciable contact with European culture through the Jesuit missionaries in the sixteenth and seventeenth centuries. Was there any real excuse for the unshakeable complacency, and the illusion of impregnable national security, which the Chinese exhibited not only in the eighteenth century, towards, for instance, Lord Macartney's famous mission, but even far into the nineteenth century, when the gunboats were already steaming up their great rivers?[1] At any rate, that complacency on the part of their rulers cost the hundreds of millions of the Chinese people dear indeed. China came within an ace of becoming the colony first of one or more of the European powers, and then, in our own time, she escaped the domination of Japan by an even smaller margin.

The Japanese when they also encountered the European problem, showed a far greater appreciation of the forces which menaced them. It is true that in the period which we are considering—namely, the first two-thirds of the nineteenth century—they dealt with the matter by means of a determined policy of non-intercourse. But when that became impossible they undertook the most remarkable, the swiftest and the most successful policy of self-development of which the world has any record. Is it not strange that the Chinese should have been so much the slower to appreciate correctly that they had encountered a new and most formidable world?

Be that as it may, what must here be noted is that even during the partial lull in imperialist expansion, between, say, 1770 and 1870, the expansion of Britain from her Indian base went steadily on in Asia. China, in the first opium war (1842) was decisively "opened up": that is to say, she was forced to trade with the West, and in particular to allow her people to buy and smoke opium, whether her own government liked it or not. Nevertheless, the first major Western aggressions on China and the completion of the conquest of India can do no more than qualify the impression that there was, in the earlier decades of the nineteenth century, a temporary recession in the tide of European imperialism. It is often forgotten, for example, that, first, the loss of the American colonies, and second, the steady movement towards independence of the other "White Dominions" after 1834, meant for Britain the dissolution of by far the greater part of her previously existing empire. With the huge, but single, exception of India, there was very little left of the eighteenth-century British Empire when you had taken away America, and were, clearly, taking away Canada, Australia and New Zealand, in the sense that you had willingly entered upon policies which implied their eventual independence. What was left was essentially the West Indies (which were not highly valued in

[1] The excuse, or at least the explanation, is to my mind to be found in the tendency of the greatest nations to get stuck at their point of maximum achievement, and so to function actually worse in a new age requiring new adaptabilities than nations which formerly were markedly inferior to them. (See Ch. XIV, below, for a discussion of this tendency.)

this period, since slavery in them had been prohibited) together with
what were little more than trading stations scattered on the African
and Asian coasts. The vast British colonial possessions of the next period
had not yet been acquired.

This was the period in which the young Disraeli made his famous
remark to the effect that the wretched colonies were millstones round
our necks. More significantly the sober apostles of industrial capital,
Bright, Cobden, the two Mills, the Gladstone of the middle period,
would all have agreed that the future lay, not with empire, but in a
free trade world of independent, self-governing states: that empire and
imperialism were declining factors in the world. Nor did these representative figures of the period hesitate to express forthright anti-
imperialist sentiments. For example, James Mill called the colonies "a
vast system of outdoor relief for the upper classes". And John Stuart
Mill made the more significant assertion that empire abroad was incompatible with democracy at home. "The government of a people
by itself has a meaning and a reality, but such a thing as government
by one people over another does not and cannot exist. One people
may keep another as a warren or preserve for its own use, a place
to make money in, a human cattle farm, to be worked for the
profit of its inhabitants; but if the good of the governed is the proper
business of a government it is utterly impossible that a people
should directly attend to it" (*Considerations on Representative Government*).

In a word, there was an anti-imperialist climate of opinion. An
economic explanation of this lull in imperialism has been attempted.
It is that the new industrial capitalisms, of which Britain was much
the most developed example, genuinely did not need to possess sovereignty over the lands with which they traded, at any rate to the same
extent as either the merchant capitalist societies had done, or as the
latter-day fully mature capitalist societies were to do. As we have seen,
the earlier mercantile imperialists drew but a feeble and wavering line
between trade and plunder. Once, however, industrial production has
got going in an imperial centre, genuine trade with less developed
countries can grow. The actual exchange of goods, of manufactured
products for food and raw materials, begins to take place. Therefore,
the physical subjection of the country traded with is not felt to be as
necessary as it was. Naturally, it is still very handy to be able to control
your customer and your supplier. We have noted, for example, that
this power enabled the Lancashire mill-owners to trade on extremely
favourable terms with the Indian peasants, to the ruin of the Indian

handloom weavers.[1] That is why it is suggested the mercantile empires did not voluntarily dissolve themselves in the first half of the nineteenth century: that is why some major examples of such empires, such as the British in India and the Dutch in Indonesia, survived right through the relatively anti-imperialist period and formed the nucleus of the new imperialism which was to follow. Nevertheless the simple fact was discovered in this period that if all you wanted was to trade with some other country, then it was not necessary to occupy it. On the basis of that discovery an ideology of Free Trade and anti-imperialism, of liberalism in one of its aspects, could and did emerge. It looked and felt to the dominant ideologists of the day as if empires were at most waning assets with which a free trade capitalist world would gradually dispense.

My own view, however, is that this explanation of "the lull" is only part of the truth. In the light of experience we can now see that another factor made British mid-nineteenth-century liberal anti-imperialism possible. Britain was so strong, economically and in every other way, that she was not subject to any challenge from trading competitors. She had a sort of natural monopoly in her trade with most of the undeveloped world. In such a situation it was often unnecessary to incur the burdens and costs of territorial acquisition. If and when the indigenous authorities were willing and anxious to trade, why conquer them? For even without acquiring sovereignty over them, the well-organised, large-scale British trading corporations had an immense bargaining power as against primitive, disorganised peasant sellers. As we shall see, the anti-imperialist climate of opinion in Britain was soon destroyed when, in the last quarter of the nineteenth century, traders from the now rapidly industrialising countries of continental Europe appeared upon the scene. And when the traders turned into *investors*, the climate of opinion in both Britain and in the rest of Europe became ferociously imperialist.

Paradoxically enough, the relatively anti-imperialist climate of much of the nineteenth century can be well appreciated from the tone and

[1] What reversals of fortune the onrush of modern history carries with it! In the nineteen-fifties it is Lancashire which is afraid of the competition of the vast Indian machine textile industry. Fortunately, however, there is no question of the bones of the Lancashire weavers whitening the streets of Oldham and Blackburn. They are steadily transferring their labour to where it can be adequately productive, making electrical equipment, jet engines, atomic piles, machine tools, and the new synthetic textiles, instead of shirts. It makes an immense difference to be (a) free and self-governing, (b) a highly developed nation, and, I may add (c) for some dawning consciousness of how social and economic change takes place to have appeared.

temper of the most famous of the declarations which helped to set the current of opinion flowing in the opposite direction. In 1883 Sir John Seeley published his two courses of lectures, delivered at Cambridge, upon *The Expansion of England* (Macmillan, 1883). This was a good ten years after the new type empires of capitalism proper, which we shall discuss in the following chapters, had begun to come into existence: and indeed Seeley is often thought of as their first apologist. Yet when we read him to-day, after three-quarters of a century, we cannot fail to be struck by his relative moderation and restraint. It is true that Seeley starts out by attacking the neglect of the imperial theme by contemporary British historians. He, rightly, complains that in their accounts of the previous 150 years of British history they concentrate their attention upon minor internal developments while neglecting the tremendous story of British expansion overseas which had resulted in the acquisition of a vast empire: the loss of the American core of that first empire: and then the process of re-expansion into Australasia, Canada and India. And it is in this connection that he uses the phrase, which is almost all that is remembered of his book to-day, that England acquired her empire "in a fit of absence of mind".

It is also true that Seeley is intent upon making his hearers, the Cambridge undergraduates of the eighteen-eighties, "empire-minded" in the sense that they are to concentrate their attention upon "the expansion of England" till she becomes as great in extent as in power. But the empire to which Seeley aspires is not the agglomeration of Asian and African possessions, the acquisition of which had just begun, and which was to dominate the lives of those Cambridge undergraduates. Seeley was almost certainly unconscious of the advent of this new sort of empire, of the imperialism of Rhodes, Stanley, Kipling and Chamberlain, of Curzon, Cromer and Milner. For him the empire consisted of two parts. First, what we should call "the old Dominions", *i.e.*, Canada, Australia, New Zealand, and (doubtfully) Cape Colony and Natal. Second, India.

It is upon the first of these two parts of the then existing British empire that Seeley concentrates his hopes. His essential message is a warning. He warns his readers that if they do not *both* rapidly develop these Dominions (confusingly to the twentieth-century readers he still calls them "the Colonies" as some of them still were) *and* make them into integral parts of the United Kingdom, Britain, in the coming twentieth century, is bound to be overshadowed by the two superpowers of America and Russia. He closes his introductory lecture with a remarkable passage in which, with, in some respects, wonderful insight into the future course of world events, he poses the alternative which he sees before Britain. He has no doubt that the Dominions will be very rapidly developed and peopled. In the 'eighties there were, he writes, 10 million "Englishmen beyond the sea". But "in not much more than half a century" (say, by 1950) "the Englishmen beyond the sea—supposing the Empire to hold together—will be equal in number to the Englishmen at home, and the total will be much more than a hundred millions". What, he considers, is in doubt is whether this empire will in fact hold together. If it does not—

"Such a separation would leave England on the same level as the states nearest to us on the Continent, populous, but less so than Germany and scarcely equal to France. But two states, Russia and the United States, would be on an altogether higher scale of magnitude, Russia having at once, and the United States perhaps before very long, twice our poulation. Our trade too would be exposed to wholly new risks."

On the other hand, if England will only become sufficiently empire minded she may enter the big class of super-powers in the twentieth century.

"The other alternative is that England may prove able to do what the United States does so easily, that is, hold together in a federal union countries very remote from each other. In that case England will take rank with Russia and the United States in the first rank of states, measured by population and area, and in a higher rank than the states of the Continent. We ought by no means to take for granted that this is desirable. Bigness is not necessarily greatness; if by remaining in the second rank of magnitude we can hold the first rank morally and intellectually, let us sacrifice mere material magnitude. But though we must not prejudge the question whether we ought to retain our Empire, we may fairly assume that it is desirable after due consideration to judge it."

We now know that neither of Seeley's prerequisites for Britain becoming an integrated super-state were to be fulfilled. First, the populations of the Dominions did not grow at anything like the speed which Seeley so confidently predicted. They lagged far behind the American rate of development. Why that has been so, why the tide of emigrants set so much more strongly towards the United States, would form the subject of an interesting study. Whether the major factor has been inferior natural resources, or differing social policies, or other factors, might be discovered. Second, the Dominions have all developed into what are in fact independent states, very loosely linked to Britain and to each other in what we now call the Commonwealth. On this issue of federal integration, Seeley is weak. His vision of what he calls "Greater Britain" required the creation of a Federal State at least as unified, as he writes in the above passage, as the United States. Indeed, it is to be in some ways more integrated, for he also writes that when a man leaves England for Canada or New Zealand we ought to regard it as no different in principle than if he moved from Kent to Cornwall. Yet he makes no suggestions whatever for the creation of federal institutions for his Greater Britain. He appears blind to the fact that in his day Dominion parliaments were already well established and that they must surely lead towards Dominion independence. There is thus something unpractical and un-thought-out about his vision of a Greater Britain.

On the other hand, Seeley's is a by no means ignoble vision. It is not really a vision of empire at all, in the sense in which that word is used throughout these pages. Seeley's Greater Britain is to be a large Federal State, the parts of which happen to be scattered over the globe, but the citizens of which are to have absolutely equal democratic and political rights. There is to be no question of England ruling over the other parts of this empire, any more than one American State rules over another. Nor must there be any possibility of one part exploiting another economically, any more than one English county exploits another. For Seeley is acutely aware that it was the remains of old-style mercantile exploitation which broke up the first British empire by alienating the American colonists. Such a British Federal State would have been (had it been practicable) an incomparably higher and better organism than the fully capitalist empires which were in fact created, both by Britain and by the other highly-developed capitalism, in the half century since he wrote. For these empires were real empires in every sense of the word: they involved the direct and arbitrary rule of one people by another and, inevitably therefore, the exploitation of one people by another.

Seeley, however, could not concentrate his vision wholly upon the Dominions. He could blind himself to the new British empire in Africa and Asia which was beginning to grow up around him, but he could not ignore the existence of the huge colony of India. In fact, he devotes many pages to India, for he is clearly worried by the issues raised by her acquisition and retention. He cannot foresee any possibility of India ever becoming part of a federal, integrated, Greater Britain. Yet he is convinced that Britain must continue to govern India. He is not wholly convinced indeed that the British conquest was originally desirable: but since it took place it must be maintained: it must be maintained, that is to say, *until Indian nationalism arises, but not a moment longer.* And he closes his fourth lecture with a memorable and enlightened passage:

"We could subdue the mutiny of 1857, formidable as it was, because it spread through only a part of the army, because the people did not actively sympathise with it, and because it was possible to find native Indian races who would fight on our side. But the moment a mutiny is but threatened, which shall be no mere mutiny, but the expression of a universal feeling of nationality, at that moment all hope is at an end, as all desire ought to be at an end, of preserving our Empire. For we are not really conquerors of India, and we cannot rule her as conquerors; if we undertook to do so, it is not necessary to inquire whether we could succeed, for we should assuredly be ruined financially by the mere attempt."

Nevertheless, Seeley, in the eighteen-eighties, cannot discern even the germ of Indian nationality. He considers that a religious movement of revolt is far more likely than a national revolt. The fact that almost as he wrote the Indian National Congress, which was destined to grow into a fully formed expression of Indian nationalism, was being founded was quite hidden from him. If he could have foreseen that in the coming half-century his condition for the British leaving India would be unmistakably met, he might have been regretful. But I do not think that he would have gone back upon his emphatic opinion that it would be suicidal to attempt to stay.

Seeley's verdict upon the consequences of British rule for India is not boastful. He does not claim any remarkable improvement in the conditions of the Indian people: if we have "removed evils of long standing", we may have "introduced new evils". But one thing, Seeley writes, we have done. He is appreciative of the traditional wealth and splendour of Indian civilisation. But he remarks that, for whatever causes, that civilisation had become arrested at a stage broadly corresponding to the European mediaeval period. Just as in mediaeval Europe men could look back upon a splendid classical past, so the Brahmin was the heir to a perhaps equal heritage and tradition.

(Seeley was still unaware of how rich, even on the political side, was the heritage of Asoka and of the Guptas.) But because, we may surmise, of the catastrophes of the Moslem invasions, there had been in India no Renaissance and no scientific development.[1] The Hindu world-view had, in northern India especially, become predominantly mystical, as a result no doubt of despair occasioned by the devastations of the Moslem conquests. Rationalism, in the Western sense, had had no opportunity to develop. Therefore "the most characteristic work of our Empire . . . is the introduction in the midst of Brahminism of the European views of the universe". This may seem even to-day fair comment, though present-day scholars will probably say that there was never any definite thing called "Brahminism". Seeley indeed under-estimated the impact of the Western world, channelled through the British connection, upon India. He might have deplored the fact that it would produce that national consciousness the appearance of which he knew must be the term of British rule. But he did realise that the introduction into Hindostan of the post-mediaeval Western world view was our essential mission in India. For this was the intellectual counterpart of the "regenerative" economic development noted by Marx.

On the whole, Seeley's thinking and feeling, in spite of his intense desire for a Greater Britain, were free from the worst aspects of imperialism. He expressly repudiated the exploitations of the mercantile empires, for he realised that they were fatal to his vision. He had not yet envisaged the new forms of imperialism which were arising even whilst he lectured at Cambridge. And we may pay him the posthumous compliment of supposing that he would have detested them. For his mind had been formed in the relatively anti-imperialist climate of opinion of early industrial, competitive capitalism.

That climate was now to change. In the last resort because, it will be submitted, of underlying changes in the nature of the economy of each of the most developed nations, an irresistible impulse towards imperial expansion was now to be experienced. Seeley's world outlook was to be engulfed by a mighty tide of imperialism of a new kind, the flood and then the ebb of which have been a principal factor in creating the world which we inhabit to-day.

[1] There had been, as I understand it, something analogous to the Reformation, in the great movement of Brahminical reform which in the end re-absorbed Buddhism and brought India back to her original faith. Moreover, that movement, in some of its phases, at some times and places (although certainly not in others) was puritanical and "protestant" in tone. But Europe would not have got very far with the aid of the Reformation alone and without the Renaissance and its associated scientific development.

CHAPTER V

THE NEW IMPERIALISM

FROM ABOUT 1870 onwards a new wave of imperialism surged out upon the world. Two countries of Western Europe, Britain and France, led the way. But they were avidly imitated. Germany, America and Japan hastened, late but formidable, to share in the partition of the world which was taking place. Even some of the smaller states—Belgium, Holland, Portugal—managed to get or retain a share. Vast but still semi-feudal structures such as Austria-Hungary and Russia were effectively stirred.

Britain, both because she still just held the lead in industrial development and because she already possessed a nucleus of empire, essentially India (but also the West Indies), held over from the mercantile epoch, took the lion's share in this new wave of imperialism. J. A. Hobson, in his book, *Imperialism*, writing in 1902, gives the table of British territorial acquisitions in the thirty years between 1870 and 1900 (see p. 80).

These acquisitions add up to a territory of 4,754,000 square miles with a population estimated in 1902 at 88 millions. It is important to remember that this whole "Colonial Office Empire", as it might be called, was, essentially, created only seventy or eighty years ago. Therefore its life span, since it is now in rapid dissolution, will prove to have been under a century.

It must not be thought, however, that the lion's share was the only one. On the contrary, French acquisitions in this period, principally in Africa (but also Indo-China), were territorially impressive (3,500,000 square miles but with only 26 million inhabitants). Belgium got what proved to be the rich prize of the Congo (900,000 square miles, $8\frac{1}{2}$ million inhabitants). Moreover, Germany at length united, and year by year becoming the most formidable industrial power in Europe, began her colonial career in this period. She annexed, in the same 30 years, a million square miles of territory with 13 million inhabitants. Japan, which only started out on her staggeringly successful course of self-modernisation under forced draft in 1867 acquired her first colonies in this period, as a result of her wars with China at the end, and with Russia just after the end, of the century.

The United States of America also gave what appeared to be

	Date of Acquisition	Area Square Miles	Population
EUROPE:			
Cyprus	1878	3,584	237,022
AFRICA:			
Zanzibar and Pemba . . .	1888 }	1,000,000 {	200,000 {
East Africa Protectorate . .	1895 }		2,500,000 {
Uganda Protectorate . . .	1894-1896	140,000	3,800,000
Somali Coast Protectorate . .	1884-1885	69,000	(?)
British Central Africa Protectorate	1889	42,217	688,049
Lagos	to 1899	21,000	3,000,000
Gambia	to 1888	3,550	215,000
Ashantee	1896-1901	70,000	2,000,000
Niger Coast Protectorate . .	1885-1898	400,000 to 500,000	25,000,000 to 40,000,000
Egypt	1882	400,000	9,734,405
Egyptian Soudan . . .	1882	950,000	10,000,000
Griqualand West . . .	1871-1880	15,197	83,373
Zululand	1879-1897	10,521	240,000
British Bechuanaland . . .	1885	51,424	72,736
Bechuanaland Protectorate . .	1891	275,000	89,216
Transkei	1879-1885	2,535	143,582
Tembuland	1885	4,155	180,130
Pondoland	1894	4,041	188,000
Griqualand East	1879-1885	7,511	152,609
British South Africa Charter .	1889	750,000	321,000
Transvaal	1900	117,732	1,354,000
Orange River Colony . .	1900	50,000	385,045
ASIA:			
Hong Kong	1898	376	102,284
Wei-hai-wei	—	270	118,000
Socotra	1886	1,382	10,000
Upper Burma	1887	83,473	2,046,933
Baluchistan	1876-1889	130,000	500,000
Sikkim	1890	2,818	30,000
Rajputana (States) . . }		128,022 {	12,186,352
Burma (States) . . }	since 1881	62,661 {	785,800
Jammu and Kashmir . . }		80,000	2,543,952
Malay Protected States . .	1883-1895	24,849	620,000
North Borneo Co . .	1881	31,106	175,000
North Borneo Protectorate .	1888	—	—
Sarawak	1888	50,000	500,000
British New Guinea . . .	1888	90,540	350,000
Fiji Islands	1874	7,740	120,124

unmistakable signs of launching herself upon the imperialist course. She cleaned up fragments of the empire of Spain (Cuba, Puerto Rico, the Philippines) and asserted, in a degree varying all the way from the establishment of a virtual protectorate in Panama to a mere reinterpretation of the Monroe Doctrine elsewhere, her general overlordship of the Americas. Finally, during the whole of this period Russia was pushing out her boundaries, eastward and southward over Asia. As usual, her development was a special case peculiar to herself. In particular, her acquisitions were landlocked and contiguous to her metropolitan mass, instead of maritime and scattered over the continents.

This dry catalogue of the territorial acquisitions of the imperial states in the heyday of the new imperialism, *i.e.*, in the forty years from 1870 to 1914, can convey but a faint impression of the overwhelming power of the Western drive towards the conquest of the world. Nor will it give us any clue as to the causes of this explosive phenomenon. Once again it will be best to describe some concrete examples. Let us briefly consider two cases of British expansion during the period, namely the acquisition of *de facto* sovereignty over the Nile Valley and the conquest of South Africa. It so happens that each of these acts of imperial acquisition had as one of its principal agents an exceptionally interesting, and articulate, imperialist: Cromer in Egypt, Milner in South Africa. The records of these two remarkable men may help us to identify the motives which drove forward the new imperialism.

Between 1880 and 1900 the whole of the Nile Valley, from the great lakes of Africa to the Mediterranean, passed under British control. In this remarkable episode of British expansion in its heyday, Sir Evelyn Baring, afterwards Lord Cromer, played the principal role. As Cromer (unlike Milner) wrote a history of the events which he, largely, directed, we may follow the story, in the main, as he himself tells it in his *Modern Egypt* (Macmillan, 1908).

Cromer opens his narrative with the following words: "The origin of the Egyptian Question in its present phase was financial." The public debt of Egypt (almost entirely held abroad), he continues, stood at some £3·25 m. in 1863. By 1876 it was some £94 m. £16 m. had been spent upon digging the Suez Canal. For the whole of the rest of the increase there was very little to show. Some part had been squandered, some part had been dissipated in corruption, but the largest part had been borrowed towards the end of the period in frantic and immensely costly efforts to pay the interest on that part of the debt which had already been incurred. The creditors were private persons and institutions in France, Britain and elsewhere.

When Cromer wrote that the origins of the Egyptian question were financial, he meant, as his narrative makes clear, that the *de facto* annexation of Egypt and the Soudan by Britain arose out of attempts on the part of the British and French Governments to collect the

interest on the above debts on behalf of the bondholders. The process
by which this happened was, however, immensely complicated. It is
pointed out by Cromer, and by nearly every subsequent historian, that
the British Government made persistent efforts, sometimes carried (as
in the Gordon affair) to the point of opening it to charges of pusillanimity, to avoid having to take upon itself the virtual annexation of
the Nile Valley. All that is quite true, *upon the assumption that, whatever
else happened, the interest on the debts, or at least the greatest practicable
part of it, had to be collected.* What the British Government really wanted
was that somehow or other the interest should be collected without
Britain having to involve herself in the complications and responsibilities of conquering Egypt. But when it became clear that that was
impossible, Britain occupied and ruled Egypt and the Soudan rather
than that the bondholders should lose their money. There would have
been no difficulty at any time in avoiding the *de facto* annexation of the
Nile Valley if the British Government had taken the view that those
of their nationals who had lent their money to the Egyptian Government had done so at their own risk. But this was an attitude foreign to
the imagination of the period, and Cromer does not seriously consider
it in the course of his two volumes.

He does mention the issue just once. By 1878 the Egyptian Government of the Khedive was about to default on its interest payments to
the bondholders. In spite of having already driven the Egyptian
Government, which was as cruel as it was incompetent, to produce
famine both in Egypt and the Soudan by its tax extortions, the British
Government joined with the French Government in representations
to the effect that there was "every reason to believe that the Khedive
could pay the coupon" (*i.e.*, the interest on the bonds) "as it fell due in
May if he chose to do so". In doing so, Cromer writes (*Modern Egypt*,
Vol. I, p. 37), the British Government departed from "the tradition
of the London Foreign Office that British subjects, who invested their
money in a foreign country, must do so at their own risk". Cromer
does not give any examples of this alleged tradition being observed,
and the main ones which I can think of are the loans to States of the
American Union and to some Latin American republics which were
with impunity defaulted. But in these cases the British Government
was hardly in a position to use force to collect the debts. It was simply not
practical politics to make war upon the United States, or even to flout
the Monroe doctrine by intervention in South America. In any case
in Egypt the money was collected from the already starving peasantry,
through the agency of the Egyptian Government, by, Cromer

writes, "two of the most iron-fisted Pashas who could be found".

Cromer, or Baring as he then was, was thus first sent to Egypt in this workaday role of a debt collector or bailiff's man. From 1877 to 1880 he served as "the British Commissioner of the Public Debt", that is to say, the British member of the international team which had been put in to extract order, and the bondholders' money, out of the chaos of Egyptian finances.[1] They had had some success in this endeavour when Cromer left Egypt in 1880. It was while he was absent that the decisive event took place which resulted in the British occupation. That event was one of the periodic upsurges of Egyptian nationalism, led on this occasion, as on a more recent one, by some of the younger officers of the Army, headed by a colonel called Arabi. These younger Army officers, together with some Egyptian civilians, attempted to stage what was in effect a *coup d'état* against the Government of the Khedive. The Khedive, it must be remembered, was technically merely a Viceroy or provincial Governor of the Sultan of Turkey, and Egypt was nominally a Turkish province. Here, as in the case of the Mogul Empire, we encounter the phenomenon of a decaying empire from which the provinces are not so much revolting as dropping off into a sort of quasi-independence. For several decades Turkish authority over Egypt had been nominal: on the other hand, the country was still ruled by Turkish nobles, or Pashas, of which the Khedive was merely the richest, just as Bengal in 1757 was still largely ruled by Moslem nobles.

Arabi's movement was nationalist, generally anti-foreign, anti-Turkish quite as much as anti-European. It expressed the convulsive effort of the Egyptians to regain some control of their own affairs by shaking off the double or triple layers of foreign rule to which they were subjected. As against the weak government of the Khedive Arabi's movement was successful. By the early months of 1882 Arabi had forced the Khedive to make him Minister of War and had got the country under his virtual control. If he had retained power he would no doubt have attempted to run the country on nationalist lines, as indeed Mahomet Ali, the existing Khedive's predecessor, had done fifty years before. And Arabi might have repudiated some or all of the debts. But even the possibility of this the British and, to start with, the French, Governments would not contemplate. They did not particularly want to annex Egypt, but they were determined to collect

[1] Cromer was not appointed, like the other Commissioners, by his Government, but by Lord Goschen on behalf of the bondholders direct. But he tells us that this made little difference in practice.

their subjects' debts come what may. The fiery M. Gambetta chanced to be the French Prime Minister for three months at the turn of 1881-2 and he persuaded the British Foreign Secretary, Lord Granville, to send a menacing joint note to the Khedive, making it pretty clear that Britain and France would not stand for a nationalist government in Egypt. This note, Cromer writes, united and galvanised the Egyptian nationalists into a real determination to achieve the independence of their country. But by the time matters came to a head in July 1882 the French Government had, as usual, changed, and was now unwilling to use force. Yet the British Government now felt committed to doing so. There was a violent anti-foreign riot in Alexandria, and British warships were sent to the port. Arabi, or the Egyptian Government, which by now hardly existed apart from him, set up batteries to defend the town. On July 11th the warships bombarded the batteries and the town, the Egyptians were driven out, and the town burnt, no one is quite certain how, probably partly by the bombardment and partly by Arabi's disorderly troops. A British expeditionary force was sent and the Egyptian Army under Arabi was routed at Tel-el-Kebir on September 13th (1882). The British occupation of Egypt, which was to last until 1956, had begun. —

Writing in 1959, it is impossible not to compare the Arabi movement of the last century with that of Nasser in our own time. Naturally the Egypt of seventy-five years ago was a much less developed place than the Egypt of to-day. Yet the similarities between the two movements are striking. Nor does Cromer himself lightly dismiss the possibility of Arabi having been able to set up an effective nationalist government, had he been allowed to do so. Cromer wrote:

"It was more than a mere military mutiny. It partook in some degree of the nature of a *bona-fide* national movement. It was not solely, or, indeed, mainly directed against Europeans and European interference in Egyptian affairs, although anti-European prejudice exercised a considerable influence on the minds of the leaders of the movement. It was, in a great degree, a movement of the Egyptians against Turkish rule. Although previous to the issue of the Joint Note some hope might have been entertained of guiding the movement, and although I am distinctly of opinion that an effort to guide it should have been made, it must be admitted that the chances of failure predominated over those of success" (Vol. I, p. 324).

Cromer goes on to discuss the question of whether Arabi could have succeeded in running a government on the basis of "Egypt for the Egyptians" and comes to the conclusion that he probably could not have done so. But this is because Cromer assumes that Arabi would have physically driven out of Egypt not only the Europeans, but also the Turkish Pashas (in whom, "in spite of many defects, the habits and traditions of a governing class still lingered"), the Syrians and Armenians, and all other foreigners. From what Cromer himself tells us of Arabi this seems unlikely. Nevertheless, it must readily be agreed that a nationalist Egyptian Government in the eighteen-eighties would have been not only an exceedingly rough-and-ready, but also, very likely, an unstable affair, which might well have collapsed after a shorter or longer period of rule. Cromer, writing in 1907, naturally concludes that some kind of foreign occupation and government of Egypt was probably indispensable and beneficial, and, equally naturally, that, if so, a British occupation was by far the best. That may or may not be so. The question is really only a special case of the far broader question of whether a period of widespread capitalist imperialism was or was not indispensable for the development of the world.

On the narrower issue of the balance-sheet of the seventy-five-year period of British imperialism in the Nile Valley we may make the following observations. In the first place, no one should doubt the remarkable character of the British constructive achievement in Egypt, and later in the Soudan. In September 1883 Cromer was recalled to Egypt, but this time as "British Agent and Consul-General". This modest title ineffectively concealed the fact that he was the absolute ruler of the country and remained so for twenty-four years, till his departure in May 1907. There is no doubt that in this quarter of a century of (disguised) colonial status the material condition of Egypt was (in some respects) transformed. And this in spite of very serious difficulties. The very first thing which Cromer had to face in his new pro-consulship was the loss of the whole of the Soudan. Maddened by the rapacity of the Egyptian Government's efforts to collect money "to pay the coupon", the Soudanese rose, in 1883, under the leadership of the Mahdi, or Moslem saviour, drove out or surrounded the feeble Egyptian garrisons, slaughtered the Egyptian expeditionary force (under a British General, Hicks) sent to reconquer them, and for some time acutely menaced Egypt's southern frontier. This led to the Gordon affair, in which an attempt was made (against the wishes of Cromer and the British Government) to reconquer the Soudan on the cheap. Gordon got himself killed at Khartoum, and it was not till 1898 (thirteen years later) that the Soudan was methodically reconquered by Kitchener.[1]

All this put a heavy strain on the new Egyptian Government, working under close British direction. Nevertheless, a very great deal was accomplished. Egypt as Cromer found it in 1883 must have been one of the most miserable countries which have ever existed. As he left her in 1907 she had become not only solvent and easily able to pay her creditors (which was undoubtedly the original object of the exercise), but also on the road at least to modern development. Competent, honest, although alien, government had been able greatly to reduce taxation on the peasants, while raising far more revenue. During the period of Cromer's rule direct taxation was reduced by £2 m. a year; the salt tax, the octroi duties, the bridge and lock dues on the Nile, and the taxes on river and fishing boats were abolished. Many other indirect taxes were greatly reduced. Good administration at the same time raised the revenue from just under £E.9 m. in 1883 to £E.15 m. in 1906 (see *Modern Egypt*, Vol. II, pp. 447-9). Above all perhaps, the irrigation upon which Egypt's life depends had been salvaged and

[1] Cromer claims, no doubt justly, that one of the major services which Britain rendered to Egypt was to force the Egyptian Government temporarily to "cut its loss" and abandon the Soudan for the first years of the British occupation. It is in this connection that he gives a delightful thumb-nail sketch of Lord Granville, Gladstone's Foreign Secretary from 1880 to 1885. Cromer had to deal with this great, bland Whig grandee throughout the first critical years of his pro-consulship. When, Cromer writes, he put to his Foreign Secretary the necessity of preventing the Egyptians from attempting a reconquest of their lost province of the Soudan, Granville concurred in the following characteristic language, which it is irresistible to quote in full:

" 'It takes away,' he said, 'somewhat of the position of a man to sell his racers and hunters, but if he cannot afford to keep them, the sooner they go to Tattersall's the better.' I have a large number of private letters from Lord Granville. Some of them are very interesting. His light touches on serious questions were inimitable, and his good humour and kindness of heart come out in every line he wrote. It was possible to disagree with him, but it was impossible to be angry with him. It was also impossible to get him to give a definite answer to a difficult question when he wished not to commit himself. His power of eluding the main point at issue was quite extraordinary. Often did I think that he was on the horns of a dilemma, and that he was in a position from which no escape was possible without the expression of a definite opinion. I was generally mistaken. With a smile and a quick little epigrammatic phrase, Lord Granville would elude one's grasp and be off without giving any opinion at all. I remember on one occasion pressing him to say what he wished me to do about one of the numerous offshoots of the general tangle, which formed the Egyptian question. The matter was one of considerable importance. All I could extract from him was the Delphic saying that my 'presence in London would be a good excuse for a dawdle'.
"I remember once comparing notes with Lord Goschen on this subject. He told me that on one occasion, when he was at Constantinople, after many unsuccessful endeavours to obtain definite answers to certain important questions which he had addressed to Lord Granville, he wrote a very lengthy and very strong private letter, intimating that unless clear answers were sent, he would resign. The only reply he received from Lord Granville was as follows: 'My dear Goschen—Thank you a thousand times for expressing your views so frankly to your old colleagues' " (*Modern Egypt*, pp. 392-3).

extended. The mediaevalisms of "the Courbash" (the rhinoceros hide whip universally used to chastise the peasant) and "the corvée", or unpaid forced labour for the annual clearance of the irrigation ditches, had gone. Justice, hygiene and education had begun. A fairly competent army had been formed. The peasant was, relatively, prosperous. The middle class was rapidly growing. Cromer could not unreasonably look forward to steady further improvement in the conditions and standard of life of the Egyptian people, if British rule were continued.

In the event, that rule was continued, although in a decreasingly direct form, for nearly fifty years more. And yet in the end, when the British did actually leave, in 1956, the final balance-sheet was not nearly so favourable as Cromer in 1907 might legitimately have hoped and expected that it would be. Egypt had been fairly effectively modernised. (It is this which enables her to lead the Arab Nationalist Movement to-day.) But it is doubtful if the standard of life of the Egyptian people, still overwhelmingly peasant, had improved nearly as much as might have been expected, as compared with 1882, or had improved at all as compared with 1907. This, no doubt, was above all due to the new menace which had arisen, in spite of—indeed precisely because of—all the civilising improvements introduced by British rule—namely, the now inordinate rate of the growth of the population. Cromer says that the population was given as 6·3 million in 1882 (although this may have been an underestimate) and 11·2 million in 1907. To-day (1959) it is over 24 million. Within the limits of the type of pre-industrial development of the British period, such an increase in population is no doubt prohibitive of any marked raising of the standard of life. At any rate, in my experience, a visitor to the Egyptian village of 1954 would find it hard indeed to imagine what conditions must have been like if and when they were even worse.

To some extent no doubt we ought to judge our success or failure in Egypt by the virtues or defects of the nationalist régime of Colonel Nasser which has succeeded it. (At any rate we are quick to take credit for the virtues of the Indian successor régime in the parallel case.) It is of course much too early to know what the verdict of history upon the Nasser régime will be. One great virtue that régime possesses: it aims at national development: at industrialisation: at the abolition of the abysmal poverty of its people. How far that constructive side is being overlaid by an appetite for larger territorial expansion and by the feud with Israel is still doubtful. But at least the spark of constructive desire is there. Moreover, criticism of the defects of the new régime must be regarded, after seventy-five years of British rule, quite as much as criticism of Britain as criticism of the Egyptians. The strict limits of the benefits which even the best form of alien rule can confer upon a people are apparent. Not materially, of course, but psychologically, the Egyptians under Nasser seem to be beginning again where they were compelled by outside power to leave off under Arabi. Once again the only form of self-government which they can produce is the no doubt appropriate but not very evolved form of an army dictatorship led by middle-rank or junior officers. Once more xenophobia has to be the main binding force which holds them together.

But the differences as well as the similarities between Arabi's movement and Nasser's are marked. This time it is clear that the attempt to create an "Egypt for the Egyptians" will not be arrested from the outside. The bombardment of Port Said in 1956 did not lead on to occupation, as did the bombardment of Alexandria in 1882. Now, as then, the only real alternatives, as Cromer so clearly saw, were to let the nationalist Egyptian movement have its way or to occupy the country and rule it. Now, as then, it was argued that the interests of "the powers" made it impossible to allow the nationalists to retain power. In 1882 it was fear that the interest on the bonds would not be paid; in 1956 it was fear that the Egyptians could not, or would not, work the Suez Canal. But this time the matter has been put to the test, and it appears that the Egyptians are experiencing no difficulty at all in this respect.

In fact, however unpleasant it may be for many people in Britain to realise, the Nasser Government is clearly quite capable of governing Egypt without foreign tutelage. Whether it will govern it ill or well is, of course, another matter. But surely there can be no doubt that once a people is capable of ruling itself at all, it must be allowed to do so. What is sad is that the historical development has been such that now that, for the first time, almost literally since the Pharaohs, Egypt became genuinely self-governing, she has become for a time the leader of anti-British feeling in the whole of her region of the world. But can we sincerely deny that the main fault for that lies with Britain, not Egypt? And yet, if we had had the statesmanship to end our period of rule in Egypt in even approximately the same way in which we ended it in India, the new Egypt might have become a most valuable friend, for our real interests do not conflict. Our record of achievement on behalf of the Egyptian people during the period in which we were responsible for their welfare is better, not worse, than our record in India, since it is not marred by an initial period of pillage. But the end spoilt everything.

An interesting passage in the conclusion of Cromer's book invites us to speculate as to what his attitude would have been to the events of the present day. Writing, let us recall, at the peak point of British imperial success, when, as we shall note, imperialism seemed even to its strongest opponent to be irresistible, he concludes his book as follows:

"Although, however, I will not venture to predict the goal which will eventually be reached, I have no hesitation in expressing an opinion as to which we should seek to attain. So far as can at present be judged, only two alternative courses are possible. Egypt must eventually either become autonomous, or it must be incorporated into the British Empire. Personally, I am decidedly in favour of moving in the direction of the former of these alternatives."

It is true that Cromer was also convinced that Britain could not withdraw from Egypt for some time to come. In fact, she did not do so for half a century after he wrote. We may easily suppose, therefore, that Cromer, faced in 1956 by the clear alternatives of once again suppressing Egyptian nationalism or of permitting Egypt to become genuinely autonomous, would have chosen the second. Instead, the British Government of 1956 half-heartedly attempted to repeat the actions which had led, in 1882, to the occupation. In the world of the mid-twentieth century they merely led to fiasco. It is unlikely that Cromer, the sanest, best-balanced and most fair-minded of the great British pro-consuls of the imperial heyday, would have approved of policies which have undone much of his lifework.

Our business, however, is to assess the motives which led Britain to annex the Nile Valley in the second half of the nineteenth century, in order to see if they throw light on the more general question of the motives which led both her and the other powers to annex in the same period much of the rest of the habitable globe. We have seen that Cromer, the man who did the job, had no doubts about the matter. The motives were "financial": it was a matter of debt-collecting. What happened was that British (and French) private citizens had lent to, or invested in, Egypt: when the Egyptian Government would not or could not "pay the coupon" an Egyptian Government which would pay had to be put in its place.

No more terse statement of the economic motives for imperial expansion has ever been made than Cromer's. But we must not accept it as conclusive just because he was the man on the spot. Cromer may have been oversimplifying the Egyptian case: or the motives for other acquisitions may have been different. And in fact it is obvious enough that motives other than the directly economic played their part, not so much perhaps in the original acquisition of Egypt as in the retention of British *de facto* sovereignty there for so long. Those motives are clearly what are often called "strategic". We held on to Egypt not so much in order to continue to "collect the coupon" as because through Egypt lay the water route and the electric telegraph to India and to the Far East. This is the "life-line of empire" argument, which was to dominate British thinking on the Middle East.

All this has led some observers to conclude that strategic considerations are more important than economic as the motivation behind empire-building. And it is quite true that in a particular case at a particular time, as in this case of the retention of Egypt, those strategic reasons may be decisive. No doubt we kept Egypt above all because we wanted to secure ourselves in India. But this fact does no more than illuminate a principle, namely that strategic reasons, however important, cannot be regarded as the primary motive behind imperial expansion. For why, in this case, did we want to secure ourselves in India? Because we had taken India. And, as we have seen, we had taken India from economic motives in a rather simple sense—because the conquest enormously enriched a very limited number of people. The strategic motive is essentially secondary. Strategy is a means to an end not an end in itself. The end is the conquest of other peoples or the avoidance of conquest by them. Therefore, however high we rate the strategic motive for particular imperial actions—and it has often been decisive—we are still left with the basic question of why people wish to conquer and to avoid being conquered.

It would be to anticipate the whole of the argument of the rest of this book to try to answer that question here. But clearly one answer would be to say that people wish to conquer rather than to be conquered because, in our epoch of history, the conquerors have usually found means of making the conquered work for them to a greater or lesser extent. And it is very much nicer to be worked for by, than to work for, other people. We shall ultimately conclude that this is an inadequate answer, both in the sense that there have been periods of human existence when it has been impracticable to make other people work for one with advantage, and that there are some signs that mankind may be about to re-enter such a period, and also in the sense that there have always been, and are, other biological and deep seated, propensities to conquest and domination. Still, it will pay us to consider this concept as an hypothesis as to the main motivation of the new imperialism of the late nineteenth and early twentieth centuries. (Readers who, rightly, regard this paragraph as an extreme simplification of an enormously complex matter are referred to Part III for an attempt at a more adequate discussion of the issue.)

Let us turn to another example of British imperial expansion in the above period: the annexation of South Africa. And for a protagonist of this event, we may follow the actions and words of Milner in South Africa in the same way that we have followed those of Cromer at the other end of the continent in Egypt. It is of course more or less arbitrary to choose Milner as the key figure in this enterprise. Joseph Chamberlain or Cecil Rhodes might equally be held typical. Milner, however, was the most intellectual and the most interesting of them. Moreover it was Milner's will power, above all, which carried through, in the face of no small obstacles, the annexation of the two Boer republics of the Orange Free State and the Transvaal.

The history of the Boer War, its origins, its course, its results, both immediate and as they are becoming apparent in the nineteen-fifties, are too well known to require re-telling here. But who can really doubt that the simple issue on which the war was fought was whether or not independent Boer sovereignty was to be cleared out of the way of the British entrepreneurs and investors who wanted to make their fortunes out of mining the diamonds and the gold which, it had been discovered, underlay the fields which the Boers were tilling? For the Boer régimes, while they did not prohibit the exploitation of these precious minerals, did hamper it, refused civil rights and citizenship to the incoming British entrepreneurs and their staffs, taxed them arbitrarily, and generally stood in the way of the full exploitation of what was turning out to be one of the most attractive of all the fields for the overseas investment of the flood of British capital which was being generated at home.

Moreover, the mines of Kimberley and the Rand were likely, it was felt, to be immensely profitable, not only because of their diamonds and their gold, but also because there was available on the spot a supply of ultra-cheap labour. This was provided by the "Kaffirs" or native African tribesmen who had been recently subdued and could be made to work for subsistence or less. The question of who should use this labour and benefit from the surpluses which it produced, the British in mining or the Boers in farming, could, it turned out, only be decided by war. That this was in truth the issue is well commemorated by the terminology in use to this day in the City of London in regard to the matter. The City has always been, and still is, in the coining of its slang at least, delightfully frank. How apt it is that South African gold-mining shares are known as "Kaffirs"! Thus in a single word the under-lying fact is revealed that what is really being exploited in South Africa is not only the gold of the Rand nor the diamonds of Kimber-ley, but the exceptionally cheap labour of the Africans, or Kaffirs, conveniently embodied in the mined gold or diamonds. Indeed, that the particular product in which the surplus created by this labour is embodied is a secondary question is illustrated by the fact that of late it has been found just as profitable to embody it in copper (from Rho-desia) or in uranium. We shall note the limits to which the exploitation of this cheap labour in fact benefits the national accounts on p. 177, below. But there was not and is not any doubt at all of the remarkable extent to which it benefited the accounts of the particular enterpreneurs engaged in exploiting it.

How much the supply of cheap labour mattered is illustrated by one of Milner's last, and most politically disastrous, acts. When, after the dislocation caused by the war, the African labour supply proved temporarily inadequate, Milner arranged to import Chinese indentured labourers. It is characteristic of the man that he was genuinely astonished that anyone in England found anything objection-able in his doing so. It would, he felt, have been very queer to have crushed Boer independence in three bloody years of war, fought primarily in order to get satisfactory conditions for working the mines, and then to let anything stand in the way of working them. But what he had failed to notice was that the great sleepy British public, which had of course never faced the fact that this was what the war had been about, could not "take" the importation of rather thinly disguised serf-labour to carry out the imperial purpose, especially when Milner, as he naïvely writes (Milner Papers, Vol. III, p. 559), had not thought twice about giving a British official authority to flog that labour without any legal process.

On the other hand it is not to-day possible to accept the somewhat naïve views of the "pro-Boer" minority of the British public. The fathers and grandfathers of the Boer farmers who are now practising apartheid, and who then held the same view of the Africans, cannot be held up as innocent victims of the British imperialists. The truth is that there were at the end of the nineteenth century two distinct layers of imperialism in South Africa. There was an in-rushing tide of British mining and land-speculating imperialism, determined to exploit "Kaffir" labour in the new and incomparably more profitable way of gold- and diamond-mining instead of in farming. But in possession was a previous layer of somewhat home-spun Boer imperialism, content to exploit African labour on a relatively small scale upon its farms. The Boer War was essentially a conflict between these two layers, or forms, of imperialism. In a sense, no doubt, the British were much the greater, more up-to-date, more powerful, imperialists. But both sides were Europeans intent upon the exploitation of the labour of far more primitive societies, either in agriculture or in the extraction of raw materials, such as gold and diamonds, for their own benefit. Thus all the generous views of the British "pro-Boers" of the turn of the century must to-day seem a little beside the point. If we accept the basic premises of up-to-date imperialism, Chamberlain, Rhodes, Milner and the British generally were in the right. The Boer republics had become an anachronism standing in the way of the effective exploitation of irresistibly attractive wealth. On the other hand, if we accept the premise of an earlier imperialism, the Boers had a right to continue to exploit "their" natives in their own primitive (but rather ruthless) way, since they had got there first. The rights, if any, of the Africans did not arise in anybody's mind, except occasionally as a talking point to throw at the other side.

Of course neither Milner, Rhodes nor Chamberlain publicly admitted what the war was about. They spoke rather of the British imperial mission. And it is quite true that for Milner the longer-term issue was whether Southern Africa was to take its place as a part of a vast super-state called the British Empire which he was utterly convinced that he and a chosen few, both of collaborators and of young disciples, had a mission to create. He gave what is in some ways the definitive expression to his imperial vision in his Johannesburg speech upon leaving South Africa in 1905.

"When we who call ourselves Imperialists talk of the British Empire, we think of a group of states, all independent in their local concerns, but all united for the defence of their own common interests and the development of a common civilization; united, not in an alliance—for alliances can be made and unmade, and are never more than nominally lasting—but in a permanent organic union. Of such a union the dominions of our Sovereign as they exist to-day are, we fully admit, only the raw material. Our ideal is still distant, but we deny that it is either visionary or unattainable. And see how such a consummation would solve, and, indeed, can alone solve, the most difficult and the most persistent of the problems of South Africa; how it would unite its white races as nothing else can" (*The Milner Papers*, Vol. II, p. 547.)

The sting of Milner's remarks is in the tail. What he was concerned with, now that the war was won, was to unite the white races in order to establish a secure white hegemony. The curious thing, however, about this vision of empire is its vagueness. On the one hand the above passage suggests that Milner had in mind something not unlike the Commonwealth as we hope to develop that association to-day. There is to be a free association of self-governing nations. On the other hand, the association must be united in "a permanent organic union", whatever that may be. Probably Milner, like Seeley before him, had taken care never to think through his imperial conception, for if he had done so its contradictions could not have escaped him. What he was actually concerned in building up, after all, was the very opposite of a free association of independent nations. On the contrary, he had just succeeded in coercing the two Boer republics into becoming parts of the British Empire, crushing, in the end, their passionate determination to remain outside it. The trouble with Milner, and the whole school of contemporary British imperialists of which he was the intellectual leader, was that they were determined to force a large part of the world voluntarily to associate with them. And that is rather a difficult thing to do.

As we have just noted, the Empire had become, by 1905, when the Johannesburg speech was delivered, above all an enormous aggregation of newly acquired colonies, together with India, which had no self-government, let alone independence, and which Milner was the first to say must not be given any in the proximate future. In a word, when Milner exulted, as he did, in his task of empire-building he was really engaged in creating an empire of the normal, old-fashioned kind, consisting of one central sovereign state, ruling and, if it so desired, exploiting a number of colonies. True, there were also "the White Dominions" and they really did enjoy an ever increasing degree of freedom and independence. But for that very reason there was every year less and less chance of them accepting any "permanent organic union", which phrase was no doubt meant to hint at some sort of super-imperial Council or Parliament with some such overriding powers in Foreign Affairs, Finance and inter-imperial commerce as those possessed by the Federal Government of the United States.

How can a man of Milner's first-rate intelligence have supposed that an imperial ideal shot through and through with such insuperable contradictions as these could ever have been realised? Perhaps a sufficiently resolute and ruthless policy of force might have kept together an orthodox type of empire for some time longer than was actually done, although certainly at the cost of ruining any possibility of the development of a voluntary commonwealth. But to think that such a policy of force could somehow be reconciled with the progressive grant of independence to "the white Dominions", and, at the same time, that the whole imperial structure could be somehow turned into a voluntary association, was a strange delusion to be entertained by, I repeat, a highly intelligent man.

Almost certainly the best chance of something constructive coming out of the two-layered South African imperialism which we have defined above was that taken by the Liberal Government which came into office in 1906, and at once gave South Africa full self-government. By hindsight we can now see that the Liberals ought to have made far-reaching guarantees for equality before the law, and for political rights, for the African population, a condition for the grant of self-government. Indeed their failure to do so makes it doubtful if, in the second half of the twentieth century South Africa will be willing to continue indefinitely to participate in an association of nations which must come increasingly to number Asiatic and African states in its membership. But to ask the Liberal statesmen of over half a century ago to have foreseen the tragedy of *apartheid* is to ask much. And certainly to have failed to apply some form of self-government to South Africa would have been to lose even the chance of a solution. Yet Milner violently opposed the Liberal attempt to apply in practice the voluntary principle to which he paid lip service.

And yet Milner was probably not a conscious hypocrite. He was rather an extremely finished product of a very special period and, in particular, of a very special form of education. He had carried all before him at Oxford. In the fabulous Balliol of Jowett, with Asquith, Gore and the elder Toynbee to compete with, he was perhaps the outstanding scholar, winning the Hertford, the Eldon and the Derby scholarships, and only missing the Ireland because he would not show up a copy of Greek verses with which he was dissatisfied. What a comment it is upon Oxford education as it then was that splendid human material such as Milner should be sent out into the late nineteenth-century world without really knowing anything about it at all. What other result could you expect if you gave all the highest, and, to a poor boy like Milner, indispensable, rewards for an ability to write verses in two of the languages of a previous civilization?[1]

We have now sketched two of the principal incidents of the process of headlong imperialist expansion undertaken by Britain and, to the utmost of their powers, by all the other highly developed capitalisms between 1870 and 1914. We have seen that the acquisition of Southern Africa and of the Nile Valley occurred from distinct, although closely related, motives. The Boer republics were overthrown and annexed because their existence hampered the exploitation of Kaffir labour in the mining of gold and diamonds by British capital. The power of the State was called in on behalf of adventurous British entrepreneurs like Rhodes investing their capital in overseas enterprises. In Egypt, on the other hand, the power of the State was used to protect bondholders, i.e., persons who had lent their money at a fixed rate of interest to a foreign government. What is common to both cases is that it was found that if the investment of British capital overseas was to be adequately promoted and protected, large slices of the world must be, in fact or in form, annexed.

On the other hand, the two examples of South Africa and Egypt provide, by themselves, quite inadequate evidence for the view that economic motives were the mainspring of the new wave of imperialism which engulfed the world after about 1870. Moreover, we should find, if we examined the other examples of imperialist acquisition in this period, that some of them fit less well with the explanation that force was being used essentially in order to promote or to protect the investments or loans of the major capital-generating powers. We should find examples of annexations of territories which had much less obvious attraction for risk capital than the Rand: and subversions of incompetent governments to which much less money had been lent than to that of the Khedive in Egypt. Evidently other powerful, if perhaps

[1] Not that, in my opinion, Milner and his contemporaries ought to have been taught technology: that would have made them still more ignorant of contemporary social relations: nor am I suggesting that knowledge of the social relations of the ancient world, derived by reading, say, Thucydides and Plato, in English (as we read the Bible) would have been irrelevant. What I am saying is that the concentration on mere linguistic feats produced a disastrous type of ignorance. (But see p. 242, below, for a further comment on this educational point.) The above note on Milner is indebted not only to Professor Headlam's two comprehensive volumes of *The Milner Papers*, but also to Mr Edward Crankshaw's recent (1950) study, *The Forsaken Idea* (Longmans, 1950).

secondary, motives, such as the strategic motive suggested above, were at work. Rather unpromising parts of the map, such as the Sahara, for instance, were annexed by powers such as France which had by no means so great a capacity for generating capital surpluses as had late-nineteenth-century Britain. Perhaps a sheer spirit of emulation, as well as military strategy, played a part in these instances.

Again, we should find that "the flag" did not invariably come to the rescue of the pound, the dollar, the franc or the mark, even when foreign investments or loans were endangered by "native" incompetence or recalcitrance. The British investors, we noted, lost a good many millions in both South America and in the southern states of North America without the British Government intervening to rescue them in the way in which it did in both Egypt and South Africa. Evidently these were situations in which it was too difficult or too dangerous to protect the foreign investor, at least by force of arms. For such an intervention would have encountered not the feeble Egyptian Government, or the small Boer republics, but the resistance of another well-developed society, in this case the United States.

Such considerations should warn us at the outset that any mechanical application of an economic interpretation of the new imperialism will not do. Still, the example of Egypt and South Africa, in which that explanation is especially clear, would, obviously, not have been chosen unless I had considered that this interpretation is the best guiding thread to an understanding of the imperialist policies of the highly developed capitalisms of the recent past. Our next task will be to set out that interpretation as it developed in the thought of those Western Europeans who were opposed to the imperialist process. Some of these anti-imperialists were liberal thinkers, of whom the British economist J. A. Hobson may be taken as the leading exponent: some were Marxists, and in this field Lenin is clearly the leading Marxist authority.

CHAPTER VI

THE HOBSON-LENIN EXPLANATION

FROM ABOUT 1870 the advanced, highly developed nations with one accord, but in ferocious rivalry with each other, turned to the annexation of the rest of the world. Why?

J. A. Hobson's book, *Imperialism* (1902), is the starting-point of any rational explanation. Moreover, a consideration of Hobson's views will give us an impression of the might, majesty and dominion which British imperialism in its heyday exercised, even over the mind of one of its most sincere opponents. Hobson never compromised his unswerving opposition to imperialism; but he was almost completely despairing as to the possibility of putting up any effective resistance to it.

Hobson's book starts out from the liberal standpoint which we noticed in the preceding chapter—namely, that for the rank and file of capitalist producers and traders, imperialism, *i.e.*, the conquest and subsequent domination of other countries, is not essential and indeed usually does not even pay its way. You do not have to conquer a country, Hobson reiterates, in order to trade with it. In fact, he shows with detailed statistics that you often do more trade with independent countries than with colonies. Is then imperialism just a gigantic intellectual error, which can be argued away by the reasoning of men of good sense and goodwill? It is a merit of Hobson's book that he sees that this can hardly be true. Imperialism must surely be in somebody's interests, or it would not have been undertaken. And Hobson proceeds to attempt to identify the motive lying behind the new surge of imperialism in which he lived, as based upon a necessity of the major capitalisms to *invest* their surplus capital abroad. This concept of the alleged necessity to invest abroad an otherwise undisposable surplus is the core of the matter. In the next chapter we shall arrive at the conclusion that the needs of particular entrepreneurs to invest abroad if they were to get the rate of profit which they demanded, and of the refusal of the property-owning classes as a whole to allow of a redistribution of the national income, were the operative factors, rather than any unconditional necessity for foreign investment. But it will be convenient to reserve comment on the theory to the next chapter. Here I am simply stating what first Hobson and then Lenin thought.

Hobson himself asks immediately, why the entrepreneurs' capital is surplus. Why can it not be profitably employed at home? He does not give a fully convincing answer. This inability to invest at home, he considers, is connected with an inability, in the capitalist societies of his day, for the demand for consumers' goods to keep pace with their production.[1] And this in turn is linked with the tendency of highly developed capitalist societies to save rather than to spend a high proportion of their national incomes. Finally this tendency is in turn associated with the extremely inequitable distribution of income which characterises them. Hobson also saw, although not very clearly, that all this was somehow linked with the growth of combinations, and the consequent atrophy of competition. But he does not go on to show how this last factor, unless powerfully offset, must upset the balance, first, of the bargaining power between capital and labour at home, and, second, between the last-stage capitalist societies and the under-developed world of atomised peasant farmers and primary producers.

Hobson had not quite the mental staying power, the sheer intellectual drive, to allow his remarkable insights to develop into a full theory of imperialism such as Lenin was immediately after him to construct out of a combination of Hobson's work with that of Marx. Nor, on the other hand, had he quite the economic technique, the analytical cutting edge to his mind, or the intellectual audacity to evolve Keynes' *General Theory*. And yet the *General Theory* is in some respects at once the proof, the extension and the application of Hobson's insights. Lenin foretold the massive revolutionary forces which must rise up against imperialism and finally overcome it. Keynes performed the even more surprising feat of indicating a possible way in which the highly developed capitalisms, by consciously redressing the balance of their economies and (although he blurred this issue) the social balance of their societies, could find ample outlets at home (albeit at relatively lower rates of return) for all the capital which they could generate. (See Chapters VII and VIII of *Contemporary Capitalism*.) With Hobson, British liberalism in its last phase came within an ace of making these two enormously important discoveries. But it just fell short.

Hobson regretfully concludes from all this that the arguments of the older generation liberals are no longer valid. The titanic new imperialist drive which surges all around him is no intellectual error to be corrected by argument. It corresponds only too closely with the real needs of the new stage of capitalist development which had set in about

[1] He has not much sense of the outlet which sufficiently rapid technical innovation might give.

1870. As such, Hobson feels in his bones that imperialism is invincible. He is convinced that it is corrupting the whole nation; that it has aborted the promise of social reform which existed up till the 'eighties or 'nineties: that it may lead to war. But there is no stopping it. He writes:

"Analysis of Imperialism, with its natural supports, militarism, oligarchy, bureaucracy, protection, concentration of capital and violent trade fluctuations, has marked it out as the supreme danger of modern national States. The power of the imperialist forces within the nation to use the national resources for their private gain, by operating the instrument of the State, can only be overthrown by the establishment of a genuine democracy, the direction of public policy by the people for the people through representatives over whom they exercise a real control. Whether this or any other nation is yet competent for such a democracy may well be a matter of grave doubt, but until and unless the external policy of a nation is 'broad-based upon a people's will' there appears little hope of remedy. The scare of a great recent war may for a brief time check the confidence of these conspirators against the commonwealth, and cause them to hold their hands, but the financial forces freshly generated will demand new outlets, and will utilize the same political alliances and the same social, religious, and philanthropic supports in their pressure for new enterprises. The circumstances of each new imperialist exploit differ from those of all preceding ones: whatever ingenuity is requisite for the perversion of the public intelligence, or the inflammation of the public sentiment, will be forthcoming.

"Imperialism is only beginning to realise its full resources, and to develop into a fine art the management of nations: the broad bestowal of a franchise, wielded by a people whose education has reached the stage of an uncritical ability to read printed matter, favours immensely the designs of keen business politicians, who, by controlling the press, the schools, and where necessary the churches, impose Imperialism upon the masses under the attractive guise of sensational patriotism" (*Imperialism*, pp. 360–1).

British imperialism in 1902 must indeed have seemed all but omnipotent. Moreover the United States of America, with all its immense future power, was, as we have noted, and as Hobson was convinced, just then taking what appeared to be its first preliminary steps along the imperialist road. She seemed to have reached the stage of economic development at which every country turned imperialist. She was duly doing so.

"The adventurous enthusiasm of President Theodore Roosevelt and his 'manifest destiny' and 'mission of civilization' party must not deceive us. It was Messrs Rockefeller, Pierpont Morgan, and their associates who needed Imperialism and who fastened it upon the shoulders of the great Republic of the West. They needed Imperialism because they desired to use the public resources of their country to find profitable employment for their capital which otherwise would be superfluous" (*Ibid.*, pp. 77-8).

Germany, too, was hurrying forward with immense power and appetite. But, curiously enough, it was not, on the whole, the imminence of that bloody collision between the imperialists which was in fact about to take place that weighed on Hobson's mind. His nightmare was different. He believed that imperialism was still in its infancy because it had not yet engulfed, absorbed and exploited what was potentially the greatest colony of all—namely, China.

"Beyond and above all this looms China. It is not easy to suppose that the lull and hesitancy of the Powers will last, or that the magnitude and manifest risks of disturbing this vast repository of incalculable forces will long deter adventurous groups of profit-seekers from driving their Government along the slippery path of commercial treaties, leases, railway and mining concessions, which must entail a growing process of political interference" (*Ibid.*, p. 224).

It was useless Hobson supposed, in a passage which reveals how little of twentieth-century development could as yet be foreseen, to expect any effective resistance from the Chinese.

"It is idle to suppose that the industrial attack on China can be ultimately evaded. Unless China can be roused quickly from the sleep of countless centuries of peace and can transform herself into a powerful military nation, she cannot escape the pressure of the external powers. To suppose that she can do this, because her individual citizens show a capacity for drill and discipline, is to mistake the issue. The whole genius of the Chinese peoples, so far as it is understood, is opposed to militant patriotism and to the strongly centralized government required to give effect to such a policy.

The notion of China organising an army of six millions under some great general, and driving 'the foreign devils' out of the country, or even entering herself upon a career of invasion and conquest, ignores the chief psychological and social factors of Chinese life" (*Ibid.*, pp. 310-11).

It was from the partition of China amongst the powers, or alternatively from its joint exploitation on the part of some super-consortium, that Hobson foresaw the greatest peril of all. He wrote a passage quoted by Lenin[1] in which he describes the social conditions which must result from a successful carrying through of the worldwide imperialist drive, including, above all, the subjugation of China.

"This would drive the logic of Imperialism far towards realisation; its inherent, necessary, tendencies towards unchecked oligarchy in politics, and parasitism in industry, would be plainly exhibited in the condition of the 'imperialist' nations. The greater part of Western Europe might then assume the appearance and character already exhibited by tracts of country in the South of England, in the Riviera, and in the tourist-ridden or residential parts of Italy and Switzerland, little clusters of wealthy aristocrats drawing dividends and pensions from the Far East, with a somewhat larger group of professional retainers and tradesmen and a large body of personal servants and workers in the transport trade and in the final stages of production of the more perishable goods: all the main arterial industries would have disappeared, the staple foods and manufactures flowing in as a tribute from Asia and Africa. It is, of course, idle to suppose that the industrialisation of China by Western methods can be achieved without effective political control, and just in proportion as Western Europe became dependent economically upon China would the maintenance of that joint imperial control react upon Western politics, subordinating all movements of domestic reform to the needs of maintaining the Empires, and checkmating the forces of democracy by a skilful use of a highly centralised bureaucracy and army" (*Ibid.*, pp. 314-15).

By hindsight we know that all this did not happen. Instead the first war of the empires, or, as Panikkar calls it, "the European civil war" flared out in 1914. Hobson partly foresaw and dreaded such a war, and yet did not quite believe in it, supposing that mutual interest must

[1] Lenin fully acknowledges his debt to Hobson.

produce an accommodation, since there was a whole world of spoils to share. And indeed the first World War did not break out directly over the imperialist rivalries of the powers. On the contrary, although these were still acute, there was apparent, by the summer of 1914, a marked tendency to accommodate their specifically overseas interests, just as Hobson supposed that there would be. The war arose, immediately, out of the rivalries of two of the land-locked, contiguous, and semi-feudal, as opposed to the oceanic, capitalist and highly developed, empires, namely Russia and Austria–Hungary.

In 1914 it was the conflict within Europe between these two obsolescent empires, rather than the overseas conflicts of the highly developed empires, which reached the flash-point of war. (This, however, may have been mere accident. After all, a conflict over who was to have North Africa, France or Germany had brought the world to the very edge of the war only two years before.) And then the fire of their conflict spread and caught the inflammable material of the overseas rivalries of the more representative, up-to-date, European capitalist empires, Britain, France and Germany. (On this occasion it touched, but did not scorch, the two non-European representatives of the imperial species, America and Japan.)

Nevertheless and however we assess its exact causes, the first war of the empires happened. It was this immense event which prevented any possibility of the realisation of Hobson's nightmare of a consolidated super-imperialism possessing and exploiting the whole earth, corrupting into servility the masses of the imperial states themselves, and distorting both their own and their colonies' economic development. The inter-imperial rivalries proved to be a factor which Hobson had gravely under-estimated. And this first war of the empires began the process of unleashing anti-imperialist counter-forces, the existence of which Hobson had not detected, but which were within half a century to destroy that towering structure of world imperialism which had so overawed him. But before discussing these developments we must examine more closely the underlying dynamics of the imperialist process.

In 1917, the year of the Russian Revolution, fifteen years after the publication of Hobson's *Imperialism*, and nineteen years before the publication of Keynes' *General Theory*, Lenin wrote a terse little book which he, too, called *Imperialism*.

In it he set out a theory of why the major capitalisms had turned, in the previous half-century, to intensely imperialist policies. For communists throughout the world this theory has in many respects become the general account of present-day capitalism. Nevertheless the basis upon which Lenin's theory of imperialism is built is often disregarded. Lenin considered that latter-day capitalisms had to become imperialist essentially because of their inherent inability profitably to dispose of their products at home. In other words, Lenin's theory of imperialism is firmly rooted in Marx's vision of the inevitable course of capitalist development, of which the theory of the ever-increasing misery of the mass of their populations is in some respect the central feature.

This underlying assumption is often overlooked by students of the remaining, and more spectacular, features of Lenin's theory. For Lenin does not argue all this at any length. Marx's diagram of capitalism had depicted the system as continually increasing production while leaving the consumption of the mass of the population constant at subsistence level, or actually declining. Lenin largely takes all that for granted: it has become part of him: he does not consider it needs arguing. What he is concerned to show is how this basic characteristic of the system, now, he is convinced, intensified by the structural changes which he goes on to describe, will produce the necessity of imperialist expansion.

He has little difficulty in doing so. If the distribution of income is becoming increasingly inequitable, the system, in order to work, will accumulate ever faster. To use Keynesian language, its propensity to save will be ever growing. To remain viable it must invest at a higher and higher rate. But its opportunities to invest at home will be limited by the very tendencies which will have increased the wherewithal of investment, namely savings. For these increased savings will tend to be subtractions from the community's capacity to consume. Therefore a time must come when lagging consumption must make further investment at home unprofitable and indeed purposeless.

Lenin would have laughed to scorn Keynes' suggestion that the State should at this point intervene by, on the one hand, lowering the rate of interest and starting public works in order to increase investment, and, on the other, by redistributing income in order to increase consumption and decrease savings. The State, he considered, will intervene all right, but it will be a state wholly owned and controlled by the monopoly capitalists. Therefore it cannot possibly be expected to intervene in order to moderate their demands. On the contrary, it is bound to intervene in order to help them to push through their programme of "maximum" profits. But at this stage such intervention must mean above all the creation of opportunities for adequately profitable and safe foreign investment: the intervention will be, in a word, imperialist.

At this point in the argument Lenin introduces one of the most important of his concepts. He calls it "the law of uneven development". This is Lenin's way of stating one of the main themes emphasised throughout the first volume of this study—namely, that highly developed capitalism, in the absence of political counter-action by the wage-earners and farmers, has developed chronic disproportions and has lost whatever automatic, self-righting, self-adjusting capacities it once possessed. Lenin picks out two main disproportions, the one at home, the other abroad.

At home the growth of oligopoly, *i.e.*, the reduction in the number of firms in any industry to the point at which competition begins to fade out, proceeds first and fastest in industry. This tends to give the major firms disproportionate bargaining power as against both the wage-earners whom they employ and the farmers, or peasants, from whom they buy and to whom they sell. Lenin was aware of this internal disequilibrium, although it was not for him the major point. He describes it briefly. He assumes, rather than argues, that the workers, already hopelessly overmatched in bargaining strength in the earlier competitive stage of capitalism, will be quite impotent to prevent their ever-increasing impoverishment when faced with the great trusts. At the same time the farmers, or peasants, will remain the last sphere of the economy in which the sellers cannot themselves influence their prices. He assumes that this must result in the ruthless exploitation of the farmers, ground between the upper and nether millstones of the two sets of oligopolists, from whom they buy and to whom they sell. He concludes that there is no chance of the population of a capitalism in its last stage raising its standard of life and so providing a growing market at home. Thus there will be no longer any room for the system to expand at home, for by impoverishing the mass of the population in the quest of profit it will have cut off the outlet for its own final products.

It was for these reasons that Lenin believed that the expansion of the giant concerns of a capitalism in its last stage must be essentially out-wards. It must be *imperialist* expansion into the hitherto under-developed parts of the world, there to repeat the whole process of capitalistic accumulation for private profit on new ground.

But there was more to the matter than that. There were more detailed reasons why the whole development of the technique of pro-duction which had set in towards the end of the nineteenth century made the acquisition of imperial possessions more and more indispensable to the great capitalisms. These technical developments were bound up, both as cause and effect, with the growth of monopoly (or oligopoly), and they supplemented its drive to imperialism in specific ways. The first of these was connected with the increasing emphasis on the export of producers', as opposed to consumers', goods to the under-developed world.

Lenin pointed out that the exchange of consumers' commodities between developed and undeveloped nations did not *necessarily* involve annexation or domination. No doubt, as a matter of historical fact, it had in practice often done so. For the temptation of the traders of a relatively advanced country to dominate a weaker country and by so doing turn the terms of the exchange in their own favour by using force in one form or another, was seldom resisted. However, Lenin considered that such temptation was relatively weak when compared to the temptation—it was, he wrote, little less than a necessity—of annexing or dominating under-developed countries when it came to the question of trading with them, not by means of exchanging consumers' goods, but by exporting capital goods to them in return for food or raw materials. For the export of capital goods is closely associated with the export of capital itself: with the act of *investment* in under-developed countries. The under-developed country can naturally seldom pay cash down for the expensive capital equipment it imports. It must get credit for it—it must borrow in one form or another, and hope to pay off the loan, or, more realistically, to pay at least the interest on it, out of the proceeds of its shipments of food and raw materials. At this point the relationship between the under-developed and the advanced country takes on the form of debtor and creditor, and that is next door to dependence and domination.

Again, Lenin saw another connection with the growth of monopoly or oligopoly within the economies of the mature capitalisms and their urge to territorial expansion. A capitalism still in its competitive stage might be willing to allow its nationals to trade, or even invest, in under-developed areas in competition with the nationals of other countries. But the whole spirit of the trusts had become anti-competitive, and it was natural for them to want to reserve for themselves the right to trade or invest in particular areas *exclusively*. This would imply, above all, the exclusion or penalisation of the nationals of other highly developed countries, and that, of course, could only be done by means of taking possession of the territory in question as a colony of one sort or another. Thus the trusts of each capitalism in its last stage tended to monopolise not only particular branches of production, but particular areas of the earth's surface. For otherwise they could not rely on being able to fix to suit themselves the terms on which they would trade in that area. The local peasants or producers of raw materials would regain some of their bargaining power if several different buyers or investors from various advanced capitalisms were dealing with them. This was to be avoided by the exclusion, in one way or another, of rival trusts from the developments of as many areas as possible. Then the full weight of superior force could be thrown into the scales in order to produce ratios of exchange extremely favourable to the trusts whose government possessed any particular territory.

The next major step in Lenin's argument was that this process of the monopolisation of particular parts of the world by particular Governments on behalf of their trusts clearly involved sharp rivalry with the trusts, and so with the Governments, which were thus excluded. Hence the above described "grab for Africa", a process competitive as between nations just because it was monopolistic as between firms. It was essentially because of this rivalry that Lenin saw in imperialism the main cause of contemporary war. Moreover, he made at this point in his argument the final, and crowning, application of his concept of "uneven development". Might it not be, it had been objected, that once the under-developed world had been completely partitioned out as colonies, protectorates, semi-colonies, spheres of influence, or satellites of the various empires, that a period of peace would ensue while each empire exploited its own colonial estate? Kautsky had implied something of this sort. Lenin's answer is that, no, this cannot be, because the empires develop at different times and at unequal speeds. The first capitalist society to reach a stage of high development will naturally acquire the largest and choicest under-developed areas as its colonies. It will become the world's dominant empire. (Lenin was, of course, thinking of Britain.)

This will not necessarily or inevitably be a cause of major war so long as that dominant empire remains also the most highly developed capitalism. But in fact it will not so remain. Other capitalisms, starting later in the race, will begin to develop more rapidly. (Lenin is thinking of Germany and America.) Perhaps they will have larger and more populous areas as their base: or they will have superior natural resources: or they will learn from the inevitable mistakes of the pioneer capitalism. For one or other or a combination of these causes they will sooner or later begin to overhaul the original empire. They will overhaul it in respect of their basic economic development, in their production of steel, power, chemicals, in the size of their shipping fleets, in their armaments industries. But these late-comers will find that the largest and most promising under-developed areas have been pre-empted as the colonies of older empires. For a time they may content themselves with annexing and exploiting those smaller and less promising areas which are still free. (Lenin was thinking of the rather meagre colonies of Imperial Germany.) But such self-denial and moderation cannot be expected to last long. The internal pressure for expansion of such later-developing capitalisms will be driving them on, because of their inability to expand their own internal markets. Soon a situation will have arisen in which relatively weak capitalisms have great colonial possessions and relatively strong capitalisms have small and inadequate colonial possessions. What is to happen? At this point, says Lenin, the world has to be not only partitioned, but re-partitioned. There can be no stable or final carving up of the world between the empires, because their relative size, wealth and strength are constantly changing. Their uneven rates of development imperatively require a periodic re-allotment of the under-developed world between them.

It what way can such a re-partition of the world take place except by a trial of strength in war? The older, weaker empires will not, indeed cannot, abdicate peacefully and hand over the spoils to their thrusting rivals. Their colonies seem, and, Lenin writes, for capitalist empires really are, necessities to them which they cannot do without. Periodic world wars, Lenin concluded, must therefore characterise the epoch of capitalist imperialism. But the outbreak of such wars, he adds, will be the signal for the outbreak also of the revolt of the colonial peoples against their exploitation from abroad, and of the revolt of the wage-earners of the empires themselves against their own exploitation by their trusts.

CHAPTER VII

THE EXPLANATION CONSIDERED

SUCH, IN BAREST outline, is the Hobson-Lenin explanation of why
the major capitalisms, at a certain stage in their development, turned
to intensive imperialist expansion. How are we to assess this theory,
which is now received doctrine from Pekin to Berlin? As the twentieth
century wears on, experience makes it clear that we cannot accept it
uncritically. Up to a point the real development of the world has
followed the path predicted. But at a certain point it has diverged in
important respects. In particular, as the next part of this volume will
be partly devoted to showing, it has been found that the major
capitalisms can divest themselves, either voluntarily or involuntarily,
of their empires without the catastrophic effects upon them which,
Lenin implied, such development must have.

It is important to examine Lenin's version of the theory in particular,
in order to see whether it contains any flaws which would be likely to
result in its predictive power failing at just this point. In fact we shall
find that there is a miscalculation at the very centre of Lenin's theoretical structure. It is, simply, that the original Marxian prediction of
ever-increasing misery within the advanced capitalisms has turned out
to be wrong. Lenin was convinced that the giant oligopolies were
bound to exert an overwhelming bargaining power as against the wage-
earners and farmers. He dismissed the possibility that democratic
institutions might turn this power into its opposite, so that the wage-
earners and farmers might become steadily richer instead of poorer.
He foresaw nothing whatsoever of the contemporary development
under which in America, Britain and Germany alike, it is precisely in
the oligopolistic industries that Trade Unionism is most successful and
most firmly established. He had no inkling that in some political
environments the industrial giants, partly freed from the pressure of
competition on their profits, would come to terms with the "counter-
cartels" for the sale of labour power, as the Trades Unions may be
called: that, moreover, they would come to terms markedly more
advantageous to the wage earners than they had ever obtained under
fully competitive capitalism. Still less did Lenin foresee that the next
stage of development in the advanced capitalisms would be neither a
revolutionary revolt of the farmers, nor their ruin by the monopolists,

but the use of their voting power, in alliance with the wage-earners, to redress the balance of the economy. Yet this is what in fact happened in the nineteen-thirties. The American farmers and wage-earners, for instance, picked up the semi-derelict Democratic Party as the instrument of their purposes. The farmers secured legislation which has in effect banded them together as an agricultural cartel, with statutory protection for their prices; and this has given them a capacity, so far at any rate, to hold their own with the formidable giants who buy from them and sell to them. (The development of British agricultural legislation, although widely different in form, has had much the same effect.)

There is not the slightest doubt that Lenin regarded the inevitability of a falling standard of life for the wage-earners and farmers within the highly developed capitalisms as the thing which made the whole imperialist process inevitable. He says so in the most striking way possible. For he expressly states, although purely for the sake of argument, that *if* the standard of life of the wage-earners and agriculturists could be raised at home, then the whole imperialist drive would no longer be inevitable. This neglected passage occurs at the beginning of his Chapter IV and reads as follows:

"It goes without saying that if capitalism could develop agriculture, which to-day lags far behind industry everywhere, if it could raise the standard of living of the masses, who are everywhere still poverty-stricken and underfed, in spite of the amazing advance in technical knowledge, there could be no talk of a superfluity of capital. This 'argument' the petit bourgeois critics of capitalism advance on every occasion. But if capitalism did these things it would not be capitalism; for uneven development and wretched conditions of the masses are the fundamental and inevitable conditions and premises of this mode of production. As long as capitalism remains what it is, surplus capital will never be used for the purpose of raising the standard of living of the masses, in a given country, for this would mean a decline in profits for the capitalists; it will be used for the purpose of increasing those profits by exporting capital abroad to the backward countries. In these backward countries, profits usually are high, for capital is scarce, the price of land is relatively low, raw materials are cheap. The possibility of exporting capital is created by the entry of numerous backward countries into international capitalist intercourse; main railways have either been built or are being built there; the elementary conditions for industrial developments have been created, etc. The necessity of exporting capital arises from the fact that in a few countries capitalism has become 'over-ripe' and (owing to the backward state of agriculture and the impoverished state of the masses) capital cannot find 'profitable' investments."

This passage is in some ways the most important in Lenin's book. For a steady increase in the standard of life of the masses and a rapid development of agriculture are precisely what *has* happened in, for example, both Britain and America. True, it is not that the controllers of the giant trusts and the rest of the property-owning classes of such societies have raised, either philanthropically or prudentially, the standard of life of the masses. It is that an all-pervasive democratic political environment has permitted the growth of counter pressures—industrial and political—which have enabled the wage-earners and farmers to force up their own standards. What can be claimed for the controllers of the trusts—though this is much—is that they have, so far, in America and Britain preferred to part with some of their potential profit to the wage-earners and farmers, rather than risk a head-on collision.[1]

In the above passage Lenin commits himself to the view that if capitalism did the two things which would, he agrees, make imperialist expansion unnecessary it would no longer be capitalism. The undeniable fact that both of these things have now happened would, therefore, presumably incline him to refuse to apply the word "capitalism" to the present economies of Britain and America. (Mr Anthony Crosland, in his recent book, *The Future of Socialism* [Cape, 1956], refuses to call them so, for example.) It seems to me convenient, however, to retain the old name for our economy, but to acknowledge that capitalism has had an extremely important modification imposed upon it. This, however, is a verbal issue. The vital consideration is that Lenin, like Marx before him, overlooked the economic consequences of democracy. For it has been the pervasive force of democracy which has wrought this highly significant change in the workings of the system. The first volume of this study discussed the interplay of

---

[1] It is often suggested that the managers, as opposed to owners, who now control most of the decisive units of the economy, have motives different in kind from that of owners. It is suggested that they genuinely and voluntarily desire to maximise general well being rather than profits; or that they yield at any rate relatively easily to Trade Union and democratic pressure to share the social surplus with their wage-earners. This is far too important an issue for adequate discussion in a chapter devoted to the Hobson-Lenin theory of imperialism. Clearly, however, there is nothing impossible about such a psychological development.

political democracy and capitalism in its last stage. The experience of
the last two and a half decades leaves no room for doubt that the effects
of political democracy upon the economic structure of a last stage
capitalism may be quite sufficient to modify its development profoundly.

All this is almost completely disregarded by Lenin. He thought of
political, parliamentary democracy simply as the contemporary form
taken by the rule of the capitalist class. In other words, from the point
of view of the mass of the population it was a sham. As a Russian he had
no experience of it; he was not really interested in its workings and he
had not the slightest faith in it as an instrument which the mass of the
population might use to raise their standard of life and so alter the balance
and character of a capitalist economy. If he had been alive to-day, he
might have been too perspicacious to subscribe to Stalin's grotesque
statement (see pp. 97-8 of *Contemporary Capitalism*) that in 1952 the
monopoly capitalisms had everywhere ground down the populations
of their countries to a bare subsistence level. But in principle he could
not have dissented from it without revising his whole theory.

Thus experience has now shown that imperialism was not the only
or necessary result of the conjunction of circumstances which Hobson
and Lenin described. True something had to be done when capitalism
became "overripe". If nothing had been done the mature capitalisms
would probably have suffered, round about the turn of the century, a
breakdown of the sort which in fact occurred in 1929. Expansion
overseas, mainly by imperialist methods, provided the necessary outlet
of new fields of investment. But instead of imperialist expansion what
might have happened, in Britain in particular, if different political forces
had been in the ascendant, was a redistribution of the national income,
making possible much increased home investment at a lower rate of
return. Hobson was right in seeing that radicalism and imperialism
were alternative solutions to the same problem. Foreign investment and
the imperialism that went with it were the solution which suited the
interests of the investing classes. A rising standard of living based upon
home investment and some redistribution of the national income
carried out by social reforms, would have been the solution which
would have suited the rest of the population. And this is what has now
largely happened. This is as much as to say that Lenin *would* have been
right, if the democratic forces had not in the end succeeded, in a few key
countries, in modifying the character of capitalist development.

We must now carefully consider an objection to this whole line of

argument. The fact is that most, though not all, contemporary economists reject the above assertion that mature capitalisms have even a
tendency to produce a plethora of capital for investment and so drive
the investors to seek foreign outlets. They consider that this hypothesis
is unnecessary in order to explain the imperialist surge of 1870-1914.
This they feel can be accounted for simply by the fact that immensely
profitable opportunities of investment presented themselves abroad.
These glittering opportunities *pulled* out the surpluses being created in
the imperialist countries: there is no need to assume "a push from
behind", as it were, caused by insufficient profitability of investment at
home. A major issue is here in question. For the view that there is
nothing inherent in even highly developed capitalism which (unless
counteracted) drives it out upon the imperialist path is in fact but one
aspect of a whole economic philosophy. The issue will come up again
and again in the second part of this volume, but it will be well to state
it here.

It is hard to exaggerate the strength of the tradition that what may
be called "the market forces" of a system of free enterprise, if uninter-
fered with, are fundamentally harmonious and equalising. Partly
consciously and partly unconsciously this is still the gospel of most of
those whose thought has not been affected by the basic critique of the
system. Of course this view is not often held with the tragic rigidity
which caused, as we noticed above (p. 55), the honourable and well-
meaning member of the I.C.S. to sacrifice the lives of millions of
Indian peasants upon the altar of the supposed laws of political
economy. Nevertheless, a sophisticated version of it is held by men and
women of many different political persuasions; and it is held all the
more strongly by those who hold it unconsciously. For then it becomes
what the late Professor Laski called "an inarticulate major premise",
almost inaccessible to argument.

What is in question here is not, be it noted, either the historical fact
of imperialism, or the present fact of an ever widening gap between the
rich and the poor nations. Both these facts can be, more or less satisfactorily, accounted for while still accepting the basic assumption that
exchanges between the developed and the undeveloped necessarily
benefit both parties. Imperialism can be accounted for by the pull of
opportunities for especially high profits in the undeveloped areas; and
the widening of the gap can be accounted for by the rapidity in the rise
of productivity in the developed, and by the rapidity of the rise of
population in the undeveloped.

What is at issue is whether Hobson, Lenin and, as we shall see immediately, a few present-day economists, were and are right in asserting something more than this. What they have all asserted in different ways is that the highly developed capitalisms, unless their pattern of income distribution is drastically altered by non-economic, political forces, have an inherent tendency to accumulation *à l'outrance*: that such economies will pile up capital, and keep down mass purchasing power, to such an extent that they will exert a ceaseless pressure upon their capitalists pushing them into foreign investment, and the imperialism that goes with it. Thus these authorities have a vision of the system as a sort of giant pressure-cooker. Moreover they believe that even after overt imperialist control has been dissolved this innate, accumulative tendency of capitalism will continue to work upon the international field. Unless drastic measures are taken by the undeveloped nations to interfere with the "natural" course of international trade, exchanges between the developed and the undeveloped will *not* benefit both parties. They may actually impoverish the undeveloped country as against its situation if the exchanges had not taken place: they will certainly fail to benefit the undeveloped country as much as they benefit the developed, and so will widen the gap between them.

For my part I have no doubt that this vision of the nature of unmodified capitalism shows an insight superior to orthodox economic doctrine. Moreover some contemporary economists who have been born and bred in the orthodox tradition; men who have slight or hostile connections with the theories of Marx and Lenin, have now worked out for themselves a theory of capitalism which either states or implies that the harmonious, equalising premise (and the rejection of the Hobson-Lenin view of imperialism which flows from it) is false. The most recent statement of this new, or rather rediscovered, view has been made by Professor Gunnar Myrdal in his two works *An International Economy* (Routledge and Kegan Paul) and *Economic Theory and Underdeveloped Regions* (Duckworth). Professor Myrdal is primarily concerned with the relations of the newly independent, undeveloped world and the handful of rich, highly developed countries, and in that connection we shall have to recur again and again to his argument in Part II.

Nevertheless, his argument is relevant to the question of the causation of modern imperialism. For Professor Myrdal is convinced that market forces, if uncontrolled, operate, both within countries and between countries, in such a way that the rich are made ever richer and the poor ever poorer. He has worked out a whole series of concepts, part economic, part sociological, with which to expound his view. He writes that a basic tendency of contemporary society is that of "circular" or spiral effects. When, that is to say, a class of citizens (*e.g.* the American negroes or the wage-earners), or a region (*e.g.* Southern Italy), or a country as a whole (*e.g.* Indonesia), has fallen markedly behind, a complex of interacting factors tends to push it still farther back and to widen the gap between it and the successful classes, regions or countries. Then only the most vigorous and sustained intervention, designed to overrule and reverse the natural "laws" of the market can effect an improvement in the lot of the disfavoured. For what he calls "the spread effects" by which, it had been assumed, the prosperity of the well-off would be diffused, are habitually overweighed by what he calls "backwash" effects, by which the misery of the miserable is made worse. Professor Myrdal sums up the innate tendency of un-counteracted market forces in the words of the Bible. "For unto every-one that hath shall be given, and he shall have in abundance; but from him that hath not shall be taken away even that which he hath" (*Economic Theory and Underdeveloped Regions*, p. 12). Professor Myrdal does not neglect to note that *within* a few of the most advanced nations remarkably successful efforts have recently been made to overcome and reverse this innate play of the market. He considers that the societies of North America, North Western Europe, and Australasia, but they almost alone, have, in the most recent decades succeeded in "integrating" themselves and overcoming what is in fact "the law of unequal development" as between their social classes and regions.

But this could not possibly be said of, for example, the Britain of 1870-1914. Then unequal development between the classes within Britain was hardly checked, and the result was the piling up of an uninvestable surplus which could only be exported. If it had been retained at home it could only have been (i) hoarded, in which case ever deepening depression would have set in, or (ii) invested at diminishing rates of return, which amounts to the same thing as saying that the market forces would have been overruled by conscious intervention and the national income redistributed. Thus the view that Hobson was right in seeing social reform and redistribution as the one alternative to imperialism is confirmed. And so for that matter is Lenin's aside (it is little more) in which (see p. 110, above) he admits for the sake of argument that social reform would be such an alternative, if it were politically practicable—which of course, he declares, it is not.

Professor Myrdal is the most recent exponent of this view that it is indispensable to overcome the innate forces of the market, both within and between nations, if socially tolerable societies are to be created. It is clearly implicit also in Professor Galbraith's theory of "countervailing power". But these (and a few others) are as yet lonely voices which have by no means shaken, or even much disturbed, the traditional presupposition of harmony. Nor do I for a moment expect to shake this presupposition here. (The argument is set out in detail in *Contemporary Capitalism*.) I would merely appeal to economists to consider carefully Professor Myrdal's most recent views, in particular, with attention. For his is a statement of what is, in effect, a general law of unequal development made by a writer against the views of whom they may not automatically shut their minds.

There is a further difficulty in emphasising this theoretical crux of the whole argument of this book (for such it is). While few economists are open to argument on this matter, many other people will consider, on the contrary, that something which is sufficiently obvious already is being laboured. Most people whose minds have not been trained in, and distorted by, traditional economic theory will find little difficulty in recognising the law, or better tendency, of unequal development of the market forces, when that tendency has not been overruled by sustained social intervention. In Britain, for example, throughout the first decade of the twentieth century, the standard of life of the British wage-earners failed to rise: the economy as a whole, and with it the gross national product, were growing steadily: ever-growing annual surpluses resulted: where could these surpluses find profitable employment except abroad? Technical change of a capital intensive character was not an adequate outlet. In abstract theory, no doubt, the rich could have used these surpluses vastly to increase their own consumption and so provide a market at home for the ever-growing product. But on any realistic assumption as to the propensity to save out of incomes of that size, that could not happen in practice. And in fact, until foreign investment took off the surpluses, a menacing tendency was felt for the rate of profit and interest to drop. Witness the late-nineteenth-century saying: "John Bull will stand many things, but he will not stand 2%."

No doubt this was an essentially long-term phenomenon. We are not here dealing with the fluctuations of the trade cycle. These are fluctuations round what would have been, in the absence of foreign lending, a long term downward pressure on the rate of interest and profit. It was not that foreign lending could suddenly be brought in to avert a collapse of the home market and consequent slump. It was that foreign lending could and did provide a method of preserving an extremely unequal distribution of the national income, thus averting social reform, and at the same time, making it possible, periodically at any rate, to run the economy at fairly near its full productive capacity.

A final objection may be made: if the capital market, and the economy generally are depressed, or menaced with depression, at home, so they will be abroad. For the foreign investments would, for the most part, be directed to producing primary products the ultimate destination of which would be the home market. So if it were unprofitable to invest at home, it would also be unprofitable to invest abroad. Again in the abstract, there is clearly force in this objection. And in practice, too, it obviously has had force from time to time, or slumps would never have been world wide. Nevertheless, it appears to me to exaggerate the degree of unification of the world market. It might still seem profitable to build a railway in the Argentine, or to sink another gold mine on the Rand, long after it had begun to seem unprofitable to sink another coal mine in South Wales. *For a time* foreign investment really could keep the economy going *without* raising the standard of life of the wage-earners and farmers or redistributing the national income.

Lenin's error was not, then, to have invented a dilemma for capitalism which did not exist. The dilemma was there all right. What he failed to see was that there was a way out, alternative to imperialism, by means of an adequate and sustained rise in the consumption of the non-capitalist nine-tenths of the population. Or rather he *did* see this way out, as we have just noted, but only as a theoretical possibility to be dismissed as utterly incompatible with what he thought was the real balance of power in any capitalist society. In all this Lenin was a child of his times. His "model" was by no means unrealistic for the Britain of 1900-14, in which he lived for a time and which he studied intensively. Unfortunately, he generalised the transient balance of social forces in Edwardian Britain into a rigid law applicable to all mature capitalisms at all times and everywhere. And even in regard to Edwardian Britain he failed altogether to see that even by 1909 Mr Lloyd George, using the pressures of the electorate, was beginning to redress the balance of society in such a way as to begin to make its functioning compatible with the investment at home, instead of imperialistically abroad, of a much larger proportion of the surplus product.

Lenin's theory of "investment imperialism", as it might be called, had then (like so much of the rest of Marxism) validity as the diagnosis of a tendency, but not as a universal law. For the basic economic tendency (namely towards an ever greater maldistribution of income) which Lenin picked out as his prime mover for the whole chain of consequences which he describes, has proved reversible. The last stage capitalisms have shown themselves to be much more flexible and capable of adapting themselves to the political pressure of their wage-earners than Lenin allowed for. This too is the underlying reason why the annexation and general domination of under-developed countries followed less rigidly and inexorably from the investment in them of the surplus capital of the developed states than would have been expected on Lenin's theory. We have given above the Egyptian and South African examples of how British domination followed what might be called British rentier and British entrepreneurial investment, respectively, exactly as Lenin's theory would have predicted. And we shall give in the next chapter another major, although more complex, example of the process, that of the exploitation of China.

On the other hand, it is quite true that other examples could be given in which no such complete political domination, at any rate, followed massive investment. British investment in the Argentine, and to a smaller extent in other South American republics, is a case in point. Two reasons why Britain never tried to annex parts of South America are at once apparent. First, as we noted above, to have done so would have involved direct conflict with the United States, which had thrown the protection of the Monroe Doctrine over them. Second, the types of governments which existed in South America, though not very stable or efficient in other respects, were comparatively well suited to the interests of foreign investors. Neither Egyptian chaos nor Boer intransigence menaced the interests of the (predominantly) British bondholders and entrepreneurs in South America. There were defaults, but there were no insuperable obstacles to successful investment such as existed in North and South Africa until the regions were annexed. There was no final necessity for whistling up the gunboats. Again, British domination did not follow as a consequence of the heavy British investment in the United States during the nineteenth century. It could not. The United States was much too powerful. Nor on the whole was such domination necessary. Again there were defaults, particularly in the case of some of the individual Southern States, but on the whole the interest on the mainly railway loans was pretty well met, or at least real efforts were made to meet it.

These considerations lead us to conclude that it would have been more accurate if Lenin had said that foreign investment, which had become necessary to the advanced capitalisms (in default, as we now see, of a steady rise in the standard of life in the mass of their populations) produced imperialism, not always or automatically, but only as and when it encountered obstacles either by way of the chaotic character, or the intransigence, of the borrowing states. And even then it did not necessarily lead to imperialism if these obstacles were too slight to be serious or too great to be overcome.

Again, it may be asked why American capitalism was only fitfully and rather ineffectively imperialist during the whole of the imperialist heyday from 1870 to 1914. Of course, the conquest and occupation of the continental United States itself had only recently been completed by the Mexican war and by the final subjugation of the Indians. And those operations can be called imperialist in the widest sense of the word. They were just as ruthless. But they were not imperialism of the same kind as the world-wide annexations undertaken during the same period by the Western European capitalisms. Indeed, the very fact that the process of occupying and rounding off the American "home base" itself had only just been completed provides the clue to why American overseas annexations remained much more modest than Hobson, for example, supposed that they would be. The fact is, surely, that American capitalism had not really reached the degree of "over-ripeness" at which imperialism, in default of an internal redistribution of the national income, becomes necessary. True, American industry was highly trustified. But the sheer size and virginity of its home territory gave it huge scope for internal development. It would have been silly for the Morgans and the Rockefellers to have gone deeply into Africa or Asia, or even South America, incurring all the inevitable risks of foreign investment, when California, Oklahoma, Texas, Washington and all the West were wide open to them. Surely it was this that gave an amateurish and imitative character to the imperialism of the first Roosevelt? It really looks as if the Americans were imperialist in the nineteen-hundreds (to the minor extent which they were) in order to be "in the swim" of the great world-wide imperialist drive rather than because they needed to make or to safeguard massive foreign investments. Indeed, we shall have to take up below (Chapter XIX) the question of whether even now, half a century later, the American economy is not still without many of the urges which drive fully mature capitalist economies towards imperialism. But to the extent that this is so, it is because an appreciable redistribution of the national income has been carried through by the American wage-earners and farmers, rather than because the Western and Southern states remain undeveloped. Exactly, as Lenin put it (although exclusively for argument's sake), in the passage quoted above, the New Deal's successful "raising of the standard of living of the masses" and "development of agriculture" did produce for some two decades a state of things in which "there could be no talk of a superfluity of capital". What Lenin conceived of as a purely theoretical hypothesis, to be defined only to be dismissed as in practice inconceivable, occurred and actually had the consequence of markedly reducing the pressure towards foreign investment and imperialist expansion. For, I repeat, even the most apparently highly developed country is only unfit for further profitable internal investment, *relatively to the standard of life achieved by the mass of the population.*

Another conclusion which is partly explicit and partly implicit in Lenin has proved false. Lenin undoubtedly thought that imperialism was highly profitable, above all, of course, to the investing classes but also, through them, to the people of the imperialist country as a whole. He re-echoes Engels' statements that a part of the British working class has been "corrupted" (*i.e.* had their standard of life improved) by being given a share in these imperial super-profits. We can now see that this plausible view was quite wrong. Mr Earl Browder, in his interesting work *Marx and America* (Gollancz, 1959), is easily able to show, for example, that there is no evidence of the British wage-earners having benefited by the outpourings of British foreign investment, and the imperialism that went with it, between 1870 and 1914. From 1900 onwards, at least, there was little or no rise in their standard of life. No doubt they would have been much better off if more of British investment had been at home. Mr Browder goes on to deduce from this truth the further proposition that nations as a whole never benefit by their imperialist conquests of other nations. So far as the present period of history is concerned, I entirely agree with him: indeed, successive chapters of the next part of this work are devoted to showing that the dissolution of much the greater part of the British Empire has proved fully compatible with a steady rise in the standard of life of the British wage-earners. It would, however, be hasty to assume that this was always true. We have seen that the British conquest of India probably played a real, if subsidiary, part in making possible the primary accumulation which got the Industrial Revolution started in Britain. And the undeniable benefits derived from successful imperialism by ancient empires are discussed in Part III.

Moreover, Browder appears to think that he has refuted Lenin's whole doctrine by refuting this particular conclusion from it. But this is not so. The fact that the British wage-earners made no gains out of the imperialism of their employers between 1870 and 1914 does not in the least mean that their employers made no gains from it. On the contrary, the British investors unquestionably made a higher rate of profit than would have been possible from investment at home. This is only another way of saying that the distribution of the national income would have had to have been more equitable to be compatible with home investment. If the standard of life of the masses of the population and the existing distribution of income are taken as fixed, then the outpourings of foreign investment which took place, and with which the surge of imperialism was associated, was not only highly profitable but indispensable to the investing classes. Everything is determined by the standard of life of the people as a whole and the distribution of income.[1]

Nevertheless, the greater flexibility which capitalism has developed does, no doubt, throw an increased importance upon the conventional motivations of imperialism, such as prestige, glory, supposed military strength and the like, the existence of which neither Hobson nor Lenin would have denied, but which they would have characterised as secondary. Secondary they may have been: but once the initial impetus to foreign investment and imperialism had been aroused by the appetites and needs of the investing classes, these other and more political factors became highly important. We noted above that the America of the first Roosevelt seems to have been drawn into a half-hearted imperialism, long before she had any real need for serious foreign investment, simply because all the other major nations were going in for it. To a certain extent this was true of some at least of the continental European states also. It is doubtful if they had much real need to open up fields for foreign investment. French peasants were no doubt piling up annual surpluses for which there was not much opportunity for investment at home in the somewhat static French economy. But these savings found a (most unfortunately chosen) outlet in loans to the Russian Government. The feverish activity of French imperialism in the period had a real element in it of sheer

---

[1] Mr Browder was for many years General Secretary of the American Communist Party. He could not stomach the super-dogmatism of the Stalinist period, broke with the communists, and is now producing valuable objective discussions of Marxism.

competitiveness. The French Government simply could not bear to see so much of Africa getting painted red on the map, even though French investors had no particular need for investment in it for the time being. And when France began to paint vast stretches of the continent with her characteristic colours, then Germany in turn felt that she "owed it to herself" not to be left behind. The Kaiser began to talk about "Germany's place in the sun": a prestige imperialism developed. Moreover, all the governments concerned firmly believed that the possession or acquisition of colonies added to their military strength. Whether they were right is another matter. Probably at that period colonies were sometimes a military asset and sometimes a military liability. The Indian Army was undoubtedly an asset to Britain, for example, and so were her African levies to France. On the other hand, weak or restive colonies were likely to be military liabilities. But no one doubted that the possession or acquisition of an empire was at once the means and the end of national greatness as well as national wealth.

It is fashionable to-day to explain imperialism in these terms. We are told that any analysis made in terms of economics is now quite out of date: that men seek power rather than wealth: that the whole modern imperialist process must be seen as a competitive struggle for power between the great nations. The first observation to make about this view is that, in this context at least, power and wealth seem to be scarcely distinguishable categories. When Gladstone spoke of "the intoxicating augmentation of wealth and power" which was accruing to the Britain of his day he was, surely, referring to one process not two. Of course, the major nations struggled, after 1870, to increase their wealth in order to increase their power, and their power in order to increase their wealth. Nevertheless, the historical commonplace that there was a great and relatively sudden increase in imperialist pressure after 1870 must be accounted for. It should be recalled that until, after 1870, the intensity of the capitalist process of accumulation was stepped up in several national centres at once there was comparatively little imperialist pressure either. It is not therefore that anyone for a moment denies the intense, power-seeking rivalries of the major states. It is that the most fruitful analysis of their activities can be made in terms of the wealth-seeking propensities of their most influential citizens. Again, it is true that neither Hobson nor Lenin attempted to provide an adequate theory of imperialism as a whole. Their theory is applicable to the period after 1870 alone. And, as the earlier chapters of this book were devoted to showing, imperialism was intense in the eighteenth century.

For that matter, imperialism is as old as human civilisation itself. In Part III an attempt will be made to sketch out a possible theory of the motivations of these earlier forms of imperialism. For they are clearly independent of those peculiar urges to foreign investment on the part of highly developed capitalisms which Lenin described. And this suggests that, contrary to Leninist theory, we may not necessarily have done with imperialism even when the phase of capitalist development which had its heyday between 1870 and 1914 has been finally transcended.

Nevertheless, and when all these qualifications have been made, I, for one, cannot deny the essential importance of the Hobson-Lenin diagnosis of the causes of the wave of intensified imperialism which set in after 1870. How can we possibly deny a connection between this outpouring of British and European capital in foreign investment between 1870 and 1914 and the vast annexations which we listed on p. 80, above? Professor Cairncross, in his *Home and Foreign Investment, 1870-1913* (Cambridge University Press), gives us figures which help us to envisage the scale of that foreign investment. In 1913, Britain was investing abroad half of her entire national savings. In the fifty years before 1914, Western Europe, as a whole, invested abroad more than the value of all the capital located in Britain. By 1914 a full tenth of the entire British national income was provided by interest on foreign investments, which equalled in value "her entire commercial and physical capital". If we wish to get an idea of what this scale of foreign investing would mean to-day we may note, Professor Cairncross adds, that in order to invest as high a proportion of her national income abroad in the nineteen-fifties as Britain did in the nineteen-hundreds, America would have to be investing some $30b a year, instead of in fact between $1b and $3b a year (on private account). And $30b a year would mean that the entire Marshall Plan was carried out every two years. In the face of such figures, is it not perverse to deny that it was primarily in order to open the way for, and then to safeguard, these outpourings of foreign investment that the west European capitalisms annexed or dominated so much of the world between 1870 and 1914? Unless we try at least to identify some such prime mover for the modern imperialist process, we shall have to retreat to the safe, respectable, but barren, view that history is an unaccountable jumble of facts and dates without interrelation or interconnections. Naturally, if we accept that view, we may be content to say that the great imperialist heyday just happened and leave it at that. But if we think that the interest and importance of history is to attempt at least to discover the interconnections of things, then we shall look for a cause. If we do that, we shall find an undeniable connection between (i) the existence of highly developed capitalist societies creating surpluses, which their distribution of income made it difficult for them to invest profitably at home, (ii) a high rate of foreign investment, and (iii) the acquisition of much of the habitable globe by these societies as their colonies. After all, each of these things undeniably co-existed. Only the intentionally blind will deny a connection between them.

CHAPTER VIII

THE RELAXING GRASP

THE CLIMAX OF MODERN imperialism was not to be, as Hobson had supposed, the joint colonisation or the partition of China. Instead, the competing empires fell upon each other in the first World War. That war did not, however, destroy imperialism. In fact, its result appeared to many observers to be not so much a blow to imperialism as a redistribution of power amongst the empires.

Territorially Britain was once again the main gainer. The major part of what colonies Germany had had, and, more important in the end (see Chapter XI, below), the main part of the Arabian domains of the Ottoman empire, now dissolved, passed, either in form or in fact, to her. But it would have been a poorly equipped observer who would have supposed that these territorial gains corresponded to any real redistribution of power in Britain's favour. True, her immediate rival, Germany, was, for the time being, knocked out of the race. But it was apparent that in fact Britain had been relatively weakened rather than strengthened. Now for the first time for 100 years she was overshadowed by another power, the United States of America.

Thus the first World War had merely redistributed the possessions of the older-established empires in a way which corresponded still less well than before to their economic and industrial potency. The two powers that were progressing least rapidly, Britain and France, had gained most. Germany, the most dynamic of the European empires, had been stripped. America, the real victor, did not, for reasons we shall discuss below, wish directly to collect any appreciable amount of the spoils. Japan had increased her power, but had in the end received no corresponding territorial rewards. The disproportion between power and possessions had been sharply increased. Such a settlement could not, and did not, last. By 1933 it had been challenged by both Germany and Japan. Germany under its now Fascist régime was clearly rearming for another challenge; Japan was already undertaking the conquest and exploitation of China, so that it seemed for a moment as if Hobson's nightmare was to be realised, albeit in a form unforeseen by him.

China, India and Turkey each provide examples of indigenous

empires of the traditional, static, Asiatic pattern, encountering, when in a process of slow disintegration, the force of Western expansion. Through the nineteenth century the Manchu Empire in China, although far from being in the hapless condition of the Mogul Empire after 1739, was in evident decline. Left to itself, it might have mouldered on for a long time, before, in the Chinese phrase, expressly coined for such situations, it had "exhausted the mandate of heaven". But it was in no condition to meet the formidable challenge of the barbarians of the West. Accordingly those barbarians began to have their will of China. The fact that China was opened up by means of two wars fought primarily in order to prevent the Chinese Government from prohibiting the import of opium has given the process a dramatically atrocious character. In fact, however, it was the familiar process of imperial expansion in its mercantile phase. The Europeans, and the Americans also, did not merely mean to force the Chinese to trade with them in opium: they were determined that China should trade with them in general, whether the Chinese Government wished to do so or not. And the treaties of Nanking (1842) and Tientsin (1860), which marked the conclusions of the two opium wars, established Western armed power throughout coastal China on a scale sufficient to ensure that no Chinese Government would again have the power to refuse to trade, whether in opium or anything else.

The imposition of these "unequal treaties" marked only the beginning of a process which, after the post-1870 resurgence of imperialism, came to the very verge of constituting a Western conquest of China. For, quite unexpectedly to the traders concerned, the China trade in its original form did not develop at anything like the speed which was desired. The nearly self-sufficient Chinese masses had the tiniest conceivable "propensity to import" foreign goods—except, perhaps, opium. Gradually it was realised that, if China was ever to become the inexhaustible treasure-house which the Europeans dreamt that it might be, it would by no means suffice to trade with her while she was still even semi-independent. China must be conquered, her static self-sufficient economy broken up; she must be "developed", and her vast reservoirs of labour must be exploited either directly or indirectly in such a way that they should produce a surplus: moreover that surplus must be expropriated for the benefit of the foreigner.

The occurrence of two major revolts on the part of the Chinese people, directed, like all such revolts, both against their own Government, which had been discredited by its inability to stand up to the foreigners, and against those foreigners themselves, greatly helped the

Europeans, and Americans, to tighten their grip. The Westerners "helped" the Chinese Imperial Government to suppress both the Taiping revolt (1850-64) and the Boxer rising (1900). By the latter date the conquest of China by the West seemed very close. The sovereignty of the Imperial Government had become thin and unreal. The huge body of China had been partitioned into spheres of influence between "the powers", France in the South, Britain in the middle, Germany in the North-East and so on. Railways were being built by European and American capital. Every major Chinese river was patrolled by the gunboats of her invaders. Hobson's apotheosis of imperialism in the crowning form of a captive China, ready for intensive exploitation by a condominium of the Western empires, seemed the logical next step.

In the meantime, however, a most remarkable thing had happened. The Western powers had been joined, in both their deliberations and their disputes as to the division of the spoils of China, by an Asiatic state, Japan. Japan, intent since 1867 on adopting every phase of Western life, took good care not to neglect this most typical of Western activities—namely, imperial expansion. In 1894 she made war on China over Korea, easily defeated her and so won the right to a seat at the table upon which the huge Chinese meal was being prepared. The old-established Western imperialists did not by any means relish the appearance of this unexpected and uninvited guest. Still, Japan carried the undeniably valid invitation card of successful aggression. She could by no means be refused admission.

Thus in the first decade of the twentieth century it seemed clear that China was to be partitioned, in one way or another, between the Western powers, plus Japan, who was to receive a modest but appropriate share. And then two further events occurred. In 1912 the Chinese Revolution broke out. The by now senile Manchu dynasty was overthrown and it seemed likely that a nationalist Chinese Government, of a progressive character, would be set up under the leadership of Sun Yat-sen. This would have been most inconvenient for the powers, who were in the very act of partitioning the country, and they were greatly relieved when (partly by their contriving) this did not happen and China began to break up into kingdoms of independent war lords, just as India had done 200 years before.

The second event was the outbreak of the first World War. It was this which gave China the breathing space she needed in order to avoid full colonisation. But for some time it seemed that, on the contrary, all that the outbreak of internecine war in Europe had meant for China was that she was to be colonised, not by the Westerners, but by her modernised Oriental neighbour, Japan. The first World War distracted, and damaged, the Europeans too much for them to be able to prosecute the colonisation of China. But Japan, their apt pupil, saw that their preoccupation was her opportunity. In 1915 she abruptly presented 21 Demands upon China. These demands, it is hardly too much to say, would have reduced China to the status of a Japanese colony, and would have effectively excluded the other imperialists. This was an appalling prospect not only for China, but for the Western imperialists also; but what could the Europeans, stuck thigh deep in the mud and blood of Flanders, do about it? In the event they did very little till after the war. China was forced on paper to accept the 21 Demands. But by a process of successful procrastination she was just able to hold off their implementation till the end of the war.

As soon as the first World War was over the position changed again. The older imperialists were no longer under a necessity to yield to the Japanese upstart. America, above all, had become an extremely formidable power. Moreover, Chinese nationalism was beginning to count. Although China had no effective Government at all, although her war-lords were always fighting each other, she had not quite fallen into the post-Mogul Indian chaos. The difference was that there was a concept of China in the hearts and minds of enough of her people (no doubt owing to her millenia of national unity) to enable her representatives, somehow or other, to assert themselves. Perhaps such inchoate national sentiment would not have availed her much against one united, effective imperialist power (it did not do so a little later, as we shall see immediately). But for the moment, faced as she was by a whole gang of imperialists each intensely jealous of the others, she was able to accomplish a good deal. At the Washington Conference in 1922 she succeeded, for the first time, in winning back a little of her sovereignty from the imperialists as a whole, and, what was far more, Japan was forced quietly to drop the 21 Demands. (She dropped them, that is to say, publicly; she did not abandon one of them as aims to be implemented the very moment that conditions became favourable.)

China had got another breathing space. And the Chinese nationalists used it well. In 1926-7 their organisation, the Kuomintang, marched north from its base at Canton, defeated the war lords (splitting with its Communist allies in the act), and made a fairly effective Chinese nationalist Government, of the modernised kind, at Nanking. From that moment it was clear that the final struggle as to whether China should be colonised or not had arrived. There was already not much doubt as to the result so far as the Western powers were concerned. The grasp of Europe on the sovereignty of the Orient was by now visibly relaxing. The first World War, although it had not fatally weakened its physical power, had done something to the spirit of European imperialism. Only momentarily, in the Nazi paroxism of the 'thirties and 'forties, did it ever again show genuine expansive power.

All this, however, was far from true of Japan. By 1930 the nationalist Government of China had completed a fairly effective unification of what had been the Empire of the Manchus. Manchuria itself was acquired by means of the adhesion of "the young Marchal", the last of the war lords, to the nationalist cause. This event set ringing all the alarm bells of Tokyo. If this were to go on: if nationalist power were to be finally consolidated in China, there would be an end of the intoxicating vision of China as the gigantic colony of Japan. Japan struck. She invaded Manchuria on September 18th, 1931. This was the beginning of a fourteen-year period of increasingly official war between Japan and China. Japanese aggression deepened and broadened by stages. In 1932 she attacked Shanghai itself. Owing partly to unexpectedly vigorous Chinese resistance, but also to the pressure of the Western powers, whose interests were thus challenged at their centre, the Japanese forces here withdrew for a time. Meanwhile, however, Japan was pushing steadily onwards from the North. Manchuria was consolidated, then the Shankaikwan pass was forced and China proper was entered. An ever-growing degree of control was established over North China and then over the nationalist Chinese Government of Chiang Kai-shek, further south at Nanking.

So far Japan had encountered only indecisive opposition, either from the other imperialists or from Chinese nationalism. China was hamstrung by the civil war which was raging between the nationalists under Chiang Kai-shek and the communists. But in 1937 the communists succeeded in kidnapping Chiang Kai-shek and forcing him to fight the Japanese instead of themselves. This again made the Japanese feel that they had no time to lose. They drove full steam ahead towards the conquest of China proper against growing Chinese resistance. By the outbreak of the second World War (which, let it be recalled, did not occur in the Far East till October 1941) some two-thirds of China (reckoned by population, less by area) was fairly effectively occupied by the Japanese. On the other hand, Chinese resistance had by no means been crushed. Chiang Kai-shek still maintained himself in the West, and what was perhaps more effective, the communists kept up a skilful and widespread guerrilla action. Nevertheless it may be said that by 1941 a Japanese conquest of China realising, albeit in a very different form, Hobson's nightmare, while not accomplished, was in sight.

It will be seen that, in the crucial instance of China, the inter-war period was marked by the relaxing grasp of the Western imperialists, but that this did not mean much respite for China from imperialist pressure. The retreating Western imperialists were replaced by the Japanese, who outdid them in respect of the ruthless determination with which they fastened upon what was, they hoped, the defenceless body of China. Clearly imperialism has nothing to do with the colour of people's skins. During the centuries in which white men alone had been in any position to practise imperialism an assumption had grown up, on the part both of the subjected peoples and of the imperialists themselves, that this was an art or crime (whichever you like to call it) peculiar to white men. The Japanese taught us otherwise.

The inter-war period in India provides a much less qualified example of imperialism in retreat. During the imperialist heyday itself, just before the outbreak of the first World War, there occurred a momentous innovation in British policy in India. This was something more than one of the series of measures by which British rule in India had been improved. It was a very short step, taken in the form of the Morley-Minto reforms, on a road which would lead to Indians taking over the task of ruling themselves. All that was done was the establishment of certain elected local government bodies with very restricted powers. Nevertheless it was by following this path that there became possible, not Indian independence itself—that would have come in any case—but the achievement of Indian independence in a far less revolutionary, violent and destructive way than might have been expected. This beginning of the process of establishing free, democratic institutions was genuinely voluntary in the sense that nothing compelled the British Government to move in this direction. Indian nationalist pressure was growing but was still by no means strong enough to have insisted on reform. The British liberal statesmen of the day seem to have had the foresight to realise that future disaster for Britain and India could only be avoided by setting the feet of both countries upon the road which led towards democracy and independence.

Under the shock of the first World War, the British Government moved further. The Montague-Chelmsford reforms were put into effect at the beginning of the inter-war period. They established a fairly significant measure of Indian responsible government in each of the provinces of British India, but they left the central government untouched in British hands and they left unsolved the problem of the Princely States which still covered, it should be recalled, two-fifths of India. Finally in 1936 an Act was passed which gave fairly complete and responsible self-government in the provinces and would have given (if Congress had been willing to accept it) some, much slighter, measure of responsible self-government at the centre. As important in some respects, there occurred a partial, but highly significant, Indianisation of the Civil Service, and to a lesser extent of the officer corps of the armed services. All this would, of course, completely misrepresent what happened in India between the wars if it suggested that there was a smooth or easy process by which reforms were benevolently handed down by the British authorities to a passive and grateful India. On the contrary, each of these steps was only taken more or less reluctantly, under Indian nationalist pressure which by 1918 was becoming really strong. This pressure was the prime mover but it was supported by much Liberal and Labour opinion in Britain itself.

The constitutional reforms thus enacted created the basic machinery of democratic, Parliamentary political life and provided, at least in the provinces, a field in which the Indian nationalists could operate democratically rather than in a purely revolutionary manner. Out of a many sided struggle with the British authorities for reforms and concessions the Indian Congress party grew up. The growth of this all-Indian nationalist movement organised upon modern lines was the decisive thing. What was being created, on the one hand by the slow retreat of British power, and on the other by the ever more vigorous assertion of Indian nationhood, was a shadow government capable of taking over and running the country if and when the British left. (Moreover this shadow government was of the democratic and parliamentary kind.) As we noted in Chapter III in regard to the mutiny, the creation of this alternative government was the indispensable prerequisite of freedom. Until and unless this could be accomplished India could not be free: she could not be free, however badly the British behaved or however much she longed for freedom. For no country can be free till she can create the institutions and political organisations necessary for ruling herself.

No visitor to present-day India can doubt that what really has made the self-government of the sub-continent possible (in addition to the British legacies of the Civil Service, the armed forces and the railways) is Congress.[1] Congress is a nation-wide political organisation with its roots in the 500,000 villages of India and at its head a group of politicians who really know each other. The leaders of Congress have worked together for twenty years and more, have been to prison together, have quarrelled and made it up, know each other's faults and strong points, have struggled not only with the British, but with each other for place and advancement—they are, in fact, a real professional leadership of a real political party in the modern sense. Such a party is not, usually, a very idealistic or starry-eyed thing: it is an intensely human thing. But the possession of one, or much better more than one, of these remarkable organisations called political parties, with their group of dominant personalities at the top, is indispensable for running a country in the contemporary democratic manner by means of parliamentary institutions. The fact that India possesses at any rate one such party is the decisive fruit of the long struggle for independence. Moreover, the fact that Congress has emerged as a democratic, parliamentary political party, permitting the existence of rival parties and conducting genuinely free elections, is the result of the *way* in which that struggle was conducted on both sides. If the British had been unyielding and had not gradually introduced parliamentary institutions into India during the last forty years of British rule, the nationalist movement must have organised itself in a revolutionary form: it must have become either a nationalist junta, like the Kuomintang in China, or, more probably in contemporary conditions, a communist party.

It cannot be claimed that the British authorities between the wars realised all this. All that they did was slowly and reluctantly to give ground before the mounting agitation of Gandhi's various campaigns. But that was enough: it was enough to enable the Indian nationalist movement to be conducted along predominantly non-revolutionary lines, even to some extent along parliamentary lines, while achieving a sufficient minimum of progress to avoid discrediting those methods.

The question remains: why did the British imperialists behave in this way? After all, no other imperialists have ever, in a major instance,

[1] Congress, of course, was originally a nationalist movement. With the 1936 reforms it began to show signs of becoming a political party, competing with other political parties, since there was now "a vote" to compete for. For example, it was then that its unity with the Moslem League was dissolved. The extraordinary Indian political achievement is that under the leadership of Nehru, Congress's doctrine and policy have been given a Socialist content. For in Indian conditions, rapid development and industrialisation are both indispensable and are possible by means of Socialist methods alone.

done anything of the sort. Faced as they repeatedly have been with ever-growing nationalist movements of revolt, all other imperialists have, on the contrary, resorted to ever-increasing force and violence, have held in check or suppressed such movements for a long time, and in the end have often perished with them in a common ruin. We encounter here for the first time a question that will repeatedly occupy our attention in the second part of this volume. For the introduction before the war of a measure of self-government into India (limited and tentative as it was) was a step of immense importance. The eventual liberation of India to which it led, much more even than the grant of self-government to the old dominions in the nineteenth century, was a decisive event. For it has led to the comparatively peaceful dissolution of by far the world's largest colonial empire, and by so doing has changed the history of the world. My own view of the motives which made the men of my nation act in this historically unique way will emerge. Here let us merely note that it is possible either to make the most lofty claims for the moral superiority of an imperial nation which has behaved in this way, or, on the other hand, to dismiss the whole thing as an exhibition of weakness and pusillanimity. It will appear that for my part, and when all allowances have been made for the inevitability of the outcome, and for our strange mixture of motives, I am immensely proud of what has been done, and of the way in which it has been done.

It is important not to overlook the part played by anti-imperialist movements of opinion in Britain at the same time as the nationalist movements were appearing in the colonised and semi-colonised parts of the world. The beginning of a revival of anti-imperialist opinion may be traced in Britain to the period immediately before the outbreak of the first World War. Hobson, writing in 1902 could, it is true, see nothing before Britain but an ever-mounting tide of imperialist passion. Revising his book for a new edition in 1905, he was still more pessimistic. He thought that the adoption of protection, or tariff reform, by Britain, which he saw as the natural concomitant at home of imperialism abroad, was inevitable. The appeal of protection, he wrote, "made to the separate interests of producers is almost certain to be successful in a people of low education and intelligence" (*Imperialism*, p. 105). Yet the very next year saw the great Liberal victory of 1906, which proved to be a victory not merely, or in the end principally, of Free Trade, but of what were at least to become anti-imperialist forces. It is true that the Liberal imperialists predominated in the ensuing Liberal administrations. Nevertheless, a genuine process of the liberalisation and democratisation of British life had begun. Never again would the hold of that ganglion of social forces which so overawed Hobson be secure. Moreover the British wage-earning class had begun, with the appearance of forty Labour Members in the Commons, the long business of securing their own parliamentary representation. The process of social reform and with it the attempt, at least, to redistribute the national income more equitably, which, as Hobson laments, had been interrupted by the new imperialism, was taken up again and pressed.

Here the basic economic issue discussed in the last chapter re-emerges. If capitalism has the inherent tendencies which Professor Myrdal, for example, attributes to it; if it always and everywhere, unless power-fully counteracted, tends to give to him that hath and take from him that hath not, then such a redistribution of the national income was indispensable if anti-imperialist policies were to be practicable. For unless it had been carried out unmanageable surpluses would have made ever more massive foreign investment, and the imperialism which went with it, inevitable. Hobson realised that this was the decisive thing: he realised, that is to say, that for such highly geared capitalist economies as the British the sole alternative to the outward surge of imperialism lay precisely in redressing the social and economic balance of the nation in favour of the wage-earners. This process was seriously begun in 1909 by the "People's Budget" of Mr Lloyd George and by the ensuing Liberal social reforms. During the war of 1914-18 the franchise was decisively extended. Between the wars the democratic tide ebbed and flowed; nevertheless on the whole it mounted, and the possibility of that decisive redressing of the balance of the economy, and of society as a whole, which could alone make imperialism unnecessary to such societies as ours, came into sight.

A very different but yet parallel process took place in the United States. For reasons which we shall seek to assess in Chapter XIX below, America paused upon, instead of pursuing, the imperialist road which in the early nineteen-hundreds certainly seemed her "manifest destiny". This pause lasted all through the second and third decades of the century. Then in the third decade the great slump, striking her with unexampled fury, and at such a moment that it happened to discredit her party of the right, enabled her also to effect, through the agency of the New Deal, a sufficient redressing of her economy and society to make it possible for her to refrain from imperialism. (Though it does not guarantee that she will do so.)

The third factor which must undoubtedly be taken into account in this connection is the emergence of the Soviet Union. The Russian Revolution of 1917 had a profound effect upon the minds of many of the leaders of the nationalist movements in the colonial territories. They saw it primarily as an anti-imperialist event. They felt that Russia, one of the world empires, had, as it were, changed sides, and was now an ally of theirs. It was not so much the change of economic system which was significant for them as the fact that the Russian Government was now for ever denouncing the imperialists, and sometimes giving help and encouragement to the nationalist movements. True, as the twenty inter-war years wore on, the ugly sides of the Stalinist régime became more and more undeniably visible: but this made much less impression upon the colonial nationalists than it did upon the European and American wage-earners. Here was the government of a great power which might at any rate help them. That was enough to still nearly all doubts in the minds of both the leaders and the rank and file of the colonial nationalisms.

Thus three new factors were emerging. There was, first, the appearance on the world stage of forces of colonial resistance to imperialism. Second, anti-imperialist, democratic pressures grew up within the remaining capitalist empires; second these pressures began to modify the distribution of the national income and so to make non-imperialist policies possible. Third, a major non-capitalist society, in however ugly a form, appeared upon the world scene. Together these three factors were to falsify Hobson's prediction that capitalist imperialism was only at the beginning of its career. But at what a cost! For these new forces only got their chance because the capitalist empires twice set about each other in world war.

Nevertheless, in 1939, at the end of the inter-war period, and in spite of each and all of the above developments, imperialism as a world system still maintained itself as the main form taken by the relationship between the developed and the under-developed parts of the world. If the grasp of the European imperialists had visibly weakened, that might be counter-balanced in the event, many observers felt, by the growth of non-European empires. Japan was already clanking forward. And if America had not yet moved, that was certainly not for lack of the power to do so: the inclination it was felt, would come in due course. The nationalist movements in the colonial territories had made progress in some places, such as India, but they were in acute danger of total suppression in China, and over much of the rest of the colonial world, including most of the rest of the British Empire, they had hardly appeared. There was little sign of the sudden end to which nearly all of the existing imperial structures were to come in the course of less than twenty years.

The events of the second World War are still close enough to a writer of 1959 for it to be difficult indeed to see them in perspective. In particular it is difficult to remember that two vast new empires, namely the empire of Germany over Europe and the empire of Japan over two-thirds of China and over much of the rest of South-East Asia (except India) were actually established, and actually functioned for two or three years, during the nineteen-forties. (The German empire over Europe was atypical in that it was, partly, exercised over highly developed and contiguous countries: but the Japanese empire over China and much of South-East Asia was similar in structure to the traditional colonial empires which we have been studying.) The momentary apparition of these major empires, and their immediate destruction, are alike of high significance. On the one hand the fact that these empires appeared, however briefly, upon the stage of history demonstrates how undeniable it is that the kind of economies which began, as we saw, to develop about 1870 typically strive to establish empires.[1] Moreover these last, momentary, empires set about their characteristic tasks of exploitation with a will. Indeed they exploited their subject peoples far more ruthlessly than any modern empire had done.

On the other hand, the fact that, after a merely momentary existence, these two vast imperial structures were totally destroyed teaches a very different lesson. It is true that they were partly destroyed by two rivals, America and Britain. But that is only part, and not the most significant part, of the story. The destruction of the two momentary empires of Germany and Japan was visibly accomplished by other forces also. The first of these forces was Russia; and Russia even in her most repulsively Stalinist form was not merely another *capitalist* empire. (Although, as we shall describe in Chapter XX below, she turned out to be quite capable of her own kind of imperialism.) Second, the anti-imperialist forces, appearing now in almost all the colonies and semi-colonies of the empires, got at this juncture their opportunity to play a real part in history. For here were the imperialists repeating their internecine

---

[1] I am not suggesting that Nazism arose solely or mainly out of a lust for empire. (I have given my views on its origins in some detail in a paper entitled *The German Tragedy* published by the *Universities and Left Review* (Spring, 1958). But it remains the case that the Nazi economy once established, exhibited the imperialist drive in its most extreme form.

conflict. It was the catastrophe of the second World War which finally drove imperialism into retreat. Moreover, in the fourteen years that have passed since 1945 the most remarkable developments in the whole bizarre history of the imperialist epoch have taken place. For these events have diverged from any pattern foreseen by any student of imperialism.

In order to realise the extent of this divergence it is only necessary to envisage what might have been expected to have happened after the second World War, if the established policies of the imperialist powers could have been pursued without interruption. In that case the vast territories of the momentary empires of Germany and Japan would have come, predominantly at least, under the rule, in one form or another, of the surviving empires, of Britain to some extent no doubt, but predominantly, of course, of America, which was now by far the stronger. But this has not occurred. In the case of Britain, instead of her imperial territories being enlarged by victory, the British Empire was, as we shall see, rapidly dissolved, in respect of territories inhabited by nearly nine-tenths of the peoples who constituted it in 1945. (And this process of British imperial dissolution goes rapidly forward in the later nineteen-fifties.)

Almost more remarkable to relate, America has not for the most part acquired the empire which Britain has relinquished; nor has she taken over the immense territories never owned by Britain, such as the Japanese occupied parts of China, which were vacated by the momentary empires. True there have been discernible tendencies for America to attempt just this. She nearly attempted to assert herself in China by force. Moreover she did fight in Korea; but this was, on the whole, in order to prevent the whole of the Far East falling into communist hands rather than seriously to attempt to establish an empire there herself. Again her immensely preponderating economic strength gave her, automatically, the dominance of Western Europe, as it re-emerged, horribly mutilated, from Hitler's Reich. But this, as is being discovered now that Western European recovery goes forward, is a very different thing from territorial sovereignty. In the event neither in the undeveloped world, nor in the ravaged and enfeebled part of the developed world, has anything which can be correctly called an American Empire been established. Finally, the other surviving, secondary, but very extensive, capitalist empires, principally the Dutch and the French, after having put up, in contrast to Britain, a futile and bloody resistance, are now, in the nineteen-fifties, in evident dissolution.

Whether or not these startling fourteen years between 1945 and

1959 can possibly mark the end of the imperialist epoch will be the subject of the next part of this study. If it proves that they do, then they will constitute one of the most extraordinary turning points in history. For never since the dawn of civilisation has there existed an even partially non-imperialist world.

PART II

IN PLACE OF EMPIRE

CHAPTER IX

THE DISSOLUTION OF THE EMPIRES

THE PERIOD OF fourteen years which has elapsed since 1945 has witnessed the dissolution of by far the greater part of the empires of developed capitalism. Above all the two major Asian peoples, who between them compose nearly half of the entire human race, have reasserted their national independence. China has become independent not only of those Western powers which were increasingly dominating her, but also of another Asian people, the Japanese. Nor, it may confidently be predicated, will she prove to have fallen under Russian domination. And India has become independent of the British. And now the same process is at work throughout Africa.

It is true that parts of the former German and Japanese "momentary empires", as we have called them, have passed under the domination, direct or indirect, of the two main victors of the second World War, Russia and America. We shall discuss in Chapter XIX the fact that some of the former possessions of the brief Japanese Empire, and, for that matter, an indeterminate portion of the rest of the world, have passed under the influence of the United States. But influence is not the same thing as empire. And in Chapter XX we shall note that a large part of the momentary Nazi Empire in Eastern Europe has passed into the power of Russia; but in this case also the result is unlikely to be a world empire. These developments are only qualifications to the remarkable fact that the main colonial empires which were upon the winning side in the second World War, namely the British, French and Dutch, endured only a few years longer than did those of the vanquished: and that they have not passed into the hands of the Americans or the Russians. Thus a great part of the world which had been, right up to 1945, the colony of this or that imperial power has now become, or is now (1959) rapidly becoming, independent, or at least as independent as any nation can be in the contemporary world. We may briefly catalogue the process, empire by empire, beginning with the British.

To an extent which is still only imperfectly realised by the British people, Britain has in the past fourteen years been divesting herself of her colonial possessions. That process began, it is true, over 100 years ago when the Durham Report laid the basis for the independence of the so-called "old" dominions, and this phase was nearly completed by the Statute of Westminster in 1931. But right up till 1945 the process of divestment was counter-balanced not only by the retention of vast colonial possessions, but also by the frequent acquisition of new colonies, semi-colonies and dependencies.[1] But in the past fourteen years the government of very substantial parts of the world's population from Whitehall has come to an end. The nations concerned have either become wholly self-governing members of the Commonwealth, or, in a few cases, they have completely severed any special relationship between themselves and Britain. Nor has this British "disim-perialism" been counter-balanced in any way. In 1945 some 550 million of the circa 2,225 million inhabitants of the world at that date were ruled from Whitehall. In addition, another 50 million people inhabited countries such as Egypt, the other Arab states, etc., which were semi-colonies of Britain. In all, then, more than a quarter of the world's population were in fact, if not in form, ruled in the last resort from Whitehall. By 1959 over 500 million of those 600 million people had become completely self-governing, either as voluntary members of the Commonwealth, or as independent states. And of the remaining, say, 80 millions over half were well on the way to self-government.

Moreover, this process of dissolution continues uninterruptedly and is evidently independent, on the whole, of whether a Conservative or a Labour government is in power in Britain. In 1951 the Conservatives returned to office. At that date the principal remaining parts of the British empire, *i.e.*, colonies governed from Whitehall, with only a minor degree of self-determination, were as follows: East Africa (Uganda, Kenya, Tanganyika); Central Africa (Nyasaland and Northern Rhodesia with a large degree of self-government exercised

---

[1] The process was, and is, also counter-balanced, in another sense, by the substitution of a voluntary connection in the form of the Commonwealth, as against the compulsory connection of the empire, for much the greater number of the former colonies. We discuss this highly important aspect of the matter in Chapters XVII and XVIII below. Here we are concerned with the British empire in the concrete sense of areas over which sovereignty (*de jure* or *de facto*) is maintained from Westminster.

by the white inhabitants); West Africa (Nigeria, the Gold Coast, Sierra Leone, Gambia), the West Indies (the Caribbean Islands, British Guiana and British Honduras), Malaya and Singapore. To these should be added the vast *de facto* Arabian empire much of which had been acquired by Britain after the first World War, *i.e.*, the Arabian and Persian Gulf states with their oil fields, plus Egypt and the Soudan (acquired at the end of the nineteenth century).

Writing in 1959, after eight years of Conservative rule, independence, either within or without the Commonwealth, has been either granted or irrevocably promised at an early date to the following: Ghana, the Soudan, Nigeria, the West Indies, Malaya and Cyprus. Egypt and some of the Arabian States (notably Iraq, which was in fact a loosely controlled British dependency) have become, it was discovered between 1956 and 1958, effectively independent. Of the remainder, the only considerable territories are in Central and East Africa. Of these Uganda is advancing towards self-government, while Kenya has passed through the horrible experience of civil war in a multi-racial society, and its future is obscure. Tanganyika is at an early but as yet peaceful stage of development. The Central African territories face the hitherto unsolved problems of multi-racial societies. And at the time of writing (early 1959) it is impossible to avoid intense anxiety as to their future.

It is true that in 1956 a curious and perfunctory (if convulsive) effort was made to reverse this whole process in the Middle East, to reoccupy the Suez Canal Zone, and re-establish British dominance in Arabia. The attempt lasted for three weeks, and merely hastened the process of dissolution in this area. Thus in a few years' time, when the existing irrevocable pledges of independence have come into effect, what will be left of the British Empire will be the difficult heritage of the East and Central African territories, themselves clearly destined to some form of independence, a scatter of islands and, perhaps, some of the oil sheikhdoms of the Persian Gulf.

The second major empire, consisting in colonies and dependencies of the traditional kind, was that of France. Indo-China, the three major Arab territories of North Africa, Tunisia, Algeria and Morocco, besides vast areas of desert and tropical Africa, Madagascar and various other islands, all still "belonged" to France, in the very real sense that their destinies were tightly controlled from Paris, as late as 1945. Moreover, there was here, until 1958, no process of voluntary, or at least agreed and "constitutional" dissolution. Until 1955 not a foot of this vast French empire was voluntarily surrendered.[1] Instead a sanguinary war was waged, year after year, in Indo-China in which, it is not too much to say, the flower of the post-war French officer corps was destroyed. But in 1959 it is possible to see that French tenacity has done little even to prolong her imperial rule; and it has had the gravest effects on her relations to her former colonies when, despite her, they have become independent.

In 1955, the French Government was compelled by the disaster of Dien-Bien-Phu to relinquish Indo-China. Soon afterwards Tunisian independence, in fact as well as in form, was accorded, and, in 1956, this was followed by the more decisive step of setting the same process in operation in Morocco. Thus by 1958 the principal remaining French colonial possessions consisted in Algeria, Madagascar, and areas of tropical Africa and of the Sahara which were vast in extent, but very thinly populated.

In these latter areas also the process of dis-imperialism has now begun. With the coming to power of General de Gaulle in 1958, a policy of moving towards a voluntary dissolution of the tropical African colonies was at length adopted. These colonies were given their choice of independence, and Guinea took it. The rest opted for a degree of self-government, which will certainly grow more and more complete, within some form of association with France. There remains Algeria. Algeria, though nominally a part of metropolitan France, is actually a colony. Here a colonial war, far less bloody indeed than that of Indo-China, but still very costly, was in 1959 still being waged, year after year, by the French in order to avoid the recognition of the necessity that even here, in the presence of some 350,000 Frenchmen,[2] the process of granting independence must be begun. However, although this colonial war is still at the time of writing being pursued with indefatigable folly, its ultimate result, after the surrender of Tunisia and Morocco, and the failure of the counter-thrust at Nasser's Egypt, is not in doubt. Therefore, in the foreseeable future the French colonial empire will be dissolved. We may conclude that in the mid-twentieth century there is little difference between fighting to retain a colonial

[1] I recollect that some of the general officers who advised me as Secretary of State for War in 1950-1 used to remark, in admiration of the French, on this fact, and politely drew my attention to the contrast between this French tenacity and the record of the government of which I was a member in granting independence to India, Pakistan, Ceylon and Burma. They genuinely supposed that in some mysterious way France would benefit by her obduracy!

[2] There are over a million French citizens in Algeria. But more than half of them are not Frenchmen by descent but Maltese, Levantines, etc., etc.

empire and agreeing voluntarily to colonies attaining their independence, in respect of the final territorial result, or even in the speed with
which that result is attained. In either case the colonies become independent. The difference, and it is an all-important one, lies in the
political and psychological consequences for both the former empire
and the former colony. If the empire in question obdurately fights a
series of hopeless and bloody "rearguard-action" colonial wars it
inflicts economic, psychological and political wounds not only on the
former colony, but also and above all, upon itself, which may have the
gravest consequences. If, on the other hand, the realities of the mid-
twentieth-century situation are recognised by the former empire,
prospects of fruitful collaboration between it and the former colony
may be opened up which can be of the highest value to both. Much of
the rest of this volume is devoted to elucidating this contrast.

In 1945 the third largest of the remaining empires of the old colonial
style was the Dutch. This consisted of the Dutch East Indies and contained a population of some 70 millions. In proportion to the possessing
country of under 10 millions, this was a vast empire. Moreover its
inhabitants were, and are, by no means primitive. On the contrary,
they are heirs to a complex and sophisticated culture. Nevertheless
they had been most scientifically exploited for the profit of a small
section of the Dutch possessing classes (see p. 31, above). In this case
also there was no question of any voluntary renunciation of empire.
On the contrary, the Dutch fought long and hard, but quite in vain,
to retain or reconquer their domains. By 1950, however, the struggle
was over and this empire, which had been established in the mercantile
epoch, but had been re-developed intensively as an up-to-date capitalist
empire, had almost[1] ceased to exist.

The British, the French and the Dutch were the three principal
colonial empires of the classical capitalist style which were extant in
1945. Belgium, it is true, possessed, and still possesses, one vast and
extremely wealthy colony, the Belgian Congo, inhabited by only 12
million till recently very primitive Africans. The intensive and highly
successful economic development of the Congo which Belgium has
undertaken has only recently begun to create a literate, self-conscious

[1] The exception is West Irian to which the Dutch cling, thus largely ruining their
relationship to the Indonesian successor state.

and therefore nationalist, African class. By 1959, however, the familiar symptoms began to appear, and the Belgian Government announced both reforms and the prospect of independence.

Lastly, Portugal still possesses two large African colonies, which appear to vegetate in undevelopment: and no doubt as long as she makes so little use of them they are likely to give relatively little trouble. But there again profitable economic development, when and if it comes, must produce its own effect in the form of a colonial nationalist movement. (There is also the absurd anomaly of Goa, which the Indian Government, with remarkable patience, continues to tolerate.)

The above summary of the dissolution since 1945 of the remaining colonial empires leaves no room for doubt that this type of empire at least is rapidly becoming extinct. It is true that other forms of imperialism, less direct than colonialism, have existed and still exist. For example the greater part of Latin America has been, and to some extent still is, subject to this indirect type of imperialism exercised by the United States. (Though here, too, there are marked signs of relaxation.) We shall discuss the whole question of these indirect forms of imperialism in some detail, and we shall conclude that though exploitation and oppression are fully possible by these methods, indirect imperialism is an unstable and transitory thing when compared to actual, direct, colonial possession. Colonialism is the hard core of imperialism: and colonialism is vanishing from the face of the earth. It is seldom recognised how remarkable a conclusion that is. We saw how only fifty years ago the whole world was dominated by organisms of this kind. Not only did the greatest of them, the British Empire, govern some quarter of all the peoples of the world; it was flanked by other secondary but still vast empires such as the French and the Dutch. It was challenged indeed, but not by colonial movements or revolt, but by other empires such as the German and the Japanese. It then seemed that even if such a challenge should be successful it would merely lead to the substitution of one empire for another.

The world of 1900 to 1914 glittered with the apparent splendour of these empires, and clanked with their accoutrements. A passionate anti-imperialist such as Hobson was at a loss to know how they could be effectively opposed. He saw the future in terms of the logical extension of the colonial system into a nightmare of world-wide imperialism exploiting the whole earth in the interests of a small class of

Western parasites. Moreover, not fifty, but only seventeen years ago, in 1942, for instance, it might well have seemed to a dispassionate observer that the imperialist system was about to be renewed and reinforced until Hobson's nightmare was realised, albeit with different beneficiaries to those which he had imagined. For, although the older empires had been seriously shaken in the first inter-imperial war, and had never wholly recovered, two new and maniacally vigorous empires, the German and the Japanese, had appeared on the world scene and had conquered, respectively, almost all Europe and two-thirds of China with much of the rest of South-East Asia.

And yet to-day, in 1959, little remains of the structure of world colonialism. In fifteen short years the whole edifice has almost disappeared. Beyond doubt this is one of the most sudden and momentous transformations in the history of the world. Can it really mean that imperialism itself is a thing of the past? Can it really be that this age-old human institution of the domination and exploitation of one people by another, which has hitherto been inseparably associated with civilisation itself, is at an end? To reach any conclusion so far-reaching after only fourteen years' experience would clearly be preposterously premature. Though a whole generation of empires, which seemed upon the point of inheriting the earth, have been swept away, it would be naïve to suppose that new generations of empires may not yet reign in their stead. Nevertheless, the fact remains that for the moment much the greater part of the world has become articulated into a series of new and relatively independent nations, two of huge size (China and India), and has not fallen under the rule of some new imperial centre. What must be the the the consequences, both economic and psychological, of the dissolution of the old colonial empires? For it is not to be supposed that so overwhelming an event can leave anything unaffected, either in the former colonies or in the old established metropolitan centres such as Britain.

CHAPTER X

DO EMPIRES STILL PAY?

(I) THE TERMS OF TRADE

THE POSSESSION OF an empire has been widely regarded as a condition for the improvement, or even the maintenance, of the standard
of life of the British people. This view used to be vehemently expressed
in conservative circles. In the imperial heyday Stead, for example,
quotes Cecil Rhodes as having said, in 1895, that the building of an
ever larger empire was a necessity in order to avoid general impoverishment and consequent civil conflict in Britain.

> "In order to save the forty million inhabitants of the United King-
> dom from a bloody civil war, our colonial statesmen must acquire
> new lands for settling the surplus population of this country, to
> provide new markets for the goods produced in the factories and
> mines. The Empire as I have always said is a bread and butter
> question. If you want to avoid civil war, you must become
> imperialists."

What would Rhodes have thought of the Britain of 1959 in which
55 million people live at a much higher standard of life, in much
increased social harmony, after having dissolved nine-tenths of their
empire? No doubt few people would to-day endorse Rhodes' view in
this extreme form. Nevertheless, the worth of empire to Britain as a
whole is still the tacit assumption of much British opinion (nor is this
opinion necessarily confined to the Conservative Party). Moreover,
this view of empire is, paradoxically enough, implicit in the communist allegation that, whatever improvement there may have been
in the condition of the British people during the past hundred years
has been due to the exploitation of colonial peoples. A view so
diversely supported deserves careful consideration. Moreover, the
matter is even now being put to the test. If, as many of the more
simple minded British imperialists have genuinely supposed, Britain
would starve without her empire, then we ought to be nearly starving
now. Again, if the slow but undeniable improvement in the standard
of life of the British people up till 1945 was attributable, as the communists allege, to the imperialist exploitation of subject peoples, then

our standard of life ought to have dropped abruptly towards subsistence since 1945. For we have lost the direct political power to exploit the labour of nearly 9 out of every 10 of those whom we may have been exploiting up till that date. Yet the fourteen years since 1945 have in fact seen a more sustained improvement in the standard of life of the British people than any previous period.

In order to elucidate the puzzle we must enquire why people suppose that the possession of an empire enriches a nation. Clearly one nation cannot, effectively, take actual money from another. (The history of "reparations" after the first World War illustrates the ludicrous consequences in modern conditions of attempting to do so.) We must, then, pull back, in Professor Pigou's ever useful phrase, "the veil of money" and enquire how one nation can take goods and services (the only wealth) from another. As we have seen nations have done so in the past by frank pillage. Clive's initial rape of Bengal was very nearly that. No one, however, suggests that this was what Britain was doing to her colonies in the first 45 years of this century. What is suggested, however, is that she was trading, *i.e.*, exchanging goods and services, with those colonies in an inequitable manner: that by means of her imperial power she was buying cheap from them and selling dear to them; and that it is this which she will be unable to continue to do now that she has lost her empire.

This more rational view of the material damage which the loss of an empire must do a country is still very generally held or assumed. To take an example almost at random, it was given recent and typical expression by an American economist, Professor Hurwitz, in the May 1957 issue of an American periodical called *Prospectus*. Professor Hurwitz wrote:

"Dependent on foreign sources of supply and foreign markets for exports, it [Britain] is particularly vulnerable to the notoriously unstable conditions of the international market. Only by ruling the world could it ever hope to exercise control over these conditions. The degree of its well being in a world which it does not dominate depends largely on being able, in the phrase of the classical economists, 'to buy cheap and sell dear'. In the nineteenth century it could do so. By the beginning of the twentieth century it was evident that it would become more difficult to do either. The terms of trade were beginning to change to Britain's disadvantage. The result was a general worsening, at least in relative terms, of Britain's position, aggravated and accentuated by two world wars."

This view sounds so plausible—so almost self-evident—that not one in a thousand of Professor Hurwitz's readers, perhaps, sought to verify it by reference to the facts. And yet readily available facts and figures show that it happens to be completely false. The degree to which Britain "sells dear and buys cheap" is expressed in what are called "the terms of trade". And the fact is that Britain's terms of trade turn out to have moved for or against her quite without reference to the contraction or expansion of her empire. It will be worth while to look into this conclusion, which is so contrary to popular assumption, in a little detail.

From the British point of view the terms of trade are the ratio of the prices of our imports and our exports. Thus the terms of trade are said to have become more favourable to Britain when the prices of the things she sells have, on the average, gone up and the prices of the things she buys have gone down.

The terms on which we trade with the world have an important effect on the British national income, for foreign trade plays an especially large part in our economy. For example, Britain's terms of trade in 1953 were 5% better than they had been in 1952, and this meant that we enjoyed an increase of between £200 million and £300 million in the national income, other things being equal. This, it will be seen, was a useful, but not overwhelming, addition to a national income for those years of some £14,000 million. In practice, of course, other things are never equal. There are other and still more important factors in the national income as well as the terms of trade, of which the most important of all is the size of the gross national product. For example, again taking the comparison of 1953 with 1952, national production appears to have gone up by 5% between the two years, which meant that the national income went up by some £500 million from that source. So the terms of trade are by no means everything. Nevertheless, the terms of trade are an important element in our national balance sheet and it would be serious if it could be shown that the loss of the empire, either the loss of the nearly nine-tenths of it which has already happened, or the foreseeable future loss of the remaining tenth, would turn the terms of trade heavily against us.

The usual method of setting out the terms of trade is to take the rate at which our exports exchanged for our imports in 1913 as 100. That is to say, the 1913 terms of trade are taken as the standard with which to compare other years. I shall quote a table kindly compiled for me from the sources indicated below by the research staff of *The Economist*. In this table it is important to note that import prices are shown as a percentage of export prices. Thus a *rise* in the figure means a movement in the ratio of exchange between our exports and imports unfavourable to Britain. In 1855 with a figure of 125, for example, we had to sell 25% more exports to pay for a given quantity of imports than we did in 1913. On the other hand, in 1935 with a figure of 70 we needed to sell 30% less exports to pay for a given quantity of imports than in 1913.[1]

BRITISH TERMS OF TRADE
1913 = 100

Year	Import prices	Export prices	Terms of Trade (import prices as a % of export prices)
1854	117	92	127
1855	114	91	125
1856	118	94	126
1857	125	97	129
1858	113	92	123
1859	113	93	122
1860	114	94	121
1861	118	94	126
1862	136	108	126
1863	141	121	117
1864	148	132	112
1865	138	124	111
1866	134	123	109
1867	127	112	113
1868	126	107	118
1869	124	108	115
1870	120	104	115
1871	115	104	111
1872	123	115	107
1873	123	119	103
1874	120	112	107
1875	116	105	110
1876	113	98	115
1877	113	95	119
1878	106	91	116
1879	102	86	119

[1] The statisticians warn us that terms of trade figures are particularly difficult to assess accurately. No doubt the following figures, especially for the nineteenth century, should be regarded as merely approximate and illustrative of general trends. But it is precisely the general trend of the figures that is important for our purposes.

Year	Import prices	Export prices	Terms of Trade (import prices as a % of export prices)
1880	107	89	120
1881	106	86	123
1882	105	87	121
1883	103	84	123
1884	98	81	121
1885	92	78	118
1886	86	74	116
1887	86	73	118
1888	88	75	117
1889	89	77	116
1890	88	81	109
1891	88	80	110
1892	86	76	113
1893	85	75	113
1894	78	73	107
1895	75	71	106
1896	77	71	108
1897	77	71	108
1898	77	70	110
1899	79	75	105
1900	85	85	100
1901	82	82	100
1902	82	79	104
1903	84	80	105
1904	85	82	104
1905	86	83	104
1906	90	88	102
1907	94	93	101
1908	90	90	100
1909	92	88	105
1910	99	93	106
1911	97	95	102
1912	98	97	101
1913	100	100	100
1920	286	360	79
1921	191	271	70
1922	153	200	77
1923	149	191	78
1924	155	190	82
1925	156	185	84
1926	142	174	82
1927	136	165	82
1928	137	163	84
1929	134	160	84

Year	Import prices	Export prices	Terms of Trade (import prices as a % of export prices)
1930	118	153	77
1931	95	137	69
1932	89	128	70
1933	86	128	67
1934	89	129	69
1935	92	131	70
1936	96	134	72
1937	110	144	76
1938	103	147	70
1939	134	156	86
1940	159	199	80
1941	169	224	75
1942	185	262	71
1943	195	281	69
1944	201	290	69
1945	201	285	71
1946	230	309	74
1947	271	359	75
1948	303	393	77
1949	306	406	75
1950	352	427	82
1951	468	502	93
1952	460	527	87
1953	418	507	82
1954	414	502	82
1955	427	512	83
1956	435	532	82
1957	442	556	79
1958	408	552	74

Sources: Up to 1913: Schlote, *British Overseas Trade from 1700 to the 1930s.* Since 1913: Various series of Board of Trade figures which have been linked together.

Several unexpected conclusions emerge from this table. First, Britain's terms of trade in, say the eighteen-eighties which are often regarded as the heyday of Victorian prosperity and empire, were not in fact by any standard at all favourable to her. On the contrary, they were in 1888, for instance, 17% worse than in 1913, and what is more significant, some 40% worse than they are to-day (1958). We see at once that any suggestion that Britain is doomed because, having lost most of her empire, the terms of trade are bound to become ruinously unfavourable to her, is ridiculously ill-founded. The fact is that they have always, since 1945, been markedly better than in the heyday of British imperial power from say, 1870 to 1913.

Let us now, however, look more closely at the figures since the end of the first World War. It will be seen that from 1918 to 1940 Britain's terms of trade improved over the 1913 level to a substantial degree. During the nineteen-twenties they were between 70 and 85; that is to say, for every pound's worth of British exports we were able to buy some 25% more imports than in 1913. In the nineteen-thirties this favourable trend was intensified, and for most of the time the figure was between 70 and 80. And in one year, 1933, the figure went to 67 so that we were in that year able to buy about a third more imports per pound's worth of exports than we could in 1913. But mark well what year that was: 1933. And 1933 was almost the worst year of the great slump: a year marked by mass unemployment: a year of the derelict areas: a year of the hunger marches: a year of bankruptcies and economic desolation. In other words, the year in which the terms of trade were more favourable to Britain than ever before or since in her history, marked, not the zenith of her prosperity, but in many respects the nadir of her economic fortunes. Here, then, is striking evidence that favourable terms of trade are by no means the only factor in British prosperity. It is clear that too high a price can be paid for favourable terms of trade: that the terms of trade can turn out to be far *too* favourable, in the sense that they may be so favourable as to bankrupt the primary producing countries which are our customers as well as our suppliers. Here, too, is evidence that the real movement of Britain's terms of trade, is far more affected by such forces as world-wide boom and slump than by the application of arbitrary colonial power.

Let us now turn to the post-1945 picture. In 1947 British terms of trade were 75. They were, that is to say, a little "worse" for Britain (and better for her suppliers) than in 1933 but still a great deal better for Britain than in 1913, and much better than in the Victorian heyday. In 1951 they had become 93, which was a good deal worse than they had been in the thirties, but still a little better than in 1913. Then they began to recover again and in 1956 they were back to 82; in 1957 they were 79 and in 1958, 74. Still it is true that our post-1945 terms of trade have been less favourable than they were in the nineteen-thirties. Is not this evidence, it may be asked, that the loss of nearly nine-tenths of the empire has, after all, affected the British standard of life? In fact the evidence only presents this impression if our attention is concentrated upon the comparison between the years since 1945 and the nineteen-thirties. If we look at the picture as a whole, we see at once that the nineteen-thirties were in fact an abnormal and exceptional period. For in the very worst year of the post-1945 period, in 1951, our terms of trade were, I repeat, better than they were in 1913 and much better than they had been in the nineteenth century. Over most of the last ten years they have been markedly better than at any period in our history except those exceptional (and disastrous) inter-war years. And yet those fourteen post-1945 years have been the period in which nearly nine-tenths of the British colonial empire has been dissolved. In other words, there is no observable correlation between the contraction or expansion of the British Empire, and the degree to which Britain can obtain supplies of food and raw materials on favourable terms. Indeed we shall find that a strong case can be made out for supposing that the terms of trade, far from turning disastrously against a now empire-less Britain, are still likely to favour Britain, and the other advanced countries, and to disfavour the undeveloped countries, to a highly undesirable degree. (Professor Gunnar Myrdal's work *An International Economy* [Routledge and Kegan Paul], especially Chapter XIII, should be consulted for this view.)

CHAPTER XI

DO EMPIRES STILL PAY?

(II) THE EMPIRE OF OIL

THERE IS, THEN, no evidence that Britain's imperial possessions enabled her to enrich herself by turning the terms of trade in her favour. This simple fact in itself disposes of the bogy that the loss of empire is likely to impoverish the British people as a whole. But it does not dispose of the economic motives of imperialism. For, as preceding chapters have emphasised, to turn the terms of trade in our favour was not the characteristic purpose of the intensified imperialism which set in after 1870. Its main purpose was rather to secure fields of investment for the surplus capital which could not be so profitably invested at home, given the existing distribution of the national income. And the successful achievement of massive foreign investment, and of the imperialism that went with it, immediately enriched, not the British people, but a narrow class of investors.

Nevertheless it may plausibly be argued that if the foreign investments were sufficiently large and sufficiently profitable, the returns on them would enrich the rest of the population to some extent at least, as the money filtered down society. It is in this connection that we must now consider what is indubitably by far the most profitable instance of foreign investment, and of the imperialism which, as usual, has accompanied it. For this instance is of particular relevance to the question of whether or not Britain is to be impoverished by the loss of her empire. I refer to oil.

The story of how British, American and to a less extent other European, capital became involved in the extraction of oil, above all in the region of the Persian Gulf, is a strange and important special case of modern imperialism. We saw (p. 125, above) that the British Empire effected one last major expansion as lately as the end of the first World War. This was the acquisition, in fact though not in form, of much of the Arabian provinces of the Turkish Empire, which was liquidated. The British had conquered Iraq, Palestine, Syria and Jordan and enabled the Arabs of Saudi Arabia to get rid of the Turks. The British Government of the day did not see why it should not acquire most of these territories, though as a sort of tribute to the times, it set up Arab kingdoms, of varying degrees of dependence, in most of them, while making an arrangement with the Zionist Jews with regard to Palestine, instead of making them into direct British colonies. The British Government of the day seems to have made these acquisitions in the general tradition of imperialism rather than with any foreknowledge of what lay below the sands which it was, not very eagerly, acquiring. (For that matter the richest oilfields of all are turning out to lie not in these new possessions but immediately beside the Persian Gulf, in tribal territories control of which the British had taken, on behalf of their empire in India, nearly a century before anyone had heard of oil.) Nevertheless, these territories, taken together and joined to British dominance in South Persia (also acquired on behalf of India) have now turned out to be by far the richest imperial acquisition which Britain ever made.

There is historical irony in all this. For centuries Britain had fought for spice islands which were often no sooner acquired than they were found to be valueless: she had conquered India itself, only to find that, though she had founded a glittering empire, India was by no means the treasure-house of her imagination. She had roamed and ransacked and peopled vast, empty continents in the southern seas. She had breached the wall of China and penetrated into the heart of unknown Africa. She had done all this, not without advantage to herself, but without ever encountering a real treasure, such as had fed the dreams of her imperialists. And then, almost at the end, when her grasp on half the world was visibly relaxing, because of the chances of world war, the dreams of an Oxford don, and the belief that she was safeguarding the route to India, Britain rather wearily took on the overlordship of Arabia Deserta. And there, at last, was the treasure.

For there is no doubt about it, for sheer wealth there has never been anything in the history of imperialism like Middle Eastern oil. True, Britain has had to share the exploitation of this treasure both with American capital and, increasingly, with the Arabs who live above it. But then there has been so much to share. A simple table will perhaps suffice to bring home the extent of Middle Eastern oil resources (see p. 156).

These figures are taken from the interim report (1957) of the Food and Agriculture Organisation's Mediterranean Development Project.

It is true that "published proved" reserves of oil are said to mean less than might be supposed, since it would probably be in the power of the oil companies greatly to increase proved reserves by a sufficiently increased expenditure on prospecting. But is there any reason to

ESTIMATED "PUBLISHED PROVED" RESERVES OF CRUDE OIL IN THE MIDDLE EAST
(*in million metric tons*)

		End of 1956
Bahrein	30
Iran	4,025
Iraq	2,900
Kuwait	6,750
Qatar	195
Neutral Zone . . .	90
Saudi Arabia . . .	5,725
Egypt	35
Total (Middle East) . .	19,750
U.S.A.	4,720
Venezuela. . . .	1,860
U.S.S.R. . . .	3,350
Total world . . .	29,680

suppose that a smaller proportion of the new oil which will undoubtedly be found in the world, will be found in the Middle East? Be that as it may, the astonishing fact remains that in 1956 some 64% of the entire world's known oil resources were thought to lie beneath these sands. No wonder that this ultimate field of empire exercises a dangerous fascination. For British imperialists are tempted to feel that with their very last throw they have found that treasure of empire which had eluded them for so long.

For that very reason it is imperative that we should keep our heads about this whole fantastic business of oil: that we should see what we have and what we have not gained as a nation by dominating some of the Middle Eastern oilfields: that we should estimate what we shall, and what we shall not, lose as that domination fades—for fade it will. We must note the extent to which we already share the oil treasure, both with the Arabs who live above it, and with the other highly developed nations, essentially of course with America, who are also actively exploiting it. For in this particular field, as in the field of imperialism generally, there is a danger that we shall allow panic fears of "losing our oil" to drive us and the world to disaster.

First of all let us agree that great damage would be done not only to Britain but also to the whole Western world if we "lost" the supplies of oil from the Middle East, in the sense that these supplies were physically cut off. The Middle East (1959) at present supplies some 20%-25% of the total non-communist world's oil supplies, and this proportion may grow. The non-communist world could, no doubt, meet its energy requirements without Middle Eastern oil, by means of developing other oil supplies, by synthesising oil from coal, by increasing coal production, by developing nuclear and hydro-power, etc. (It is often forgotten that Hitler fought a six years' world war largely by doing just these things, and did so before the existence of nuclear power.) But the cost and the dislocation would be very considerable.

What risk is there, however, of the physical cutting off of Middle Eastern oil supplies? It must be remembered that though such a thing would damage us, it would ruin every one of the Arab oil-producing states. These states have come to depend for their large development programmes, for the luxury of their governing classes, for their military establishments, and for much of their general revenues, on the ever-growing share of the oil profits which they draw in the form of royalties. It is barely conceivable that so long as they remained genuinely independent, they would or could for long cut off this oil revenue by their own voluntary actions. It may be said, however, that the Russians might come to control the Middle East to the same extent and in the same way that they control Eastern Europe, and that they might then institute an oil blockade of the West. But such a development would, no doubt, take us far down the fatal road towards an East-West conflict. So there is little point in speculating about its economic consequences, for neither we nor the Russians would be there to experience them. On either hypothesis, therefore, the threat of the physical cutting off of Middle Eastern oil supplies is unreal.[1]

The physical cutting off of the oil is not, however, the threat with which the British Government, and the Anglo-American oil interests, are principally concerned. What is on their minds is rather that in one way or another the extremely high profits which are yielded by the extraction of Middle Eastern oil should be lost to their present recipients, and acquired, either by the Arabs, or by rival oil companies: and no one can deny that this is a real fear. In fact it is not too much to say that the Arab States, for the past ten years at least, have been steadily taking a greater and greater share in the profits of extracting this oil: that this process will continue, and, what is more, that it ought to continue.

[1] But see p. 174, below, for consideration of by far the least pleasant real possibility, i.e., that partly as a result of our suicidal attack on the Arab nationalists, some of the oil fields should come into the control of communist or pro-communist Arab governments, without overt Russian intervention.

We must next consider the consequences for Britain of this gradual but inevitable process whereby a growing proportion of the very high profits of the extraction of Middle Eastern oil will have to be shared with others. In order to do so we must try to disentangle (i) the part which imperialism, *i.e.*, the acquisition of sovereignty, or, in this case, of disguised sovereignty, over the territories involved, played in the acquisition of these profits; (ii) the remarkable manner in which the pricing policy of the world-wide oil industry causes these "super-profits" (as they may be called) to arise in the Middle East; (iii) how the super-profits are distributed; and (iv) their significance in relation to the total British national income in general and to the British balance of payments in particular.

First then, there is no reason to doubt the fact that British overlord-ship of many Arabian and Persian Gulf oil-bearing territories greatly helped the British oil companies to acquire the ownership of much, though by no means all, of the highly profitable process by which the oil is tapped, transported and refined. The fact that, in the late eighteenth and early nineteenth centuries, the British Government in India had acquired, for strategic reasons, the overlordship of South Persia and of the Sheikhdoms round the Persian Gulf, greatly assisted the early British oil prospectors, when they established the Anglo-Persian Oil Company in the first decade of the twentieth century. Again, the fact that at the end of the first World War Britain took over Iraq from the Turks decisively helped the Anglo-Persian Oil Company (now British Petroleum) to extend into the oilfields which were then being discovered, as well as into the still richer fields in the Sheikhdoms in and around Kuwait. It was no accident that the main share went to British rather than to French or Italian companies. Here was a genuine example of the acquisition of political sovereignty (*de facto*) actually bringing major economic gain. Nevertheless, it is note-worthy that the profits of the oil had to be shared with the great American companies. One major field, that of Saudi Arabia, became exclusively American, and the exploitation of the Iraqi fields and of the richest field of all, Kuwait, was undertaken on a "fifty-fifty" basis. Evidently territorial possession, even in this case, was by no means all important.

Second, it is not the case that the exceptional profits which arise from extracting Middle Eastern oil are due to the semi-colonisation of the area by Britain. On the contrary they arise, in the main, from the price policy of the world oil industry which is, on the whole, controlled by the American companies, and controlled in the interests of the native

American oilfields. That policy is an excellent example of how some prices are fixed in the present monopolistic, or as it was termed in the first volume of this study, oligopolistic, stage of capitalist development. For the world price of crude oil is so fixed that its extraction from the relatively high cost oilfields of the United States will be profitable. But such a price automatically makes its extraction from the low cost fields of the Persian Gulf enormously profitable. A second table will express the full extent of that profitability in terms of Iraqi oil, which is typical, under the current agreement between the Iraqi Petroleum Company and the Iraq Government.

TABLE IR/1, P. 75 OF F.A.O. MEDITERRANEAN DEVELOPMENT PROJECT
TERMS OF PAYMENT UNDER THE 1952 OIL AGREEMENT (SHILLINGS AND PENCE)

	Basic posted prices for 36¹ API per ton[1]	Cost of production per ton	Profit per ton	Iraq's share per ton
I.P.C.				
Before revision[2] .	93/1	13/–	80/1	40/0½
after ,, .	108/4	13/–	95/4	47/8
B.P.C.				
Before revision .	89/7	13/–	76/7	38/3½
after ,, .	100/6	13/–	87/6	43/9
M.P.C.				
Before revision .	85/8	13/–	72/8	36/4
after ,, .	99/11	13/–	86/11	43/5½

Source: National Bank of Iraq.

To sell for about 100 shillings a ton something which costs you 13 shillings a ton to produce is a remarkable achievement. Such a margin of profitability makes it far from ruinous to have to give back to the Arab States half (or more) of the profit. Truly, contemporary capitalist oligopoly "moves in a mysterious way its wonders to perform". But it would be hasty to assume that all the consequences of this extraordinary pricing policy are necessarily bad. It will be seen that, in effect, the American oil companies, in order to preserve the profitability of their own high-cost operations in the United States, present huge profits to the partly British owned companies operating round the Persian Gulf. They do so all the more readily, of course, because,

---

[1] 36¹ API designates quality of oil.
[2] The 1952 Oil Agreement specifying equal sharing of profits was revised in March 1955, retroactive to January 1954.

as we noted, they too have substantial interests in these fields and share in the resultant super-profits.

Several rather unfamiliar conclusions arise from this fact. If Britain, and the rest of the oil consumers of the world, had as their object the acquisition of oil at the minimum possible price, thus improving their terms of trade appreciably, the best thing that could happen for us would no doubt be for the Arab Governments immediately to nationalise the Middle East oilfields and (if they could, which they perhaps could not) to begin to operate them in real price competition with all other oil suppliers. In that event the marginal prices of oil in the world would no doubt fall substantially and all oil consumers such as Britain would benefit proportionately.

On the other hand, of course, the largely British owned oil companies would lose some of their very high profits, and in this unique case, these profits really are big enough to have a significant counterbalancing effect upon the British balance of payments and national income. Mr Andrew Shonfield, in a recent work entitled *British Economic Policy Since the War* (Penguin Books, 1958), which we shall have occasion to cite again, estimates that in 1956 our oil investments were bringing in £323 million a year gross profit out of a total profit from all overseas investment of £667 million gross, or £95 million net out of a total of £178 million net. Thus our profits from oil account for more than half of our net receipts from all overseas investments. On the other hand, the part which income from overseas investments plays in our balance of payments is often greatly exaggerated: for our receipts from overseas from all sources run at over £4,000 million gross.

Whether the British national income and the British balance of payments would be more benefited by cheap oil than it would be injured by the loss of the oil profits is probably an open question. However, it would not be merely the British oil companies which would lose their profits. (And an important part of these profits go to the British Government both as a majority shareholder in British Petroleum, and by way of taxation.) The Arabian Governments would also lose heavily. For they now get approximately half of these profits by way of oil royalties. And the ambitious schemes of economic and social development on which some of them (notably Iraq) are engaged, and on which the hopes of the Arab world largely depend, would be halted in their tracks, since they are wholly financed out of these oil royalties. Finally, the oil industry would no longer be able to finance, as it does now, the major part of its immense development programme out of its own retained profits, but would have either to raise vast amounts of new capital on the market, or to curtail development. It is evident that "the loss of Middle Eastern oil", in the sense of the loss of the ability to draw the present exceptionally high profits from its extraction, would have far more complex effects both upon Britain and upon everyone else concerned, than is usually supposed. It would injure the British economy in so far as Britain is an oil producer, but would actually benefit her in so far as she is an oil consumer.

The recent case of the loss of the monopolistic position of the Anglo-Iranian Company (British Petroleum) in South Persia is instructive in this connection. When the dispute broke out in 1951, I was Secretary of State for War in the Attlee administration. My colleagues and I were unofficially advised, both by the advocates of using armed force and by the opponents of such a course, of three things. We were told that if the dispute was not resolved it was certain that, in a matter of months, (i) Persia would be ruined; (ii) not only would the Anglo-Iranian Company be ruined, but the British economy itself would be crippled for lack of oil, and (iii) the Persians could in no circumstances succeed in arranging for the extraction of the oil or the operation of the Abadan refinery. All three propositions turned out to be without foundation. The dispute dragged on for nearly three years: the Persian people appeared to be no more, if no less, destitute at the end of the period than at the beginning;[1] the Anglo-Iranian Oil Company was not greatly affected; British oil supplies were without undue difficulty maintained from other sources; finally when a settlement was at length reached, the Persians were able to hire an international consortium which is successfully operating the oilfields and the refinery, on terms still profitable to that consortium. Britain could have retained a greater share in the profits from Persian oil if she had not (until it was too late) refused to give the now customary half of them to the Persian Government. But even the quite unnecessarily unfavourable settlement which was reached had no significantly adverse effects upon the British economy.

The Abadan crisis will also serve to remind us of the fact that the emergence of Middle Eastern oil as a major factor in the world is far more recent than is always recollected. It is not too much to say that it

---

[1] This was because the Persian Government had at that time not begun to use its oil revenues for constructive development. So Persia had not much to lose. It remains true that Iraq to-day (1959) might have her development destroyed by a long interruption of her oil revenues.

is only in the past nine years, since 1950, that really important quantities of oil have begun to flow out of the region. The following table taken from *The Economist* (July 2nd, 1955) *Supplement*, "Oil and Social Change", gives the earlier figures: after 1954 the figures are supplied by the Iraqi Petroleum Company.

CRUDE OIL PRODUCTION
(million metric tons)

	Bahrain	Iran	Iraq	Kuwait	Qatar	Saudi Arabia	Neutral Zone
1938	1·1	10·3	4·2	—	—	0·067	—
1940	0·9	8·8	3·2	—	—	0·67	—
1950	1·5	32·1	6·2	17·3	1·6	26·2	—
1951	1·5	16·8	8·2	28·2	2·4	37·2	—
1952	1·5	1·4	18·3	37·6	3·3	40·5	—
1953	1·5	1·3	27·7	43·3	4·1	41·4	0·03
1954	1·5	4·8	30·1	47·7	4·8	46·6	0·75
1955	1·46	15·53	31·75	53·20	5·28	45·67	—
1956	1·46	25·60	30·42	53·39	5·71	46·80	—
1957	1·57	33·98	21·35	55·62	6·42	46·95	—
1958	1·98	36·89	34·75	68·06	7·82	48·93	—

It will be seen that, except in the case of Persia, production was small right up to the second World War. Persia is in several respects a special case. Even here, moreover, production trebled between 1938 and 1950. It was then interrupted by the Abadan crisis, but is now, in 1957, well above its old level. In Kuwait, Saudi Arabia and Iraq the oil began to flow in bulk after 1950, or after the late 'forties in the case of Saudi Arabia. Moreover, 1950 is an important date in another respect. It was then and in the immediately following years that a substantial share in the profits of the now substantial flow of oil began to flow to the Arab Governments. A second table illustrates the point (see p. 163). (Figures from *The Economist* to 1954, after that year from *Petroleum in the Eastern Hemisphere*. First National City Bank.)

Thus it is only in the last nine years that the present extraordinary situation in the Middle East has arisen. Indeed, as we shall note below, the economic development financed by the oil revenues, has only been on any substantial scale in the last three or four years since 1955. For, even in the case of Iraq, where the development programme is much better organised than elsewhere, delays, whether inevitable or not,

ESTIMATED DIRECT PAYMENTS BY COMPANIES TO GOVERNMENTS
(*equivalent in million U.S. dollars*)

	Iran	Iraq	Kuwait	Saudi Arabia
1940	16·0	8·1	—	1·5
1950	44·9	14·8	12·4	112·0
1951	23·3	38·5	30·0	158·0
1952	—	110·0	165·2	160·0
1953	—	143·7	191·8	166·0
1954	—	191·4	217·3	260·0
1955	89·5	206·5	305·0	282·2
1956	152·0	192·6	306·0	290·9
1957	214·0	156·9	365·0	296·9
1958	246·0	235·0	415·0	310·7

postponed the actual spending of much money till 1955, at the earliest
(see p. 169, below).

The inferences which may be drawn from the story of Middle
Eastern oil and of the imperialism which has been associated with it
seem to be somewhat as follows. There is no doubt that British
imperialism in the Middle East did appreciably (though largely
accidentally)[1] help the British economy by facilitating the acquisition,
by (largely) British owned oil companies, of an important position in
the extraction, transport, and refining of the oil which has been discovered around the Persian Gulf. This was probably the most
financially successful piece of imperialism that there has ever been. But
even in this case, the results should not be exaggerated. For the fact
is that the oil companies' huge profits are earned, to an important
degree, at the expense of the consumers, including the British consumers, of oil. It is a matter of genuine doubt what the net effect upon
the British economy would be if these profits were diminished, as
they would be, by an outbreak of price competition in the world oil
industry, such as might (or might not) follow from the relinquishment
of the remaining British imperial positions in the Middle East. Indeed
it could be argued that the main sufferers from such an event would be,
not the British people who might get cheap oil (as at least an important
offset to the loss of profits) but the Arab Governments, and the further

[1] Accidentally in the sense that the end result was quite different from what was originally
intended. Sir Winston Churchill may be thought of as having started off the process when
he invested a large sum of public money in the Anglo-Persian Oil Company before the
first World War. His object was to increase the power of the fleet by going over from
coal to oil burning: the end result has been the involvement of large British interests in
the extraction of Middle Eastern oil.

development of the oil industry by means of self-financed investment.[1]

If, however, it is considered to be in the British interest, on balance, to maintain the present situation, in which the British oil companies can earn such profits as these, this can in all probability be done for a long time yet. For it is a clear Arab interest to preserve these exceptional profits, which the price policy of the American oil companies has, as it were, thrown into their laps. What is needed is to remain calm and clear-headed before the demands which Arab nationalism will, from now on, certainly make for an ever-growing participation, in one way or another, in the industry. We must be prepared for the fact that Arab Governments of whatever character will ultimately demand an ever-growing share of the profits of the actual extraction of the oil. Why shouldn't they? We should think it strange if the Arabs demanded even a share in the profits of mining South Yorkshire coal. It is true that the capital for the extraction of the oil has had to be provided by the West, owing to the primitive level of Arab technique. But this capital is being amortised, even on a strict accounting basis, over quite a limited number of years. In the end it will gradually pass, in one way or another, into the hands of the inhabitants of Arabia. Nor should it be thought that this will ruin the oil companies. Apart from the compensation which, if they are sensible, they will be able to negotiate for their local fixed capital, they will retain the immensely important facilities for the transport, refining and distribution of the oil.

The extent of the profits which they would derive from these "non-productive" facilities (as they are called) is becoming a matter of controversy. On the one hand some of the spokesmen of the Arab Governments evidently believe that most of the oil profits might, in certain circumstances, be concentrated upon these transporting, refining and distributing processes, in which many hundreds of millions of pounds of capital have been invested, and which are, for the most part, carried on outside of Arabia. They fear, it appears, that at some future time the oil companies will lower the price which they pay for crude as it flows into the tankers, without correspondingly lowering the price at which it is resold to the transporters, refiners and distributors who are, in many cases, their own subsidiaries. Thus they might divert the major part of the profits to these latter agencies and away from the point of production. Consequently, Arab spokesmen in the early

---

[1] It will be noted that cheap oil would probably benefit almost the whole British people, while low oil profits would, directly at least, hurt the limited number of shareholders in the oil companies. But this contrast is in this particular case much modified by the substantial public participation in the profits by way of both shareholding and tax.

months of 1959 were raising a demand for participation in these transporting, refining and distributing processes and indeed emphasising
this demand rather than a demand for the nationalisation of the
producing process or even for an immediate increase in their share in
the profit "on first sale", as it were.

The oil companies tend to reply to this demand by denying that the
processes of transporting, refining and distributing their oil are carried
on at a profit at all. They cite figures, for example, from a pamphlet
entitled *Petroleum in the Eastern Hemisphere* by William S. Evans, the
economist of The First National City Bank of New York. Mr Evans
points out (p. 12 of his pamphlet) that in 1958 the oil companies of the
Eastern Hemisphere (the Middle East is overwhelmingly predominant)
appear actually to have made a loss of $260·1 millions on their non-
productive activities. Why, it is implied, should the Arab Governments want to participate in this unprofitable business?

It is to be feared that this at first sight effective argument will make
less impression in Arabia than might be supposed. In the first place,
1958 was an unique year: in all other years there have been, on Mr
Evans' calculations, profits, though they declined from $164 million
in 1953 to $27 million in 1957. Second, the reasons given for this
decreasing profitability of the non-productive activities of the
companies are revealing. The relative excess of the supply over the
demand for oil now appearing in the world has exercised, even upon
this highly organised industry, some depressing effect upon the price
realised for the end products as sold to the ultimate consumer. At the
same time "the posted prices", as they are called, "of crude sold to their
subsidiaries" have been kept high. Thus in 1958 these same oil companies had a net income of $976·9 million from their productive
activities after paying $1,237·0 million to the (mainly Arab) Govern-
ments.

Naturally no one can forecast precisely what would happen if the
Arab Governments took over, in whole or in part, the business of the
actual production of oil within their territories. What the Arab spokesmen are beginning, it is evident, to fear is that in that event the oil
companies could and would so lower the prices for crude, F.O.B. the
tankers, that all or most of the profit would be diverted to the non-
productive activities. Probably such fears are exaggerated. Much would
depend upon the strength of the respective bargaining positions of the
Governments and the companies. And this would in turn depend upon
such factors as the relative solidarity of the Governments on the one
hand and the companies on the other: on the number of "free" tankers

available: on the world demand and supply position: on the growth of alternative sources of oil supply: upon the availability and price of alternative energy sources, etc.

But if the Arab fears of being relentlessly "squeezed" if they do not obtain participation in this momentarily profitless "non-productive" side of the oil business are no doubt exaggerated, so also are the fears of the oil companies that they would lose everything if they lost their productive activities. On the contrary experience during the Abadan crisis indicates that their bargaining position would be strong. They would almost certainly be able to arrange price schedules which gave them fine profits on their vast "non-productive" activities. On the other hand, they might consider the Arab demand for association in these "non-productive" activities, so that a conflict of interest would not arise.

So far we have considered the Middle East and its oil exclusively from the point of view of a Britain which is in the process of a rapid general liquidation of her empire; for the prospects and problems of a post-imperial Britain are the main subjects of this volume. But it is impossible even to suggest a viable policy for Britain in the Middle East without at least glancing at the matter from the standpoint of an Arab civilisation which is struggling to be reborn. At the cost then of going, for a few pages at least, outside the proper scope of this volume, we must look at the situation from the other side. For unless we do so we shall ignore political, social and psychological factors which are at least as important and relevant as the pounds, shillings and pence of oil revenue with which we have so far dealt.

It will be fascinating to observe the course of Arabian development during the remainder of the century. Let us never forget that we are here concerned with the descendants of one of the major civilisations, and major empires, of the world. We all know, of course, that while we in Western Europe were sunk in our dark ages, the Caliphate of Bagdad was the centre of a civilisation stretching from the Euphrates to the Zambezi, to the Pyrenees. And this civilisation developed algebra, invented the concept of Zero, preserved Aristotle (a more doubtful blessing in my opinion) and in general was by far the highest culture extant in the world this side of India and China. Again we know, in a sort of academic way, that Western Europe only revived from the dark ages by means of a life and death struggle, conducted over many centuries, with the Moslem powers, whether

Saracens or Moors, or, later, Turks; that that struggle lasted from before the Crusades to long after the Western reconquest of Spain; and, finally, that the first Western penetrations of both Africa and Asia, which led to the founding of the modern empires which we have studied, were undertaken by the Portuguese essentially as an out-flanking counter-attack in the course of a still desperate struggle with the Moslem power.

We know all this, but we know it in a very tepid, torpid sort of way as compared with the way in which a present-day Arab nationalist knows it. For him these events of a millennium ago are just as actual as, and are far more important than, the two World Wars of the twentieth century are for us. For him the fall of the Bagdad Caliphate, in our thirteenth century, is the main event and tragedy in history. How could it be otherwise? For that disaster was one of the most complete and terrible that has ever overtaken a civilisation. Though the Bagdad Caliphate was in full decline, the Arab world was still very strong. The Crusades were being finally repulsed. Iraq, perhaps the most advanced state of Arab civilisation, was inhabited, it is estimated, by over 20 million highly civilised citizens, living on the elaborately irrigated plain of the two rivers. Suddenly this heart of contemporary civilisation was destroyed by a series of invasions from Central Asia: it was physically destroyed in a way that few other civilisations could be destroyed, by means of the ruin of its irrigation system so that the valley of the two rivers became what it has largely remained until to-day, a desert.

And now, after nearly ten centuries, the oil royalties are beginning to pay for the rebuilding of those irrigation works, in some cases actually in the old channels. The population of Iraq which had sunk to little more than 4 million is now rising and will probably rise again beyond the old figure. And not only in Iraq, but all over the Arab world, which is as big and as diverse, and now perhaps as rich in natural resources, as all Europe, an immense if uneven, a decisive if distorted, development is going on. It is a startling moment in history. For in some parts at least of this undeveloped world there is no short-age of capital. Oil pays for everything. It is true that the Arab states face every other obstacle to development which confronts the whole pre-industrial world. Indeed they face them in what seem to the Western observer at least particularly aggravated forms. It would be outside the scope of this volume to attempt even a sketch of the social problems of the Arab oil states. Nevertheless it may be worth while to attempt to illustrate the sort of situation which they face in order to suggest what may be the right post-imperial British attitude to them. We may do so by quoting one or two of the outstanding facts and figures in relation to Iraq. In choosing Iraq as our example we may be confident that we are choosing the Arab oil state with the best record of development. The social situation in the other major oil states is in other words much more difficult still.

It is important in fairness to the Iraq authorities, and the pre-1958 Iraqi régime in particular, to re-emphasise one fact at the outset. And that is that it is only in the last nine years that they have had really considerable oil revenues, capable of transforming their country, at their disposal (see p. 162, above). The table on p. 169 from the F.A.O. Report made in the last years of the Nuri régime shows that it was not in fact until the years 1954-5 and 1955-6 that development expenditure really got going.

It will be seen at once that there were no expenditures of a magnitude which could quickly or greatly affect the lives of the people of Iraq until about 1954. *And what is more it is the considered opinion of expert students of the situation that right up to the revolution of 1958 the development programme has had very little direct impact upon the standard of life of the fellah, or share-cropping cultivator, who forms the basic element in the Iraqi population.*

It is true that one great thing was done. For the first time for many centuries both the Euphrates and the Tigris were in 1957 brought under control. This will prevent the appalling floods which, every four or five years devastated large areas of Iraqi agriculture, as well as whole quarters of Bagdad. This is an indispensable achievement; nevertheless all it will do, in itself, is to *prevent* recurrent disaster for the Iraqi *fellah*. It would not, probably, in itself have improved his abysmal standard of life by a single dinar. In order to do that it will be necessary not only to control but also to utilise the water of the two rivers; it will be necessary both to irrigate and to drain the land. And in order to do that it will be necessary, in the opinion of most experts, drastically to modify the land-holding system of Iraq. For it is the opinion of those who have studied the matter (as we shall note) that nothing can, substantially, help the Iraqi *fellah* until that is done. For Iraq, as one of the opening sentences of the report of the International Bank[1] puts it was up till 1958 "almost wholly devoid of peasant proprietors". This

[1] *The Economic Development of Iraq,* published for the International Bank for Reconstruction and Development by Johns Hopkins Press, 1952.

IRAQ: REVENUES AND EXPENDITURES OF THE DEVELOPMENT BOARD
(*In million dinars*)

	April 51 March 52	April 52 March 53	April 53 March 54	April 54 March 55	April 55 March 56
Revenues					
Oil revenues	6·7	22·9	34·8	40	59·1 (*a*)
Miscellaneous	·8	1·1	·5	·7	1·5
Total revenues	7·5	24·0	35·3	40·7	60·6
Expenditures					
Budgeted expenditures (*b*)	9·4	20·5	28·4	31·6	46·6
Actual Expenditures					
Administration: studies and organisation	·1	·2	·3	·3	2·6
Irrigation projects	·8	2·5	4·8	8·5	8·8
Principal roads and bridges	·6	1·8	1·9	4·3	6·5
Bldgs and establishments	·8	2·3	2·5	2·7	1·4
Land reclamation	·8	1·0	2·3	3·0	0·3
Industries	—	·1	·5	2·0	2·4
Other expenditures	—	5·0	—	—	7·5
Total expenditures	3·1	12·9	12·3	20·8	29·5
Actual surplus (+) or deficit (−)	+4·4	+11·1	+23·0	+19·9	+31·1
Foreign Reserve (*c*)	9·4	20·5	64·6	83·3	102·2 (*d*)

(*a*) To February 1956.
(*b*) Sources—Development Laws No. 35 (1951), No. 25 (1952), No. 45 (1955), No. 54 (1956).
(*c*) On December of financial year covered.
(*d*) On December 1956, the foreign reserve amounted to I.D. 121·2 million. *Source:* Quarterly Bulletin of Central Bank of Iraq, October–December 1956.

means that Iraqi agriculture was in a pre-peasant condition, compared with which the situation of even the Bengali peasant on his rice patch is advanced and progressive.

The Iraqi cultivator was (until 1958) a sharecropper, and a share-cropper working under what were some of the most onerous terms of agreement with his landlord which could be found anywhere in the world. According to the F.A.O. Report the landlord under the Nuri régime, if he provided any services, such as water, or working capital, received up to 75% of the crop: if the landlord provided nothing, he received 50%. The results of such a system on the distribution of the national income were as follows. Out of a total agricultural output valued at 70 million dinars[1] only 38 million dinars went to the cultivators, entirely in kind. This gave each cultivator an average annual income of 12·7 dinars, again in kind; an income that is to say, which implies an entirely sub-human standard of life. (As Professor Myrdal points out [op. cit.], this is actually a lower income than that on which the Palestinian refugees are existing on their dole from the United Nations.) 57% of the active population were cultivators. Total rent, profit and interest, at 120 millions, were two-fifths of total national income and over half of that generated outside the oil industry. Agricultural rent and interest paid no taxation.

The consequences of all this upon the prospect of improving agricultural output were summed up in the F.A.O. Report as follows:

"This inequality, together with the system of sharecropping, render any change in productive practices difficult. The labourer has no claim on any particular piece of land. In the South he usually has to move to a new abode built by himself every year. He therefore has no interest in improving or even maintaining the land, and is quite incapable of introducing a new system of cultivation. The land or pump owner on his part is satisfied with his income and more interested in preserving his status than in any possible increase in his revenue or in agricultural development under present conditions" (p. 23).

Such was the heritage of the new régime which came to power in Iraq in 1958. How it will tackle the social problem remains to be seen: but it appears that a widespread division of the land is beginning. Nor should the consequences of this be underestimated. For most of the development under the previous régime had benefited the towns rather than the countryside, since in the towns development was not blocked by the system of land tenure. But this in turn made for a painfully lopsided and distorted development. Nothing, surely, in the long run can decisively benefit the people of Iraq till their whole agricultural and land holding system can be transformed. For on this will depend, in turn, a genuine self-generating and self-perpetuating process of development and capital formation.

But, how in the social setting of Iraq was such a transformation to be effective without, as a first step, a distribution of the land? So

[1] The Iraqi dinar is exactly equal to the British pound.

conservative an authority as Lord Salter, who prepared a report for the
Iraq Government in 1955 made this comment:

"The great water schemes, the dams, reservoirs, main irrigation
works and main drainage outfalls, etc., are being constructed wholly
at the expense of public revenue, derived from the oil royalties,
which belong to the whole country and not to any one section of it.
These water schemes will, of course, increase the productivity of the
land, and therefore its value—to an extent that in time will equal,
and indeed ultimately exceed, their cost. It is not unnatural that
sections of the community should regard it as unjust that one section,
already more privileged than others, should now be further enriched
to such an extent at the public expense, and should resent a policy
which would have that effect. They may well have an ultimate power
which is altogether out of proportion to their present representation
in Parliament and their ability to influence legislation by constitutional means. It is this contrast between immediate and potential
political power that constitutes the danger and the difficulty of the
problem" (p. 24).

The phraseology is almost comically restrained. Nevertheless, the
stark outlines of the situation which exploded in 1958 emerge from
Lord Salter's Report. Destitute cultivators, without political rights and
a landlord class which did not even pay taxes were both suddenly
confronted with rapid economic development. Moreover, the Nuri
régime which perpetuated this suicidal situation was unconditionally
supported by a foreign empire, which thus drew upon itself much of
the odium of every class in Iraq except the feudal landlords. The catastrophe for British interests in the Middle East caused by this blind
support of an unviable régime was very great. Moreover, writing in
early 1959, it is impossible to avoid the foreboding that we have not
even yet experienced the worst consequences of the Suez operation.
That armed attack upon the Arab nationalists has made it difficult
indeed for the British Government to see in them the one remaining
force with which we can and must co-operate in the Middle East.
Yet it is becoming ominously clear that unless we do so the area may
become increasingly controlled by the communists.

The social situation in the other major oil-producing states is, I
repeat, almost certainly still more difficult than that of Iraq. Moreover,

throughout the Arab world there are no doubt very real barriers, as well as those created by archaic social structures, to successful development. The prostration of the high Arab civilisation of a millennium ago has been so complete and has continued for so many centuries that the human raw material now available for revival is in some places both scanty in numbers[1] and damaged in quality.

And at the same time the whole area has become a manœuvring ground in the cold war between East and West (however, the Arabs often draw advantage from this by playing off one side against the other).

Nevertheless, and in spite of everything, the sheer inflow of the oil millions, which are already being used, at least in the key state of Iraq, for physical development, are almost certain in the end, and in one way or another, to ensure the rebirth of Arabian civilisation. Local feudalists, imperialists nervous for their millions, strategists of the cold war, the feud with Israel, the anachronism of French imperialism in the Magreb, and divisions between pro-nationalist and pro-communist Arab states, will distort and disturb that development, but they can hardly stop it. What is vital for the West in general and for Britain in particular, is to realise that this profound transformation is now under way. Unfortunately, however, many of us seem, it must be confessed, peculiarly unsuited to appreciate the contemporary Arabian situation. Some of the British experts on the Arab world are men of the old school, convinced that the methods by which we have dealt with, for example, the Persian Gulf Sheikhdoms since 1780 are still the best. Some are enthusiasts dominated by the British-Arabophil tradition which goes back far beyond Lawrence. But the Arabs whom this kind of Englishman knows and loves may prove the least likely and the least suited to guide the development of their countries. The Arabophil tradition is romantic in the worst sense of the term, in that it sees in the present-day Arab a kind of "noble savage". But contemporary Arabs are neither savage on the one hand nor more nor less noble than other people, on the other. Like the rest of us they are a mixture of all sorts of good and bad qualities. The essential thing about them is that the best and most influential of them passionately reject an impotent, pre-industrial condition for their countries. Consequently they are determined to acquire precisely those Western qualities of urban development which Lawrence and many another Englishman

[1] In other parts of the Arab world, such as Egypt, it is tragically excessive in numbers. There is, in other words, an extreme maldistribution of population as well as wealth, both as between states, and as between classes, in the Arab world.

have so loved them for being without. If we do not genuinely and whole-heartedly help them they will turn elsewhere.

Others of our representatives in the Arab world see the new states essentially as pawns in a desperate game of chess which they are playing against Russian communism. The defect of this view is that the supposed pawns simply will not play that game. Most non-communist Arabs are, naturally enough, interested in the East-West struggle only in so far as they can get advantages for themselves by playing off one side against the other. For themselves, they are interested in only two things, namely their vendetta with Israel, which they see as a part of a struggle against Western imperialism, and their own development; it is to be feared in that order of priority.

What in these circumstances should be the general line of British policy in regard to this last acquired, this richest, and in many ways strangest of British empires, the empire of oil?

First of all let us face the fact that like all our empires, and like everybody else's for that matter, our oil empire is fast fading and that it will finally pass away altogether. The issue is not whether we should keep our oil; the issue is in what way should the relationship between the (partly) British owned oil companies and the emergent Arab states be handled? If we are to avoid costly and unnecessary catastrophes such as the Abadan dispute with Persia, we must clearly envisage that relationship as the steady transfer of the actual extraction of the oil from their own soil to Arab hands. Already, after all, the Arabs take half of the profit of that process by way of royalties. We must actively seek to associate them with the operation of the process itself. For many years they will need the vast expertise and resources of the oil companies in order to help them to get the oil, and they will have to pay us well for that help. But ultimately this end of the business will and should pass into their hands, leaving the oil companies with the immense work of transporting and refining the oil.

The political counterpart of such a view is the progressive transfer of our support, even in the Gulf Sheikhdoms, from semi-feudal interests to the rising middle-class Arab nationalists. No doubt the difficulty of such a swopping of horses while crossing the turgid streams of Arab politics can hardly be overestimated. We start with the immense handicap of having indulged in the Suez insanity, so that it will be far harder than it would otherwise have been to convince the Arabs that we are not pursuing some subtle, new imperialist policy. Moreover, such a change of policy is so much at variance with the whole tradition of our representatives that it will be difficult indeed to find men able to carry it out.

There is the additional and formidable difficulty of Israel. The burning Arab desire to exterminate the Israelis presents a most serious obstacle to genuinely good Anglo-Arab relationships. For, whatever the Arab outcry, we must refuse to discriminate against the Israelis, whether in the supply of arms or in trade or in any other way. Nevertheless, the events of 1956 have had at least this advantage. The Arabs have seen for themselves that for many years at least they have about as much chance of exterminating the Israelis, or for that matter of avoiding defeat at their hands, if it comes to war, as they have of invading Australia. So anxiety for the Israeli experiment in democratic socialism will be unnecessary so long as we do not undertake an arms blockade of Israel while pouring arms into the Arab states, under the pathetic delusion that they will be used to stop the Russians.

In spite of all these formidable difficulties, what other policy than the progressive withdrawal of British support from the Arab feudalists offers even the possibility of a successful outcome? Blind support of the feudalist-based régime of Nuri Pasha in Iraq led in 1958 to a catastrophe to British interests and prestige which may prove at least as disastrous as the Suez incident of 1956. Are we to pursue the same fatal policies to the end in each one of the relatively small but (in some cases) immensely rich oil-bearing sheikhdoms of the Persian Gulf? Can anybody in his right mind genuinely suppose that the feudal-based régimes can indefinitely survive even there? Their survival is impossible if only because they must either use their oil revenues productively and so create the social conditions which must inevitably lead to their own transformation; or they must squander them, in which case they must ultimately become too outrageously scandalous to exist. If when the crash comes we are still firmly riding the feudal horse we shall lose (partly to the Arabs, partly to rival oil interests) far more of our oil profits, and lose them far more quickly, than necessary. And this will be to our own, and probably to the Arabs', considerable disadvantage. Moreover, the time left to us for undertaking a revolution, however difficult and painful it may be to execute, in our policy in and around the Persian Gulf would seem to be short. If we persist in maintaining the oil sheikhdoms as semi-colonies, ineffectively run half by us and half by the local feudalists, we shall run an acute risk of seeing them pass into the hands, not of Arab nationalists, but of communist or communist controlled régimes. We have only, surely, a short time left in which to realise that the coming to power of the Arab nationalist in this area, far from being a disaster for us would be by far the best eventuality.

It has been important to consider this last British empire, the empire of oil. For undoubtedly it has "paid" better than any other. Significant benefit to the British economy has arisen. In particular the recent rise in the British standard of life may have been sustained during the past ten years in which Middle East oil profits have really got going, to an appreciable, though not major, degree by the fact that British domination of the lands round the Persian Gulf decisively helped British oil companies to get a large share in the profits of extracting, transporting and refining the oil which is now pouring out of the area. It is prohibitively difficult exactly to quantify such a factor as this, if only because there are so many possible hypotheses as to what would have happened if we had not had an oil empire. For instance is it to be assumed that Britain would, in that event, have had no profits from the transport and refining of the oil? Next, is it to be assumed that if British oil companies had not made these huge profits, the price of oil would have dropped and Britain as a major oil importer and consumer would have had a corresponding benefit? Or is it to be assumed that other people, say the Americans, would have kept the price up and got all the profits, Britain thus losing on both scores? Such uncertainties make it impossible to set a figure of what we should have lost in say the last ten years if we had not had a major stake in Middle Eastern oil. I can only record the conviction that even in this, by far the most financially successful of all imperialist ventures, the gross loss would have been of the order of say 1 or 2% of the gross national product.

Moreover, once again dominance in the Middle East has not been maintained for nothing. The military and diplomatic bill has been considerable. Till 1956 we were paying, year in year out, a subsidy of £12 m. a year to one puppet government, that of Jordan, alone, for example. All this suggests that the specifically imperialist element in our Middle Eastern oil enterprises has been less profitable, net, than is often supposed and that as this element has to be abandoned the loss to the British economy will not be serious. For it will be precisely by abandoning in good time and with a good grace our imperialist pretensions to dominate the area; it will be by coming to terms with Arab nationalism, that we shall be enabled to carry on, for many years yet, a highly profitable business in oil. Of course the rate of profit on oil extraction will slowly drop as and when other people are free to make competitive tenders for doing this or that part of the job, and as the Arabs become capable of doing some of it themselves. But what have we got to complain of in that?

The bizarre story of the British oil empire in the Middle East illustrates two facts. First, there may be gains from imperial possessions that do not necessarily reveal themselves in the terms of trade. (As we shall see immediately, however, these gains are often greatly exaggerated.) Second, it illustrates the fact that there can undoubtedly be imperialism without the formal annexation, or colonialisation, of one country by another. The Persian Gulf oil-bearing area has never been "painted red on the map". Various forms of indirect domination have been employed, ranging all the way from the long-established British near-colonisation of the Gulf Sheikhdoms, to British relations with Persia, which have always been to some extent those of independent states. And this leads towards general considerations which must be taken up in the next two chapters.

CHAPTER XII

DO EMPIRES STILL PAY? (III) SUMMARY

THERE ARE, OF COURSE, other instances, as well as oil, of high profits derived from investments in colonies or semi-colonies. In general if a firm which exports, say, primary products from a British colony is itself British owned, it may be making an extremely high rate of profit even if it gets no more than the world price for its products. And this profit may be wholly or partly transferred to Britain in the form of dividends to British shareholders.

An instance of this process is afforded by the British-owned copper mines in Northern Rhodesia. Figures which have become famous were given by Miss Phyllis Deane in her authoritative study entitled *Colonial Social Accounting* (Cambridge University Press, 1953), a work issued under the auspices of the National Insitute of Economic and Social Research. Her Table 14 (op. cit., p. 37) shows what happened in the year 1949 to the values created by the mining companies of the copper belt.

EXPENDITURE BY MINING INDUSTRY IN NORTHERN RHODESIA

1. European salaries, wages, bonuses	. .	£4,100
2. African wages and bonuses	. . .	1,400
3. African rations	. . . .	600
4. Payments to contractors .	. .	1,000
5. Payments to Rhodesia Railways[1]	. .	1,800
6. Income Tax ⎱		3,600
7. Customs[2] ⎰		
8. Total expenditure	.	£12,500
9. Gross value of output . . .	.	£36,742

We note that of the £36·7 m. realised, only £12·5 m. was spent in Northern Rhodesia at all. A gross profit or surplus, call it what you will, of some £24 m., or two-thirds of the total, was transferred to the

---

[1] This excludes freight divisible with South African Railways but includes payments for transport outside Northern Rhodesia. As Rhodesia Railways is not a Northern Rhodesian concern this is only partly a payment to the Northern Rhodesia economy.

[2] This includes only payments made direct to Northern Rhodesian customs and not payments made to South African or Southern Rhodesian customs and later received by the Northern Rhodesian Government under the terms of the Customs Agreement.

United Kingdom and America. Moreover, it will be noted that of the £12·5 m. spent in Northern Rhodesia, £4·1 m. was paid to Europeans, mainly British, living and working there. Only £2 m. in money and rations out of the £36·7 m. went to the Africans working in the mines.

Such are the fantastic results produced by the discovery of valuable raw materials such as copper in what was at the time an ultra-primitive country such as Northern Rhodesia. It is impossible to become aware of them without understanding the sense of outrage which possesses a subject people as soon as it comes to know what is happening to it under imperialism. Needless to say, the Africans of Northern Rhodesia ought to be receiving, in one way or another, a much higher proportion of the values which they are helping to create. They ought to be receiving something comparable to the oil royalties which the Arab states have, as we saw, now extracted from the oil companies. They are not nearly sufficiently developed to be able to produce these values themselves or even to be able to spend such sums individually; but royalties comparable to those received by the Arabs ought to be financing Northern Rhodesian development on a major scale. (A very little has now been done in this direction. A proportion of the royalties paid by the copper companies to the "landlord" British South Africa Company now goes to the Northern Rhodesian Government.) Nevertheless, it would be wrong to jump to the conclusion either that the Africans had got no benefit from the gusher of wealth which has been found in their country, or that this sort of "colonial" super-profit is an important element in the British national income. On the first issue Miss Deane calculated that in 1945 the average income of all the Africans in the colony was about £27 a year per adult male. But the 33,000 Africans then engaged in mining had incomes of £41 a year.[1] Moreover, the Africans still living in the villages off subsistence agriculture had much lower incomes still, though difficult to express in money terms. Miss Deane's calculations give the impression that the African copper-miners are, say, two or three times as well off as the African subsistence farmers. The conclusion seems to be that even ultra-imperialist development of this kind, in which the native population is too weak in influence to get more than a fractional share of the values created, may be, nevertheless, better than no development.

Turning to the effect upon the British economy, no one would seek to deny that it has been advantageous to get some of our copper in this way. But again it is important to compare the order of magnitude of

[1] By 1958 this had risen to £189 a year according to the year-book of the Northern Rhodesian Chamber of Mines.

the sums involved. We made about £24 m. (in 1949) by owning the Northern Rhodesian copper mines—and even that is not allowing for the foreign shareholding in the companies concerned. But this compares with a national income rising from £10,000 m. to £18,000 m. a year. It may be objected that Northern Rhodesian copper is merely an instance. Still copper is perhaps the outstanding remaining example, after oil. Moreover a further consideration must be kept in mind. It is not the whole of the profit on the British capital invested in these enterprises which is in question. For much of it could have been earned in alternative non-imperialist enterprises at home or abroad. After all, British firms can and do invest on a great scale and very profitably both at home and in countries such as the United States, Canada and Australia over which they can exercise no element of imperialist coercion. What is in question is the extra profit added on by the imperialist control over the lives and labours of subject peoples.

I know of only one attempt to separate this element of imperialistically derived extra-profit. This attempt was made by Mr Dutt, the principal theoretician of the British Communist Party, in a work to be discussed in the next chapter.[1]

He gives (pp. 56-8) instances of the high profits earned by some of the great firms which operate, to a large extent, in the British colonies or former colonies. For instance, he shows that 817 such companies earned profits of £438 m. in 1951. This was a 47% gross profit (before tax). Mr Dutt contrasts this with the record of 1,970 companies operating mainly at home, which earned £1,437 m. in 1951. This was a gross profit of 34%. "In the difference between these two figures we have a partial indication of colonial super-profit within the general structure of monopoly profits", Mr Dutt writes. But, although he gives the corresponding figures, Mr Dutt does not compare the respective profit rates for 1950—a more representative year than 1951. In 1950 his mainly "colonial" firms made £277 m. and his "home" firms £1,154 m. This was a rate of gross profit on their respective capitals of some 29% for the "colonial" firms and some 25% for the "home" firms; a much less striking contrast. More important, the size of the figures in fact gives little support to the theory that the whole structure of British life rests upon a basis of imperialist exploitation. Mr Dutt fails to compare his figures of £277 m. or £438 m. a year gross profits for his "colonial" firms with a gross national income of £11,464 m. for 1950 and £12,537 m. for 1951. Again, Mr Dutt does not attempt to

[1] The Crisis of Britain and the British Empire (Lawrence and Wishart, 1953).

say what proportion of the activities of his "overseas" firms took place in countries under effective British sovereignty and what proportion in foreign countries.

A more interesting calculation is made by Mr Andrew Shonfield in his previously mentioned *British Economic Policy Since the War*, pp. 110-16. Mr Shonfield is concerned to compare the results of overseas investment as a whole, whether in British colonies or not, with the results of home investments. Taking the test of profits he concludes, on the basis of a Bank of England Survey for 1955, that the overseas investments of British companies in that year were yielding, on the average, rather less than 10% net, and he estimates that the average rate of profit on home investments was of the order of 8% net. So that if we are to accept profit as the sole criterion of national interest there is a perceptible, though not very large, advantage in overseas investment. But Mr Shonfield does not accept net profit as a criterion of the national interest. For he calculates that capital invested at home yields an increase in British physical output, or Gross National Product, at the rate of 33% per annum per pound invested. He concludes that the national interest will only be served by investing overseas instead of at home if our "enterprise overseas is going to pour out profits to be brought home to Britain so enormously faster—at least three or four times faster—than our exporting manufacturing enterprise now looking for funds at home". For what matters to the nation is not just the amount of realised profit going to shareholders, but the total of values created, going to Labour, Management and everybody else concerned. In the case of overseas investment these values, other than profits, do not come to Britain at all.

Thus Mr Dutt's and Mr Shonfield's conclusions could hardly be more opposite. Mr Dutt is persuaded that overseas investment, and imperial investment in particular, is the one way in which Britain can obtain the "super-profits" which, he supposes, alone sustain her economy. Mr Shonfield, on the other hand, while admitting that overseas investment is rather more profitable to the investors than home investment is convinced that the latter is by far the more advantageous to the British people as a whole. Thus the two observers come to diametrically opposed conclusions. Perhaps they have insufficiently elucidated the major premises of their respective arguments. The fact is that it is impossible to answer the question, "Which is better, overseas or home investment?" until we have asked the counter question, "Better for whom?" On Mr Schonfield's figures overseas investment is better by about 2% *for the investors*. If the national interest is still identified exclusively with the interests of the holders of income-bearing shares and bonds (some 10% of the population), as to a remarkable extent it still is, then there is a rational basis for the immense importance usually attached to overseas investment for private profit, and to the imperialism which has been associated with it. But if we identify the national interest with the welfare of the wage and salary earners of Britain (some 90% of the population)[1] then the advantage (for Britain) is overwhelmingly with home investment.

Overseas investment, and the imperialism which goes with it, are, or at any rate tend to be, a logical interest for the shareholding, property-owning tenth of the population. For this section of British society foreign investment as a whole certainly did pay, and the empire, with all its costs, could be rationally thought of as a necessary overhead. It is doubtful if empire any longer pays even this section of the population. And it is obvious that empire no longer "pays" (if indeed it ever did) in the sense of procuring material benefits to the great majority of the people of Britain. Mr Shonfield comes to much the same conclusion as Hobson did half a century ago: "if . . . we devote more British capital to investment in the up and coming industry abroad, we shall end up with a lot of very rich individual British investors and our productive capacity enfeebled to the point where we are incapable of selling anything of our own anywhere in the world against foreign competition. No doubt the investors will then decide to emigrate, because the country has no future."

Especially high profits from imperialistically fostered foreign investments are not the only other source (apart from the terms of trade) from which imperial gains may be derived. In particular, Britain is often alleged to be continuing to exploit large parts of the undeveloped world by means of the arrangements which have grown up amongst the members of the British Commonwealth, both self-governing and colonies (plus the Irish Republic and Iceland, but minus Canada), for pooling their currency reserves, including their gold and dollars. Broadly, this means that in respect of the rest of the world, and of the dollar countries in particular, "the sterling area", as it is called, trades as a unit. When, for example, Malaya sells rubber, or Ghana cocoa, to America or Canada, the receipts in dollars go into a common pool together with the receipts from the sale for dollars of British motor cars and whisky, or Australian wool. Equally, when Australia buys

[1] See *Contemporary Capitalism*, Chapter VIII.

American precision instruments or bulldozers, or India buys American steel, or the United Kingdom buys Canadian aluminium, the dollars to pay for these things come out of the common pool.

As everybody knows only too well, the inhabitants of the sterling area, in common with the rest of the world, have ever since 1945 desired to buy, and have tended to buy, more from the Americans than they have sold to them. Therefore, there was a constant pressure on the sterling area's gold and dollar reserves. For every member of the sterling area would like to allow its citizens to buy more and more dollar goods. Under the pooling arrangement, however, the sterling area has no system by which what a particular country can draw out of the common pool is related to what it has put into it. A member-country may be a great dollar-earner and yet draw very little by way of dollar spending; another member-country may earn very few dollars and spend a great many. It would not be surprising to find that such a system produces results which seem, at any rate, unfair to some members of the sterling area as against others. And so it does. More-over, upon examination, it emerges that the large dollar-earners and the small dollar-spenders were precisely the remaining British colonies. The figures show that they, and they alone, in the years immediately after 1945, earned substantially more dollars than they spent. The avidity with which Mr Dutt and other communist com-mentators seize upon these figures may be imagined. Here, they feel, is proof that Britain is seeking to meet her chronic dollar deficit by means of ever-increasing exploitation of her remaining colonies, and to some extent, her ex-colonies: that these colonies are made to earn the dollars for Britain to spend.

The matter is not so simple. It is true that the colonies put more into the dollar pool than they took out. But the principal beneficiary was not the United Kingdom. The countries which, quite as much as Britain, took more out of the pool than they put in were precisely the other independent members of the Commonwealth, including India. It could be argued that it was actually India, Pakistan, and the other independent members of the Commonwealth, including Australia and New Zealand, rather than the United Kingdom which were "exploit-ing" the remaining colonies. For they have financed their own dollar deficits by drawing on the dollar surpluses of the colonies.[1] Moreover, there was nothing necessarily wrong in using the colonies' dollar surpluses for the common purposes of the sterling area pool, *if* the

[1] Mr Anthony Crosland, in his book, *Britain's Economic Problem* (Cape, 1955), made a careful study of the relevant figures in the immediately post-war years.

colonies were fully and adequately paid for those dollar surpluses. For the colonies' dollar surpluses were not simply taken from them. They were credited with the full amounts in sterling. At this point in the story there arises a critical question: how much was that sterling worth to them? Was it an adequate compensation for the dollar earnings which they surrendered? The answer depends on whether they could buy an adequate supply of goods from Britain, or elsewhere, with that sterling. To put the point in terms of goods, if the colonies are to be deprived of the right to buy transatlantic goods with their dollars, they must be given, if the transaction is to be equitable, the right to buy equally suitable goods at competitive prices from sterling sources. And the fact is that this was not adequately achieved. For their sterling depreciated seriously during the period.

Mr Dutt naturally makes great play with all this (see particularly pp. 265-71 of the *Crisis of Britain and the British Empire*). It is true he oversimplifies the issue. For example, he ignores the flow of British capital into the colonies during the period. Again he represents the produce boards for cocoa, cotton, oil and fats, etc., which have been established in, for example, Ghana, Nigeria and Uganda as designed permanently to withhold the full price of their products from the producers of these countries. The best evidence that this is not so is afforded by the fact that after Ghana became independent she decided to continue the cocoa board, when she was certainly in a position to scrap it. In fact, now (1959) that the prices of primary products have fallen, the accumulated funds of the produce boards will stand the African producers in good stead.

When all such qualifications have been made, however, the charge that no adequate return for their invaluable dollar surpluses has yet been made, either by the United Kingdom or the rest of the sterling area, to the remaining British colonies, is a very serious one. If the account between the colonies and the rest of the members of the Commonwealth were to be closed to-morrow, it would be impossible to deny that the colonial peoples had suffered grave exploitation for the benefit of the self-governing peoples of the Commonwealth. When it is recalled that these colonial peoples are far poorer than are the peoples of the countries of the independent sterling area (with the huge exception of India), the gravity of the issue will be appreciated.

Fortunately, the sterling area accounts are by no means closed, and it is still possible for the independent sterling countries, and the United Kingdom in particular, to discharge their debt in part at least to the colonies and ex-colonies. For that it is first of all necessary that they should be allowed and enabled steadily to draw down their sterling balances. This will mean that, instead of exporting more than they have imported, as they have been doing, they will import more than they export. And that, of course, will cost the rest of us something in terms of exports for which we get no return. But the truth is that we have already had that return, when we most needed it, and that we must now pay off in full what is a debt to the colonies if ever there was one.

These considerations throw light upon the question of the investment of British capital in the remaining colonies and in the Commonwealth as a whole. By far the best use which the colonies can make of their accumulated sterling balances is to spend a good part of them, not on imported consumers' goods for immediate consumption, but on, first, capital goods for their economic development and, second, such necessities for cultural development as schools, hospitals, and medical and welfare services generally. Again, it is the very least we can do to supply them. Moreover, considering what we have caused the colonies to do for us, it is the least we can do to supply them, not in the form of British private capital seeking high profits, but in the form of publicly allotted capital, consciously undertaking projects of development and welfare, even though such projects may have poor financial prospects.

As a particular instance, the *circa* £500 million with which the colonies provided the sterling area (in dollars too) in the years 1946-52 may be thought to put into perspective the £36 million expenditure which we incurred during these same years on the abortive groundnuts scheme, with which I was so closely associated. It may be that this particular scheme was doomed to failure in any case: it is clearly impossible for me to judge. But it is surely tragic that the British people should be led to suppose that we were squandering their money, without need or obligation, on the attempt to develop the colonies. The truth is that it is our elementary duty to undertake development schemes in the colonies and ex-colonies, even when the chance of any financial return is small, if we are ever to repay the massive financial support with which the colonies have furnished us. The groundnuts scheme was only one of the development projects undertaken by the British Government in the colonies in this period. Many others were undertaken both in the development and in the welfare fields. But even so, the total sum so expended goes only a small way towards recompensing the colonial peoples for the financial support which we were drawing from them. Moreover, even the full discharge by the United

Kingdom and the other independent sterling countries, of their debts to the colonies will not alter the fact that in the post-war years those colonies were, temporarily at least, exploited without their consent. It is difficult to believe that if they had been self-governing they would have been willing to fall in with quite so altruistic an arrangement. The acid test of this issue is now rapidly approaching. The colonial dollar surpluses arise mainly in Malaya, Uganda and Ghana and Nigeria. Ghana and Malaya have now achieved, and Nigeria is approaching, self-government; Uganda also is entering on the same path. There is little doubt that when these colonies become independent members of the sterling area they will insist upon better treatment. It is a sad fact, but it is a fact, that there is no substitute for being in a position to look after oneself.

We now encounter a remarkable paradox. While it is clear that the sterling area arrangement benefited Britain and some of the newly independent states of the Commonwealth at the expense of the remaining colonies in the immediately post-war years, quite another position had arisen by the nineteen-fifties. In the opinion of one school of economic thought at least, the sterling area had become by 1959 a sheer liability for Britain. Far from being a mechanism for the exploitation of the colonies, it has now become in their view something of which Britain had better rid herself as soon as possible. Mr Andrew Shonfield takes this view.

In order, Mr Shonfield considers, for Britain to maintain this arrangement, which now benefits her hardly at all, she has to allow a completely free and undirected export of private capital to the sterling area. This capital, which Britain ought to be using at home to increase her own rate of investment, is flowing not to India or the other undeveloped areas, but predominantly to South Africa and Rhodesia. He quotes the following table of British investment, both private and public, in the sterling area between 1946-55 from A. C. Coran's work, *The Changing Pattern of Industrial Investment in Selected Sterling Countries* (Princeton University, 1956):

South Africa	.	.	.	£500 m.
Colonies	.	.	.	£450 m.
Australia	.	.	.	£350 m.
Rhodesia	.	.	.	£250 m.
India	.	.	.	£100 m.

In Mr Shonfield's view, this substantial outflow of ill-directed invest-ment is one of the prime causes of Britain's recurrent balance of pay-ment difficulties. "The Third British Empire", as the sterling area has been called is, it is suggested, becoming on balance a dead loss to Britain. This remarkable view may or may not be correct. But at least it shows that there is not a great deal in the accusation that Britain, for example, continues directly to exploit her ex-colonies by means of the sterling area arrangement. For it is at least arguable that she is now the actual loser by it. On the contrary it may well be argued that it would be cynical for Britain to drop the sterling area, from which she un-doubtedly benefited in the past, now that it may become a liability to her. Perhaps this issue will solve itself, however. As the remaining large dollar-earning colonies (Malaya, Ghana, Nigeria) become independent they will insist upon a dominant voice in deciding the future of the arrangement. Perhaps they will wish to continue it upon a more equitable basis. Perhaps they will wish to end it. (We shall discuss the future of the sterling area in a Commonwealth of which almost all the members have become politically independent in Chapter XVIII below.) In either case the effect upon the British economy is a matter of argument. We may be slightly enriched or slightly impoverished. To such manageable proportions has this question been reduced.

Especially high profits on overseas investments or special arrange-ments like the sterling area are not the only source (even apart from the terms of trade) of the increased national income which Britain may derive from the existence of her overseas possessions. There are all sorts of salaries, expenses, "connections" and jobs, which derive directly or indirectly from colonial possessions. These are very impor-tant to individuals, but quantitatively they cannot be considered as a really significant part of the national income. We come back, therefore, to the terms of trade, including the question of the running up of balances between the empire in question and its colonies, and especially high profits on overseas investments, as the substantial factors in the whole question of empire. For these are the only factors consider-able enough to be significant for the economies of the empires in question.

We encounter at this point, however, a most important considera-tion which has been implicit in many preceding chapters, but must now be made explicit. The fact that imperialist gains now play a minor and doubtful part in the national income of the highly developed countries does not mean, as might be supposed, that the losses suffered as a result of imperialism by the undeveloped, colonial or exploited countries have been minor in any sense. And this for two reasons. First, as we noted in the case of the initial pillage of India by Britain, many kinds of imperialism are immensely wasteful. Comparatively small overall gains by the exploiting country are often only secured by means of the dislocation and semi-devastation of the exploited country. (For an extreme example one can think of the Arab empire in East Africa where, it is said, the slave raiders reckoned that they were doing well if one in ten of their captives survived the march to the coast, and if, again, one in ten of these survivors survived in the holds of the dhows on the voyage back to Arabia. Or again, one may think of those same Arab imperialists when their turn came to be conquered. The destruction of the irrigation system of the Bagdad Caliphate destroyed a great civilisation. But it brought little wealth to the Central Asian Mongols who perpetrated it.)

In the case of recent and present-day imperialism, there is a more important reason, however. It is simply that the highly developed countries have such immensely higher per capita national incomes than the pre-industrial countries that the unrequited transfer of say £100 m. a year may mean a minor addition to the wealth of the former but the imposition of a crushing burden upon the poverty of the latter. This is clearly an immensely significant consideration politically. It makes the continuation of specifically imperialist exploitation not only a crime but a downright mistake. The thing is no longer good sense even from the imperialist's or ex-imperialist's own point of view. They would almost certainly make much more by the devotion of the proportion of the national energy, talent and resources which they now devote to hanging on to positions of imperialist exploitation, to making further progress in technique. And this is to say nothing of the fatal odium which they incur, since their exploitive activities may still injure the exploited most gravely.

This consideration should help to clear up a rather barren controversy between communist, or near communist, economists and their critics. Communist economists when presented with facts and figures showing that Marx's prediction of ever-increasing misery for the wage-earners of the advanced capitalisms has been falsified, are accustomed to reply with a flood of facts and figures designed to show that the peoples of the undeveloped world continue to live at or near subsistence, and that their standard of life may be falling rather than rising.[1] Their figures are only too true. But then they are not in question. What the communist economists are implying, however, is the Leninist contention that any improvement in the standard of life of the wage-earners of the advanced capitalisms has been made at the expense of intensified imperialist exploitation of the undeveloped peoples. We have seen that this is not so. The fact is that stagnation and even decline in the undeveloped world have probably harmed the wage-earners of the developed world rather than benefited them. (For example, the paradox of the 1933 terms of trade: see p. 152, above.) The only people it may have benefited are a handful of the rich in the highly developed capitalisms.

On the other hand imperialism has undoubtedly distorted the development of the undeveloped world. Paradoxically and sadly it has done so not only by its exploitive, but also by its beneficent, activities. By establishing law and order, and more recently by introducing hygiene and preventative drugs, without promoting the all-round economic development which should go with them, it has produced the terrible population pressure which is in many cases (e.g., India and Egypt) one of the principal problems of the undeveloped world. But here again, we begin to pass out of the sphere of imperialism and into the vast field of world development and how it is now to take place. For the injury (not unmixed of course, as Marx showed, with long term advantage) which imperialist exploitation has done, and to some extent is still doing, to the undeveloped peoples is closely bound up with the whole burning issue of how these peoples are to develop in the post-imperialist period which the world may be entering. This vast subject will have to be taken up at a later point in this study. In this volume we are concerned with the process, going on all round us, of the actual liquidation of the colonial imperialist system as it has existed in recent centuries, and in particular with the major special case of the dissolution of the British Empire.

It seems probable, therefore, that any economic loss which the British people may suffer as they relinquish their residual ability to exploit their ex-colonies, will be far less than is usually supposed. The main remaining potential loss is oil profits. This would be some £323 m. gross, if it is assumed that non-imperialist policies would result in us losing the whole of our oil profits. But this is a wholly

---

[1] See, for example, Mr Charles Bettleheim's reaction to the figures given in the previous volume of this study (Contemporary Capitalism, Chapter VIII) in Cahiers Internationals.

unrealistic assumption. The most that would be likely to happen is that those profits of £323 m. gross or £93 m. net, as Shonfield estimates them, would gradually diminish. Thus we might think of the total potential loss as of the order of a per cent or so at the very most of the gross national income (£18,000 m. in 1957). This, let it be reiterated, would be the *gross* loss. To set against it are the expenses entailed in attempting to maintain British power over peoples which have reached, or are reaching, the stage at which they are determined to make the attempt to govern themselves; these are very considerable. It is difficult to distinguish this element in our defence budget of £1,400 m. But Mr Shonfield (op. cit.) makes an attempt to do so. He calculates that we are spending about £160 m. a year on defence overseas. To this sum he adds £40 m. for subsidies of one kind or another paid to colonies, dependencies and satellites. This gives a direct drain of some £200 m. a year, and this is a drain not only upon our resources in general but upon our earnings of foreign currency. Mr Shonfield seems to imply that we could save the whole of this £200 m. a year. This is no doubt an exaggeration. But it is clear from these figures that, quite contrary to what is almost universally supposed, it is by no means certain that there will be any net loss at all to the British people in forgoing their remaining opportunities for imperialist exploitation. In other words, it is probable that the remaining elements of British imperialism no longer pay even on the narrowest book-keeping view of the matter.

All this may cause us to speculate as to whether Hobson's foreboding of a totally imperialist world, was not always a mere nightmare. Even, if for example the European powers, or later Japan, had conquered China, as they so nearly did, would they not have given up the enterprise when they found that it did not pay? But the fact that imperialism can be shown to be no longer bringing any gains to the mass of the populations of the possessing countries (if it ever did) is not really a refutation of the possibility that a "total imperialism" might have been established by the conquest of China. What we have shown is that for purposes of *trade* between countries imperialism is often unnecessary or even harmful. But we have also shown that such trade, by becoming first, trade in capital goods, and then investment, tends to pass over into the direct exploitation of the wage-earners and peasants of a colony. And no one can deny that such direct exploitation of, for example, the labour of 600 million Chinese *could* have provided unearned incomes for considerable sections of the populations of the West. What Hobson, and Lenin too I believe, had not fully realised was the profound change in the structure, and therefore the nature, of capitalism which such total imperialism would have involved. After all the first effects of harnessing the labour of 600 million Chinese to the task, as Hobson suggests, of supplying all the products of the basic industries of the West, would have been to ruin those industries. Theoretically no doubt the wage-earners, salary-earners and capitalists in those industries could have been pensioned off out of the gigantic profits made out of exploitation in China. In the end large sections of the Western population could have lived in idleness. Something like the later Roman social pattern of limitless unearned wealth for patricians and bread and circuses for the plebs could have been reproduced. But to do this would have meant so radical a reconstruction of capitalism that there would have been little of the system left. Experience suggests, therefore, that imperialism, if it had not destroyed itself in its internecine struggles, would have had to abolish capitalist relations of production as such, and substitute for them some sort of industrial feudalism, with a much more fixed and rigid social system. (The Nazis and the Japanese militarists might have done it.)

I do not, therefore, think that there is a contradiction in saying that imperialism has ceased to bring appreciable benefits to the advanced countries (without ceasing to be ruinous for the undeveloped) and agreeing that, in theory at least, Hobson's nightmare was real. Only that nightmare was hardly capable of realisation without a much more thoroughgoing change in the existing social and economic system than he, or Lenin, or anyone else, realised.

The conclusion of this and the two preceding chapters is so contrary to what is usually supposed that it deserves some further emphasis. For many people—from conservatives to communists—sincerely believe that "if we lose the empire we shall be ruined". They ignore the fact that we have "lost" nearly nine-tenths of the empire already, with, as we have seen, no observable effect on the rate at which we exchange our products with those of the rest of the world. They suffer under the illusion that it is possible, by means of governmental authority, based in the last resort on armed force, to turn our terms of trade as a whole substantially in our favour. Certainly this was done in particular instances in the past, and it is still being done, to some extent, in the case of that, after all, relatively minor part of our trade which we do with the remaining colonies. But the main, decisive part of our overseas trade is already conducted, as we have seen, with nations, both members and non-members of the Commonwealth, which are completely self-governing and against which we could not possibly use force, even if we would. Whether or not we exploit their primary producers, as we certainly did in the 'thirties (but almost as much to our own detriment as to theirs) has not, as we have seen, much to do with imperialism (in the strict sense of the rule of one people by another) but is governed by the much broader question of what the terms of trade between primary producers and manufacturers in general are likely to be. When we are no longer able to use force to exploit anyone, we may indeed suffer some economic loss but it will be of the order of 1% or so of the national income and even that is without taking into account the possibly greater expense of attempting to continue our rule in areas which are determined that they will no longer remain our colonies.

The specifically Marxist contention that any improvement which, it is sometimes reluctantly admitted, may have taken place in the standard of life of the wage-earners in the advanced capitalisms, is simply due to intensified imperialist exploitation has at length been adequately answered. That contention was noted and briefly denied, in the first volume of this study. But comprehensive comment upon it had to be postponed to the part of the study dealing specifically with imperialism. We are now in a position to see that if we use the term imperialism in its habitual, and surely proper, sense of the rule (open or concealed) of one country over another, there is to-day little substance in the communist assertion. If on the other hand we extend the term, as contemporary communist writers habitually if tacitly do to mean any bargaining advantage which the developed countries can exert against the undeveloped, then indeed it is entirely true that this is one of the factors which tend to keep the poor countries poor and the rich countries rich. But if we extend the term imperialism as widely as this it ceases to have any very clear meaning.

What is then really at issue is the far broader question of the tendency of highly developed countries continually to widen the gap in wealth between themselves and the undeveloped world. And we shall note that this tendency, whether it is to be called imperialism or not, is not confined to the capitalist part of the world. It seems therefore better to use the word imperialism to mean some degree at least of political, and in the last resort physical, power of one country over another. But if we do adopt this narrower usage we must not for one moment seem to deny that the wider issue—call it what you will— of the economic relationship, between the developed and the un-developed world, is of crucial importance. The best way, perhaps, to express that issue is to write that we shall find that the liquidation of the specifically imperial, or colonial, relationship which is going on so fast to-day, will prove to be not enough. In order to make a viable world it will not be enough for imperial or ex-imperial states such as Britain to cease from ruling and exploiting their colonies: it will prove indispensable for them actively to help those ex-colonies—and the un-developed world as a whole for that matter—to develop. That will be the subject of a later stage in this study. Here we are concerned to overcome the fear of national ruin which obstructs the indispensable preliminary process of freeing the colonies, as this becomes feasible, from external rule.

We have seen that the fear that without her empire Britain will not be able to obtain her food and raw materials, or will have to obtain them at ruinously high prices, will not stand up to an examination of the figures. There are however more than figures to prove the point. There is striking evidence to be derived from the fortunes of two neighbours of Britain's.

We have already noted the tragic circumstances of contemporary France. There can be few observers still left to deny that the largest single cause of her misfortunes is the passion with which she clings to the remainder of her empire. True, France emerged from the second World War far more severely injured, both materially and morally than Britain; for she had had the searing experience of occupation. None the less, her innate powers of recovery are second to none, and, sure enough, the industry and good sense of her people have been steadily rebuilding her in these last fourteen years. To-day, in 1959, she would be far along the road to complete recovery, were it not for the fact that since 1945 she has not known a single year of peace. She has been engaged in colonial warfare, often on the largest scale, from the very moment of her liberation until the present, and, if her imperial policies continue, there seems little prospect of relief. We have already mentioned the havoc that the struggle in Indo-China wrought in the military, financial and moral strength of France. But no sooner was she quit of that, than the struggle in North Africa became intense. Though,

I repeat, it is far less sanguinary, it is perhaps equally costly. France is in 1959 said to be maintaining the almost incredible number of five hundred thousand troops, permanently under arms, in North Africa. No wonder that she has been reduced to almost total military impotence in Europe, unable any longer even to make her promised contribution to the N.A.T.O. forces guarding Europe's eastern frontiers. And at home she was up till 1958 unable to check the increasingly grave inflationary disorder of her finances. (One has only to think of what Britain's plight would be if we tried to maintain five hundred thousand men abroad, continuously under arms, in order to seek for no further explanations of France's difficulties.)

And what is it all for? The loss of Indo-China when it came turned out to have no observable evil effects upon the French economy. Algeria is a far less rich possession. The fact is that a settlement with the Algerians upon the basis of their independence, far from reducing France to "a Portugal", as is suggested, would immediately restore her to her natural position as a leading European nation. For then she would have troops and money and energy to spare. No concern for the future of the French settlers in Algeria, natural as such concern is, should really weigh with a patriotic Frenchman on this issue. For the brutal fact is that her imperial policy is ruining France. Still less should any hopes of immense profits from Saharan oil be allowed seriously to weigh in the balance. No doubt certain French companies may make high profits out of the oil: but France will not if she has to sink the wells, run the oil trains and guard the pipe-lines in the midst of a chronic civil war. Actually the only hope of the really profitable operation of the Saharan wells is an Algerian settlement. And such a settlement must involve at the very least half of the profits going to the Algerians, just as it has in Arabia. In any case, the profits which can possibly be got from such oil will form a far smaller fraction of the French national income than is usually imagined. France is ruining herself for a reminiscence of glory and a mirage of oil profits.

If the French warning were not conclusive, the Western German example would be. Lack of imperialism on the part of Western German capitalism is, perhaps, involuntary. Nevertheless the fact remains that West Germany, besides all the other consequences which she suffered as a result of the most catastrophic defeat of recent history, was stripped of every acre of her imperial possessions. And what is the result? She is universally held up as an example of the most prosperous, the strongest, the most stable economy of Europe. As a matter of fact some of the praise is exaggerated. Nevertheless present-day Western

Germany incontestably demonstrates that it is possible to maintain a stable, prosperous and progressive economy without imperial possessions. Of course there are many other facts to account for the so-called "West German miracle". There is the influx of skilled refugees from East Germany combined with German power of organisation and German industry; there is the apparently undestroyable asset of mature industrial know-how; there is American help. Nevertheless the fact that Germany has not had to devote any of her resources to trying to maintain threatened imperial possessions has been one of her most useful assets. The position of influence and general importance which West Germany has already achieved in the world, only fourteen years after her utter prostration, proves conclusively that imperial possessions are not, to say the least of it, indispensable for material strength. It suggests strongly that, on the contrary, they are likely to prove "running sores" which destroy both the economic and the moral vigour of a nation's life. Exactly contrary to popular prejudice, a nation is likely to-day to be strong or weak in inverse ratio to her imperial possessions.

CHAPTER XIII

NON-COLONIAL EMPIRES

Much of the above evidence of the irrelevance of imperial possessions to a nation's standard of life rests upon the assumption that the British and other empires either have been, or are being, liquidated. But it may be suggested that this assumption is false: that nothing of the sort has taken place: that behind the political changes involved on paper, in this or that act of independence, the exploitation of the native peoples by the British and other imperialists goes on, only now in a different way. This, we may be told, is the simple and sufficient explanation of why the terms of trade have not turned against Britain as her empire has (apparently) dissolved, and in general of why our standard of life has not suffered.

This is essentially the communist account of the matter. It is for example the main argument used by Mr R. P. Dutt, a principal exponent of Marxist-Leninist views in the English language, in his full-dress study of contemporary British imperialism entitled *The Crisis of Britain and the British Empire* (Lawrence and Wishart, 1953). Again Professor Paul Baran, that unique phenomenon, a Marxist working at an American university, has expressed similar views about contemporary imperialism generally in his book, *The Political Economy of Growth* (*Monthly Review* Press, 1957). It is an advantage to possess these authoritative statements of the orthodox Marxist view of the matter, and it will be convenient to discuss the issue in connection with them.

Mr Dutt duly puts forward the Leninist thesis that the whole British economic and social system rests upon imperialist exploitation and that in particular any increase in the standard of life of any section of the British people, which, he reluctantly implies, may have taken place, is the result of the further degradation of many millions of primary producers in a continuing British empire. Mr Dutt sweeps aside the blank contradiction for this view which arises from the simultaneous achievement of independence by nine-tenths of the inhabitants of the former British empire and the existence of terms of trade considerably better for Britain than in her empire's heyday. He simply denies that any dissolution of the British Empire has occurred. India, Pakistan, Ceylon and Burma, he holds, were just as much British colonies when he wrote in 1953 as ever they had been. Britain, he alleges, can and does exploit their populations just as grossly as ever. Nothing has changed: or rather, nothing has changed in the substance of the imperialist relationship; there has merely been a change in the form and method by which exploitation is carried on.

The test adopted in these pages of whether or not a particular country is a colony, *de facto* or *de jure*, of another is the simple one of where effective *sovereignty* lies. Can or cannot some foreign country impose its will without war or the threat of war upon the country in question? Of course we must not be misled by whether or not the official forms of colonisation have been established. It would be formalistic in the extreme to deny that the Egypt of Cromer was a British colony because that absolute ruler of the country was called "British Agent and Consul-General" instead of Governor, as in most other colonies. Nor can it be denied that there are borderline cases. Was or was not Iraq between 1918 and 1958 a British colony? On the whole up till 1945 she was. For if we apply the simple test of war-making, we find that in the second World War, Iraq was used by British forces and the anti-British revolt of Rashid Ali unhesitatingly put down by British troops. On the other hand, after 1945 the British hold on the country was visibly relaxing and a considerable measure of self-determination was achieved even under the Nuri régime, although British troops (the R.A.F.) remained in occupation. Full independence was clearly achieved in the revolution of 1958 and British troops left. And the same transition over roughly the same period took place in Egypt. Again it can be very plausibly argued that some of the "banana republics", as they are contemptuously called, in Central America are effectively American colonies, even though they have never been, for long, occupied by American troops. For as was recently demonstrated in the case of Guatemala, the State Department exercises a veto over the kinds of government which they may elect.

Nevertheless, and although each case must be examined on its merits, it will not usually be difficult to apply the above test of whether a country is *effectively* sovereign over itself or not. To return to the great case of India, for example, can the British Government to-day decide, as up till 1947 it undoubtedly could do, the height of India's tariffs, her rates of income tax, her foreign trade and payments policy, her economic policy in general and, surest test of all, whether or not India shall go to war in any given situation? By this obvious test India is to-day as unequivocally independent as she was unequivocally a colony up till 1947. It was, as a matter of fact, this very issue of the right to decide on peace or war which brought matters to a head. With remarkable folly the British Government of 1939 caused the Government of India to declare war on Germany without any attempt at consultation with the Indian people. This was one of the factors which caused the final determination of almost all politically conscious Indians to be rid of British rule. And the fact is that they are rid of it. No one can possibly pretend that a British Government could to-day declare war on India's behalf.

Mr Dutt, of course, makes much of the fact that India, Pakistan and Ceylon have chosen to remain part of the British Commonwealth. He does not put it like that. For him Britain "imposed the Mountbatten settlement", including partition, upon the unwilling peoples of India and Pakistan, who were striving to make a united revolutionary republic. It does not disturb Mr Dutt that this allegation of an imposed settlement is in flat contradiction to another of his allegations, in which there is much more truth. This second allegation is that there was nothing else which Britain could do after 1945 than to come to terms with the Asian nationalist movements. This is basically correct. The real credit which may be claimed for the British Government of the day is not that it magnanimously "gave" India her freedom, when it need not have done so, but that it appreciated the necessity of recognising Indian independence instead of fighting futilely against it. For, if we had not recognised this necessity, we should inevitably (as Seeley foresaw, see p. 77, above) have ruined both India and Britain. And, after all, this recognition was no small achievement. I am aware of no other important instance of imperial authorities recognising such a necessity when they encountered it. It was Frederick Engels who cited the Hegelian maxim that freedom was the recognition of necessity. If so, the British Government's recognition of the necessity of Indian independence in 1947 was one of the most truly free acts in history. The truth is that in 1947 Britain had neither the capacity nor the intention of continuing to govern the sub-continent herself or of compelling the Indians and Pakistanis either to remain within the Commonwealth or to partition the peninsula.

Professor Baran (op. cit.) takes the same view as Mr Dutt but he expresses it in more general terms. He assumes without question that imperialism, mainly on the part of Britain and America, is still in full swing, and that the fact that in the last fourteen years Britain has relinquished, and America has not acquired, political sovereignty over the greater part of the non-communist pre-industrial world, is largely irrelevant. He assumes, rather than argues, that Britain and above all America, are continuing to exploit the pre-industrial peoples just as atrociously as ever.

His view appears to be that the imperial powers have succeeded in setting up in most of their ex-colonies, and for that matter in other pre-industrial countries also, what he calls "comprador govern-ments".[1] These governments are run, he writes, by the native merch-ants and other business men who have large and close commercial relations with the major firms of the imperialist powers, and they run their pre-industrial countries strictly in the interests of the imperial powers, either arresting development entirely or distorting it to a fatal degree. Usually, he writes, they only permit development in (i) the extraction of raw materials for the imperialists (ii) in light consumer industries and (iii) in agriculture. They prevent development in the basic heavy industries. In return the imperialist powers heartily support such "comprador régimes". It is true that Professor Baran occasionally notices that some of the governments of the non-communist pre-industrial world do not fit into this description, in particular the Indian Government. He calls these "New Deal type governments" and credits them with rather better intentions, but not with much else. In general he too is evidently convinced that no undeveloped or pre-industrial society which has not become communist has really escaped from imperialist exploitation.

What are we to say of this communist thesis, put forward in the more plausible version of Professor Baran? No impartial observer would wish to deny that it is possible to carry on the imperialist control and exploitation of an undeveloped country without retaining it as, or making it into, a direct and formal colony. Many instances of imperial-ism by means of puppet or satellite governments have been given above, and many more will be given below, from both the non-communist and the communist worlds. Of course it is possible to rule and exploit people in this way. Every experienced imperialist will tell Professor Baran, however, that such indirect rule and exploitation is by no means the same thing as possession of the country in question as a direct colony. Once an even nominally sovereign local government is established, forces are invariably set in motion which tend in the direction of genuine independence. Imperialist control can go on, often for some time, but it becomes more and more precarious. To say that

[1] A comprador was one of the Chinese merchants engaged in trade with the foreigners.

the advent of even partial political independence makes no difference is a grotesque oversimplification.

Again Professor Baran represents the Western powers as determined to prevent the development of the pre-industrial nations at all costs. He writes:

"Western big business heavily engaged in raw materials exploitation leaves no stone unturned to obstruct the evolution of social and political conditions in under-developed countries that might be conducive to their economic development. It uses its tremendous power to prop up the backward areas' comprador administrations, to disrupt and corrupt the social and political movements that oppose them, and to overthrow whatever progressive governments may rise to power and refuse to do the bidding of their imperialist overlords. Where and when its own impressive resources do not suffice to keep matters under control, or where and when the costs of the operations involved can be shifted to their home countries' national governments—or nowadays to international agencies such as the International Bank for Reconstruction and Development—the diplomatic, financial and, if need be, military facilities of the imperialist power are rapidly and efficiently mobilized to help private enterprise in distress to do the required job" (op. cit., p. 198).

This is carrying overstatement to the point of falsification. It is entirely true that there are examples in which Western power has been used (though usually with greater folly than success) to prop up reactionary governments in the pre-industrial world. Morever, the Western powers could and should be arraigned for failing whole-heartedly to support with adequate funds the development of the pre-industrial world. But, after all, for the first time in history, a good deal of money has been actually given by the rich countries to the poor countries for the express purpose of development. It is perverse to make no distinction between say, the monies provided under the Colombo Plan, or the American Point Four programme and traditional imperialist investment for profit by private enterprise. And it is equally perverse to assume that, say, £50 million lent by Russia to India to build a steel works is an act of the purest philanthropy, while £50 million lent by Britain to India to build another steel works, is an act of imperialist exploitation. Again it is true that there is a tendency for the Western powers, for selfish reasons, to try to bias development in the direction of extractive and consumer goods industries, and towards agriculture, to the prejudice of heavy industry. But after all, there is something to be said for some development, at least, taking one or other of these forms. It is not true that all the profits of the extractive industries go to foreigners. (As we have just seen, the Arab oil states have now got hold of half of them.) Consumer industries are very useful to consumers, and concentration upon agricultural development does not *necessarily* mean being kept as hewers of wood and drawers of water for the imperialists. It *may* do so—as for example in the East Indies under the Dutch. But it may not, if the pre-industrial country's government is both independent and capable. The cardinal example of this is New Zealand, which by reason of, precisely, a heavy concentration upon agricultural development with some development of consumer industries, was actually able for one year at least (1956) to raise the per capita income of her people to the highest in the world, exceeding that of the United States themselves by a narrow margin. (And if she could not retain that world leadership, she yet maintains very great prosperity.)

Thus the whole question is far more complex than communist and Marxist writers are willing to admit. It is quite true that the dissolution of imperial sovereignty over most of the undeveloped world is no proof that its exploitation for the benefit of the highly developed countries has ceased. But it is a prerequisite for it ceasing.

It is particularly unfortunate that communist and Marxist writers give such a travesty of the relationship between the ex-imperial states and the newly enfranchised under-developed world. For behind that travesty there is an overwhelmingly important issue.

In order to comprehend it we must recur to Professor Gunnar Myrdal's analysis of the matter, which we glanced at in Chapter VII, above, in connection with the discussion of the Hobson-Lenin explanation of imperialism. For the truth is that everything turns on the basic economic issue to which we then referred. If we accept the traditional "harmonious" view of the way in which the market forces work under conditions of *laisser faire*, then there is no problem. If "the play of the market", acting by means of the price mechanism (classically studied under the form of demand and supply curves), is the central and decisive factor in the situation, then there is no special problem in the relationship between the developed and the under-developed world. Just as (we saw) within countries there could be no problem of the maldistribution of the national income, which could in turn produce the pressure to foreign investment and its accompanying imperialism, if the economic system worked as it does in the text books, so between rich and poor nations also, on the same comfortable hypothesis, there would be no particular difficulties. The flow of international trade, if left to itself would continually tend to spread prosperity round the world. The far lower labour costs of the poor countries would continually be attracting capital out of the rich countries, and generally tending to equalise the standard of life of the peoples of the world.

Professor Myrdal's essential, and profoundly disturbing, message is that there is no such beneficent equalising tendency. Just as he sees that within nations, as between their classes and their regions, the real tendency of unregulated capitalism is summed up in the biblical aphorism "unto him that hath shall be given", so between nations also the real consequence of unregulated international exchanges—the real effects of breaking down the trade barriers—will be to enrich the rich and to impoverish the poor. "The main idea I want to convey", he writes, "is that the play of the forces of the market normally tends to increase, rather than to decrease, the inequalities. . . ." This is not the place to attempt to prove the correctness of Professor Myrdal's vision. The reader who doubts it must both study his recent works (*The International Economy* and *Economic Theory and Underdeveloped Regions*) and, which is perhaps even more convincing, look around him. At this stage in our argument I am merely pointing out that if Myrdal's vision does correspond with contemporary reality, many of the puzzling paradoxes which we have discovered in the recent history of imperialism and its dissolution fall into place. For it follows from his premise that the true curse of imperialism was a negative one: its bane lay in what it prevented even more than in what it did. Myrdal puts it like this:

"From one point of view, the most important effect of colonialism was related to the negative fact that the colony was deprived of effective nationhood, and had no government of its own which could feel an urge to take constructive measures to promote the balanced growth of a national economy.

"The country and the people were laid bare and defenceless to the play of the market forces as redirected only by the interests of the foreign metropolitan power. This by itself thwarted individual initiatives, at the same time as it prevented the formation of a public policy motivated by the common interests of the people."

The truth is that the empires did not really need artificially to bias the terms of trade in their favour: all they had to do was to prevent any autonomous authority arising which could "interfere" with the market forces in such a way that development could get started in the colonies. It follows that independence is by no means an automatic cure. If the ex-colony's government takes no drastic action to break the invisible bonds of the market there may be no improvement at all in its condition. Myrdal continues:

"When a poor and backward nation becomes politically independent, it will find out, even if it did not know before, that political independence most certainly does not mean that it is automatically on the road to economic development. It will still be up against cumulative social processes holding it down in stagnation or regression: the 'natural' play of the forces in the markets will be working all the time to increase internal and international inequalities as long as its general level of development is low."

There are plenty of historical examples where precisely this has happened. Latin America, as a whole, over more than 100 years, derived very little benefit from her liberation from Spain. The governments of the successor states proved, on the whole, incapable of making use of their freedom. Of course there was some development, but most of the states tended to drift into the economic control of either America, or Britain, or simply of the developed world as a whole. They remained in Myrdal's phrase "bare and defenceless to the play of the market forces". (It is only in the last fifteen years that they have really begun an independent development. But now in some cases they have. Mexico, in particular, is developing as fast or faster than any other country in the world, and Brazil, the potential great power amongst them, is evidently on the move.) Whether this state of things ought to be called "the continuance of imperialism by other means" is largely a terminological question. When there is direct, even if intermittent, interference by military force, such as the United States has periodically undertaken in Central America, an element of imperialism, within the sense used in these pages, is clearly involved. But when it is simply a question of the local government being incapable of taking the measures of interference with "the free flow of international trade" necessary to the development of its country, even though no one is preventing it from doing so, it seems better to say simply that even national independence is no good unless it is used.

Myrdal has many eloquent passages upon the necessity of independent under-developed nations adopting conscious, purposive measures which taken together form a national plan of development. He writes:

"Under-developed countries, utilising their newly won independent status, can by purposive policy interferences manage to alter considerably the direction of the market processes under the impact of which they have hitherto remained backward. The cumulative nature of these processes, which has pressed them down, holds out, on the other hand, the promise of high returns from their policy efforts, if they manage to plan them intelligently and carry them out effectively. This, however, is a very big 'if'.

"From that point of view, the political independence they have won for themselves, or are now winning, is their most precious asset. It gives them freedom to organise their own life according to their own interests. In the absence of a world state, their policies have to be nationalistic in the sense of being directed with a single-minded intensity to raising their own economic standards and reaching greater equality of opportunity with the rest of the world. It is not up to them, who are the poor, to take into account international considerations, except those that are also in their own interest."

It will thus become apparent that the grain of truth behind the communist dogma that no under-developed country can become genuinely independent unless it goes communist is simply this. No under-developed country can become genuinely independent, in the sense of being able to develop its own resources, unless it can establish a government able and willing to interfere drastically in, first, its own internal economic life and second, and in particular, with "the free flow of international trade". For leaving the matter to the forces of market will produce stagnation and disaster. But such conscious planning need involve neither communist methods nor communist aims.

We shall pursue this theme: but first we must complete the discussion of the consequences of the dissolution of the empires upon the imperial nations themselves. So far we have considered only the economic consequences. We have found that they are not particularly considerable. Now, however, we must take up the social, political and psychological consequences. For they are much the more important.

CHAPTER XIV

THE CLOSE SHAVE

THE MORALE, THE SPIRIT, the mental health even, of all of us in Britain are deeply involved in the question of the dissolution of our empire. The whole tone of our national life will partly depend on whether we can comprehend the process in the perspective of history. For in the British upper and middle classes in particular, but extending widely amongst the wage-earners also, there exists what the psychologists would call an "identification" with the empire. Quite apart from whether or not they suppose that their economic interests will be affected, many people in Britain feel a sense of personal loss—almost of amputation—when some colony or semi-colony, Burma or the Soudan for example, becomes independent. The hauling down of the Union Jack in yet another part of the world has a depressing effect. This feeling of personal loss from the fact that the writ of the Parliament of Westminster no longer runs in some territory is all the more difficult to deal with because it is essentially irrational.

Such a feeling is the entirely natural result of several centuries of historical development. The British Empire was much the greatest and most successful of the colonial domains of mature capitalism. Moreover, the specifically capitalist British empire, which, as we have seen, was for the most part created as recently as the fourth quarter of the nineteenth century, was itself deeply rooted in one of the greatest of the mercantile empires. And that earlier British empire, although suffering major vicissitudes, such as the loss of America and the gradual grant of independence to "the old dominions", had yet persisted, in large measure, right up to the middle of the twentieth century.

So tremendous an imperial tradition could not but have profound effects upon the national psychology. To a considerable degree (though never quite wholeheartedly) the British people became an imperial people, with the characteristic faults and virtues of such peoples. The moral and psychological shock of the rapid dissolution, whether voluntarily or involuntarily, of such an empire must inevitably be great. Moreover the psychological effect upon the nation is intensified by the Cassandra-like pronouncements of those who are opposing the process of voluntary dissolution. As each imperial possession is relinquished, we are told by influential voices that "we are losing the will to rule"; that nations which do that are "done for": that unless we "put up a fight", either to retain, or to regain, this or that imperial possession we are "comitting national suicide". Natural and inevitable as are such feelings and their expression, there cannot be the slightest doubt but that it would be precisely the retention by Britain of such imperialist attitudes of mind as these which would lead us to national suicide. Nothing could be more obvious than that irretrievable disaster must result from an attempt on the part of Britain to cling to the vestiges of her empire, or, worse still, to engage, by means of a sort of imperial quixotry, in attempts to regain this or that part of it. And yet a painful and protracted process will be necessary in order to readjust the national psychology to the broad future which is in fact open to the British people.

If anyone is inclined to doubt the existence of this measure of residual imperialist feeling in the British people, they should recall the Suez episode and the simple, almost tribal, emotions, with which about half the population of all classes (according to successive Gallup Polls) reacted on that occasion. It will be our next task to analyse this imperial sentiment, which is made up of many different elements, good and bad. It is made up on the one hand of a genuine concern for the welfare of peoples once entrusted to our charge: but it is also made up of possessiveness. Thus even when the imperial sentiment expresses a genuine love of some subject people, it is nearly always a possessive kind of love. And we all know the tragedies to which possessive love leads in family life. The same tragedies await the expression of this kind of love by the old matriarch of the Commonwealth.

Nations, like men, become wedded to their own pasts. And the more brilliant that past has been, the more acute is the danger that the nation in question will be unable to show the power of adaptation to a changing environment which is a condition of survival. It is just because we British were certainly the most successful and, we at any rate are convinced, the most enlightened, of the latter-day imperialists, that it is such a difficult task for us to find the quite different, but equally significant, role which now awaits us in the world.

This tendency of nations to become "fixated", to use another of the expressive terms of modern psychology, upon some glorious feature of their own pasts is not confined to an irrational attachment to vanishing empires. Nations which have for a time led the world in any field of endeavour are apt to fail in adaptability when the world-scene

changes and new roles become indispensable for them. For they are
sure that they alone possess unchanging formulae of triumph: that they
have nothing to learn and nothing to change. In order to appreciate
the full magnitude of the task of psychological adaptation which now
faces the British people, it may be worth while to glance at some of the
outstanding historical examples of this fixation upon some feature of a
glorious national past. In doing so we shall be following a theme of
Professor Toynbee's, to which he largely devotes the fourth volume of
his *Study of History*. Professor Toynbee, as usual, elaborates this, in
itself, simple idea with a glittering net of generalisations which need
not concern us. But his main conception, which is that nations tend to
get stuck at a certain point in their development, and that particularly
successful nations are particularly prone to this disaster, since they are
apt to become profoundly self-satisfied, is, surely, both valid and
valuable.

Perhaps the most famous of all the examples of this fatal process is
afforded by the Hellenic devotion to the political institutions of the
City State, or polis. The Greek City State was one of the main political
inventions of human history. For it provided the first institution in
which a relatively free political life could be lived by a proportion, at
least, of the inhabitants of developed urban communities. Till then
the achievement of civilisation had been dependent upon the creation
of despotic empires. Men had had to give up their primitive tribal
freedom in order to become civilised. (See p. 321 below.) The evolution of the City State—of, that is to say, the more or less democratic
government of society by its free males—was the supreme political
achievement of the Greeks. It was the pre-condition of all the rest of
their unsurpassed creativeness. No wonder that the Greeks regarded it
as the indispensable condition of Greek civilisation itself: no wonder
they preserved it literally at all costs.

Yet at a certain stage of development the City State became a
limiting and constricting institution, instead of a liberating one. As
soon as the creation of communities bigger than the city state became
a condition of survival, its retention became impossible. For in its
democratic form it could only be worked in a community small
enough for all the free male citizens to gather in one place and transact
business. This strict limit was set simply because, so far as I can see, the
ancient world never developed the political device—in itself it is no
more—of representation. The consequence was that the Greek world
could only grow by the proliferation of more and more city states, each
independent of all the others. It is true that federations and alliances

(which tended to become miniature empires) were often attempted, but they could never be successfully maintained. Thus internecine war between the city states could never be abolished, and the back of Greek freedom and civilisation was broken in the greatest of these, the Peloponnesian war between Athens and Sparta. The Greeks were faced by the agonising dilemma of abandoning the only form of democracy and freedom which had been evolved, or of abandoning all hope to unifying their civilisation and thus escaping conquest. Yet to abandon the city state was to cease, the Greeks felt in their bones, to be Greeks at all. For Greeks were, precisely, beings at once free and civilised. Their civil institutions alone enabled them to be themselves. Because they were incapable, for good as well as ill, of breaking the mould of the city state they were conquered, and ultimately enslaved and destroyed, by the unfree, tyrannously ruled, semi-Greek or non-Greek superpowers of Macedon and Rome.

Professor Toynbee, writing in the nineteen-thirties (op. cit., Vol. IV, pp. 414-18), speculated as to whether Britain, its originator, was not going to prove fatally fixed upon another major invention in the political field, namely parliamentary, representative, democracy. He wondered whether we were not going to cling to this, our own peculiar political institution, until it had long passed through its period of creative usefulness. In that event he feared that Britain would find herself surpassed by the political creativeness of other peoples, who would invent mechanisms for the exercise of free self-rule in large, highly developed societies, other than parliamentary democracy.

It was a plausible view. For no doubt it would be easy to become irrationally wedded to a political mechanism such as parliamentary democracy, by means of which a degree, at least, of freedom can be combined with the material advantages and strength of large, highly organised communities. It might be fatally easy to fail to distinguish between the all-important *purpose* of the institution, in this case the largest possible degree of freedom and self-rule, and the indifferent means by which that purpose is sought to be achieved. Yet, writing two decades later, in the nineteen-fifties, a British parliamentarian may be pardoned for supposing that the danger to which the British people are for the time being exposed is quite different. Parliamentary democracy (in its various forms) is proving to be a remarkably flexible institution. It may prove capable of much development of its basic mechanism. But even in its present rather crude form it may yet show itself capable of coping with the immense task of establishing effective democratic control over highly developed economies.

Moreover, the only really new form of democracy which has been even suggested in the twentieth century,[1] namely the original Soviet democracy, as conceived by Lenin, consisting in representation by occupational instead of geographical categories, appears to have been still-born. For it has been abandoned in the communist world. It has been abandoned not only in the sense that the practice of any sort of democracy has been abandoned in favour of rule by a single party. It has been abandoned also in the sense that the democratic constitutions which have been kept in formal existence in each of the communist states (although totally disregarded in practice) have now reverted, in every case I think, to ordinary geographical representation.

Thus when in 1956 the immensely hopeful possibility appeared that in some of the satellite states of Eastern Europe these apparently dead democratic constitutions might be brought to life and begin to function, it did not seem likely that even then Soviet democracy, in its original occupational form, would be tried out. If any form of democracy spreads into the communist world, it looks as if it would be some variant of the old, originally British, model of the Parliamentary representation of geographical constituencies or, of course, of the American Presidential model. It does not seem, therefore, that Britain is in any danger of becoming fixated upon a dying institution, even if she continues to regard Parliamentary democracy as the very heart of her national life. On the contrary, it seems probable that her peculiar institution has still an immensely important role to play in the world. Britain can do no greater service than to develop and perfect this institution for the essential social purpose of to-day, which is the democratic control of economic life.

The danger of a subsidiary but potentially very damaging fixation on our own form of democracy undoubtedly exists for Britain however. This is the danger that we should suppose that our whole democratic machinery might be, or can be, immediately applied in all the new successor, independent, nations of the Commonwealth, or the undeveloped world generally. In some cases, notably India, it has so far proved possible to do almost literally this. But in 1959 it is becoming clear that India is an exceptional case; that Indian democracy, with real

---

[1] Presidential democracy, on the American, or now French, models, though it has important advantages and disadvantages as compared to parliamentary democracy, has always seemed to me to be merely a variant of the fundamental institution of representative democracy. So long as there are genuine electors, genuinely capable of throwing out a government of one particular political tendency and replacing it with another of a different tendency, the shape given to the system is a secondary, though important, issue. (See *Contemporary Capitalism*, Chapter IX, for a discussion of all this.)

contested elections, a genuinely exercised universal franchise, competing political parties and a remarkably high degree of liberty of
opinion, association etc. is a marvellous, if precarious, achievement
for an under-developed country. If we suppose that this achievement
can be reproduced all over the world, and become disillusioned and
hostile to those new nations which fail to reproduce it, we shall make
fools of ourselves. It is becoming clear that many of the under-developed nations can only develop, or even exist, if they institute much
simpler and cruder forms of government. The first essential for them
is a strong central authority: if that authority has to be arbitrary and
unrepresentative it will exhibit all the normal and shocking defects of
arbitrary and unrepresentative governments. That will be just too bad:
but it will do nothing to show that there is an alternative. For experience indicates that in many cases the attempt to reproduce our full
democratic system leads merely towards a dissolution of society in a
welter of meaningless political cliques, or alternatively to a particularly
corrupt form of concealed authoritarian rule in the interests, for instance, of a landlord class. In these cases rule by a group of Army
colonels, or by some individual who has emerged out of the struggle
for independence, may be not only inevitable but preferable.

This does not mean, however, that it ceases to matter whether such
under-developed, and as it were sub-democratic, societies retain the
more elementary democratic freedoms. This will matter very much to
them in the long run. After all democracy is by no means an "all or
nothing" system. On the contrary whether or not a society is democratic is essentially a matter of degree. Britain evolved most important
democratic rights and liberties, such as Habeas Corpus, a good deal of
freedom of expression, etc., centuries before she could be called a
democracy in the present-day, representative, sense of the word. If the
new nations can retain, or develop, some of these liberties they will
retain the capacity to evolve towards genuine self-government.
Therefore a comprehension of what is happening when some of them
abandon forms of democracy which experience shows to have been
instituted quite prematurely, as some of them are doing in 1959, should
not even qualify our dedication to the democratic ideal itself and for
ourselves. We cannot much influence the course of development in the
new nations by any direct means: if we attempt to do so we shall
probably produce exactly the opposite effect to that which we intend.
If we lecture and abuse them for their abandonment of democracy
to-day we shall do nothing but harm. But we can influence them,
probably decisively, in the long run by the sheer force of the example

of an effectively functioning democracy in existence in Britain. As their level of economic, educational and cultural development rises first this and then that element of democracy will become applicable to these societies. If we have stayed true to democracy we may rely upon their peoples to insist, in due time, upon its application or re-application to themselves. For if and when it can be made effective the sheer practical advantages of democracy are decisive.

Political institutions are by no means the only things upon which nations can become fixated. A particular stage of industrial technique may also become their idol. This fixation is also one from which Britain in the twentieth century is obviously in danger of suffering. As the world-originator of modern industrialism she could hardly escape from a tendency to find in the early forms of industrialism a permanent answer to the economic problem. And in fact it is proving a hard, although on the whole a successful, struggle for Britain to rid herself of a complacent faith in what might be called the steam-engine era of industrialism. In the nineteenth century the steam-engine almost became the household god of Britain. One may still go into Birmingham or Lancashire works and find in some inner shed or bay of the factory a beautiful old beam engine, carefully preserved in full working order, polished, tended, enshrined: clearly one of the *lares et penates* of the establishment. Such industrial *pietas* is to be commended so long as it is accompanied by resolute determination to see that actual production is carried on by the very latest methods which are appropriate. And on the whole since 1945, and in distinct contrast to her dismal record between the wars, Britain has striven hard and successfully to transcend her potentially fatal priority in industrialisation.

The danger for Britain is, then, a different one from that foreseen by Professor Toynbee. Nations and states often become fixated upon other, and less worthy, things than the political institutions or industrial techniques which they have created. In fact by far the commonest and crudest object of such a fixation has been conquest and empire. From Assyria, with her speciality for total ruthlessness, to Hitler with his, what most men have meant by national greatness has had little or nothing to do with a particular political institution. What has been idolised has been simply the capacity to conquer and to enslave, or otherwise exploit, other peoples. For by far the greater number of states, over by far the greater part of their histories, this has been the single test of national greatness. No state which had not subdued, and was not exploiting, other peoples, has been considered great. Prowess in war has been all that has really counted. And necessarily so, for the social environment of nations and states has been of such a kind that there has been little alternative between conquering and being conquered, between enslaving and being enslaved. Goethe's famous phrase has been even more true of nations and states than of men: "You must rise or you must fall. You must rule and win, or serve and lose, you must suffer or triumph, you must be anvil or hammer." In such a world, empire and the means of empire, namely military power, almost inevitably became not only indispensable, but the sole criterion of greatness.[1] It dominated the imaginations of both men and nations. Accordingly both past imperial achievement, and the military means which have proved effective in making and maintaining that achievement, have become idols which men and nations have blindly and obstinately worshipped.

Here we encounter the possibility, indeed the probability, of a fixation within a fixation. Not only do great old nations tend to idolise their military greatness as a whole, since it has made them empires instead of colonies, conquerors instead of conquered. They tend also to pick out the particular feature of their military technique which has always in the past led them to triumph. But in so doing they open themselves to the most terrible danger. For military techniques also become obsolete, and therefore fatal for their exponents, with the passage of time. Accordingly the nations which have become wedded to obsolete techniques for making war have tended to perish with them. The Macedonian phalanx, the Roman foot soldier in the formation of the legion, the mediaeval armoured cavalry man, the Spanish pikeman, the German soldier of the panzer division of yesterday, and, for our own nation, the British sailor in his oaken or armoured ship of the line, each became, in its day and hour, an object of national worship. For each was thought to be, for a time correctly, the invincible instrument of empire. Yet time after time such a national commitment to a particular military technique, after the historical scene had changed, or the technique itself had been superseded, has led as infallibly to

[1] This is why the controversy about whether the motives of empire building are strategic or economic seems to me so barren. Of course the strategic reasons—the search for power and military security—have at one level been all important. But why have nations wanted power over and security from each other? In order I am convinced that they should exploit rather than be exploited. This seems to me to have been true since the dawn of civilisation, though not before (see Chapter XXII, below).

catastrophe as it had hitherto led to triumph. In our own case an un-thinking "navalism" is surely one of the dangers which besets Britain to-day. After three hundred years of national triumph, founded essentially upon naval supremacy, it is a British conditioned reflex to feel that in the last resort what matters is naval predominance. It is no longer so.[1]

But the main danger which faced Britain in the mid-twentieth century was neither that of fixation on her creative political achievement of Parliamentary democracy, nor on a "steam engine industrialism", nor on her "navalism". Her main danger was a fixation upon her imperial past. British imperialism had been so triumphant, so relatively enlightened, and so recent, that when, in 1945, it suddenly became apparent that the imperialist epoch was over (at least for Britain), there seemed little possibility of Britain avoiding an agonising period of national exhaustion and humiliation, sustained in the cause of unsuccessful attempts to retain her world-wide domains.

There are, of course, only too many historical examples of an empire the metropolis of which has been unnecessarily ruined by such unsuccessful attempts to preserve its imperial domain. In antiquity Athens herself perished, partly, in attempting to retain her empire of ex-allies, whom she had enslaved into semi-colonies or satellites, and partly in a major attempt to extend her empire by the Syracusan expedition. Moreover, it does not seem to have been her material losses, which might have been reparable, but the fact that she could never again feel satisfaction with herself, which undid her. The fate of Spain contains the most obvious warning in the modern age. Here, too, there seems no material or objective reasons why Spain should not have become, after she lost her empire at the beginning of the nineteenth century, a successful member-state of the European community. What undid her was that the Spaniards were unable to see any tolerable way of life now that their country's grandeur was gone. Indeed, the Spanish temperament seems even now hardly to have broken out of the imperial mould in which it set fast in the sixteenth century. And the result has been more than three centuries of uninterrupted sterility and

---

[1] I recollect meeting Lord Keynes on the day after the *Repulse* and the *Prince of Wales* had been sunk by Japanese aircraft off the east coast of Malaya in December 1941. He was immensely moved. "We all feel," he said, "quite different about the loss of capital ships to any other loss. It's the only thing that gives us a sinking feeling in the pit of our stomachs. I suppose it's because if the last of them was gone we should all be gone." It was still just true in 1941.

rancour. Portugal has followed the same path, although in her case a softer decay has seemed to ease the descent. In our own time there has been one lucky escape from this, the normal fate of imperial peoples: that of Holland. There was nothing voluntary, as we have noted, in the dissolution of her vast Indonesian domains. On the contrary, she fought to retain them with true Dutch obduracy. Yet when they were lost the Dutch people have, in the last decade, shown a splendid common sense. Instead of declining into a Spain or a Portugal, they have rebuilt their country into a marked prosperity and afford perhaps the most striking of all the examples of the combination of a rising standard of life with the dissolution of empire.

We have already discussed a major contemporary example of the failure to overcome an imperial fixation. In the last twelve years France has been losing her former empire the hard way, with most of her former colonies only obtaining their independence at the cost of inflicting a military defeat upon their former "motherland", and so creating a wound of antagonism which must make their future relations, which to their mutual advantage should be close, particularly difficult. (Tunis and Morocco, however, were let go just, but only just, before the worst had come to the worst.) But up till 1958 it was impossible to close one's eyes to the dreadful symptoms of a fixation of the French spirit upon the barren dream of the retention, or re-conquest, of her empire. That so great, so brilliant, so humane a people as the French could be seriously threatened with such a fate was tragic indeed. Now at the eleventh hour the events of 1958 enable us to hope at least that France will solve this terrible problem. For whatever harm de Gaulle's coming to power has done to French internal democracy (and it may be very great) his Government has undeniably taken a vital step forward in the colonial field. Throughout tropical Africa the way to peaceful and sane development seems to have been opened. The frightful question of Algiers alone remains unsolved. General de Gaulle has shown the desire for a liberal approach here too; but at the time of writing he has not made it (Spring, 1959). We can only pray that, above all for the sake of France herself, she will in the end "let her people go".

Yet even the example of France gives only a faint impression of what would have happened to Britain if she had decided in 1945 to fight to retain her empire. Her empire was so much greater, and the political movements for independence in her main colonies (e.g. India) were so much more powerful than the corresponding movements in the French or Dutch Empires, that total and rapid national ruin must almost certainly have resulted from any British attempt to retain her empire by force. In 1959 it is already possible to say confidently that this peril has been avoided. In spite of the incomparable dazzle of our imperial heyday, we have freed ourselves from our imperial fixation sufficiently, at least, to avoid destroying ourselves by fighting to preserve India, Pakistan, Ceylon, Burma and the rest. Moreover, as we have noted, the return of a Conservative government in 1951 has caused only minor interruptions in the steady march of a voluntary, or at least largely non-violent, process of dis-imperialism.

In all the circumstances this is a record of remarkable flexibility. The British people, in the last fourteen years, have shown a power both to recognise a sudden and rapid change in their environment and to adapt themselves to it, which is for a British writer an irresistible subject of self-congratulation. By 1959 Britain was almost certainly out of the imperialist wood, in the sense that it was now clear that she was not going to destroy herself by clinging obstinately and hopelessly to an imperial heritage suddenly become untenable. But how close a shave it was! Extraordinary feats of statesmanship, exhibited, intermittently, by both political parties, were necessary to induce this imperial people, in defiance of some of their deepest instincts, peacefully to relinquish their rule over nearly a quarter of the entire human race. We may appreciate both the *expertise* of this political operation, and the dire consequences which must have ensued if it had failed, not only from foreign examples but also from the actual course of events in those relatively minor cases in which this statesmanship was absent.

Up to 1958, for example, the British Government pig-headedly refused to allow self-determination to the little Mediterranean island of Cyprus. It did not do so, in my view, in the main for the avowed military reasons, although these have counted. One of the real reasons may have been psychological. Part of the explanation for the mystery of why Britain would not let the Cypriots go, as she has let, or is letting, hundreds of millions of Asians and Africans go, is that the majority of the islanders had affronted British feelings by expressing the desire, not for independence within the Commonwealth, or even for independence outside it, but for union with another country. In 1958 this obstacle was removed by the Cypriots' declared willingness to abandon the demand for Enosis. But by then passions had become so hot, and the Turkish minority had been stimulated into such intransigence that the obvious, simple solution of steadily extending self-government had become very difficult. Fortunately, at the eleventh hour a patched-up solution was reached between the Greek and Turkish Governments, and was acquiesced in by the Cypriots and the British Government. It may well be true that by 1959 passions had become so violent that only such a solution as this was possible. Nevertheless it remains to be seen how well it will work. And it is entirely untrue, in my view (derived from a visit to the island at the time), that the far simpler and better solution of normal self-government and, later, self-determination, was unavailable in the earlier nineteen-fifties, before the Turkish minority on the island had been activated. Thus the refusal to pursue, for several years, and even in this relatively small instance of Cyprus, the general British policy of allowing self-determination to any sufficiently developed people which effectively, vehemently and persistently demanded it, did significant damage to Britain, economically and militarily (chiefly by way of the cost of maintaining 30,000 troops in Cyprus). And it did immense damage to us morally in the eyes of the world by spoiling our otherwise splendid record of liberalism towards our dependencies.

The damage done us by the wrongful detention of this one little island of half a million people gives us a measure of what would have happened to us, both economically and morally, if we had tried to maintain our rule over, for example, 360 million Indians. The marvel is that there has turned out to be enough sanity amongst us to make it possible for Britain to avoid destroying herself in the attempt to retain the untenable.

For this relative freedom from a fixation on empire we must partly thank the anti-imperialist tradition of a part of the British Liberal and Labour movements. Sometimes that tradition has been naïve, impractical and foolish, expressing itself in an "impossibilist" pacificism. Nevertheless, its existence may well prove to have been the salvation of the country. For without this traditional anti-imperialism on the part of many of the most politically conscious of the British people, we should almost certainly have been doomed to fight out a series of rearguard actions which would have ruined us, without preventing, or even significantly postponing, the dissolution of the empire.

The anti-imperialist tradition of the British Labour movement in particular arose partly no doubt because the main material gains of empire were always confined to a narrow range of property owners: to, at most, that 10% of the population which, as we noted in the first volume of this study, could be counted as the substantial beneficiaries of the system. In the heyday, between 1900 and 1910, the high rate of British capital accumulation was not mainly used, even indirectly, for the benefit of the British wage-earners by way of the development of Britain, but, to the extent of some 7% of the national product, was going overseas and, to a large extent, into the empire.[1] Behind these figures lies the fact that this Edwardian imperial heyday was also the period of an almost static standard of life for the British people. It was the heyday of a degree of economic insecurity for the wage-earners almost inconceivable to us in 1959, and of extremes of class stratification. It was the epoch of *The Ragged Trousered Philanthropists*.[2] In such conditions the most independently minded section of the British wage-earners managed to escape, to a lesser or greater degree, from the pervasive imperialist mental climate of the day. They absorbed the doctrines of Hobson, Brailsford, Buxton, Morel and the other anti-imperialist middle-class radicals, founded their own political party, and gave to that party a marked, though not very clear, anti-imperialist character. The degree of social fission within British society which these developments revealed was never very great, but it was just deep enough to be significant. It is only because all this happened that to-day a majority of the British people can, just, escape from the national fixation upon empire.

This separate and distinct world outlook of some of the British wage-earners, incipient and incomplete as it was, made it possible for the Attlee government to take the decisive steps towards a peaceful and voluntary, instead of a bloody and ruinous, dissolution of the empire. For no government could have done this if the entire British people had retained those imperialist attitudes which characterised, in the main, the British upper classes. If all the wage-earners also had looked upon the empire as their own, had idolised this national achievement as the be-all and end-all of national life, then there would have been no hope or possibility of the present remarkable process of adaptation to a swiftly changing world environment. It was only because at least the most politically conscious sections of the British wage-earners felt a sympathy and identification with the colonial peoples as, to some extent, joint victims of the exploitation of the imperialist system, that the national situation has been saved.

[1] This figure—an estimate of course—is given by Mr Harold Wilson in his *War on World Poverty* (Gollancz).
[2] *The Ragged Trousered Philanthropists*, by Robert Tressell (Grant Richards, 1914).

CHAPTER XV

BRITAIN WITHOUT AN EMPIRE

By the skin of our teeth, by good sense and by good luck, some-how or other, we have been saved from the fate which has overtaken most nations which have lost their empires. We have not suffered that searing succession of national defeats, frustrations and humiliations which habitually mark the decline of empires which have exhausted the mandate of heaven.

We have been saved: but for what? It will not do us much good to exhibit all the wisdom and moderation in the world, if we do not find some fresh national purpose, capable of inspiring the spirit and energies of the British people. For to a considerable extent the enlargement or maintenance of the empire has been our national purpose. What is to be put in its place? That daemonic will to conquer, to rule, and some-times to exploit, which first possessed us as a sort of emanation from the Gangetic plain two hundred years ago, has left us. And thank heaven it has. For its continuance to-day after British material power has been overshadowed could lead only to catastrophe. Yet we shall stagnate unless we can find other purposes to satisfy our hearts. What can they be?

In this enquiry the experience of other peoples should be instructive. After all Britain is far from being the first nation to lose an empire. We should be able to gain some insight into our own situation by taking into account what may be called the post-imperial periods of other peoples. For it is by no means the case that all post-imperial nations have wrapped the Spanish cloak of despair and disdain about them. On the contrary, many have found highly successful employ-ments for their national genius. Some of these post-imperial national concerns have been of a markedly more creative character than others, but all are instructive. It may be useful briefly to survey the question of what unexhausted nations do with themselves when they lose their empires.

We may consider first the least satisfactory of the alternatives to empire. When a still vigorous nation loses, for one reason or another, its ability to conquer and rule others—by age-old tradition, the main purpose of powerful nations—its citizens are apt to turn to personal self-enrichment as the be-all and end-all of human life. This can in one sense hardly be called a national purpose at all. For personal enrichment, above all in the context of traditional capitalism, is competitive, narrowly individualistic, non-co-operative, even anti-national. Still it is for many temperaments a most absorbing pursuit and many peoples in their post-imperial phases have devoted themselves to it.

We may think of the Dutch after the War of the Spanish Succession; of the French in what might be called their Balzacian period after the Napoleonic wars. (And this is the underlying mood of the French people to-day, it may be suspected, if they could rid themselves of the disastrous anachronisms of their imperial rearguard actions.) And now it seems probable that the West Germans have gone the same way. We might perhaps describe this process as the total commercialisation of the national life. Leon Trotsky, that master of the phrase, called it "Belgianisation". Trotsky took the Belgians as the archetype of a totally commercialised people: of a people, worthy, industrious, stable, indeed, but of a people who had renounced all national visions, dreams, ideals; of a people whose almost universal ambition had become individual wealth and comfort. Such a people have in a sense given up; they have given up because altogether too much has happened to them; they have endured too many disasters, humiliations and defeats, too many enemy occupations, too many alien armies marching across them.[1] Such a people receives a thoroughgoing impression of its own impotence to decide its fate. Even its boldest and most energetic spirits are apt to opt for personal comfort and security at all costs. In politics they become neither left nor right, neither progressive nor reactionary, neither nationalist nor internationalist: they become Belgianised.

Of course, there is something to be said for such national commercialisation or Belgianisation—call it what you will. Her neighbours, for example, may be pardoned if they devoutly hope that a substantial measure of such commercialisation of spirit has overtaken the German people. For the ubiquitous German salesman is at any rate much to be preferred to the ubiquitous German Panzer division. Moreover, nations which, like West Germany and Britain, satisfy a large and indispensable part of their needs by means of foreign trade, must in any case pay close attention to the essentially commercial task of discovering what are the things which the world most wants and which they can produce as well or better than anyone else.

[1] In the Belgian case national frustration began as long ago as their failure to wrench themselves free from the Spanish Empire at the turn of the sixteenth and seventeenth centuries, when they were leading the world in commercial and industrial development, and when, by a miracle, the Dutch won their freedom.

Again, a commercialisation of the national spirit is a development likely enough for any people who have had a long and full experience of the capitalist system. For when it is not imperialist, the capitalist spirit is essentially commercial. Perhaps the most judicious economist of all those who have striven to draw the portrait of capitalism, Joseph Schumpeter, wrote of "the unromantic and unheroic civilisation of capitalism". Only by way of rare exception, he concluded, can capitalism generate an ideal outside and beyond personal enrichment. He quotes, but only by way of an exception illuminating his rule, the inscription on the house of an old Bremen merchant, *"navigare necesse est, vivere non necesse est*—to voyage is necessary to live is not necessary" (*Capitalism, Socialism and Democracy*, p. 160). But such a spirit, he continues, is profoundly atypical of capitalism. It can only appear in the system's hot youth of mercantile adventure, before it has settled down to the real business of money making. Thus, apart from a few early "heroic" periods in its development, for the most part connected with the sea, such as the periods of the Hansa, the Venetian, the Dutch and the English merchants, the ethos of capitalism has been *terre à terre*. It is prosaic and, above all, self-seeking in the most direct sense of finding in personal enrichment the aim of life. And necessarily so, for the essence of its philosophy is that a striving for such individual enrichment will infallibly benefit, by means of the invisible hand of competition, the whole community to the maximum possible extent.

For contemporary Britain, however, the main danger is not, precisely, "Belgianisation". It is rather a related, yet distinct, variety of commercialisation. It is, in a word, Americanisation. In America we have before us by far the greatest example of a nation which has taken personal enrichment as its ideal. True, she has adopted almost total commercialisation for different, even opposite, reasons. It is not that she has experienced too much, but too little. No searing disasters (except the Civil War) have ever happened to her. But for whatever reasons (and Marxist allegations to the contrary) America remains to-day, in the nineteen-fifties, a community with an essentially non-imperial climate of opinion. The national ideal is personal enrichment, not the conquest and rule of other peoples. The business man, not the pro-consul, is the exemplar for the people. The business of America is still business. As such she must be an object of intense interest to a post-imperial Britain, seeking instinctively for a new "way of life" incarnating a new national ideal. Does or does not the famed "American way of life" provide us with an example to follow?

Contemporary America is an immense test case of the results of placing personal enrichment above every other goal of human endeavour. And let it be said immediately that in the marvellously favourable American circumstances the results are impressive. Nurtured by a virgin continent's immense natural resources, played upon continually by powerful democratic forces, the American ideal has resulted in raising the general standard of life to the highest point yet achieved by the human race.[1] With a median family income of just under $4,000 (1956), the Americans, with significant but on the whole minor exceptions, have largely got what they set out to achieve. They have got rich. And no one, especially from amongst the better-circumstanced classes of poorer communities, should underestimate this achievement.

If, however, we study American society in order to learn what satisfying national purpose can take the place of empire, we may conclude that the ideal of personal self-enrichment will hardly suffice. Indeed, when all the other peoples of the world cast their eyes upon America in appraisal, as they do, their verdict is clearly by no means wholly favourable. If it were, American leadership would be far more widely and willingly followed than it is. American affluence in itself would be immensely impressive, but what, it seems, the rest of the world senses is the paradox that it is just at the moment when personal self-enrichment as a national ideal has largely achieved its purpose, that its inadequacies become apparent.

The student is fortunate in this connection in possessing a self-criticism of present-day American society of the very highest quality. Professor John Kenneth Galbraith's major work, *The Affluent Society* (Hamish Hamilton, London, 1958), enables us to comprehend, as never before, the perplexities and dilemmas which face, in the very hour of its triumph, a society which chooses personal enrichment as the national ideal. Professor Galbraith's book is at once massive and intricate and no adequate summary of it can be attempted here. Nevertheless, certain of its themes closely concern our present enquiry into what should be the national purposes of a non-imperial society such as Britain has suddenly become. His first proposition is that Americans, much more than any other people, have set up *the production of things* as their true object of worship. That which promotes production is good, that which hampers it is bad. But (though here Professor Galbraith is, in my opinion, inadequately specific) the production to

[1] With, as noted on p. 200, the interesting minor exception, in 1956, of contemporary New Zealand.

be thus worshipped must be of a specific sort. Because personal enrich-ment is the national ideal, it must be production for profit. It is the profit, or surplus, given off like some precious vapour from the act of production rather than that act itself, which is the national objective. The emergence of profit alone sanctifies the act of production: whether or not any particular activity will yield a profit is the criterion of its desirability.

Consequences of the utmost magnitude flow from the adoption of this national idea. On the positive side, to engage in all acts of produc-tion which will yield a profit becomes a categorical imperative. In what Professor Galbraith calls "the conventional wisdom" this is justi-fied by the explanation that what is most profitable to produce will be at the same time what best satisfies a human want. Professor Galbraith agrees that in the epoch of scarcity so to some extent it was. The criterion of profitability had a relation, discernible if never exact, to the satisfaction of primary human needs. It could be argued at least that if only the distribution of income were not too inequitable, the criterion of profitability would serve the essential purpose of allotting the resources of the community in such a way as best to satisfy the needs of the population.

In "the affluent society" it is no longer so. And here Professor Galbraith introduces what is perhaps his most important concept, "the dependence effect". The dependence effect is in the main simply advertising. But it is advertising raised to the American level in which some $1 billion a year—an appreciable part of the gross national product—is spent on it. Such advertising has ceased to be a useful, if noisy, accompaniment of the production and marketing of goods. Such advertising has become an independent force. *It has become nothing less than the prior production of the wants or needs which the produc-tion of goods is to satisfy.*

When this happens, advertising—in the widest sense of the word—becomes a prime mover of the whole economic system. When a society becomes so affluent that, far from its wants and needs crying out of themselves for satisfaction, it becomes necessary to devote a very real part of the national effort to fabricating them artificially, everything in both the theory and practice of economics has been overturned. When the majority of all families have already had not only their primary needs, but their desires for television receivers, for automobiles, for refrigerators and the full catalogue of "consumer durables", satisfied: when it becomes imperatively necessary, in order to continue to pro-duce at a profit, to convince them that they need *another* television receiver, *another* refrigerator and *another* much longer, larger and more glittering automobile, the whole *rationale* of production for profit begins to totter. At that point the needs of men, the satisfaction of which is the sole rational object of economic activity, have like the fibres of our clothing become synthetic: they have become secondary and derivative from the productive process itself. And with that the whole process has become circular. For the justification of capitalism the consumer and his wants must be sovereign. But where is that sovereignty if the consumer's wants must first be elaborately and expensively manufactured for him, as a pre-condition of manufacturing the goods to satisfy those wants? The consumer and his wants have become the mere puppets of the categorical imperative to produce at a profit. And if we ask the question why should we produce at a profit if not to satisfy natural human wants, the answer of the conventional wisdom will be that the distillation of profit is the aim and object of human activity, the primary of which it is impious to question. When a capitalist society has reached the American degree of affluence, the manufacture of wants must at all costs be kept one step ahead of the manufacture of the goods to satisfy those wants. The image of the caged squirrel turning its wheel with every busy step inevitably occurs to Professor Galbraith. The worship of production for profit now that it no longer serves the satisfaction of natural wants, has become an idolatry: how can such a thing for long provide a satisfying national purpose for grown men?

But personal enrichment as a national ideal has another consequence. Not only must everything and anything be produced which will yield a profit, however little unsynthesised need there is for it, but nothing, or at least the lowest minimum, of those things the production of which will *not* yield a profit, must be produced. This negative side of the worship of production for profit results in a condition which Professor Galbraith calls "social unbalance". For it so happens that some of the most important and urgent of the real needs of an affluent society, cannot, in practice, be satisfied by production for profit. These are broadly the needs which cannot be satisfied by the sale of goods or services to individuals, but must be catered for by the provision of a public service. They range all the way from such *terre à terre*, but not unimportant, services as refuse collection, street cleaning, town planning and satisfactory housing for the mass of the community, to such life and death matters as the maintenance of law and order, education and, finally, defence.

In a series of striking chapters, Professor Galbraith shows that twentieth-century America, by far the richest society which the world has ever known, is stinting itself to an almost insane degree on some or all of these public services. Nor is the reason far to seek. Because their provision cannot be left to private profit-seeking entrepreneurs who will themselves provide (or borrow) the necessary resources in the expectation that they will in due course be recouped manyfold, these services must be provided out of public funds raised by taxation. But in the ideology of a society which has taken personal enrichment as its goal, this has come to mean that their provision is not counted as a form of production at all. On the contrary, they are regarded as grievous burdens upon the community, the size of which must be minimised almost at all costs if they are not to break the back of the economy. The more television sets, the more refrigerators, the more automobiles the country produces the richer, everyone agrees, it will become. But the more municipal services, the more city planning, the more roads (without which the automobiles, incidentally, cannot be either parked or run), the more schools and the more arms the country produces, the poorer it is thought to become. And yet, all unknown to the public, the economists of all political persuasions add together roads and automobiles, schools and refrigerators, arms and television sets, to reach their total of the gross national product, which no one challenges as the measure of the wealth of the nation.

The consequences of the illusion that only that which is produced for profit constitutes wealth—that all the rest is burden and loss—would be comic if they were not so grave. Here is America, the Croesus of the nations, so rich that she diverts a significant part of her resources to an ever more frantic attempt to make people want things for which they have little rational use, half-starving herself of essential public services. The American people have been persuaded that they cannot afford to have their garbage adequately collected, their cities properly cleaned, their slums cleared, or even enough parking places and roads built to enable them to use their third or fourth automobile. All this, however, is inconvenient and silly rather than tragic. Far more serious for the future of the Republic is the fact that the American people have been led to deny themselves anything approaching an adequate educational system for a community as rich as they are.

Finally, we come to the most curious effect of the illusion that production which is not directly for private profit is not production at all. This is the effect upon defence. Now, nothing is more rooted in the lore of "left wing" criticism of capitalism than that defence is the one field in which a capitalist government will never stint its public expenditure. Yet present-day American experience bears out this dictum—which I have made a dozen times myself—but partially. The capacity of events in the twentieth century to outstrip our current comprehension of them and to render "the conventional wisdom", either in its classical capitalist or its Marxist form, almost comically wrong, has become very great. In the economic field itself, the Marxist prediction of ever-increasing misery has turned out to be the reverse of the truth. It is ever-increasing affluence which is in America becoming increasingly incompatible with an unmodified capitalism. And, so curiously does history tease the prophets, that in the field of defence, a similar, if by no means so absolute, a reversal has taken place. It has not turned out to be the wicked armament contractor, avid for dividends from cannon, who rules the roost in the most advanced capitalisms. It has been, on the contrary, the American business man, fanatically determined on business as usual, and regarding defence expenditure, since it has to be paid for out of taxation, as a most unpleasant necessity, who has become the representative figure. True, dominant American opinion has not nearly the same degree of hostility to public expenditure upon defence as upon expenditure upon education and the social services. Up to a point, contemporary America, with a defence expenditure of nearly $40b, or over 10% of her gross national product, confirms the traditional radical view that this is the one field in which public expenditure is respectable. Nevertheless, Professor Galbraith points out that *on the hypothesis upon which the American Government is working* (he is careful to point out that he considers it a false hypothesis)—namely, the hypothesis of an implacable and irremediable conflict between America and the communist world —this is certainly an inadequate expenditure. It is an expenditure which was proved inadequate in the autumn of 1957 when the Russian sputniks revealed to a horrified America that even in some aspects of nuclear warfare, the Russians were already ahead of them. More importantly, perhaps, if less dramatically, it was a rate of defence expenditure which had clearly left America with painfully exiguous conventional forces with which to counter communist moves in various parts of the world, without resorting to the mutual suicide of nuclear war.

Thus the world was presented with the astonishing spectacle of an American big business Administration which steadfastly refused to make any real attempt to negotiate seriously with the communist powers, either for a limitation in armaments or anything else; which indeed refused ostentatiously to recognise the very existence of the

Chinese communist state, but which at the same time refused to arm itself at what, it is now clear, would have been the level necessary for such a policy of intransigence. Mr Dulles' announced policy of "negotiating from strength" had turned in practice into a policy of no serious negotiations and not much strength either. Sir Winston Churchill at an early stage of the British rearmament programme said that "we arm to parley". In 1958 the most powerful nation on earth seemed to be getting herself into a position in which she would neither parley nor arm herself on the scale which would have been necessary to support her intransigent policy. The reason why the "businessman's administration" of President Eisenhower felt it necessary to cut American defence spending is apparent. The President announced the conclusion of his economic sages that there was a mystic figure of some $38b which American defence spending could not exceed without gravely damaging the American economy. He did so at a moment when it was necessary somehow to persuade as many American families as possible that they needed a fourth automobile, with tail-fins twice as long as before, in order to keep that economy going. For the tail-fins were produced for private profit, while the arms would have had to be paid for out of taxation. So remarkable are the effects of a fanatical adherence to the national ideal of personal self-enrichment in conditions of great affluence.

Of course, we must not let the present aberrations of the American mood mislead us. After all, Professor Galbraith's great book is as much an American product as are the silly tail-fins of her latest and shiniest automobiles. America still has the capacity for self-criticism. And so long as she retains that we may confidently hope for her recovery from her aberrations (which for that matter are no worse than other people's: only they show more because she is so large). Such criticisms as the above are merely criticisms of certain aspects of American life at a particular time. She is so vast and so rapidly developing a community that she is sure to change and grow, and change again, many times in the remainder of the century. Nevertheless, we British at the present juncture in our affairs should look long and hard at the result of the contemporary American worship of self-enrichment. For it would be disastrous indeed if we took over that worship, in place of imperialism, as our national ideal, just at the moment when it is showing its inability to guide the people of affluent societies. To be sure it would not in Britain produce as yet the aberrations which it has done in America, for we are not yet so affluent. But let us take note of the material pitfalls and the spiritual deserts towards which we should inevitably march if we took "the American way of life" as our national ideal.

The danger is real, for the ideal of personal self-enrichment is likely to have a strong appeal to an immediately post-imperial society such as Britain. For example that same prudent climate of opinion which has enabled us to escape from imperialism is apt to carry us on into a belief that we need not have, or cannot afford the defences of an independent nation. It may be, paradoxically enough, that some British conservatives will be especially prone to this fallacy. When they finally realise that the empire really has gone (as to some extent happened after the Suez fiasco in 1956), they are apt to become more radical, in one sense, than anyone else. In particular they are apt suddenly to question all need for maintaining defence forces. If, they evidently feel, our armed forces have proved unable to preserve our empire, what is the use of them? Let us scrap the lot, save the money, and live in prosperous impotence. No judgment could be more hasty. The fact that a country has irrevocably entered its post-imperial period does not mean that she can afford to be defenceless. We shall indeed suggest below that the world as a whole may possibly be entering a post-imperial period. But even if that proves to be so, it does not, unfortunately, mean that the world is about to become a peaceful, placid lake upon the still waters of which it will be safe to navigate in an open boat. On the contrary, the world is almost certainly entering a period of intense storm and stress. Young, vast, thrusting, formidable nations are everywhere jostling each other. The developed world is partitioned into the two hostile groups of communism and capitalism; the underdeveloped world hovers undecided between the two. Anything more reckless than to divest ourselves unilaterally of the possibility of armed defence in such a world could scarcely be imagined. A vigorous nation determined to play in its post-imperial period as significant a role in the world as ever (although a different role) must, unfortunately, maintain, as long as others do, the best defences which it can afford. Moreover, pending an effective measure of international disarmament, such a nation must maintain the particular types of armaments which are decisive for that time and place.

It is no doubt psychologically difficult for a nation to resign its imperial role and yet at the same time to realise that if it means to sustain for itself that independence which it is granting to others it must maintain adequate defences. The anti-imperialist mood passes over, all too easily, into a sort of commercialised pacifism. It is possible, nevertheless, for post-imperial nations to maintain both the will and the means with which to preserve a sturdy independence. The example of Sweden comes to mind. I shall always recollect the answer given to me by my military advisers to one of the first questions which I asked them when in 1950 I became Secretary of State for War. I asked them what was the strongest army in Western Europe at that time. They replied without hesitation that it was the Swedish. We must, of course, beware of drawing a direct analogy between present-day Britain and Sweden. A nation of over 50 millions is inevitably of a different type, and with a different role in the world, from a nation of 7 millions. None the less, if we wish to retain a true independence (although not necessarily nor probably an independence of all alliances in the way Sweden has done), we shall have to cultivate a proper regard for our ultimate power of defence. For the world is still a place in which the weak go to the wall. Despite Goethe, it *is* possible for a nation to avoid being hammer or anvil, to avoid either conquering or being conquered. Not only the Swedish (and the Swiss), but other examples testify that this is possible. But it is only possible if both the spirit of independence and the expression of that spirit in adequate defence forces are maintained.

There is, it is true, another possibility in this field of defence. It is possible for a post-imperial nation to neglect its means of self-preservation and yet to preserve itself, for a time at least, by means of declining into dependence upon an all-powerful ally. And there are those who see such a role for Britain, in the form of dependence upon America which, it is assumed, probably wrongly, will always be adequately strong for both. The present British-American alliance is indeed a necessary response to the unmistakably expansionist policies pursued by Russia in the post-1945 decade. But support for that alliance is one thing and resignation to a position of total dependence upon America is another. Those who advocate such a position for Britain should study the lessons of history in this case also. They will surely find that, precisely for the sake of genuinely good Anglo-American relations, a self-respecting British independence in defence, as in all other matters, is indispensable.

The classical example of total dependence upon a neighbouring super-power is that afforded by the dependence of the Greeks, upon Rome, after their conquest in the Hellenistic period. Moreover the post-1945 relationship between Britain and America has been sometimes compared, especially by the present (1959) British Prime Minister, Mr Macmillan, with the Greco-Roman relationship in the

Hellenistic period. And no doubt the comparison is instructive, so long as it is given as a warning, not as an example. The Greeks, of course, had been conquered by the Romans, not merely surpassed by them in power as we have been by the Americans. Nevertheless, the Romans did not wish to rule the Greeks directly: they wanted (partly out of a genuine reverence for Greek civilisation) to recreate a measure at least of Greek freedom. The following is a description, from the pen of Mommsen, of the consequences for both the Romans and the Greeks of such a situation.

"There was a profound justice and still more a profound melancholy in the fact that Rome, however earnestly she endeavoured to establish the freedom and earn the thanks of the Hellenes, yet gave them nothing but anarchy and reaped nothing but ingratitude. Undoubtedly very generous sentiments lay at the bottom of the Hellenic antipathies to the protecting power, and the personal bravery of some of the men who took the lead in the movement was unquestionable; but this Achaean patriotism remained not the less a folly and a genuine historical caricature. With all that ambition and all that national susceptibility the whole nation was, from highest to the lowest, pervaded by the most thorough sense of impotence. Everyone was constantly listening to learn the sentiments of Rome, the liberal man no less than the servile: they thanked heaven when the dreaded decree was not issued: they were sulky when the Senate gave them to understand that they would do well to yield voluntarily in order that they might not need to be compelled; they did what they were obliged to do, if possible in a way offensive to the Romans, to save form: they reported, explained, postponed, evaded, and when all this would no longer avail, they yielded with a patriotic sigh" (Mommsen's *History of Rome*, Volume II, p. 479).

It might be possible for Britain to live thus, undefended and prosperous, in total dependence upon America. It would be the logical end of a process of "Belgianisation". It may be said that we could then become very rich. But even this is not so certain. It is possible that a people who had renounced all other ideals than personal enrichment would not succeed very well even in that. For the undiluted capitalist ethos pushes individual enrichment to the point at which it conflicts with, and may frustrate, the enrichment of the nation as a whole. So far from the invisible hand maximising the general gain, national moods may be generated (such as that which seems to beset contemporary

France as well as contemporary America) in which the struggle for individual gain positively impoverishes the community by frustrating the degree of co-operation needed for successful large scale economic development at the present level of technique.

But, far more important, it is doubtful if major nations can long content themselves with a wholly commercial ideal. Nations which have known empire may simply break their hearts if they do not find a higher ideal than personal enrichment by which to live. Britain will find no tolerable substitute for empire as the national goal in the narrow purpose of personal self-enrichment. On the other hand, and without at this point leaving the consideration of material things and their production, there is a purpose which, though in no conflict with personal enrichment, can and indeed must form a part of a new national purpose for Britain.

This is the welfare ideal. The welfare ideal is also one which involves the enrichment of the population—in economic terms a rising standard of life. But it is distinct from and much superior to personal enrichment in that it is much less self-centred and self-seeking: it takes the material welfare of the whole community as its concern: it is generous and co-operative as compared with the ideal of individual self-enrichment.

Moreover, to an ever-increasing extent it will be found that such a community as Britain will not be able effectively to earn her living in the world unless she simultaneously evolves an appropriate and equitable system for the distribution of the fruits of her productive effort amongst the 50-odd millions of us. For it is increasingly true that unless the distribution of its results is felt to be equitable, the productive effort will not be made. Thus equitable (rather than equal) distribution must remain a first task of British statesmanship. This national ideal is not badly summed up in the one word, welfare. The welfare ideal may sometimes, it is true, seem a limited and even selfish one. But properly regarded and pursued it is neither. The truth is that if any nation can so arrange its political and economic life that it eliminates poverty, disseminates both equity and opportunity, and withal fosters personal liberty and human diversity, it will perform an incomparable service, by example, for the whole world.

Mr David Lloyd George was asked in his old age what he considered was the main achievement of his life. To his interrogator's surprise, he did not reply that it was his leadership of Britain to victory in the first World War. He declared instead that he should be remembered in history as the man who started in Britain the process by which the stark contrasts and conflicts of class were to be increasingly softened and mitigated by means of a more equitable distribution of the national income. In this striking piece of self-adjudication the first statesman of the welfare state foresaw the immense consequences of the process which he set under way in the People's Budget of 1909. By the nineteen-fifties that process had been taken far enough, not only in Britain but also in all the other highly developed democracies, for Professor Myrdal in his book, *An International Economy*, to found much of his argument upon the growing realisation of what he calls "national integration". The advanced democratic nations are succeeding, he considers, in making themselves into genuine communities. They look after the welfare of all their citizens, as distinct from a favoured class of their citizens, to a sufficient degree, he continues, to make their peoples feel a sense of national unity and solidarity which in actual practice can be observed increasingly to transcend the conflicts of class.

But the realisation of this welfare ideal is still incomplete and above all still precarious. A major failure to control the workings of the economy could still plunge our highly developed societies into rending social conflicts. Therefore, to the extent that any nation can exhibit the model of an effectively functioning society, successfully controlling its economy, and equitably distributing its benefits, that nation will become for the contemporary world what Pericles claimed Athens to be in her own time and place—namely, "the education of Hellas". It would be arrogant to assume that Britain will fulfil any such role as that. On the other hand, she certainly ought to aspire to such a role and strive to fulfil it.

In the event, of course, many mature nations will make themselves into examples by their achievements, some in one field, some in another. An instance of both the importance and the limitations of welfare as a national ideal is afforded by a relatively small nation which entered its post-imperial period 250 years ago, just as Britain was fairly entering on her imperial mission. In the eighteenth century, Sweden, exhausted by the vast empire she had built but could not maintain, even by means of the frantic militarism of Charles XII, sank into apparent lethargy for nearly two centuries. But in our own day she has become the "pilot plant" of the welfare state, achieving a steady, and yet rapid, material progress which repays and receives the study of the world. On the other hand, critics of Sweden, and of the welfare state, point to the fact that she has the highest suicide rate in the world,[1] that alcoholism is a very serious social problem, and that, they allege, there is something unpleasantly smug and self-satisfied about Swedish society. Whether the suicide rate would be lower and the Swedes soberer if they were poorer and more insecure is by no means proven, of course. Nevertheless, the Swedish example is surely well worth our attention for both its negative as well as its positive lessons. It does suggest to us that the welfare ideal, while certainly much superior to the crude ideal of personal self-enrichment, is not enough. Nations, it seems, must aspire as well as simply live well, if they are to be healthy.

The fact is that economic progress, in our highly favoured part of the world (about one-sixth of the non-communist world by population), though nowhere else, is becoming too easy to be exciting. Accordingly for us the welfare ideal is ceasing to glitter in the way which it did, and still does in the pre-industrial world of grinding poverty. The suspicion is beginning to dawn that the way to achieve a steadily rising standard of life—if that is all we want—is becoming pretty obvious. On the one hand, all but the most rigidly minded socialists should be by now aware that the profit motive, the criterion of profitability, the price system generally, and the urge of self-enrichment, if they are kept under strict and effective social control, can in appropriate circumstances be powerful means for attaining the purely material purpose of a steadily rising standard of life. The profit motive and the price system, in other words, can be made into useful servants, though they remain disastrous masters. On the other hand, all but the most die-hard supporters of capitalism must be increasingly aware that private profit simply will not do as either the mainspring or the sole regulator of mature and affluent societies such as ours. Exclusive dependence upon personal enrichment as the national purpose produces the most unfortunate results even in the material field, by way of both instability and irrationality. But over and above that it is becoming clearer every day that it is imperative that a mature people should possess itself of some national purpose apart from and beyond national enrichment. We have a desperate need for a national purpose or ideal which stands outside and beyond the workings of our economic system: an ideal for the sake of which the system is worked.

[1] Professor Myrdal informs me that the high Swedish suicide rate may be a mere statistical illusion, the result of the superior records kept by the Swedish authorities as to the causes of death.

CHAPTER XVI

BY BREAD ALONE?

To put the conclusion of the last chapter in another way: concern with the economic problem is a paradoxical business. Until a certain degree of general well-being is reached, it is, and it should be, overwhelmingly important. Below the degree of affluence and security which has only been even approached in our time and in our corner of the world, the poor will be, and the rich ought to be, concerned to raise the national standard of life as by far the highest social priority. But at or near the present American standard of affluence, concern with sheer material welfare, narrowly considered as the median purchasing power over commodities of the population, will and should drop very sharply. Once we have secured our bread, it will be puerile to go on piling up the loaves. There will be a whole universe of other concerns awaiting us. The first of these non-material, or only semi-material, concerns is, in my opinion, the attempt to solve the problem of social equality.

It might have seemed natural to classify this problem, with welfare, under the economic head: but it has become largely unreal to do so. The fact is that a further redistribution of the British national income will have only indirect and uncertain effects upon the standard of life of the British wage-earners. (The figures are given in Chapters VIII to X of *Contemporary Capitalism*, the first volume of this study.) That this is so is sensed by the British electorate. Moreover, the present distribution of the national income appears largely to satisfy their feeling for social equity. There is, for the moment at least, no passionate demand for further redistribution in the equalitarian direction. Or at least that demand is minor compared with the population's unremitting pressure for a steadily rising standard of life, however achieved. These are political facts. And yet the social settlement, lately arrived at in Britain and expressed in the post-1940 redistribution of the national income, carried within itself one highly irrational element.

The general pattern of wages and salaries and of profits of small businesses—of earned incomes in general (net of taxation)—evidently does not seem by any means wholly unjustified to the majority of the nation. And it is this vast mass of earned incomes—something like 90% of the whole (see *Contemporary Capitalism*, p. 144) which dominates the national consciousness. The majority of the electorate seems almost unconscious of the existence of the remaining (*circa*) 10% of property derived, unearned, and to-day overwhelmingly inherited, income. They see, and many of the lower-paid resent, whether justly or unjustly, the high salaries, large expense accounts, and other privileges and emoluments of the recipients of large, earned, salaries. But the existence of the often much larger inherited and wholly unearned incomes, which, too, have far more scope for evading taxation, largely escapes them. So long as this psychological situation persists the whole question of unearned income has not reached the agenda of practical politics.[1] Nevertheless, it is hard to imagine that so curious a position will persist indefinitely. For the anomaly is very great. Only the most elaborate economic casuistry can now argue that inherited, unearned, incomes represent payment for one of the factors of production.

A little more, perhaps, remains of the traditional Marshallian argument that such incomes represent a necessary reward for risk bearing: but not much. The big distributions of unearned income increasingly come from the major oligopolistic corporations, the shareholders of which encounter an almost negligible degree of risk. For the real risks of launching out on new processes are increasingly borne, not by individual enterprise, but by these corporations, which average out their successes and failures in these new fields without significant effect upon their distribution to their shareholders.[2]

The truth is that large inherited, unearned, incomes have become, in effect, pensions drawn in respect of their recipients having taken the precaution to be born in the right cradles, and very little else. It is this arbitrary, because hereditary, element in them which must, surely, lead towards their eventual abolition. For historical evidence tends to show that once such privileges have become functionless, they do begin, though often only very slowly, to atrophy.

It would be an illusion to suppose, however, that even if all large, inherited incomes could be abolished outright (which is not practicable), the re-allocation of the productive resources at present employed

[1] The far larger scope for the legal evasion of taxation (of which taking capital gains as income is only one method) enjoyed by the large, unearned incomes gives the issue its acuteness. The undeniable impression derived from the British social scene to-day that we are a far less equalitarian country than the Treasury's figures of distributed, post-tax, personal income would imply, is accounted for by the relative immunity from the full impact of taxation of those with considerable capital holdings, as compared with wage- and salary-earners. From these latter alone is taxation inexorably deducted at source. Of all this the mass of the wage-earners are still largely unconscious.

[2] All these considerations were discussed in much greater detail in *Contemporary Capitalism*, to which volume the reader who, rightly, considers this chapter to contain many apparently unproven statements, is referred.

in providing them would transform the general standard of life. On the other hand, the provision of these unearned, inherited, incomes can hardly be regarded as a negligible burden on our productive resources. If Mr Dudley Sears' figures (given on p. 144 of *Contemporary Capitalism*) are still approximately correct, property-derived incomes are of a comparable order of magnitude to, for example, our expenditure on defence. And we are not accustomed to say that our defence burden is negligible. (Or, again, the sums involved in providing these incomes would pay several times over, for the major expansion of the educational system suggested below.) So the matter can hardly be written off as not worth bothering about.

On the other hand, the difficulties, and for that matter social dangers, of reopening the question of social equality should not be underrated. We are here dealing with the burning question of the rights of property. This issue has always generated an almost thermo-nuclear social heat. The passion with which the recipients of large inherited, unearned, incomes may be expected to defend them against further encroachment must not be underestimated. (It should be recalled that the share of post-tax distributed personal income going to unearned, property-derived, income appears to have been approximately halved, having dropped from 20% to 10% between 1939 and 1949; see *Contemporary Capitalism*, p. 144; it has no doubt since risen again, however.) Nor should the power of the, by themselves, tiny number of the recipients of such incomes to rally to them all those who believe (usually quite erroneously) that their fortunes depend "on the rights of property" remaining inviolate, be underestimated. Any attempt further to curtail the receipt of functionless, large, inherited, unearned, incomes will certainly be represented as an attempt to destroy the rights of "the small man", meaning the, usually modest, profits of small businesses and the savings of families out of earned income against old age and other contingencies of life, etc. These categories of property derived incomes cannot and should not be abolished, or even curtailed. For they are in the main, either the postponed spending of earned incomes, or are earned incomes taken, nominally in the form of profits, but actually as the often hard earned wages of management of small, or even medium-sized, businesses. And it is perfectly practicable to distinguish between such necessary, and in effect earned, though property-derived, incomes, and large, functionless, inherited incomes which are unearned in the true sense of the word. For it is socially meaningless to class together the "profits" a man derives from working a garage, a small business, a shop, or a farm which he has himself built up, and the "profits" a man derives from inheriting £200,000 worth of shares in the leading companies of the country.

In what way and to what extent the British electorate will, over the decades, curtail or even in the end abolish, large, unearned, inherited, incomes I do not pretend to be able to foresee. But that they will and should move in that direction appears certain. One obvious way to effect this social change would be by means of a sufficiently rigorous use of death duties. What would be necessary would be to make evasion impossible, and also no doubt to raise the rates upon the great mass of fortunes in the middle brackets of say £10,000 to £100,000.[1] If it was made impossible to inherit much more than, say, £10,000 (or any other figure which satisfied the contemporary sense of social justice), the receipt of considerable, inherited, unearned incomes would be gradually abolished, while the passing on of personal property, including, after all, even quite large houses and small businesses, would still be possible.

No doubt it may be objected that the sort of non-hereditary capitalism which would result from such a policy would not work. This may be true, if no other economic or social changes had been made at the same time. But in practice of course, unearned, hereditary income could not be progressively abolished by, for example, the extension of death duties to this extent without a simultaneous extension of social ownership of one kind or another. It would be necessary for the Treasury to accept both shares and land in kind in order to make death duties on this scale practicable. Again the Labour Party's proposals in this field, entitled *Industry and Society*, contemplate the gradual but steady acquisition of shares in the ownership of the major corporations. The object of this essentially long-term policy is not, as both its opponents and its protagonists sometimes appear to suppose, the acquisition of managerial control over these corporations. As a matter of fact, many of them are efficiently managed already. The objective is that a measure of social ownership and responsibility should spread steadily through society in parallel with the steady extinction of large, inherited, unearned incomes. For, I repeat, the electorate is sure, whether we like it or not, in the end progressively to diminish these now indefensible incomes. And disorganisation might well result if the parallel process of extending social ownership had been neglected. There seems little reason to suppose that the increasingly mixed

---

[1] As well as stopping the obvious loopholes, it would be necessary no doubt to impose gift taxes, *inter vivos*, on approximately the same rates as the duties themselves. It is impossible to discuss the fiscal details here. But see Mr N. Kaldor's work on the related question of death duties, expenditure—taxes, etc.

society which such measures will produce, will not work on what will be, in effect, a non-hereditary basis. However, the death duty, share-buying, and generally fiscal methods are only noted by way of examples. It may be that the British electorate will pursue the ideal of social equality (when in due course they take it up) by different means. The point is that pursue it they will.

For the social, as opposed to the economic, consequences of the steady extinction of large, unearned, hereditary incomes would be profound. The injustices which are based upon the existence of the great block of hereditary wealth, power and privilege, of which those incomes are the fruits, can hardly be exaggerated. The greatest of them is the least noticed. Throughout large parts of British industry the direction of the companies concerned is still largely hereditary; inevitably so, so long as income-bearing property in their ownership passes from father to son. No more irrational method of selecting the directors of contemporary industrial concerns than by heredity can well be imagined. Indeed, no apologist of the capitalist system has ever attempted to defend such an arrangement. It has been assumed that the force of competition acting on the principle of the survival of the fittest, would weed out the ineffectively, because hereditarily, directed firm. The reasons why this assumption has become unrealistic in our epoch of the atrophy of competition and the rise of oligopoly have been discussed in the first volume of this study. Here it is only relevant to point out the profound injustice of retaining a large hereditary element in the direction of firms, the operations of which are becoming ever less competitive, in the real life and death sense of that term. The truth is that to talk of even approaching genuine equality of opportunity is impossible in such circumstances.

The second major anomaly built upon hereditary, unearned, income is Britain's "pecular institution" of a separate educational system largely reserved for the children of the recipients of such incomes. The far-reaching inequalities resulting from the existence of this extraordinary institution have often been emphasised. For some at least of these consequential anomalies are now beginning to be noticed. But what is still not realised is that they are all based on the existence of large, inherited, unearned, incomes. Yet when reformers have approached this institution, as in the case of the public schools they have recently done, they have found it difficult even to suggest modifications of them, let alone to suggest their abolition. For the fact is that they cannot be abolished, without creating new anomalies and injustices, unless the pattern of income distribution, and in particular the inherited, unearned, element in that pattern, which sustains them, is itself abolished. For example, if you try to abolish the public schools system while leaving such incomes untouched, you soon find yourself in the untenable position of infringing the important personal liberty of letting a man send his children to the school of his choice. It is only as and when the major inherited incomes are dried up at their source that the public school system in its present form will cease to be appropriate to the British social scene. Till then it can hardly with advantage be touched: then everyone will see at once the necessity, not necessarily of abolishing it, but of modifying drastically the method of selecting its pupils.

In general, it will be found that this is the only fruitful approach to the modification of those features of our society which will be more and more felt to be indefensible. The truth is that any society which had succeeded in making incomes of this type a negligible element in its economy would have gone far in having created in practice "a classless society". It is now only too painfully apparent that a classless society has not been created by the Russian Revolution. The absence of elementary democratic rights has allowed new and different, but apparently gross, privileges to be erected in place of the old privileges based on income-bearing private property in the means of production. But add the progressive extinction of large, hereditary, unearned income to the democratic institutions of contemporary Britain, and you would have achieved the basis of a socialist society, in its specifically economic aspect at least. True, the socialist ideal is far richer and higher than this. But the steady extinction of grossly irrational privilege will alone keep that ideal in touch with real life. Whether or not we wish to create a classless or socialist society, in which every child really enjoys something approaching equality of opportunity, is a question of ultimate value—judgment. Each of us must answer that question for himself. I can only affirm that, for my part, and in spite of everything, the creation of such a society still seems to me in the words of the old English Chartist, George Julian Harney, "the only worthy object of political warfare".

Socialists will work consciously for the attainment of this social ideal. But we should flatter ourselves if we supposed that our conscious endeavours are likely to be the principal agent in bringing it about. The decisive influence is likely to be that immense majority of the British electorate which earns its living, whether or not it holds conscious socialist opinions. After all, why *should* the British people continue indefinitely to pay immense pensions to a million or so quite arbitrarily selected men and women? The British wage-earners will not need to become conscious socialists in order that, in due course, the progressive abolition of such anomalies will seem to them to be the obvious thing to do. (Indeed, the thing may well be done, in part, by the pressure of wage-earning members of the Conservative Party.) No doubt the British people, in its good sense and sangfroid, will take its own time about all this. No one is likely in the second half of the twentieth century to underestimate the disastrous effects of attempting to push through social reorganisation before men's hearts and minds are prepared for it. We see that those consequences are as appalling as are the consequences which flow from a rigid refusal to reorganise society when the time *is* ripe; and one cannot say more than that.

This task of pressing on steadily with the process of making our country into a classless society of genuinely equal opportunity is an immensely difficult one: for that very reason it should occupy much of our national energies in our post-imperial period. This is a social purpose for which the British people will be sure, in due course, to use the democratic institutions they have developed.

Another national purpose will be the perfection of these democratic political institutions. Nor is this a small nor an easy matter. Contemporary democracy, based on effective universal suffrage, is a far more precious, but also a far more precarious, achievement than is usually realised. Hard experience shows that unless a people can itself ensure by its own self-rule that its productive resources are devoted to raising the general welfare, they will not be so devoted. Much of them will be diverted, on the contrary, to the enrichment of a narrow class or to other purposes. Nobody else will look after the mass of the population if that population proves incapable of looking after itself. Again, an effectively functioning democratic system is likely to prove in the twentieth century the only way in which the peoples of complex communities can conduct their national life, and adjust their differences, without tearing themselves to pieces. In this field Britain undoubtedly possesses advantages. British democracy, although crude and ineffective in the extreme by any ideal standard, probably works better than any other which has yet been devised.

Moreover, in perfecting and using the mechanism of her own democracy Britain can provide an immensely valuable example to the world. For that matter, British democracy already *is* serving as a model for large parts of the world. This too has become possible because of the unique British achievement of acquiescing in the dissolution of her empire by a process far less violent and more voluntary than any comparable process hitherto known to history. If each of her former colonies had had to detach itself from Britain by means of armed conflict there would have been no possibility of their adopting British institutions in general and parliamentary democracy in particular. But, as it is, and even in such cases as India, in which the winning of independence has been neither a smooth nor an easy process, enough respect for British political institutions has been both generated and preserved to allow them at least the possibility of taking root in the soil of the newly independent nation.

For example, it is a remarkable experience for a British Member of Parliament to visit the Lok Sabba, the Federal Parliament of the Indian Union, when that sovereign body of nearly 400 million human beings —far and away the largest aggregation of human beings that has ever attempted to rule itself through representative institutions—is in session. If he enters it at "question time", in particular, the mixture of familiarity and difference, as compared with his own House at Westminister, is positively eerie. The order paper which he is handed, the questions, and the supplementary questions, which he hears Honourable Members asking, and the answers which he hears the Ministers giving, at present predominantly in English, are almost identical in form with those of Westminster. And yet this Parliament is dealing with the very different problems of an undeveloped, tropical sub-continent. Moreover, that sub-continent was for 200 years, and until only yesterday, the politically impotent colony of Westminster.

We have noted, in the previous part of this volume, some of the grimmer results of the rule of India by Britain. And yet, in spite of everything: in spite of the pillage of Bengal in the seventeen-seventies, over which indeed oblivion may by now have fallen: but in spite also of the often bitter, personal memories of their struggle with Britain carried by almost every one of the leaders of present-day India, the central British institution of parliamentary democracy is at the moment finding in India by far the most ambitious application which it has yet had in history. This must mean, not only that "the regenerative role" of the nineteenth-century period of arbitrary British rule was not unsuccessful; it must mean, that, in the nick of time, in the last twenty-five years of British rule, parliamentary institutions into which the flood of Indian independence could pour itself, had been established.

India is only the most striking instance of a world-wide development.

For more than a century parliaments have sat in the old dominions. And in the last twelve years of "dis-imperialism" new parliaments have positively proliferated in former British colonies. When in 1950 the rebuilt House of Commons was opened at Westminster, no part of the proceedings could, I thought, compare in impressiveness with the procession of African, Asian, Australian and Canadian Speakers, Lord Chief Justices and Prime Ministers. Here, in those white, brown, and black faces, was animate evidence that the retreating British Raj had left, scattered across the continents, a whole series of parliaments, each struggling with the problems of human government as conducted by methods more civilised than the simple fiats of dictatorship. Some of course of these new democracies will fail: some have failed already. And nothing is worse than to attempt to continue with "a pseudo-democracy", in a country which is evidently below the level of development which makes a democratic system possible. Nevertheless as economic and social development has its effect some form of the democratic process will become the most important single political institution for such states. Here was proof that, in spite of everything, British rule had had enough positive features and, above all, had known well enough how to make an end of itself, to cause its former subjects to wish to imitate instead of to spurn the institutions of their former masters. If this is not national greatness, what is?

Perfecting our democracy, both for our own sake and for the sake of the example which we can give the world, is an immensely important national purpose. But we shall not carry it very far unless we link with it another purpose which both we, and the other relatively affluent societies at present neglect most scandalously. I refer to education in the very broadest sense of the term. For it is obvious that only a population at a very much higher level of general education than has yet anywhere been achieved, will be able to solve the increasingly complex problems of self-rule with which advanced communities will be confronted. Only an educated democracy will survive.

Once the question of education is envisaged in quantitative terms, it becomes clear that none of the affluent or semi-affluent non-communist societies have yet begun to take education seriously. We in Britain, for example, are estimated to be spending (in 1958) between 3% and 4% of our gross national product upon education. This compares with some 10% to 15% on new investment in physical capital resources and some 8% on defence. This raises the issue of whether

further resources could be spared for the three taken together, either
from taking up the slack in the economy (in 1958 quite considerable),
or from the consumption of the richer part of the population. But
apart from this larger question, the *allocation* of resources as between
net investment, defence and education is certainly grossly irrational.
Say, for the sake of argument that resources equalling 1% of the gross
national product could be taken either from slack or from the consumption of the better-off, 1% from net investment and 1% from
defence, and that these released resources could then be devoted to
education. This would nearly double our present educational expenditure. No doubt the educationalists would tell us that it could not be
done in under something like ten years, in order to make the transfer
of resources practicable. Again, only educationalists could even sketch
for us the immense programme of educational expansion which such
a transfer of resources would imply, at every level of the educational
system, primary, secondary and university. But what the layman can
do is to envisage the gains which the community might obtain by
taking education seriously in the specific sense of devoting to it a
proportion of our gross national product comparable to that which we
devote to defence, and much less than that which we devote to net
physical investment.

The starvation of education has become irrational and inefficient,
even on the strictly utilitarian grounds of increasing our material
welfare at the highest possible rate. We are already reaping the rewards
of our folly. One clear advantage of the highly central Russian
economy (offsetting some of its obvious and important disadvantages)
is that a really adequate proportion of the national resources can be set
aside for the training of men and women who will, in turn, rapidly
increase those productive resources. The far less affluent Russian society
is, in the nineteen-fifties, turning out more university-trained engineers
than the whole of the West put together. The criterion of profitability
will not, if it is left to itself, win us any economic contests with societies
which work on different principles.

Nevertheless, neither the urge to increase our already considerable
material well-being, nor the desire to keep ahead of the Russians, is a
sufficiently inspiring ideal to cause us to begin to take education
seriously. The only thing which really is inspiring is precisely education
for its own sake; education in the widest sense of the development of
men and women to the maximum extent of which they are inherently
capable. This is surely an absolute good.

The distinction between an expansion of education which took as its purpose the subsequent expansion of national production at the maximum possible rate, and education for the sake of the development of the human being as such, may be thought of as corresponding to some extent at least with the distinction between an emphasis upon the exact sciences and what are generally called "the arts". In Britain at the moment an effort is being made to expand our output of exact scientists and technicians. From a bread-and-butter point of view, no money could be better invested. Nevertheless, it would be a thousand pities if the British higher educational system, which was largely stuck for several centuries in the mediaevalism of teaching a couple of dead languages, now went to the other extreme and swung over to an equally lopsided concentration upon the exact sciences. After all, man's battle for command over his *natural* environment is clearly going to be won. What is in doubt is the result of the battle for command over his *social* environment. We can live well enough with the forces of nature, even at our present level of technique. It is each other that we cannot live with: unless we find out how to manage our societies and their relations with each other a little better, at least, than we do at present, we face, as we all now know, extinction.

In sheer self-preservation we should concentrate on the so-called inexact, the social sciences: on political economy, sociology, psychology, political theory, history. As yet educationalists of both schools appear to neglect this, I should have thought, sufficiently obvious proposition. The scientists, it is hardly too much to say, know nothing except science in its narrower sense and at heart do not believe that there is any other kind of knowledge (except perhaps music). Hence their remarkably naïve pronouncements when they comment on social, economic or political phenomena. And the humanists, it is hardly more of an exaggeration to say, know nothing but Latin and Greek: and they do not, at heart, believe that there is any other worthy object of study but the culture of the ancient civilisations taught in their defunct vernaculars.

The history of Greek and Roman civilisation is indeed one of the most fascinating and illuminating social studies imaginable. We can learn as much about our contemporary problems from reading *The Peloponnesian War* and *The Republic* as any two other books in the world. But the attempt to make the non-specialist student read them in Greek has been, for several centuries, an almost perfectly effective bar to their comprehension. Even for that minority of students who acquired the linguistic aptitude necessary, it prevented real comprehension, for the simple reason that it left no time to read the equally important texts of the modern world—to read Newton's *Principia*,[1] *The Origin of Species, Capital, The General Theory* and *The Study of History*, for instance, without the comparison of which Thucydides and Plato are robbed of nine-tenths of their meaning. (Compare the fantastic fact that Plato was taught in our universities for several centuries [until the commentaries of Crossman and Popper, indeed] without anyone pointing out that *The Republic* [in its political aspect] was a blue-print, drawn out of its author's social despair, for what we now call a totalitarian society.) It will not be until the humanists have shaken off the ludicrous mediaevalism of attempting to teach their subject in Latin and Greek that they will be in a position to offer a viable alternative to a narrowly scientific and technical predominance in our education. In recent decades a beginning has been made at Oxford to overcome this dreadful situation by the institution of "Modern Greats": but it is only a beginning and, surely, by no means a satisfactory one as yet.

The cumulative improvement of our social and political institutions and of our educational system are merely examples of the kind of things to which a post-imperial society can and must devote some of its energies. There are plenty more: but it would be out of place to do more than mention some of them here. There is the whole field of aesthetics: nor is this a question outside of public affairs. It is very much a responsibility of contemporary government to use (a tiny) part of the social surplus for the patronage of the arts, as we have now begun very tentatively to do in Britain. For unless material resources are made available in this way, there can be little aesthetic achievement in such societies as ours: with them there may be. We must not expect greater certainty in this field than that. Again, there are an ever-increasing number of men and women who feel passionately about the development and preservation of the physical beauty of our country and our cities. And that is no small task.

Such national objectives as these will seem more satisfying to some people than to others. It may be objected that there is an implication about them all that we should try to become a nation of highbrows, scientists, scholars, dons, writers, artists. That, of course, would be as undesirable as it would be impossible. Nevertheless, a change in the relative esteem in which achievement in different spheres of life is held,

[1] And to acquire the very considerable mathematical equipment needed to do so as a good, hard, solid bit of "mental gymnastics".

is now overdue in Britain. This is an important matter, since it is becoming increasingly clear that the relative esteem in which achievement in, for example, politics, business, science or the arts is held, is as effective an incentive to that achievement as financial reward. A revision of the scale of esteem in which, say, an eminent financier, admiral or administrator on the one hand, and an eminent scientist, economist, painter or musician on the other, is held in Britain, is now imperative. If Britain is to be as great in the future as she has been in the past, we shall have to take the things of the mind and the spirit much more seriously than we have hitherto done. A cheerful philistinism will no longer do.

Again, there is the overriding ideal of the pacification of our conflict-racked world. It is an overriding ideal in the very practical sense that if we fail to pursue it successfully, we shall soon all be dead. Nevertheless, Britain as such can only make a contribution to world pacification: she cannot command it. We may believe that she is especially well placed to act in this field; but she is one nation amongst many.

When all is said and done, the kind of national ideals or objectives considered above will hardly, by themselves, fire the spirit of the British people. The abolition of unearned income would be an epoch-making thing: but it can only come about (beneficently) over many decades: education on a quite new scale might transform our society: but again only in a new generation: the arts are, perhaps, the highest things in life; but we cannot command them. Peace is a prerequisite of life: but we can only contribute to its preservation. Moreover all these things, except the last, are merely ways of perfecting our own insular society. To some temperaments this will seem an adequately inspiring ideal: but to others such an ideal will seem too stay-at-home, too self-regarding, too smug. Such temperaments will feel undiminished the old, deep, British instinct to go out into the world to seek both their material and their spiritual fortunes.

It is by lifting our eyes and looking outwards upon the whole world that we shall find an ideal high enough, difficult enough of attainment, and therefore inspiring enough, to fire the national imagination. The highest mission of Britain in our day is to help the under-developed world. It is a mission that cannot be fulfilled by means of government-sponsored loans and grants alone: though these are its necessary foundation. It must be fulfilled also by individual men and women going out themselves into the struggling, surging four-fifths of the world which are to-day in the throes of "the great awakening". In doing so they will be building upon, though at the same time transforming, one of our deepest national traditions. For interlaced with all the worst of imperialism, there has always been a genuinely self-sacrificing—a missionary—spirit in the men who have put the stamp of Britain (for good and ill) upon so much of the world. In the imperialist form which it has hitherto mainly taken there is no room at all left for that spirit. But so long as it is given a new social form, and pursued in a new way, this adventurous, hardy, often self-sacrificing as well as self-regarding, impulse should in our day find far more scope than ever before. The greater part of the world is entering a far more dynamic period than it has ever yet known; it is plunging into the cataracts of the industrial revolution. Such a world will have more need than ever before for men and women of the British nation who will go out into it and there apply their skills and experience for the benefit both of the peoples of the world and of themselves. Only they must find a new frame of reference, in place of the imperial one, within which to act. Above all they must achieve a new attitude of mind in regard to the peoples with whom they will work. They need not pretend, indeed, to an impossible altruism: we cannot become a nation of international "do good-ers". But neither must we be even tainted with what are now insufferable pretensions of national or, far worse still, racial superiority.

And here, it must be admitted, we are undeniably handicapped by our imperial past. As compared, for example, with many Americans (from the Northern states at least), we are apt to be definitely inferior in the simplicity, the directness, and, for that matter, in the common humanity, of our approach to men and women of other races. Especially in the culminating phases of our empire, during the first half of the twentieth century, the nauseating ideology of racial intolerance made inroads into the British national psychology. Now that we have lost our empire such attitudes have become ludicrous without ceasing to be vile. We need not pretend to be at the same stage of development as the more primitive peoples of the world. But we must never claim that the higher stage of development which historical opportunity has enabled us to reach has the slightest connection with any ascertainable innate superiority. The truth is that the highly developed peoples *are* the highly developed peoples: that and nothing more. If, however, we rid ourselves of what are now pathetically inappropriate imperialist attitudes, we shall be in a position to perform indispensable services for the undeveloped peoples. They will be willing to pay us well for our expertise. But what they will not suffer a moment longer is an attempt either to rule them or to despise them.

To abstain from imperialism is not enough. To turn our backs in well-fed indifference upon the hundreds of millions of striving and suffering men and women whom we once ruled would be as great a crime as to try to continue ruling them against their will. The opposite of imperialism is not isolation in a Little England, prosperous, tidy, smug. If we wish to be as great in the future as in the past, we must work and serve wherever we once ruled and—sometimes—robbed.

It is a question of developing in action a genuine sense of human solidarity with peoples in a very different stage of development from our own. It has not yet been done. In our own day we have seen some degree of actual solidarity grow up between the different social classes within our own country and within the countries of the highly developed West. Inadequately, uncertainly, clumsily, but yet already with highly significant social consequences, we have begun to override deeply entrenched privileges and interests, and deeply ingrained intellectual prejudices, in order to care for all the people of our communities. No such advance in elementary human solidarity can be recorded upon a world-wide scale. The ex-imperial powers have let or are letting their subject peoples go—sometimes with a good grace, sometimes with a very bad grace. But they have hardly yet begun to do more than talk about the next, far more difficult, but equally indispensable task, of turning back towards their former subjects and extending to them the hand of true aid and friendship.

It seems to me that this is above all the field in which Britain is called upon to lead the world. For she has succeeded, at the end of her period of empire, in creating an institution which gives promise at least of providing the necessary institutional and emotional links by means of which Britain may fulfil her destiny. That institution is the Commonwealth. I call the Commonwealth a promise rather than an achievement advisedly: for it would be rash and premature in the extreme to claim that this extraordinary institution has yet taken firm root in the world. Nevertheless, if it *can* be firmly planted: if it can be nurtured by all its members, if it grows and thrives, then it may provide precisely the means by which Britain can creatively concern herself with those vast parts of the under-developed world with which she has been long associated. The next two chapters are devoted to the question of the Commonwealth: for it is by means of this daring experiment in the relations between a whole group of very different nations that

Britain may add to the indispensable, but yet in a sense limited, tasks of internal improvement, just that higher, less self-seeking, national ideal, which, as it seems to me, she will especially need.

To sum up this section of the argument. It cannot be denied that the dissolution of her empire has, to some degree, affected the spirit of the British people. Yet once the new type of opportunities opening before Britain both at home and abroad are realised, there should be no question of that fatal droop in the national spirit which has been the fate of many peoples who have lost their empires. It is precisely in its post-imperial period that a people can best show its creative powers. There is nothing original about an empire. Conquest has been, since the dawn of civilisation, the monotonously repeated exploit of all vigorous peoples. Our empire, we like to think, was, on balance, less oppressive and more beneficent than the others. But that is the most that can be said for it. It is now and to-morrow, in our post-imperial period, that the British people can really show what they are made of. It is now, if ever, that the British people can make a name for themselves which will be remembered when their empire, along with all the other empires, is only a name in a list which the bored student will have to memorise. But for that we have to develop a capacity to conceive of national greatness in terms less primitive than those of physical conquest and exploitation. We have to realise, as we have hardly done as yet, that the things of the mind and the spirit are not, after all, mere fads of a few intellectuals but may actually make or mar the national fortunes.

It will be by serving the peoples of the world that we can be great. We can serve them by a sustained effort to provide them with both the material means and the technical skills which they so desperately need. This is perhaps the highest, most aspiring ideal which we can set before ourselves. But it is in no conflict with the ideal of continually improving and perfecting our own society. On the contrary we can also help the world by the example of a successfully functioning, progressing, self-adapting, society as much as by direct aid. Therefore it would be wrong to place the two kinds of national ideal in opposition to each other. As the necessary complement of our direct help to the undeveloped world, we must strive with all our power and skill to make our own island a better and better place. What is now demanded of us by history is in some respects no more than a return to an older national ideal. The imperial fever lasted in Britain less than three centuries in all.

Before ever there was a British empire, our greatest poets expressed their love of country in a way which was almost the opposite of imperial. True, their patriotism was always ready to be martial if need be, but it was inspired by the beauty and grace of our country rather than by its power. Moreover there was something about the geographical fact of being an island which stirred in them a peculiar intensity of emotion. Seeley, writing nearly a hundred years ago on the expansion of England, foresaw the day on which that expansion would be over and he quotes the line from Shakespeare's *Cymbeline*, calling our island. ". . . In a great pool, a swan's nest." The symbols of beauty, grace and peace magically invoked in those seven words will prove more enduring than all the symbols of empire.

CHAPTER XVII

THE COMMONWEALTH

Preceding chapters have been based on the assumption that the British people are conscious of the dissolution of the empire. But this assumption may be only partially true. If the empire was acquired in Seeley's fit of absence of mind, it is being relinquished with half averted attention. And this is no bad thing: the national assent could, perhaps, not have been obtained if the process of relinquishment had ever been consciously realised for what it was. The thing could only happen because, on the one hand, it happened piecemeal, and on the other because of a factor which we have not yet considered. To a very considerable extent the whole process has been seen not as the dissolution of the empire but as its transformation into the Commonwealth. But what is "the Commonwealth"?

The first thing to say about the Commonwealth is that it is not the empire under another name, as some conservative opinion has tended to assume. It is instructive to follow in this connection the various changes in the nomenclature used, both in official documents and in the press, during the immediately post-1945 years. At first the old term "The British Empire" was still widely used. For a time this was replaced by "The British Commonwealth". But then it was discovered that this phrase also was not popular outside the United Kingdom. To whom did the Commonwealth belong, after all? What right had Britain to assert possession of it in its very title? Accordingly the word "British" has been dropped and the term almost universally used is now simply "The Commonwealth". Naturally, if these terminological changes had been the only ones, they would have gone far to confirm the views of any other body of opinion which loudly asserts that the Commonwealth is simply a new and hypocritical name for the British Empire. For this (as we noted in the case of Mr R. P. Dutt) is the emphatic contention of communist or near communist spokesmen.

At the cost of flatly contradicting this coalition of the right and the extreme left, it must be asserted that experience has now demonstrated that both the above views are false. When a people, the Indians, the people of Ghana, or another, become independent within the Commonwealth they in fact gain either immediately or within a relatively short period, the power to control their own destinies, to the extent at least to which any but the most powerful or fortunate peoples can hope to do so on this increasingly inter-dependent planet. The old imperial relationship, of which the substance was that the fate of such peoples was decided at Westminster, is ended. Therefore both the assertions of the communists and the hopes, usually unspoken, of British imperialists of the old school, that nothing would be changed, have proved ill-founded.

The second thing to say about the Commonwealth is that just because it is not the empire under another name; just because it is attempting to become an association of genuinely free nations (which is almost the logical opposite of an empire) it is one of the most imaginative and fascinating enterprises in history.

We have said advisedly, however, that the Commonwealth is attempting to become, rather than that it actually is, an association of free peoples. For when we come to examine the actual links which bind the Commonwealth we shall not find them easy to describe or to define. Indeed, the sceptic may ask, what links could possibly hold together peoples so geographically, racially and economically disparate as these? What is it that these peoples have in common, except the one historical fact that at one time they have all been ruled from Westminster? Has that one fact caused the Bengali and the French Canadian: the cultivated West Indian descendant of slaves kidnapped from West Africa and the entrenched Australian Trade Unionist: the sons of Chinese indentured labourers brought to Malaya and the sons of Boer commandos who fought at Ladysmith: the cocoa-growing peasant of Ghana and the New Zealand sheep farmer: the pious Buddhist of Ceylon and the Coventry shop steward—all to possess qualities in respect of which they are profoundly akin to each other and different from the rest of the world?

On examination, however, it will be found that this is not a mere rhetorical question, expecting an answer in the negative. Certain effects, hitherto at least indelible, have actually resulted from British rule. The peoples which have passed through this experience *have* something in common. That something ranges all the way from an addiction to cricket to a capacity for parliamentarianism. (And these are important things. To know a no-ball from a googly, and a point of order from a supplementary question, are genuinely to have something in common.) Nevertheless, can it really be contended that such stigmata of British rule as these are sufficient to enable a coherent association of nations voluntarily to arise out of the materials which once formed the British empire? Is it not fantastic to suppose that this extreme diversity of peoples, who were once held together by British power, will wish to form and to maintain an especially close association with each other?

The supposition may prove fantastic; history may decide against the Commonwealth. Yet the mere fact that such a voluntary association is even a possibility: more, that, up till now at least, it has actually come into existence, in respect of the great majority of the former British possessions, is evidence that British rule really did have many of those positive features on which we like to plume ourselves. If the empire had been merely tyranny and exploitation, it is inconceivable that the Commonwealth attempt could ever have been made. In that case our former colonies, as soon as they had become independent, would have wished to associate themselves with any other nation rather than Britain. If their and our statesmanship can build a voluntarily cohering association of nations out of the materials which once formed an empire it will be a feat unparalleled.

What, then, can we point to as characteristic of members of the Commonwealth, differentiating them from other states? There are certain things. In the first place, the Commonwealth nations have essentially similar political structures. They are nearly all, in form at least, parliamentary democracies built broadly upon the original British model.[1] They possess, that is to say, sovereign parliaments elected in most cases by adult suffrage,[2] to which prime ministers and their cabinets are responsible, and of which they are members. They possess also similar party systems, and for that matter similar parliamentary procedure. They possess independent judiciaries, and last, but not least, professional, powerful civil servants, hierarchically organised, who do not come and go with changes in governments. Now this particular political structure has its advantages and disadvantages. But it is certainly striking to find it reproduced, almost unchanged, in countries as different in every other respect as India and New Zealand, Ghana and the United Kingdom. Mr Patrick Gordon Walker, M.P. (an ex-Secretary of State for Commonwealth Affairs) in his contribution entitled *Policy for the Commonwealth* to *Fabian International Essays*

---

[1] Pakistan is now (1959) a military dictatorship: but we may hope that this will not last. Again some members of the Commonwealth (Canada, India, Australia) are of course Federal structures resembling in this respect the United States rather than Britain. But as I have maintained elsewhere these differences between democracies, *i.e.*, Federal or unitary, parliamentary or presidential, republican or monarchic, though important at one level of discussion, are not particularly significant for our present purposes. It would be political pedantry to put much emphasis upon them.

[2] South Africa is, of course, here the great exception, since she excludes the vast majority of her people from the franchise.

(Hogarth Press, 1957) describes the effect of this near identity of political structure as between the Commonwealth nations. He writes that "it produces in every Commonwealth country 'natural opposite numbers' in a way that is unknown outside the Commonwealth. All Commonwealth Prime Ministers are the same sort of constitutional creature: they have identical status, rights and duties in their own countries, and they conceive of Parliament and Cabinet in similar terms. The same thing is true of other Ministers, of civil servants, members of the opposition, judges, lawyers, generals. Commonwealth countries can always meet on the same level and their representatives at all levels speak the same political language." (Mr Gordon Walker's essay should in general be consulted both for its broad similarity of approach to that attempted here, and for certain interesting differences.)

This near identity of political structure as between the Commonwealth nations, amidst their extreme diversity in every other respect, is the imprint of Britain upon them. Mr Gordon Walker writes of the Commonwealth being "the product of British Imperialism—or rather of the propensity of British Imperialism to transform itself into its opposite". In this highly dialectical concept he makes the best description of this extraordinary historical development.

The second respect in which the members of the Commonwealth have something in common relates to what they do, rather than to what they are. Members of the Commonwealth do two things in common: they meet in periodic conferences of either Prime Ministers or Ministers of Finance. And they exchange state papers. Of these two links the second is potentially much the more important. This exchange of state papers is at present very incomplete. But let no one underestimate the degree of solidarity and intimacy which would grow up between governments which invariably let each other see all their state papers, including their Cabinet minutes. They could have no permanent secrets from each other. They could hardly act without all-round prior consultation. Such a system of invariable and all-inclusive consultation would, in fact, amount to much more than an alliance (allies are habitually far less intimate with each other). Thus this simple and largely unnoticed act of the exchange of state papers would constitute a very close Commonwealth link.

The matter must be put in the conditional mood, however, for, so far, the Commonwealth system for the exchange of information is by no means complete either in respect of the papers circulated, or in respect of the Commonwealth governments included in the circulation lists. Some papers are not circulated at all, others have a restricted circulation. Perhaps this is inevitable in the present state of the Commonwealth, when the relations between some members are at least as bad as those between foreign countries (*i.e.*, India and Pakistan), and when new and quite inexperienced governments are steadily being added to membership. Nevertheless, if the Commonwealth is in fact to grow into a fully effective association, the growth and standardisation of the practice of the exchange of papers must occur. This would be both the cause and the effect of a growth of confidence and intimacy between the member governments: it would be the very basis of a a system of uninterrupted consultation which, if it could be developed, would do more than anything else to make the Commonwealth into an effective force in world affairs.

At present (1959), however, no fully effective system of Commonwealth consultation has been evolved. Indeed, the British Government's action in the Suez episode in the autumn of 1956 represented the worst example of a breakdown in Commonwealth consultation which has yet occurred. For the British Government acted, not only without informing important Commonwealth governments (Canada and India), but, it is impossible to avoid concluding, without informing them precisely because it knew that they would not agree. For the plea that the British Government had no time to inform the Commonwealth comes perilously near the implication that the British Government had no time for the Commonwealth. The result was that the Commonwealth, in the words of the Canadian Prime Minister of the day, "was subjected to great strain". Nevertheless, the forecast may be hazarded that precisely because the Commonwealth connection did— by however narrow a margin—stand the strain to which it was subjected in 1956, the prospects of its endurance and development may actually have improved.[1] Indeed, Mr Nehru's firm refusal in the face of much hostile domestic opinion to leave it in 1956 may come to be seen as a turning-point in Commonwealth development. For what may be seen as so significant in that refusal was that Mr Nehru, and the Indian Government, evidently saw that they were by no means faced

[1] This argument is, of course, analogous to Sir Anthony Eden's contention that his invasion of Egypt strengthened the United Nations by forcing it to turn him out again with an international force. In both cases this is the plea of the transgressor that he has really done good by "proving" and testing the forces of law and order. As a matter of fact, there may be something in the argument—only the transgressor does not usually get much credit for the entirely unintended good that may have resulted from his transgression.

with the choice of either agreeing with Britain or leaving the Commonwealth. They saw that a third and preferable course remained open to them. They could remain in the association but at the same time express—as they certainly did—dissent from the British action in the most unequivocal terms. Moreover, Mr Nehru and his colleagues found that other powerful members of the Commonwealth, including above all, Canada, were on their side and not on Britain's. Therefore what was tested out by the experience of 1956 was the assertion, undoubtedly true in theory, but not fully realised or accepted in practice, that Britain could not unilaterally control Commonwealth policy. The events of 1956 proved once and for all that the second change in nomenclature, from "British Commonwealth" to "Commonwealth", had also been no empty form, but had expressed the reality that Britain was becoming simply one member of an association of genuinely equal nations.

All those in Britain who in their hearts suppose that the Commonwealth is "really" only the old British empire under another name are, after 1956, visibly and audibly finding this development very hard to endure. But all those who believe most strongly in the Commonwealth and its future will wholeheartedly welcome it. For it may prove an immense gain for Britain to be a member of a world-wide, multiracial association of genuinely equal nations: that, indeed, would be the highest possible reward which she could win for her unique good sense in making possible the peaceful dissolution of her old empire. For the alternative to such membership of an association of equals is the quite tolerable, indeed, in some ways advantageous, but rather unadventurous role of a medium-sized European industrial nation, like West Germany for instance, without particular connections or responsibilities in the outside world. That, and not, as our lingering imperialists suppose, some impossible return to imperial "greatness", is the alternative to the evolution of a Commonwealth of equals.

We must now look more closely into the origins of this extraordinary entity, the Commonwealth, shot through and through with anomalies and contradictions, but yet indubitably living and growing. Hitherto we have written of the Commonwealth as a creation of the last fourteen years since 1945. And so in essence it is. For before 1945 much the greater part of its peoples were still ruled arbitrarily from Whitehall, so that, whatever name it was given, the association was, in fact, predominantly an empire. Nevertheless it is equally true that the present attempt to develop a true Commonwealth could never have been made if there had not been, within the old empire, a nucleus of nations between which genuinely free relations had already been firmly established. These were "the Old Dominions", as they were then often called, essentially Canada, Australia, New Zealand and, after 1909, South Africa. The first three were characterised by the fact that their evolution towards self-government had begun over 100 years before 1945, with the Durham Report upon Canada. By 1945 there existed, then, a Commonwealth within the empire. That was the model which made it possible to imagine the continuance of the connection, if and when the great colonies, with populations not of European descent, in Asia and Africa, became self-governing and independent. The effort of imagination required of both the British and their former subject peoples of Asian or African descent was to see that there was nothing but race prejudice to prevent an evolution in the relationships of British Asia and British Africa to Britain, in the twentieth century, similar to the evolution in the relationship between Canada, New Zealand and Australia to Britain in the nineteenth century. The attempt to build such relationships is the attempt to build the Commonwealth. Therefore we must feel deeply indebted to those Whig and Liberal statesmen of the last century, from "Radical Jack" Durham onwards, who, by their gradual discovery or adoption of the Dominion status concept, provided the indispensable model.

At the other end of the scale of political development from the old-established self-governing Dominions, there remain fairly considerable colonies, still governed more or less arbitrarily from Westminster, as a sort of imperial vestige within the Commonwealth. They are a steadily shrinking factor, as colony after colony becomes independent. But some at least are likely to remain more or less dependent upon Britain for some time; for some of them contain peoples at a very early stage of development. Such peoples must remain incapable, for some time to come, of forming a state or nation in the contemporary sense of those terms. It is impossible to generalise about these remaining colonies. Some, like Malta, are very small, although highly civilised. Some are very large, but containing genuine primitives, like the East African colonies. Some are free from, and some, like Kenya, are by no means free from, the tragic complication of the existence within them of white settlers and, in some cases, of a third group of Asian settlers as well as their native inhabitants.

The fact that the old empire, forcibly maintained and governed by Britain, has already passed away, as to nearly nine-tenths of its inhabitants, does not mean that we can hastily apply self-government to each and all of these remaining colonies. Where their peoples have, obviously, some way to travel before they can reach independent nationhood, we must continue to govern them for a time to the best of our ability. Nor must we dodge the implication that we cannot be sure that we shall be able to avoid the repugnant task of putting down rebellions, such as the Mau Mau rebellion in Kenya: rebellions, that is to say, of people who, in our judgment, could not possibly take over the colony and govern it as a going concern. Ghastly as have been some of the methods used in the suppression of the Kenya rebellion, and wholly unjustified as are some of the views and claims of some of the white settlers, nevertheless, I for one, can see no alternative to the decision to repress the Mau Mau movement. The victory of Mau Mau could not have been permitted, since, far from even pointing in the direction of the progress and well-being of the African peoples, it was unmistakably regressive and atavistic.

Again, although for quite different reasons, I have always taken, and still take, the view that we were justified in refusing to allow the predominantly Chinese Malayan communist party forcibly to capture the government of Malaya, which it would almost certainly have done if we had not exerted a very considerable degree of force against it. I have never seen any reason why 4,000 or 5,000 militant Chinese communists had any more right to govern the Malay Peninsula than we had. The only people who have that right are the Malays themselves, together with such of the Chinese and Indian immigrants as have thrown in their lot with the country of their adoption. And this is what is now taking place. British rule in Malaya is coming to an end, but it is not being succeeded by the equally arbitrary rule of a handful of Malayan communists, almost all of whom are Chinese. On the contrary, it is being succeeded by a democratically elected Malayan government.

Thus we must face the fact that in some colonies we must continue to govern for a time. Our rule is imperfect and alien, but in these cases it is the best rule available. We cannot allow it to be replaced either by atavistic tribal movements or by *coups d'états* promoted by tiny communist minorities. No doubt it is only too true that it may be difficult in some cases to distinguish between genuine national movements, ready to take over the government of a former colony with a fair chance at least of carrying on organised and civilised life, on the one hand, and either communist tyrannies or tribal throw-backs on the other. No doubt we may make mistakes and yield too soon and to the wrong forces in some cases, and refuse to yield until too late to genuine national forces in others. We must simply do our best to avoid such errors.

One way in which we may help ourselves is to call freely on the advice of the native leaders of neighbouring parts of the Commonwealth, which have themselves achieved independence or are well on the way to doing so. In one of the most perplexing cases of recent years, that of British Guiana, this advice was sought. Events in British Guiana raised the extremely difficult issue of whether or not it is the duty of democrats to allow the democratic election of non-democratic forces. A communist, or pro-communist, government was elected, quite legally, in this British colony. If the votes of the British Guianaians at this election had been regarded as valid, then, it is probable, this would have been the last time which they would ever have had the opportunity freely to vote. Should, to generalise the issue, anti-democratic parties, such as the communists and fascists, be allowed to take part in the democratic process, the rules of which they have no intention of observing? Or should democrats refuse to allow people still under their rule to vote themselves into a dictatorship? I, for one, knew too little of the real situation in Guiana to form a view of what should have been done there. But I was impressed by the fact that the most prominent leaders of the West Indian colonies, themselves socialists and men of African descent, took the view that the suppression of the communist—or semi-communist—government of British Guiana, in spite of the fact that it had undoubtedly been duly elected, was justified. If the Commonwealth is to grow and flourish, Britain must more and more take into consultation its independent members in dealing with the problems which will inevitably arise in the remaining colonies. For the rest we and the statesmen of the Commonwealth must judge each case on its merits; for there is no alternative.

The most difficult situations of all are likely to arise in those colonies or ex-colonies which contain white settlers and, in some cases, Asian middle classes as well. The principal examples are Kenya and the Central African Federation (Northern and Southern Rhodesia and Nyasaland). The issues here are complicated in the extreme, and bedevilled at every point by the intractable passions of racialism. In Kenya it is true that in 1959, after several years of horror, a gleam of hope is said to be visible. It is credibly reported that the experiences which the colony underwent in the course of the repression of the Mau Mau rebellion were so terrible that they have made at least some of the leaders of the white, brown and black races realise that their only hope is the building of a multi-racial society. And efforts at least in this direction are now being made. The difficulties of creating an effectively functioning democracy out of peoples at so enormously different stages in their development as the white settlers, the Indian traders and the African tribesmen can hardly be exaggerated, however. We can only pray that these difficulties can somehow be surmounted. For what other hope is there for Kenya?

The position in the newly formed Central African Federation may prove even more intractable. There the situation is dominated by the demand of the tiny minority of white settlers and business men for a Federation with an ever greater degree of independence of Britain. But this, of course, is an utterly different matter from the demand of a homogeneous native population for its independence. Indeed, the vast majority of the population of British Central Africa are passionately opposed to the early grant of independence in this sense, since they know that the rule of the local whites is likely to be far more oppressive and race-conscious than that of the Colonial Office. Again, the presence of South Africa to the south and the inclusion in the new Federation of the immensely rich copper belt in the north are complicating factors. In the copper belt imperialist exploitation, in the classical sense that an immensely high proportion of the values being produced is siphoned off from the actual Rhodesian producers, in one way or another, is still going on, as we have noted. In Southern Rhodesia the British Government, having, in my view most unwisely, surrendered far too much of its power into the hands of the local white population, is no longer in a position to control events. But it may be able to assert itself in Northern Rhodesia and Nyasaland before the position becomes intolerable.

At the time of writing, in early 1959, the tensions were coming to a head, particularly in Nyasaland, where conflict with the African Congress Movement had begun. The intolerable prospect of Britain becoming involved in an "Algerian" situation, unless a sharply different approach were made, had loomed over the British political horizon. It will be a supreme tragedy if Britain, after having emerged with such credit from so many of the difficulties involved in the dissolution of the greatest of colonial empires, were to fall at this last fence. In order to avoid disaster for both ourselves and for Central Africa it is, surely, indispensable that we should assert three principles in practice. First, that the majority of the inhabitants of the territory or territories should have the right to choose their own destiny. Second, that precisely in order to preserve that right the British Government must not surrender any power to the present Central African Federation until and unless it is asked to do so by a majority of the African population. Third we must make it clear that if the Federation is to survive and succeed ultimate power must be vested in the hands of a majority of *all* its inhabitants. If we are told that any such democratic system is there impossible, then the Federation is impossible.

Finally, there is South Africa: that large, wealthy, independent and rapidly developing member of the Commonwealth. Her government is now expressly founded upon the doctrine of racial supremacy. Those principles of racial equality which, it is universally conceded, must be the very corner-stone of the Commonwealth if it is to survive, are here systematically repudiated. Moreover, beside the main racial conflict, of which the very purpose is to segregate and dominate the Africans who form the immense majority of the population, there exists also a subsidiary conflict between the white ruling minority and the fairly substantial body of Indians: and, finally, the white minority itself is divided by sharp hostility between those of Dutch and British descent.

The problem of South Africa is not a problem with which the British Government can deal. Nevertheless, South Africa is a member of the Commonwealth and the character of South African society is to that extent unavoidably a Commonwealth problem. It will be intensely interesting to see whether a body of Commonwealth public opinion on such basic matters as racial equality arises, and what effect, if any, such Commonwealth opinion has upon South Africa. So far as Britain is concerned, the correct policy for the British Government is surely to adhere unhesitatingly to the principle of racial equality: to support without reservation the views of non-European members of the Commonwealth on such issues, but not itself to take any initiative hostile to the membership of South Africa in the Commonwealth. If South Africa finds membership of an essentially multi-racial association incompatible with racial policies which she will not abandon that is a matter for her. On this crucial issue the emergence, in 1957, of the first Negro nation, Ghana, as a full member of the Commonwealth can hardly fail to be of decisive importance in the end. South Africa has wisely offered no objection to the admission of Ghana, and no doubt in the immediate future of Nigeria, to the Commonwealth. Yet can we really suppose that the apparition on the world stage of independent

Negro states will ultimately prove compatible, within the same association of nations, with *apartheid* in South Africa? The outcome cannot be exactly foreseen. But it is certain that Britain, if she wishes the Commonwealth to be preserved, must throw all her weight and influence within its councils behind those who stand for genuine racial equality.

Meanwhile, the British Government must concentrate upon solving its own Commonwealth problems. For we simply cannot afford, if the Commonwealth is to survive, any more tragedies and disasters such as that which occurred in Cyprus. No arguments derived from the (in this case largely spurious) claims of military necessity; no complications (real enough though they were in Cyprus) over the position of dissident minorities within the local population, can possibly excuse the return in the matter of Cyprus to an imperialism which was totally out of keeping with everything which we have recently done, and are doing, in the rest of the world. Of two things, one. Either our conduct in Cyprus was utterly wrong, or else what we have done, and are doing, in India, Pakistan, Burma, Ceylon, the Soudan, Ghana, Nigeria, the West Indies, and elsewhere, is an inexcusable betrayal of our imperial position. Both policies cannot be right. And, of course, it is our main policy of attempting to turn the empire into a voluntarily associating Commonwealth that is right, and our conduct in Cyprus that was wrong. It was so wrong that, if it had been persisted in, or if it is indulged in elsewhere, it would and will wreck the whole of the rest of our policies.

This raises the question of Commonwealth defence. It must be admitted that a good deal of portentous nonsense is sometimes talked on this subject. For we should commit a sad mistake if we supposed that the armed forces of each of the Commonwealth governments can be added together as a general Commonwealth force, to be used in a common defence against any outside menace, whether that of Russia, China, or any other. For example, the armed forces of Pakistan and of India are not maintained for the purpose of a combined defence against Russia or China. On the contrary, we must face the unpalatable fact that the armed forces of each of these important members of the Commonwealth are primarily maintained as a defence against the other. In other words, the relations of these two member states are more, not less, hostile to each other than to the rest of the world.

What, then, can be the role and conception of Commonwealth defence? As in the case of the other Commonwealth institutions which we have listed, we must conclude that, for the present at any rate, it must be a modest one. Nevertheless, the leading Commonwealth nations will undoubtedly be wise, in this dangerous world, and until and unless international disarmament can be secured, to maintain the best armed forces which they can reasonably afford. They should do so, not, as is sometimes argued, in order to form a common front against "the communist menace". The part which military power can play in that respect must be fulfilled not by the Commonwealth, but by the nations of the North Atlantic Alliance and their associates. Again, the nations of the Commonwealth differ widely amongst themselves in their attitude to the major communist states, *e.g.*, South Africa's, as compared with India's, attitude to Russia and China. The purpose of adequate Commonwealth armed forces is rather, and simply, to provide against quite unforeseeable emergencies and contingencies which are nevertheless sure to arise. It would go far to dissolve the Commonwealth connection if its member nations became helpless, powerless states unable to defend themselves or each other, and so at the mercy of anyone who made arbitrary demands upon them.

The chief burden of providing armed forces has always hitherto fallen upon Britain because she has been so much the richest of the Commonwealth states. But as Canada, in particular, and later Australia and India develop, this burden should be more equitably shared; indeed it must be if the Commonwealth is to be properly balanced. But again this can be only a matter of gradual evolution.

This brief survey of the political connection between the members of the Commonwealth, as they exist in the middle of the twentieth century, may well seem depressing to enthusiastic supporters of the Commonwealth who have never clearly envisaged what it is that they are being enthusiastic about. Nevertheless, it is important that these limitations in the Commonwealth as it exists to-day should be brought into our full consciousness. For, if they are not, we may attempt to make the Commonwealth play roles of which it is incapable. And then the results will be disillusionment and even disaster. But to face the realities of the Commonwealth should certainly not be to despair of its growth and development. The wisest advice on that score which

I have encountered comes from that eminent Indian scholar and public servant, Mr Panikkar. Mr Panikkar, an outstanding champion in India of the maintenance of the Commonwealth connection, when asked what policy we should pursue in order to foster its development, is accustomed to say that the great thing, for the moment, is not to put too great a weight upon the links which hold the Commonwealth together. These links are still but newly forged in many cases, he points out, and could snap if made to carry too much strain. But if no premature moves are made, either to put burdens upon the Commonwealth which it cannot bear, or artificially to articulate it into a more formal organisation—why, then, who knows but that it may grow into a strong and immensely beneficial association?

Such cautious, Whiggish, advice should surely be agreeable to the British tradition of gradual, empirical development. No doubt the Commonwealth is a much less logical and much less ambitious institution than the United Nations. Nevertheless, there may prove to be ample room for both of them in the world. In fact, there will certainly be room for both of them so long as men with such utterly different backgrounds as, for example, Mr Diefenbaker of Canada and Mr Nehru of India, Mr Nkrumah of Ghana and Mr Menzies of Australia, feel that there is. Who knows how the world is to develop? It may be that this extraordinary institution, the Commonwealth, is destined to prove one of the vehicles of its development. It may be that we are only at the very beginning of its potentialities: it may be that nations which never formed part of the old British Empire will wish at some time or another to join it and that they will be admitted.[1] It may be that some of its contradictions and difficulties which now look formidable will solve themselves with the passage of time and the rapid economic and social development upon which almost all its member nations are now embarked.

Finally, there is the simplest reason of all for maintaining, if it can be done, the Commonwealth connection. It is that in the world as it is to-day it would be wrong to disrupt any connection between nations. As Mr Nehru put it in his explanation to America of why he did not leave the Commonwealth over the Suez crisis of 1956, it would be a retrograde step in the present world to break down *any* link which exists between the nations. The degree of co-operation, limited and

[1] This question arose at the end of 1958 over the question of the proposed merger between Ghana and Guinea. Mr Gordon Walker (op. cit.) comes down against this possibility. He considers that to have been a part of the old British Empire must be a condition of Commonwealth membership. I am inclined to think that to possess a political structure similar to the existing Commonwealth model would be a better criterion.

imperfect as it is, which exists between the members of the Commonwealth is, after all, an example of international co-operation. The
periodic conferences, the exchange of State papers, the economic
arrangements (which we shall consider in the next chapter), these
things do all help to break down the absolutism of national sovereignty. And surely we can ill dispense with any institution which does
that. For absolute national sovereignty bids fair to become one of the
Molochs of our epoch. How much inter-Commonwealth co-operation
can accomplish in this respect we do not know. But in this rough
world it may yet prove of immense value to the member nations—to
Canada, to India, to Ghana, to the United Kingdom, or to Australia—
to find themselves standing with the other members of the Commonwealth in some future international emergency.

CHAPTER XVIII

AN ECONOMIC BASIS FOR THE COMMONWEALTH?

THE POLITICAL interconnections of the Commonwealth are undeniably tenuous. For the last fifty years, however, there has existed a school of thought which has sought to create an economic basis, at first for the empire in its old form, and more recently for the Commonwealth. Its adherents have persistently suggested that this should be done by somehow canalising trade into inter-imperial or inter-Commonwealth channels. Moreover something has actually been done in this direction, in the form of the system of imperial preferences which came into existence in the nineteen-thirties.

A presumption of this school of thought in its less sophisticated form is that the economies of the various Commonwealth countries are what is called "complementary" rather than competitive. The relatively undeveloped Commonwealth countries are thought of, that is to say, as producers of food and raw materials, and Britain as a producer of industrial products, so that a "natural" exchange of products between them can occur. The first comment on this reasoning is, surely, that in so far as this picture of the Commonwealth is correct such a natural exchange of products will occur without any need for special arrangements to promote it. Britain will buy Canadian wheat and New Zealand meat because she needs them, and Canada and Australia will continue to buy British manufactures, mainly because they need them for their own development, and also because it will be difficult in the long run to sell to us if they do not buy from us. But any attempt to make either the older, or still more the new, members of the Commonwealth buy British manufactures *exclusively* would be bitterly resented and resisted by them. For they would see in it an attempt to introduce by the back door a shifting of the terms of trade in favour of Britain. Moreover all the members of the Commonwealth are intensely suspicious of any tendency on the part of Britain to assign to them the role of raw material and agricultural producers, while taking to herself the role of the provider of advanced industrial products. For, from historical experience, they are convinced that this would mean their relegation to mere hewers of wood and drawers of water at a far inferior standard of life.

Recent trends in world trade may not suggest that this suspicion is necessarily well founded. After all, there is no inherent reason why those who specialise in the production of food and primary raw materials should exchange their products at a disadvantage with those who specialise in producing machine tools and jet engines. As we saw the people of New Zealand, with their intensive agricultural specialisation, had in 1956 returned the highest per capita income of any country in the world, including the United States. This fact suggests that the matter is much more one of the intelligent organisation of the production and marketing of agricultural and primary products than had been supposed. Nevertheless, it would take the undeveloped peoples decades, if not centuries, to become convinced that agriculture and primary production rather than industrialisation offered the way to wealth. And, of course, they are right in supposing that in the long run industrialisation is the only way to successful and balanced national development, to say nothing of military and economic power. Hence nothing could do more to disrupt the Commonwealth than to attempt to organise its development upon this assumption that its parts are "complementary" to each other, in the sense that some are, and should remain, producers of food and raw materials while the United Kingdom should provide the industrial products.

Thus the fact that the economies of some of the members of the Commonwealth can be said to be complementary to others is very much less important than it appears to be at first sight. For the less-developed, under-industrialised, members of the Commonwealth are each and all determined to change that condition by developing themselves. Moreover, although this seems almost impossible for some minds in Britain to realise, Britain has little to fear and much to gain from that process. It is precisely for the purposes of industrialisation that the whole undeveloped world, within and without the Commonwealth, will need to buy ever-increasing quantities of industrial products from us. True they will be increasingly industrial products of a different kind from those which they bought in the nineteenth century. No one will ever sell appreciable quantities of grey cotton cloth to India again. What India and the undeveloped world as a whole will buy is ever-growing quantities of producers' goods, means of production, capital goods, call them what you will, rather than industrial consumers' goods. But what of that? Such a development is very much to our advantage, for Britain is far better placed to produce this sort of export profitably than she is to attempt to compete in the production of the simpler sort of consumers' goods.

True the Commonwealth members will not buy their capital goods imports exclusively from Britain. For instance, in the nineteen-fifties India is buying each of her four steel mills from America, Germany, Russia and Britain respectively. But then on the other hand, Britain will not sell exclusively to the Commonwealth. She will market her manufactures anywhere she can. She will do so, in particular, in other highly industrialised countries such as Germany and America, as well as in the under-developed world. For it is a common, persistent and disastrous fallacy to suppose that nations even tend to cease to trade with each other as and when they industrialise. Again, some people fear that the undeveloped countries of the Commonwealth, and for that matter outside it, as they industrialise, will have no raw materials or food left to sell to Britain. The answer to this apprehension is that in that case they would be unable to pay for those imports of manufactures without which they could not industrialise themselves. They will find that they have to go on producing a surplus of food and raw materials over and above their own consumption precisely in order to pay for the imports of capital equipment which they must have.[1]

Finally, there is no validity either in the argument that all this may be true for the period during which the undeveloped countries are industrialising themselves, but that when this process is complete they will no longer have any need of British manufactures, and that then, at any rate, Britain will not be able to pay for her imports. This foreboding is based on the fallacy that the process of industrialisation comes to an end after some definite period. This is not so. Industrialisation goes on indefinitely, and, indeed, appears always to accelerate. The most industrialised countries are, that is to say, continuing to industrialise themselves at an ever-increasing speed. Their industrialisation must, of course, include the industrialisation of agriculture, i.e., the application of science to the production of food and raw materials, as well as to manufactures. But so long as this balance is preserved what we call industrialisation is simply the never-ending process of man's assertion of his command over his material environment. There is no fear of it coming to an end and so of the demand for capital goods tapering off.

What remains, then, of all these dire apprehensions as to the effect upon Britain of the industrial development of the Commonwealth, and of the rest of the under-developed world, apprehensions which are probably the underlying motive for all those vast and vague schemes of "Empire Free Trade" and the like, which would unfailingly wreck the

---

[1] And, of course, service the loans which they will have had to contract in order to get capital goods which they cannot pay for on the nail.

Commonwealth if an attempt were ever made to implement them? There is just this grain of truth in them, but no more: countries which do not succeed in maintaining themselves in the forefront of technical progress will not succeed in remaining so well off as those which do. Countries which have only, say, coarse cotton textiles to offer the rest of the world in exchange for the food and raw materials which they want to buy must not expect very favourable terms of trade. But countries which take care to have the latest jet engines, machine tools, terylene, titanium, and atomic piles ready for delivery, are most unlikely to lack for customers who will pay them attractive prices. This is indeed a very important consideration for Britain to keep in mind. But it has only a limited connection with the economic arrangements of the Commonwealth.

Therefore the fact that the Commonwealth consists in both highly developed and in under-developed countries does not really provide any special economic basis for the association. The major under-developed Commonwealth countries, such as India and Nigeria, for instance, will want to buy British machinery and capital goods of all sorts, but only if they are competitive in price and quality with comparable goods obtainable elsewhere. And any attempt to persuade such Commonwealth countries (to say nothing of trying to force them) to buy British when they do not want to, would be quite the shortest road to the break-up of the Commonwealth. Similarly, Britain will want to sell her engineering products, and manufactures generally, to India, Australia and the rest of the Commonwealth. But she will want to sell them to America, to Germany, to China and to Argentina and to the rest of the world as well. There is really very little in the idea of the Commonwealth as an area of complementary economies marked off by tariffs or preferences from the rest of the world.

Such crude schemes as empire Free Trade can thus be refuted by repeating, as has just been done, what is in effect the classical free trade case. Yet this is the very view which, because of its effects upon the undeveloped world, we have criticised so sharply above. We now see that, naturally enough, there is little wrong with the free trade argument when we look at the matter from the point of view of purely self-regarding United Kingdom interests, at any rate in the short run. If we are trying simply and solely to maximise British wealth then the best way to do it will seem to be to let the market forces operate throughout the world unchecked and uncontrolled. For Britain is one of the more highly developed countries and, as we have seen, the market forces will favour such countries and penalise the under-developed countries with deadly efficiency. All interference with the way the market forces work would be almost certainly harmful to United Kingdom interests, narrowly conceived, as nearly all experienced British officials have realised.

But if we look at the matter from the point of view of the development of the world, with which British interests themselves are after all in the long run identified, almost the opposite of all this is true. In this context, as we have seen, the market forces, unchecked and uncontrolled, are certain to prove ruinous. They will ruthlessly give to him that has and take from him that has not. They will do so until in the end (as they did in the great slump of the 'thirties) they have so utterly ruined the have-not nations that their ruin will spread to the rich countries also; for international trade will become so one-sided that it can hardly be carried on. Therefore in the immediate and urgent interest of the world as a whole, and in Britain's own long-term interests too, we cannot uncritically accept the *laisser-faire*, free trade argument. From this point of view the necessity for the dissolution of the imperial relationship arose because that relationship imposed un-regulated market forces upon the under-developed world. But the dissolution of the empires was only the first, negative, step: the second step must be positive. A genuinely fair and constructive relationship between the developed and the undeveloped world must be created, to fill the vacuum left by the end of empire. And in the difficult and complex business of building up this new relationship, the Commonwealth may play an important part.

How, then, ought we to set about fostering Commonwealth trade upon a genuinely fair and mutually beneficial basis? There exists, already, one form of international trading arrangement which, in practice, has a special application to the Commonwealth. Bulk purchase agreements, long-term contracts, and price stabilisation schemes were tried out between, in particular, the United Kingdom and several other Commonwealth countries, both in the war and in the immediately post-1945 years. Under these arrangements the United Kingdom agreed to buy, either directly on government account, or using the existing trading organisations as agents, supplies of, for example, Canadian wheat, Australian meat, New Zealand dairy products, West African fats and West Indian sugar at fixed prices, or at prices which were allowed to vary only within fixed limits, over a term of years.

The attraction for primary producers of such arrangements proved very considerable. The security against the wilder fluctuations in the prices of primary products on the international markets proved ample recompense against the risk of failing to benefit fully in times of high prices. All except one of these arrangements have now been ended by the present (1959) Conservative Government, but that one, on sugar, is still in force and may well prove of high value to the Commonwealth sugar-producers. Logically no doubt there is no reason why the United Kingdom should make such arrangements exclusively with Commonwealth countries. And, in fact, similar arrangements were made with foreign countries, including the Argentine, Denmark, Holland and Poland. As a result of a good deal of personal experience of such arrangements as United Kingdom Minister of Food between 1946 and 1950 I should say, however, that it is often easier to make and to work such contracts with Commonwealth countries. The "identity of political structure" is a real advantage. There is a relative understanding and confidence between Commonwealth members which undoubtedly helps to create the conditions in which intimate economic relations, such as these, can work well. If, then, a means for strengthening the economic ties within the Commonwealth is sought, it may be found in re-creating arrangements of this sort, and not in tariffs or preferences. A secure market at relatively stable prices is the main positive advantage that the United Kingdom can offer the primary producers of the Commonwealth. And it should do so in its own interests, in theirs, and in the interests of the development of the Commonwealth, as a part of the under-developed world.

It is significant in this connection that Professor Myrdal (*An International Economy*) though not writing particularly of the Commonwealth, regards the stabilisation of the prices of the foodstuffs and raw materials exported by the undeveloped world as one of the most important benefits which the advanced nations can confer on them. He points out that the gyrations of these prices play havoc with the planning of any under-developed country which is striving to emerge from economic stagnation. And he concludes that the negotiation of long-term contracts and bulk-buying agreements between them and their customer is one of the best ways of helping them. The political connection of the Commonwealth, loosely-knit as it is, may provide a most useful framework for such arrangements.

Let us next consider the future of that semi-Commonwealth institution, the Sterling Area. The fact that most members of the

Commonwealth (less Canada and, for some purposes, South Africa, but plus Kuwait, Eire and Iceland) at present pool their earnings of gold and dollars, *i.e.*, the sole universally accepted means of international payment, drawing on that pool without close regard to what they, individually, have put into it, is certainly an economic fact of great importance.

In a previous chapter doubt was expressed as to whether this arrangement could continue at least in its present form. For now, one by one, the remaining major dollar-earning colonies are ceasing to be colonies. In particular, in 1957, the two main dollar-earners of the system, Ghana and Malaya, became independent nations. It seems clear that they do not desire to leave the Sterling Area. Nevertheless, it is hard to believe that the arrangement will in future work in quite the same way as before. Moreover, when we look more closely at the Sterling Area, its structure, which at first sight looked relatively simple, is found to be exceedingly complex. It is shot through and through with exceptions, special cases and anomalies. No two members have exactly the same relationship to the Bank of England in which they keep their reserves. Some remaining colonies have, in effect, no separate currencies of their own: their currency notes are backed pound for pound at the Bank of England and are to all intents and purposes British pound notes. Others, such as South Africa, do not even pool the whole of their foreign exchange earnings with the system. Others again, like India, have a vast and highly developed currency system of their own, while they are linked with sterling, and are making full use (as we have noted) of sterling balances in London. Others, again, as we saw in the case of Pakistan at the devaluation of the pound in 1948, do not necessarily even shift the exchange value of their currency and the dollar in step with the British pound.

All this is not to say that the Sterling Area will necessarily dissolve. It has real convenience and advantages for some of its members. Paradoxically enough, however, and exactly contrary to the opinions of those who like Mr Dutt see in the Sterling Area an instrument of continuing British imperialism, it is beginning to look, in 1959, as if its main disadvantages may be experienced by the United Kingdom. It is argued, by Mr Shonfield, for example, that if we reinvested our capital at home instead of exporting a good deal of it to (some) countries of the Sterling Area, our economy would in general be strengthened and in particular our reserves would become less vulnerable. On the other hand, it would be selfish abruptly to dissolve the Sterling Area simply because it was thought to have ceased to serve United

Kingdom interests. What the Sterling Area may become is a group of countries, at various stages of development, which wish to be able, at need, to discriminate collectively against dollar imports or the export of capital to dollar countries. And it may prove useful to have such an association which is a good deal stronger than any of its members taken alone would be. For the fact is that even Britain, though a highly developed country relatively to India or Nigeria, is to some extent at least herself an under-developed country relatively to America. Therefore just as many kinds of interferences and controls are indispensable to India and Nigeria if they wish to trade with Britain without being progressively impoverished by the process, so interferences and controls may be indispensable for Britain if she wishes to trade with America without impoverishment. This may prove a difficult lesson for dominant British opinion to learn, for we have been for so long the stronger in our trade relations, that free trade has become a dogma. Such uncontrolled trade is still very much in our selfish, short-term interests *vis-à-vis* the undeveloped world. But in our trade with America we shall have to learn the lesson that blind obedience to the market forces is not necessarily in the interests of all parties, as we have supposed and preached for so long: it is simply in the interests of the stronger.

These considerations were reinforced, in 1958, by the intention of six European countries to set up a customs union amongst themselves, and to do so in a form which made it difficult if not impossible for Britain to join them. If, of course, trade between these six nations is canalised so that it is increased inter-se and decreased with the rest of the world, then the case for any genuinely mutual arrangements for fostering inter-Commonwealth trade will be reinforced. As the reader will have gathered from preceding sections of this chapter, these pages are written in a spirit of considerable scepticism as to the utility of preferential systems for this purpose. Contrary to much "imperial" opinion, the Commonwealth would almost certainly be disrupted, rather than built up, by any attempt to canalise by increased preferences the trade of its members into inter-Commonwealth channels, thus inevitably impairing the right of members to trade with equal facility with the rest of the world. This is not to say, however, that it would be wise to suggest the dismantling of the existing system of imperial preferences. It is probable, indeed, that if this system had not been established a quarter of a century ago, and was now proposed for the first time by the United Kingdom, the newly emancipated members of the Commonwealth, at least, would be hot against it. They would see in it an attempt to reimpose, by economic means, an imperial bondage from which they had escaped politically. They would not consider the advantage which their products received in the British market as sufficient recompense for the advantage which they were called upon to give British products in their own markets. As, however, the system of inter-Commonwealth preferences is in existence, most Commonwealth statesmen appear to look at the matter quite differently and would deplore and resent any suggestion that they should lose their advantage in the British market. They have evidently not found the advantage which they have to give to British products unduly irksome. And of course, vested interests have been created, on both sides, which would be injured by any change or abolition of the system. Thus it would, unquestionably, be a blow to the Commonwealth, and a disturbance to the existing pattern of trade, if imperial preferences were disturbed.

Nevertheless the future development of the Commonwealth cannot be effectively promoted by such negative means as preferences, tariffs and the like. On the contrary, the Commonwealth can only be built up by the positive action of each of its members, by means of the above-mentioned price stabilisation, long-term contract and bulk-produce arrangements, and by loans, grants, credits and technical assistance: in a word, each member must positively help the development of the others. The prosperity of Britain and the world alike will rest upon such positive action. For what really matters is that both the Commonwealth and the under-developed world as a whole, shall press on with their industrialisation and development generally at a steady, uninterrupted pace. Controls over the market forces there should and must be, but they should be predominantly of a positive type: they should consist above all in the planned purposive investment of capital where it is most needed instead of where it is most profitable, and in the stabilisation of the prices of the products of the primary producers.

The economists now tell us that there is some critical proportion, of the order of 12% net of its gross national product, which a nation must accumulate and invest in order really to "get going" on the tremendous process of industrialisation. If the giant states of Asia with their vast populations, and the less populous but territorially vast states of Africa and Latin America, achieve during the rest of the century some such rate of accumulation as this; if, in general the *circa* 80% of the living generation of mankind who are still at the peasant level of production and consumption, are swung into the industrial revolution, it is hardly too much to say that every other factor in the economic situation of the world will sink into insignificance. It would be rash to pretend that the reactions of so portentous an event as this on the economy of the old industrial centres such as Britain can be accurately foreseen. But there can surely be no doubt that, always on condition that we devote ourselves to producing the industrial specialities which the awakening world will most need, there will be an almost illimitable demand for our products, and for the products of the other industrial centres. This type of consideration sets such schemes as Commonwealth preference and the European common market in perspective. They must be seen and judged by whether or not they contribute to the development of the part of the undeveloped world with which we are associated, and by so doing to world development as a whole. Moreover, it is certain that world development cannot be promoted by a blind attempt to bind the world to a *laisser-faire* dogma of everywhere allowing the market forces free play. Discriminatory devices such as the Sterling Area may have a part to play. The purposive direction of capital export upon government account or under government control certainly will. But whatever the methods used the Commonwealth will grow and flourish economically if the half-dozen existing centres of industrialism succeed in helping the undeveloped world as a whole through the storm and stress which necessarily faces it during its period of primary accumulation. No other consideration compares in importance to this.

The above account of its economic possibilities may seem discouraging to enthusiasts for the Commonwealth ideal. And yet it is indispensable for the sake of that ideal itself that they should face these realities. I yield to none in my enthusiasm for the potentialities for good in the Commonwealth conception so long as tasks which it cannot possibly accomplish are not put upon it. For when we have reviewed all its limitations, the Commonwealth possesses one asset which may prove priceless, precisely for the purpose of world economic development. Professor Myrdal, both in *An International Economy* and in *Economic Theory and Undeveloped Regions*, reiterates that the underlying difficulty which threatens to delay, perhaps fatally, world economic development, is the lack of what he calls "elementary human solidarity" between the peoples of the advanced and the undeveloped nations. We have hardly begun to develop between nations he writes (out of the bitter experience of an international official of the United Nations) even that degree of "human solidarity" which we are learning to create, and to act upon, within each of the advanced industrial nations. When sections of the population of our own nation are in danger of being thrust down into destitution we have, recently, come to their assistance to a greater or lesser extent. We have flouted the market forces. We have broken with the dogma of *laisser faire* and done the less profitable rather than the more profitable thing, in order to sustain and to save "under-privileged" sections of the population or derelict regions of our own countries.

Moreover, through our democratic institutions we have given such threatened sections of the population fairly effective means of insisting that we do come to their assistance. All this is far less true of our rela-tionship with the peoples of the undeveloped world. And this has been above all because they have not had the political power to insist upon their needs being met. In the existing climate of opinion their fate has not really been considered our concern; for they have had no votes in our communities. This last consideration is the decisive one. British, American or West German politicians may be good, humanitarianly minded men, but professionally, as politicians, they cannot go far be-yond what is sanctioned by the state of mind of their peoples. Until and unless their electorates can be made to begin to feel a genuine concern in the matter, democratic politicians of the West cannot concern them-selves about the subsistence standards of a Brazilian or an Indonesian peasant in the same way in which they can, and indeed must, worry about the standard of life of their own people. Until there is the necessary evolution in the opinion of their own countries, they cannot beyond a certain limited degree care for the fates and fortunes of the undeveloped peoples. For if they attempt to do so they will simply cease to represent their electorate and others will replace them. It is the duty of every conscientious democratic politician in the highly developed countries to do everything in his power to change this situation. But he can only do so by using and extending to the utmost every existing element of solidarity between the developed and the undeveloped peoples. Now the Commonwealth is such an element of existing human solidarity: it is something already in people's minds, to a lesser or greater degree: something on which a concern for the still destitute peoples of the world can be built.

Some human solidarity at least is actually felt by the British people for the people of the undeveloped parts of the Commonwealth. For example, it is definitely easier to get the British people to forgo the full advantage of their bargaining position in importing some raw material or foodstuff at the cheapest possible price if the commodity in question comes from Commonwealth sources. (The Commonwealth Sugar Agreement may again be instanced.) Again, it has proved possible to induce the British tax payer to make some sacrifices by way of grants and loans under the Colombo Plan, the Colonial Development Corporation and the Colonial Development and Welfare Fund, largely, I think, because the money is going towards the development of parts of the Commonwealth. None of this is particularly logical. There is no purely logical reason why the British people should be able to feel more of a concern for the welfare of an Indian or a Ghanaian peasant than they do for the welfare of an Indonesian peasant. But the fact is that they do: at least a little more. Even this small beginning of basic human solidarity as between the developed and the undeveloped world is of immense importance. It is above all in this respect that the Commonwealth ideal is precious. It is a bridge across the immense abyss which separates these two worlds. The Commonwealth, precisely because it includes in some undefined zone of human solidarity, nations as disparate in every respect as Canada, Ghana, India and New Zealand, the United Kingdom and Nigeria, should be maintained and developed, if this proves in any way practicable. The Commonwealth is a part of the main: it involves us with mankind.

CHAPTER XIX

NEW EMPIRES FOR OLD?
(I) AN AMERICAN EMPIRE?

THE FABLE TELLS US that the fox who had lost his tail sought to persuade the other animals of the virtues and advantages of taillessness. American, Russian, and perhaps Chinese, readers of these pages may well entertain the suspicion that any contemporary British writer who preaches against imperialism has similar motives to those of the fox.

"What," such readers may remark, "is all this talk about the world entering a post-imperial period? All that has happened is a repetition of the familiar historical process by which the sceptre passes from one hand to another. It is true enough that the British Empire, and for that matter the other European empires have had their day. But why should anyone suppose that the great super-states of the world will forbear to impose their empires upon it? This is the end of a chapter in the book of imperialism, not the end of the book."

It may be so. But we may notice that if the Russians, the Chinese, or the Americans do say things of this kind, they will almost certainly say them under their breaths. No one will come out now in the old forthright way and proclaim that he is out to build an empire for his country. No Russian or Chinese could possibly make any such avowal. For imperialism is one of the worst of all the sins in the communist canon. Nor is an American likely to do so. For in his case, too, imperialism directly contradicts his oldest national tradition, which is one of liberation from British imperial domination. On the other hand, the fact that an avowal of imperialism runs counter to the ideology or the traditions of each of the giant nations, which are to-day alone in a position to make an attempt to dominate the world, does not, it must readily be admitted, mean that they will in fact abstain from making that attempt. It may only mean that they must find new forms, new methods and a new vocabulary for imperialist expansion, if they should undertake it. In this chapter and the next we must examine, therefore, the prospects of the world re-entering an imperialist epoch under the domination of one, or of each, of the super-powers of the twentieth century.

The question of whether or not America attempts to establish her empire over all or much of the world does not depend upon whether the Americans are morally good or bad people. As it happens, they are in this matter exceptionally "good" people. Their whole tradition, I repeat, is far more anti-imperialist than the British tradition, for example. Nevertheless, they may find themselves embarked upon the imperial attempt, whether they like it or not, and whether they know it or not, unless they avoid certain patterns of development within their own economy. In assessing the likelihood or the reverse of America launching herself upon an attempt at world empire let us, then, first of all review the economic factors which could drive her on to this course. For in this matter also economic development, while it is not everything, is at least one major determining factor.

To pose the question in its simplest form: does the fact that America has become by far the largest, richest and strongest capitalism inevitably mean that she will attempt, by means of imperialist expansion, to subjugate and exploit both the other capitalist societies and the un-developed world, and in the end to fight a third world war, either with them or with the communist world? Contemporary communist writers, at least until recently, have given an unhesitating yes as their answer to this question. Stalin, for example, in his political testament, *Economic Problems of Socialism in the U.S.S.R.* (1952), painted a picture of the capitalist world as already intolerably exploited by an all-embracing American imperialism.

"The U.S.A.", he writes, "has put Western Europe, Japan and the other capitalist countries on rations; Germany (Western), Britain, France, Italy and Japan have fallen into the clutches of the U.S.A. . . . The major vanquished countries, Germany (Western) and Japan, are now languishing under the jackboot of American imperialism" (p. 33).

Taken literally, Stalin's picture has little relation to reality. To give a man almost $40 billions[1] as the United States has given Europe since 1945, is rather an odd way to put him on rations. And the assertion that the vanquished Germany and Japan are "languishing under the jackboot of American imperialism" will strike the British observer as particularly ill-conceived. In fact, of course, Germany and Japan have been in the post-war period the favourite sons of the State Department, the recipients of unstinted American assistance. Far from their peoples

[1] Foreign Grants and Credits by the United States Government, September 1958 quarter, U.S. Dept. of Commerce.

"languishing in misery" they have been enabled to stage a recovery in their standard of life which startles every observer.

Stalin's flatfooted denials of the most obvious contemporary facts tempt one to pay no more attention to his argument. And yet his general account of the situation has obvious elements of truth in it. It is true that American *power* has been extended over Western Europe and Japan to an unprecedented extent. But that power, far from having been used to ruin these countries, as Stalin, with his really insane bigotry, assumed that it must have been, has been used in a desperate attempt to succour and sustain them. (The *motives*, in fact, of course, mixed, which have led America to perform this gigantic salvage operation are, as the communists would be the first to emphasise, irrelevant at this stage in the argument.) On the other hand, the benevolent use which has hitherto been made of it does not alter the *fact* of the extension of American power over the whole of the rest of the non-communist world. No other capitalism has ever before extended its general influence, as opposed to its annexations of territory, to this degree. What will be the consequences? Again the communists have no doubts. Stalin, for instance, concluded the passage just cited by committing himself to the assertion, which caused much comment at the time, that there was more likelihood of a war of revolt against America from the, in his view, miserably exploited secondary capitalisms than of a war between America and Russia. This conviction of the primacy of "the inter-imperialist contradictions", even over the capitalist-communist struggle itself, is, I think, one of the things which give Stalin's successors that self-confidence, which, in spite of their recent misadventures in Eastern Europe, Western statesmen who have come in contact with them have observed.[1]

A true account of the effect upon the world of American power and wealth in the mid-twentieth century would have to be far more complex than Stalin's. The first factor to lay hold on is undoubtedly the disproportionate economic magnitude of United States capitalism. Here is the economy of a country which, though large, contains, after all, only 170 of the 2,650 million inhabitants of the world (some 6%), and which yet is responsible for something like half the entire world's industrial production. It is true that industrial production is by no means everything. Nevertheless industrial production is

[1] All this stems from the present-day communist interpretation of Lenin's theory of imperialism (see Chapter VII, above). The communists regard imperialism not merely as the invariable and inevitable consequence of mature capitalism, but as virtually synonymous with contemporary capitalism. And they do so far more mechanically than did Lenin.

unquestionably the basis of *disposable* economic, political and military power.

Such a degree of predominance as America now possesses is a new thing in history. These 170 million Americans consume, for example, more than half of the entire world's production of copper, aluminium, wood pulp, and several other staples. Such statistics could be multiplied, but the fact of American wealth is familiar and undisputed. Evidence of it is some times recited as if Americans were to blame for being so rich. But this is merely the silly voice of envy. American wealth is the perfectly natural result of well-known geographical and historical factors, not the least important of which has been the vast energy of the American people, combined with their overwhelming concentration upon production for private profit almost to the exclusion, as Professor Galbraith has described, of all other human purposes. But the historically comprehensible causes of American wealth do not explain away the unprecedented phenomenon presented by the mid-twentieth-century American economy.

That phenomenon is, in one of its aspects, an extreme example of the principle of the uneven development of capitalist societies which we have already discussed. Just as the superior bargaining power of the large corporate employers tends to suck up a disproportionate part of the national wealth from the wage-earners and the agriculturists within capitalist societies (unless these classes develop commensurate leverage by combination), so the few highly developed capitalisms, and especially the most highly developed of all, tend to suck up a disproportionate part of the wealth even of other well developed capitalisms. The principle of "to him that hath shall be given" operates not only as between the developed and the under-developed world, but also as between capitalisms at different stages of development. It will enrich the richest and impoverish the less rich, since power in general and bargaining power in particular tend to become concentrated in fewer and fewer hands. This is no one's fault: no one consciously plans such a development. It is simply the inevitable result of those who take the key economic decisions of the world obeying the normal capitalist incentives to maximise the returns upon their enterprises. The result, however, unless it is consciously counteracted is an extreme heaping up of wealth and power in one place.[1]

This formidable centripetal drive of capitalism expresses itself, above

[1] Readers who are inclined to regard all this as outdated Marxist harping on the alleged "contradictions of capitalism" are again recommended to consult Professor Myrdal's *Economic Theory and Underdeveloped Regions*.

all, in the appearance of large masses of disposable capital in the principal centre, or centres, of industrial activity, and in a corresponding shortage of capital everywhere else in the world. But it will be asked, does capitalism have no device to meet this situation? Surely there must be some way in which the capital generated in the industrial centres may be spread throughout the world? For, if not, surely the system must long ago have become unworkable? We have seen that there is such a device, and its operation in the past has alone prevented the uneven development of the system, as between country and country, from getting wholly out of hand. This is precisely that device of foreign lending, of the investment of capital on private account, and in the expectation of profit, which we considered to be the basis of modern imperialism. Now we must note that capitalism would nevertheless produce monstrous disproportions in the absence of such a device.

In the classical theory of capitalism, as fast as capital accumulates in one place—for example, America—it will be pumped out into the rest of the world. For its plentiful supply in America[1] and its scarcity elsewhere will create so marked a differential in its yield within and without her borders that it will flow outwards. This, indeed, as we saw in Chapter VII, is broadly what did happen in an earlier case of disproportionate development, during the nineteenth century, when the British was the main capital generating economy of the world. A steady stream of British foreign lending, maintained by private British citizens in search of maximum profits, alone enabled the capitalism of that period to function and develop on a world scale. For in the theory of classical capitalism national frontiers and boundaries are simply disregarded. The reinvestment of profits earned in Blackburn is considered to be just the same kind of economic act, whether it takes place in Birmingham or in Brazil. Of course, in practice national frontiers could never be thus disregarded. The *foreign* investment of the surplus given off by an economy was always an act very different in its political consequences from the reinvestment of that surplus in further industrialisation at home. It had different political consequences for a dozen obvious reasons. Those different political consequences flowed in particular from the fact that, if the investment took place overseas, it exposed the investor to all the risks consequent upon his money having come under the jurisdiction of a foreign government; at least it did so unless his own

[1] We shall note in a moment that it is only now in the nineteen-fifties that it is becoming genuinely plentiful in America. Up till now America has had large undeveloped regions within her, and she still has some.

government's writ followed his money. We came to the conclusion that this was not indeed the sole, but that it was on the whole the most important, reason why the outward flowing stream of profit-seeking British foreign investment from about 1870 onwards carried on its current the paraphernalia of British imperialism. This was the stream of wealth which carried British power outward from the borders of the island till, as we have seen, the British Government directly ruled over some quarter of the human race. We saw that this world-wide power was, as it were, the hard deposit left by the stream of British capital exports, and it was this power against which the later coming German capitalism beat itself in the two world wars.

The question is, will this process be repeated in the case of America in the second half of the twentieth century? If a sufficiently broad, deep, and sustained stream of private profit-seeking American foreign lending were to start to flow out, political and military consequences corresponding to those which occurred in the case of nineteenth-century Britain might be expected to appear. If it were on a sufficient scale such private American foreign lending could relieve, at a price, both any plethora of capital being generated in America, and the dearth of capital in the rest of the world. But it is hard to see how the price of the spread of American capital through the world by this traditional method of private profit-seeking foreign lending could be anything but American imperialism on a world-wide scale. In that event Stalin's picture of the world as he saw it in his closing years, although it was a travesty of reality as it actually existed in 1952, would begin to come true.

It is crucial in this connection to emphasise and re-emphasise the connection which exists between *private, profit-seeking,* foreign investment and the extension of the imperialist power of the foreign investor's government. The essential reason for this connection is that the profit-seeking foreign investor will not usually or adequately invest unless he is given the degree of security which in many cases only the extension of his own government's power can give him. How considerable that extension would have to be, in order to induce a significant flow of American foreign lending upon private account, can be gauged from a passage in the well-known report of the American Paley Commission on raw material supplies. As a method of inducing American private investors to put their money into schemes for producing the raw materials which America will need to import from overseas, the Paley Commission recommended that the American Government should negotiate a series of "investment treaties" with what the report called "resource countries", *i.e.,* countries which could supply natural resources needed by America. These treaties would provide that

> "The resource country's government would pledge its co-operation in removing the uncertainties which chiefly deter investors, in return for guaranteed prices or purchase commitments by the United States Government, plus an assurance that the United States would facilitate investment in both resource and general economic development. The agreement could cover tax laws, regulations applying to foreign ownership and management, administration of the labour code, export regulations, exchange restrictions, import permits, the right to bring in foreign technicians, transport facilities, compensation in the event of expropriation, and other matters of concern to investors."

It is precisely this necessity "to remove the uncertainties which chiefly deter investors" which has made the whole portentous development of imperialism the concomitant of large scale foreign lending on private account and for profit. For who can doubt that such wide provisions as those recommended above by the Paley Commission would inevitably lead on to a system of domination, under whatever name, on the part of the investing power?

The question is, then, to what extent will America's present economic predominance express itself in imperialist expansion, even if that expansion takes on new forms? Before we mechanically conclude, with Stalin and the communists, that such a development is inevitable, we should take certain counter-considerations into account. There is, first, the aforementioned anti-imperialist tradition in America itself; second, there are characteristics of the American economy which mean that it is still in some respects pre-imperialist in character; third, there is the quite new strength and effectiveness of nationalism in the undeveloped world: fourth, a "middle class" of largely post-imperial, independent but quite strong nations are now in existence, and, finally, there is the existence of the counter-power of Russia and China. Let us take up these five matters in turn.

First, there is the American anti-imperialist tradition. Historically American anti-imperialism derives from the fact that the nucleus of the United States was a rebellious province of the British Empire. Moreover, built into that tradition there is, for good as well as ill, that spirit of personal self-enrichment as the be-all and end-all of life, which we discussed in Chapter XV, above. We now note that from the point of view of the rest of the world there is a lot to be said for the Americans resting content with this limited ideal of self-enrichment, at any rate as against their becoming imbued with the ideals of glory, expansion, destiny, mission, and the like, which always accompany the onset of an imperialist climate of opinion.

It is extraordinarily difficult to assess the true weight which should be given to such non-material factors as these in affecting actual American policy in the second half of the twentieth century. We can set limits perhaps to their importance by saying that it is clear that, on the one hand, it would be wrong to think that their effect is likely to be negligible, or, on the other, that by themselves they could possibly prevent an era of American imperialism. After all, as we have noted, America did, at the end of the last century, take part, fairly actively, in the contemporary imperialist expansion. She began, moreover, at that time to develop an imperialist ideology and to talk of her "manifest destiny". Nor, I think, can it be argued that it was her anti-imperialist origins which put a stop to this embryo-imperialism of the America of the first Roosevelt. It was rather the swing of the pendulum in American domestic politics, with the election of Wilson (on domestic issues) and, in particular, the first World War. The first World War brought America into world politics indeed, but in a different way. She began to be less, rather than more, interested in the acquisition of colonies. She rather naïvely felt it, on the contrary, to be her mission to organise a world society. And the post-war recoil from this involvement in the world was isolationist, not imperialist. It tended to take her out of colonisation as well as out of the League of Nations.

It is true that this first half-abortive phase of American imperialism has left behind it one important and persisting effect—namely, a varying but considerable degree of American domination over the successor states of the old Spanish empire to the south of her. American power is unquestionably predominant all over Central and South America, and there are limits to the degree of independence of Washington enjoyed by any of the Latin American states. Nevertheless, it is also necessary to notice that there have proved to be limits to the degree to which Latin America has become an American domain. None of this vast area, with the single exception of Puerto Rico, became an actual American colony. Thus the results of this first phase of American imperialism surprised us much more by their limitation than by their extent. Moreover, most observers of the Latin American scene report that American domination of this region of the world is on the whole diminishing rather than increasing. As more competent indigenous

governments emerge, and as, above all, the actual process of economic
development goes forward, it is by no means certain that even here an
American empire will be consolidated.

We now come to our second consideration, namely, the character of
the American economy. There was an economic reason for the evident
half-heartedness of this initial American inclination towards imperialism. As we noted in Chapter VII, fifty years ago the American economy
was not really ready for an empire. Her own vast homeland had not
been by any means adequately exploited. It may be said that that homeland itself had been acquired by imperialist means. And undoubtedly
from a moral point of view the destruction or dispersion of the Red
Indian nomads, both by the British colonists before the seventeen-
seventies and by the Americans afterwards, was one of the more
ruthless episodes in the whole story of the world-wide expansion of the
European peoples. Again, at a later stage important parts of the
American homeland were acquired by war with Mexico, the most
northerly of the successor states of the old Spanish empire. If the
subject of this enquiry were the relative morality or immorality of these
American aggressions as compared, say, with the British conquest of
India, a good deal could be said on both sides. But this is not what our
enquiry is about. Under the view of the nature of imperialism which,
it is to be hoped, is emerging from these pages, the conquest of the
American homeland was not imperialism in the same sense at least as
the acquisition of colonies. The difference does not indeed lie in whether
the colonies are overseas or contiguous with the homeland of the
conqueror. It is rather a question of whether the conqueror's rule is
imposed, in the main, for the purpose of using directly or indirectly
the labour of the conquered people for his own benefit. Acts of conquest which do not have this as their objective, or result, are better
seen as acts of simple aggression rather than imperialism. All this,
however, is largely a matter of definition and like all definitions the
one used here for imperialism is to some extent arbitrary. It is, I believe,
nevertheless consistent. (It is stated briefly in the Preface, and in some
detail in Part III, below.)

At all events and however we choose to characterise the Americans'
acquisition of their homeland, once they had acquired it there existed
for them huge opportunities for internal development, which it was
far more profitable, far safer, and far more natural for their entrepreneurs to exploit, than to enter the exciting, but risky and not
necessarily immediately profitable, imperial race. And even to-day,
half a century later, this is still partly true. By means of a readjustment

of the American economy, and a redistribution of the American national income, the crisis of the nineteen-thirties was overcome *internally*, instead of by means of imperialist expansion. And this in turn has meant that the whole structure of American capitalism, and the effective political forces arising from that structure, still look inwards rather than outwards. It is no more than an over-simplification to say that to-day the greatest barrier, within America, to the growth of an American empire is the fact that the American entrepreneurs and investors, with the single, although important, exception of the oil industry, are simply not much interested in it. They see no urgent reasons for large scale foreign investments when they can still find scope for safer and equally profitable investments at home. Accordingly, they see no urgent reasons for the subjugation of large parts of the world in order to safeguard investments which they are not very keen to make. Their relative indifference enables the American anti-imperialist tradition to survive.[1]

Nevertheless, if the above were the only safeguards against an epoch of American imperialism we should be bound to judge them to be wasting assets. Sooner or later the great American corporations would find that much the most profitable opportunities open to them were abroad. Then the American people would be likely to be subjected to the same sort of intensive imperialist propaganda as formed the mental climate of Britain in the nineteen-hundreds. No doubt it would be necessary to conceal American imperialist expansion under new names. New and probably actually anti-imperialist sounding slogans would have to be coined in order to reassure a people who really have a sturdy tradition of regard for the principle of the independence of nations. But it is to be feared that this would not prove a particularly difficult task for the professional manipulators of public opinion. The Americans are a generous but a gullible people. We have had a foretaste of the kind of watchwords which would be issued in Mr Henry Luce's propaganda on the theme of "the American century".

The question is, will American liberalism be strong enough to resist such a propaganda? Americans liberals would not lack indeed a rational basis for an anti-imperialist stand. It has emerged from our whole discussion of the establishment and dissolution of the British Empire that it is almost certain that the immense majority of the people

---

[1] Investment in Canada is an exception. There the inflow of American capital is so strong that even the highly competent Canadian Government feels threatened by it. But so far at least the result appears to have been an intensification of Canadian nationalism rather than the gradual establishment of an American empire.

of a mature capitalism gain nothing from the outpouring of foreign investment which is the material basis of the latter day empires. On the contrary, they will be much better off, as Mr Shonfield has shown, if these investments are made at home. It is only a limited class of investors—at the very most 10% of the population—who will be benefited by the maintenance, by means of foreign investment, of a higher rate of profit than would otherwise have been possible. The mass of the American people would be better off if surplus American resources were devoted to expanding their exiguous public services than to private profit-seeking foreign investment, and to the imperialism which would inevitably accompany it. (On the other hand, the whole undeveloped world desperately needs an inflow of American capital: but if it gets it on a private profit-seeking basis it will be accompanied by an imperialism which is now unacceptable. The real solution is neither home investment nor foreign investment for profit but foreign investment on public account.) Nevertheless, the fact that American liberals would have an excellent rational case for resisting American imperialism is no guarantee whatever that they would be successful in doing so. The same issue which was fought out in the 'eighties and 'nineties in Britain, i.e., should there be further social reform and a further redistribution of the national income—or imperialism—may prove to be the great issue in American public life in the second half of the twentieth century. There would be no foretelling the outcome of such a struggle within America. There are, however, other obstacles, exterior to America, to the growth of a major American imperialism.

The third counter-consideration is the fact that any future outward drive of American imperialism would encounter a world very different from that in which the European imperialists operated, even as lately as the turn of the nineteenth and twentieth centuries. In the history of the last fifty years the birth of passionate nationalisms all over the undeveloped world may perhaps prove even more important than either the appearance of communism or of the recent mutation of capitalism. Alike in the then semi-derelict societies of China and India, in the South and Central American successor states of the Spanish empire, amongst African societies which were purely tribal only a few decades ago, in the Arab successor states of the Ottoman Empire, with their princely revenues from oil—over the whole earth there has been a universal and simultaneous birth, or in some cases re-birth, of passionate national self-consciousness. It is, in Professor Myrdal's phrase, "the great awakening".

For us, the citizens of the old nations of Western Europe, with anything up to ten centuries of independent national existence and national consciousness behind us, there is nothing particularly inspiring about such nationalist passion. On the contrary, we are all beginning to appreciate the negative side of nationalism. Nationalism is indeed still immensely strong in the peoples of Europe. Nevertheless, Europe has been torn to pieces twice in a generation by wars which started as European national wars, although they both developed into world wars. Nationalism is thus hardly likely to seem anything very new or very hopeful to us. But how parochial we shall once again show ourselves to be if we think that nationalism feels in the least like that to the peoples of the rest of the world. It is hardly too much to say that for them to articulate themselves into modern nation-states, with full national consciousness, seems salvation itself. Or at least it seems the prerequisite of salvation. They feel that they cannot be either progressive or reactionary, capitalist or communist, dictatorial or democratic, that they cannot exist at all, until and unless they exist as nation-states.

How cruel a joke history has played upon the predictions of Marx in this respect. A hundred years ago Marx, a Western European, could already see the seamy side of nationalism. In the new world of capitalism which had just come into being, the proletarian, he felt, "had no fatherland". Socialism could only be realised in the international commonwealth of the future. It is true that Marx was not so unrealistic as to fail to support in practice the struggles of contemporary nations for their independence. Nevertheless, it remains true that he never really believed that the workers as such could, or would, identify themselves with their own nation-states. To-day it would seem truer to say that both workers and peasants, far from having no fatherland, have nothing until they have a fatherland. They cannot even pursue their class ends until they possess the framework of a national fatherland within which to pursue them. For the force of nationalism is overwhelmingly strong precisely in those "have-not" nations which are adopting one form or another of socialism. This immense underestimate of the strength of nationalism is surely Marx's greatest error in the political field. It arose, it would seem, from a deficiency in his basic theory of human society. It arose from his failure, that is to say, to attempt even (he could not possibly have succeeded 100 years ago) to think of man biologically as well as economically. He did not allow (in practice) for a biological substratum of human nature, which would impel large, fierce mammals to put their own *pack* before everything else: which would make them feel it necessary to attempt to realise all their class, social, economic aspirations through and by means of their nations.

Be all that as it may, the fact is that nationalism is to-day the strongest single sentiment in the world. Class, race, religion, all move men greatly; all are intertwined with nationalism. But where they conflict with nationalism they usually prove the weaker. Poland, Hungary and Yugoslavia are the most recent examples in the communist, India, Pakistan, Egypt, Israel, Cyprus, Iraq and the Sudan in the non-communist, worlds of countries in which people have been clearly moved to act by nationalist sentiments which have over-ridden all other considerations. There is little need to set out the disadvantages and perils which this enormous, and still growing, force of nationalism presents for the contemporary world. Nevertheless, it does form an important barrier to the re-enaction, this time under American auspices, of the sequence of heavy foreign lending on private profit-making account, leading by the series of consequences which we have traced, to imperialist domination in one form or another. In the whole world to-day there is, perhaps, no determination as great as the determination of the ex-colonial peoples to remain independent. There is a similar determination in even the most immature peoples to achieve their independence, often enough with little regard to their own material interests. There exists, as has been recently (1956) revealed to the world, an equal determination on the part of the historic nations of Eastern Europe to resume their independence. Again the peoples of India and China unquestionably put their national independence first— far above the question of whether they should organise their economic and political life upon the capitalist or the communist model, or upon some model of their own. Finally, the "millionaire" states of the un-developed world, the oil states of Arabia, show that they are more excited by the passions of nationalism even than by desire for oil royalties.

It is upon a world such as this that a new wave of American imperialist expansion would break. It would be an exaggeration to say that the existence of nationalism even upon this scale made the creation of a twentieth-century American empire impossible. After all, the powers of physical resistance possessed by the new nations of the un-developed world are relatively small. Given sufficient determination and ruthlessness, they, or at least the weaker amongst them, could no doubt even be re-colonised, without much military difficulty, by American imperialism. Short of that, an effective American empire could perhaps be built up without the actual colonisation of the states into which American private capital flowed. It is more difficult and far less satisfactory for an imperial power to exercise its rule indirectly, covertly and by means of coercing satellite or puppet governments, but the thing can be done.

Another factor is, however, beginning to appear in this connection. The world is ceasing to consist simply of imperialist states and impotent, undeveloped nations. There now also exist a number of fairly powerful nation-states of two other kinds. First, a number of the old states of Western Europe have entered their post-imperial period. And then there are a number of ex-colonies which are becoming relatively developed. Just as a middle class has grown up between the capitalists and the proletarians within the advanced capitalisms, so a middle class of nation-states is emerging on the world scene. Britain is on the whole the most powerful of the nations of this middle class. But Western Germany, Italy, Australia, Canada, India, France, and, on a smaller scale, Holland, Sweden and Yugoslavia, are other examples. Naturally, in so far as the post-imperial nations cling to remnants of their empires, as France has done in North Africa, or as Britain did in the case of Egypt in a moment of aberration in 1956, they both exhaust themselves materially and, far worse, forfeit all possibility of becoming rallying points for independent nations attempting to resist the pressure of potential new imperialisms. But as and when they give up this futile role they have the capacity to become extremely important additional factors of resistance to the rise of new empires, either in the West or the East. These middle nations are by no means materially or militarily impotent. They will become increasingly a factor to be reckoned with. And it may well prove that one of Britain's most important future roles will lie in an enlightened participation in and even, on occasions, leadership of, this body of world opinion.

Nevertheless, and in spite of this very considerable addition to the non-imperialist forces of the world, it is probably true that if no more than (i) the American anti-imperialist tradition, (ii) the still partly pre-imperialist pattern of the American economy, (iii) the flood tide of nationalism in the undeveloped world, and (iv) the emergence of a

"middle class" of post-imperialist, or non-imperialist, nations, stood
in the way, the establishment of an American empire, in one form or
another, over all or much of the world would still be probable. The
economic and military strength of America is gigantic. If she set out
with determination upon the road of empire-building, it would be
rash to deny that the most probable future for the world might be to
enter a period of American domination, exercised no doubt by somewhat new methods, but not likely to be very different in its consequences from the imperialisms of history.

There is, however, still another factor in the contemporary situation. There is the existence of other and comparable power-centres,
namely the two major communist states of Russia and China. We
shall discuss in the next chapter the question of whether these communist states are liable themselves to take the road of empire. Here we
have merely to note that the existence of these alternative power-
centres, genuinely and completely independent of America—and
whether they are themselves imperialist or not—undoubtedly constitutes another factor adverse to the possibility of the creation of an
American world empire.

For, from the point of view of the independent, or potentially
independent, nations of the world, the existence of two or more
imperialist powers is decidedly better than one. Until and unless an
actual partition of the world between them is arranged, and maintained, even nations with quite limited military power may be able to
sustain a real measure of independence by balancing between these
rival powers, and the *blocs* which they create. This is what the states of
the undeveloped world have been doing since 1945. They are using
the existence of the two major world power-centres, America on the
one hand and Russia (and, in a rather different sense, China) on the
other, to maintain their own independence. They would be maladroit
indeed if they were not. To "swither" (to use an expressive Scottish
term) between two overwhelmingly strong but mutually hostile
powers is, of course, a policy which has been pursued by weaker states
since time immemorial.

This policy is well seen in the case of India. But it can be readily
enough detected all over the undeveloped, or to give it its latest, and
significant, name, the "uncommitted" world. Such a policy excites
great annoyance in the West (as also in the East, it may be hazarded,
but the rulers of Russia and China seem much more capable of con-
cealing their chagrin). American and sometimes British spokesmen are
outraged because countries like India or Egypt or Indonesia do not

whole-heartedly throw in their lot with the West and make common cause against "the communist menace". There is an unconquerable *naïveté* and parochialism about this Western attitude. To suppose that nations which were only yesterday the rebellious colonies of one or other of the Western imperialisms will regard as their salvation the powers from which they have just escaped: or will regard Russia and China, which they see arrayed against the older imperialisms, as their deadly antagonists, is indeed to ask for the moon. The fact is that hitherto the new or re-born nations of the world have, on the contrary, regarded Russia and, especially, China as their natural associates in their struggle for independence, even if these two nations have taken to organising their economic life in a particular way which may or may not appeal to the new nations. It may be that this attitude upon the part of the new nations will not indefinitely survive the evidence of Russian and Chinese imperialist policies which we discuss below. But, even if the new nations come to regard Russia and China also as imperialist, or potentially imperialist, powers, that in itself is unlikely to make them "throw in their lot with the West". They are much more likely to conclude that the way to maintain and develop their national independence is to pursue the aforementioned policy of watchful balancing between these formidable forces.

Nor does such a policy seem foredoomed to failure. In particular it may give substance to the other barriers against the establishment of an American world empire which we have noted. The ability of otherwise militarily impotent nations to turn towards the communist bloc for assistance and support if threatened by the vast economic and military power of America, and, *vice versa*, to turn to the West when encroached upon in the same way from the East, is a far from negligible factor in the world scene. Together with the aforementioned factors of (i) the American anti-imperialist tradition, (ii) the relative immaturity of the American economy for empire, (iii) the new passion of nationalism running through the undeveloped world, and (iv) the rise of a middle tier of, largely, post-imperial states, it renders an epoch of American imperial domination a much more dubious prediction than it must seem at first sight. Before, however, attempting to evaluate the possibility of the world escaping from a new epoch of imperialism we must consider the opposite possibility of a Russian, or perhaps Sino-Russian, world imperialism.

CHAPTER XX

NEW EMPIRES FOR OLD?
(II) A RUSSIAN EMPIRE

COMMUNISTS ASSERT THAT no socialist society can be imperialist. It lacks, they maintain, all those social relations, such as private traders, and investors looking for especially high profit, which are the prime movers in the process which ended in the imperialist partitioning and re-partitioning of the world in this century. Only slanderers of a socialist society could even suggest, therefore, they continue, that it could conceivably become imperialist.

If we define imperialism in this narrow sense of the governmental protection of the profit-seeking overseas transactions of private citizens, then they are right. For the citizens of a communist society cannot undertake foreign commercial transactions for their own profit. But in the Preface, imperialism was defined more broadly, and I think more realistically. It was defined as the imposition of the power of one nation on another, with the intention of ruling the subjected nation for an indefinite period. The question of whether or not its purpose was always that of securing economic gain by exploiting the labour resources of the subjugated nation was left over in the hope that a conclusion would emerge from our account of the historical record. In my view it does emerge that such gain is the single most important factor in the imperialist process. We have seen, indeed, that at least in recent times the gains of imperialism have not gone to the conquering peoples as a whole but to a narrow investing section. We have seen that the gain is often acquired simply by preventing the weaker people from intefering with the normal workings of international trade rather than by overt acts of exploitation. We have seen that once the imperialist process has got going then all sorts of other motives—strategic, power-seeking, prestige-seeking—nationalist motives—have become extremely powerful. On any given occasion they may well be more important in forming the decisions of the imperial power than the expectation of economic gain. Again we have seen that imperialist domination does not invariably follow private profit-seeking foreign investment: there may be no pressing need for it when the local government is amenable already, or there may be insuperable obstacles, where the local government is strong.

Nevertheless, the historical evidence does appear to me to show that the expectation of gain has been the primary motivation around which all other considerations, passions, prejudices, illusions and, for that matter, sincere views of duties and obligations, have clustered. But *to whom* the expected economic gain will go, whether to private individuals, to institutions, or to the conquering state itself, is another matter. There is nothing in the definition of imperialism here adopted which precludes the possibility that the state itself should attempt to acquire such gains. Under this definition, then, there is nothing about a socialised economy which precludes it from acting imperialistically. And in fact, of course, the whole non-communist world does accuse Soviet Russia of acting imperialistically towards those other nations over which she now exercises paramount power.

What truth is there, however, in this accusation that Russia has, in fact, developed a neo-imperialism on a socialised economic basis? We have had fourteen years' experience (1945-59) of Russian paramountcy over a group of Eastern European nations. No one can really pretend that anything can be done between the "Iron Curtain" and the Chinese border without Russian consent.[1] How is she treating her dependencies? According to Stalin and to all communist spokesmen, she has treated the nations of Eastern Europe with an altruism more perfect than has ever before been exhibited by one state to another in human history. For example, Stalin wrote:

"Not a single capitalist country could have rendered such effective and technically competent assistance to the People's Democracies as the Soviet Union is rendering them. The point is not only that this assistance is the cheapest possible and technically superb. The chief point is that at the bottom of this co-operation lies a sincere desire to help one another and to promote the economic progress of all" (*Economic Problems of Socialism in the U.S.S.R.*, p. 35).

This account of the situation in Eastern Europe always seemed inherently improbable. And after the break with Yugoslavia in 1948 first-hand evidence became available that this was not at all how some at least of the "People's Democracies" felt about the matter. Since 1948 the Yugoslav Government has been in the unique position of being an ex-satellite. It has experienced the treatment accorded by Russia to its dependent states and is in a position to say what that treatment has

---

[1] Even if, as in the case of Poland in 1956, extremely reluctant consent.

been like. On the other hand, we must not expect a government which has emerged from a desperate and potentially mortal conflict with the Soviets to take an impartial or even a temperate view of its experiences. The earliest available account, of which I am aware, of the dealings of the Soviet Government with Yugoslavia, while the latter was still its satellite, is contained in a series of articles by the Yugoslav statesman, M. Djilas (now imprisoned in his own country for expressing critical views), in the official Yugoslav newspaper, *Borba*, for November 26th, 1950. (For a fuller account of M. Djilas' views on imperialism in general see *New Fabian Essays*, pp. 204-6.) M. Djilas had not the slightest doubt that Russia had become imperialist. He wrote:

"But where in this respect does the new, 'soviet' imperialism stand? Are there new developments in this too, such as those characteristic of the old private capitalist monopolies? All that is new here is the fact that the state which all, or nearly all, believed to be socialist, has through its own internal state capitalist development, turned into an imperialist power of the first order. But as for the actual forms, through the relatively poor development of its forces of production, what characterises this new, state-capitalist, imperialism is precisely that it has the old, colonial-conquest imperialist forms accompanied, albeit, in 'socialist' uniforms, by the old political relations: the export of capital is accompanied by a semi-military occupation, by the rule of an official caste and the police, by the strangling of any democratic tendencies, by the establishment of obedient governments, by the most extensive corruption and by unscrupulous deception of the working people."

M. Djilas' article goes on to allege that the Soviet Government exploited Yugoslavia more ruthlessly than capitalist states are accustomed to exploit their dependencies. It would be wrong, I repeat, to consider M. Djilas' as other than an *ex parte* statement. Not only Djilas, however, but many Yugoslav economists have now described in detail the consequences of the establishment by the Russians of "mixed companies" in Yugoslavia, by means of which they gained complete control of sectors of the Yugoslav economy. They have asserted that the Russian Government, in the post-war years, deliberately and ruthlessly used both these economic means and also its power of military coercion to turn the terms of trade in its own favour to a monstrous degree: that in particular Yugoslav food and raw materials were made to exchange with Russian manufactures at ratios much worse for the Yugoslavs than those obtainable by them in exchange with capitalist states.

Until the year 1956 there existed no other conclusive evidence as to whether or not these charges of Russian imperialist exploitation were well founded. But in that year, first in Poland and then, tragically, in Hungary, the veil was torn away and none, except those who were determined to be self-deceived, could deny the existence of a Russian imperialism, albeit of a new kind. No visitor, for example, to Poland during the events of the autumn of 1956 could doubt that there was a universal conviction that Russia was buying goods from Poland (coal in particular) at too low a price, and selling Russian goods to Poland at too high a price. All the typical attitudes of the people of an exploited colony, resentment, distrust, fear, cynical acquiescence, were to be found amongst the Poles, including the Polish communists, towards Russia. To what *extent* the Russians had thus economically exploited the Poles: how *much* difference it would have made to the Polish standard of life (and how much it would have cost Russia) if the world price had been paid for all Polish coal, for example, or for other Polish exports to Russia, I have never been able to estimate. (It is quite possible that the Poles exaggerated their exploitation: semi-colonial peoples habitually do.) But of the fact of some degree of exploitation, and of a burning resentment against it, there can be no doubt. I have no first-hand evidence of Hungarian attitudes in this respect: perhaps none are needed. For it is clear that the Hungarian people were united in the most passionate resentment against Russian rule in general and Russian economic exploitation in particular.

A forcible turning of the terms of trade in her own favour, to the grave disadvantage of her satellites, was not indeed the only, or perhaps even the principal complaint which, the world discovered, was entertained against the Russians by the peoples of Eastern Europe, and for that matter by some at least of the satellite communist Governments themselves. What, it was found, the peoples of Poland and Hungary, and it may be surmised the peoples of the other "People's Democracies", resented with passion was something deeper and simpler than that. What they resented was not this or that aspect of Russian rule. What they resented, above all, was Russian rule itself. For that rule was exercised, not only or principally to impoverish them for the sake of Russia, but also to impose upon them an economic and political system which they had never chosen. Their demand was for freedom in the simplest and most classic sense: for freedom to determine their own destinies. It is probable that they would have used such freedom to establish a form of democratic socialism. There is evidence that, at any rate in Poland,[1] this was the inclination of the more articulate sections of the population. Capitalism had probably become unreal and was in any case a by no means pleasant memory. Be that as it may, what the Polish people and the Hungarian people unmistakably and unanimously demanded was independence, as nations, and after that, democratic institutions so that they might order their own affairs as they thought fit.

But that was precisely what the Russians, like all other imperialists, could not grant them, without progressively ceasing to be imperialists. It made no difference in practice that many of the Russian leaders, perhaps sincerely, could not conceive that the Polish and Hungarian industrial workers, in particular, were determined, if need be by violence, to repudiate Russian communism. Imperialists never can believe that "their" subject peoples "really" want to repudiate them. If they show that they do so, they must have been "misled by agitators", "corrupted by the subversive agents of hostile powers", or, as the Russians put it, suborned by "Fascists, Americans, Horthyists, Pilsudskyists, imperialists, etc., etc., etc." They must be protected from themselves, imperialists always conclude, and at all costs prevented from deciding their own futures. In Budapest, as in Cyprus, the same dreary process of self-deception is at work, and the Russians may be heard using all the futile arguments with which we are so familiar from our own imperialists. The result of the Russian régime in Eastern Europe is to have made it certain that, if any actual democracy were established in any of "the people's democracies", the people would repudiate any economic system which had been enforced upon them by the Russians. After the autumn of 1956, therefore, it is perfectly clear that Russia has pursued an imperialist policy in respect of her Eastern European dependencies. All the only too familiar circumstances of imperialism have been reproduced: some degree at least of economic exploitation: the ever-growing resentment of the exploited peoples: the attempt to rule by acquiescent "puppet" governments: the attempt, when that fails, to arrive at compromises with more or less nationalist governments: and finally, when

[1] I was in Warsaw during "the October days" of 1956 and had some opportunity at least to guess at the desires and attitudes of mind of the Polish people.

that fails, the ruthless suppression of all opposition by a policy of "firmness".

But why did the Russian Government become imperialist? Surely it was not necessary for it to have exploited its satellites in this way? Surely, whatever cash benefits may have been derived from selling dear to them and buying cheap from them, must have been enormously outweighed by the savage hatred which has been produced in peoples whose attitude to her must always be of great importance to Russia. This is incontestable for the long run. And yet it may not be impossible to understand how and why the Russian planners, in the immediately post-1945 years, yielded to the temptation to exploit the peoples subject to their rule. That temptation must have been considerable. Russia was still in those years in the throes of primary accumulation. She had still, that is to say, somehow to wring a surplus out of her own pitiably poor agriculturists in order to sustain her industrial development. Why, her planners must have felt, should not the, after all, much better off peasants of Eastern Europe be made to make their contribution? And as for the European industrial workers, why should not these, on Russian standard, very well-to-do people, who moreover in the case of the Eastern Germans at least had been devastating Russia for four years, be made to pay up?

For the Russian people were still miserably poor. *Let it never be forgotten that we now know from the official figures of the Russian Government that there were still, as lately as 1953, no more cattle in Russia per head than in 1916.* No accounts, however factual, and in the main they undoubtedly are factual, of Russian prodigies of industrial progress can any longer, in view of these figures, conceal from the world the degree of sheer privation, in terms of such basic foodstuffs as milk and meat, from which the Russians are only now emerging. For in terms of actual, present human welfare, though not, of course, in terms of present power, or possible future wealth, cows are far more important than blast furnaces. It is, therefore, comprehensible that the Russian planners did not feel that they were imposing anything out of the way on the population of Eastern Europe, when in fact they used their power to commit what seemed to those populations acts of extreme exploitation.

Russian exploitation of her satellites demonstrates, then, that a society which has eliminated the relations of production characteristic of capitalism is yet capable of imperialist exploitation. It is true that the proceeds of this exploitation will go, not, as they do in the case of a capitalist society, into the pockets of a small class of wealthy private individuals, but will be used to add to the general resources of the state. But will that be much consolation to the people of the exploited dependency? Moreover, Russia has shown itelf exposed, as a result of such policies, to all the difficulties, the expenses, the complications and the odium which face every imperialist power when it attempts to enforce its rule upon unwilling, and in the end rebellious, subject peoples. The best that could possibly be said for the Russians was that they were doing no more than other empires had done before them. A basic question is posed by this tragic experience. Has it now been demonstrated that a change in the economic mechanism and motivations of an economy, such as Russia has no doubt achieved, provides no guarantee that the mental climate of the society in question will change also? Does, for example, the change from production for profit to production for use do nothing after all to change the relations of a given society to weaker societies outside it, to change those relations from imperialism to co-operation? For my part I am quite unwilling to agree with the idealist (in the philosophical sense) view, which has now become so fashionable, that there is no connection between the nature of an economic system and the tone and temper of the society that is built upon it. But that that connection is far more complex and indirect than had been supposed, appears proven. In particular the political institutions which form the connective tissue, as it were, between the economic base and the moral superstructure of a society have turned out to be both far more important, and to vary far more independently, than the Marxist scheme had allowed for. If Russia had had democratic political institutions, as well as a socialised economy, it would have been more difficult, at least, for her rulers to have committed their crimes and errors of imperialist domination in Eastern Europe. For the Russian people could at least have been appealed to by the Poles and the other subject peoples.

About the existence of Russian imperialism there can be, then, no doubt. The question is, is this Russian imperialism likely to dominate the world, or, alternatively to partition the world with an equal and opposite American imperialism, thus inaugurating a new imperialist epoch? Calmly regarded, the establishment of a wide and enduring empire by Russia, although clearly a possibility, does not seem likely.

In fact, in 1959, only fourteen years after its establishment, the Russian Empire of Eastern Europe is visibly in disarray. Power was lost in one considerable part of it, Yugoslavia, as early as 1948. In 1956 a compromise had to be reached with Poland. It is true that Poland is still held firmly within the Russian power system, and that a good deal, though by no means all, of the internal liberty which was briefly achieved in 1956, has now been taken back. Nevertheless, "the October Days", as the Poles call their defiance of Russian authority in 1956, may yet in the long run prove to have been that first short, but fateful, step, upon the road to the achievement of independence by a colony with which other imperialists are so familiar. Again in the spring of 1957 it became evident that leading communist theoreticians of East Germany, under the leadership of Professor Harrich, had completely repudiated the whole structure of Russian ideology. They were duly imprisoned, but the necessity to imprison such personalities in a colony is by no means a sign of the stability of an empire, as every experienced imperialist would confirm. Finally, the most extreme, and even to the imperialists themselves most unwelcome, degree of force had to be used in Hungary in order to avoid a complete loss of power. This certainly does not look like the successful consolidation, still less extension, of a Russian Empire.

On the other hand, Eastern Europe is by no means everything. And it is true that Russian expansionist tendencies have recently found much more scope elsewhere. Major errors on the part of Britain and France in the Middle East, committed at the same moment as the Russian Empire in Eastern Europe appeared to be cracking up, presented Russia with unhoped for opportunities for the penetration of that area. Naturally, Russia is anxious enough to use such opportunities. Nevertheless it remains to be seen how far the expansion of Russian power in the Middle East can go without running up against Arab nationalism.[1] Such Arab nationalism will surely find ready material support from the West when we have come to our senses. If that Western support becomes genuinely free from a counter-attempt to re-impose its own domination over the area (as it has never been hitherto), the prospects of Russian domination here also do not seem high. Moreover, since the Middle East holds a crucial part of the oil resources of the world, Russia knows that an attempt to push matters to extremes in this part of the world might be a cause of general war.

[1] This has now (May 1959) occurred, with the breach between Nasser and the communists.

Africa is often considered to be a favourable field for the expansion of Russian power, essentially by means of the fostering of communist movements. And some parts of Africa, above all, of course, South Africa, where racial tension is at its highest, undoubtedly offer such prospects. But over the greater part of this continent it begins to look as if here, too, the future lay with an indigenous nationalism. With the independence of Ghana in 1957 the pattern has clearly been laid down for the emergence of a series of African nations (whether federated or not) upon the sites of the British and French West African colonies. And there seems small prospect of their desiring to become, or being compelled to become, Russian satellites. (But there is still acute danger of us driving the inhabitants of Central Africa into the hands of the communists by attempting to impose white settler rule upon them.) Even in Moslem North Africa, and in spite of the continuance of a desperately dangerous situation in Algeria, the achievement of even partial independence on the part of Tunis and Morocco will probably prove to have been decisive, in the sense that independent nations, rather than colonies of the Western, or satellites of the Eastern, super-states, will be the pattern of the future.

Turning to the greatest potential field for Russian expansion, to the mainland of Asia, we find that the spread of Russian power is here opposed, partly by the same obstacle, namely the rise of indigenous, non-communist, nationalisms (in India for example) but partly by an obstacle of another kind altogether, namely the emergence of a second communist power, China, of a magnitude far too great for there to be any question of her becoming a Russian satellite. In fact, if there is to be a communist imperialism in Asia, it is more likely to be conducted by China than by Russia. (We note below the possibilities of a Sino-imperialist epoch.)

The obstacle to Russian expansion presented by the new nationalism of the under-developed world must be emphasised both because of its intrinsic importance and because it is habitually underestimated and misappreciated in the West. This is natural because the new nationalism is apparently directed much more against the West, since much of it had arisen in Western colonies and semi-colonies, than against Russia or China. Therefore the West feels this nationalism as hostile, and tends to overlook the fact that it is potentially hostile to Russian expansionism also (cf. the West's attitude to Nasser). Of course if the West strives to continue with wholly impossible colonial policies the new nationalism will be thrown more and more on to reliance upon Russian support. But this will be highly dangerous to it. For experience shows that once

Russian domination is firmly established in a country it is exceedingly difficult to shake off. A dictatorship finds it easier than a democracy to continue indefinitely the domination by ruthless force of a subject people: for its own people may never know about the process at all. Examples of any retreat or relaxation even of Russian rule over other people, once it has been established, are rare. Yugoslavia was, just, able to free herself without being attacked; Finland, in spite of the fact that she was first attacked by, and then, as a German satellite, attacked, Russia has been treated, for some reason, with marked relative liberality: half of Austria was evacuated; Persian Azerbaijan was occupied briefly just after the end of the second World War and then evacuated; and a relaxation of Russian control has been obtained by Poland. But that is a short list of retreats from and relaxations of Russian exterior rule compared with the immense process of "disimperialism" which has been partly undertaken and partly undergone by the West.[1]

Nevertheless, we in the West shall undoubtedly deceive ourselves if we suppose that a realistic view of the expansionist tendencies of Russia (and China) on the one hand and of the Western powers on the other, will be held, or still more expressed, in the "uncommitted' world. In this matter it is still true that Russia will be more readily forgiven for stealing the horse than we shall be for looking over the gate. And this for a number of reasons, about which we cannot, in the short run at any rate, do very much; we must simply accept them as part of the facts of life. There is, first, the whole colonialist history of the West, together with the irritating colonialist vestiges of the present day. There is, second, the undeniable fact that the Russians, as communists, but also traditionally as Russians, are far less racialist than we are. They genuinely show that they do not think that Asians and Africans are their inferiors. And we often still do. (How many sputniks was Lord Malvern's recent [April 1959] remark in the House of Lords that all Africans were liars worth to the Russians?) It is impossible to overestimate the advantage which the Russians derive from a moral superiority over us in this matter. Third, there is the fact that, so far at least, the Russians have shown themselves unreservedly anxious to encourage, and to a fairly generous degree, considering their own

---

[1] I have said nothing about those huge parts of Russia which the present régime inherited in both Europe and Asia which are ethnically non-Russian. For I do not pretend to know whether the frequent allegations that the Great Russians are ruling unwilling peoples in these regions imperialistically, are well founded or not.

resources, to help, the under-developed countries to set up heavy industry bases of their own, and so to achieve genuine economic independence. Fourth the Russians, and the Chinese, where they have conquered and dominated other countries, have been most careful to institute methods of "indirect" rule, mainly through and by means of the local communists. This has enabled them, in the short run at least, to give a more or less convincing local colour to their domination.

This last reason for the far greater tolerance of uncommitted world opinion for Sino-Russian as against Western expansionism may prove something of a wasting asset, however. There is nothing new, as we have noted repeatedly, in this device of indirect rule. Britain has employed it again and again and, naturally, it is used widely in those parts of the world which are under a relatively high degree of American domination. Therefore we can speak from experience on the matter. And experience suggests that the Russians will discover the disadvantages of "indirect rule": indeed, they have already done so in Hungary. For an especial degree of detestation is often reserved for the native agents of an occupying power. Again there is the depressing problem of what kind of puppets the occupying power is to choose. Shall they be efficient and sensible but, almost inevitably, independently inclined? Or shall they be worthless but dependably subservient? We may recall Colonel Calliaud's cautious protests against the deposition of Mir Jaffier from the Nawobship in the Bengal of the seventeen-sixties (see p. 34, above). The Russians or Chinese may find themselves wondering whether or not to "raise a man to the dignity just as unfit to govern and as little to be depended upon, and in short as great a rogue, as our Nabob, but perhaps not so great a coward, nor so great a fool, and of consequence much more difficult to manage". Worse still in many ways for the occupying power you may pick a man who is not only able but a genuine patriot, a Tito or a Gomulka.

This trying dilemma is not confined to Russian or Chinese ruled dependencies: but Russian and Chinese ruled dependencies are not exempt from it. The truth is that whether in Seoul or in Warsaw, in Manilla or in Budapest, in Mecca or in Pankow, in Guatemala or in Tibet this same old difficulty, which confronted the British in Bengal, may be seen reappearing. Thus the advantages of the Russian reliance on indirect rule may prove in the end to be short-term advantages. Nevertheless and taken together with their other solid advantages over us in the matter of influencing uncommitted opinion we must not suppose that we shall get anything like what will seem to us a fair hearing on this matter in much of the world. Nor will it do us anything but harm to reiterate our irritation with what may seem to us unaccountable Asian and African partiality for the Sino-Russian side. We should be far wiser to let experience alone decide the matter. In Eastern Europe at least experience is working fast.

It would be unreal to discuss all this without taking into account the effect of the communist ideology held by the Russian Government. For it is commonly supposed in the West that the Russian Government intends "to conquer the world for communism" or that at any rate a Messianic communism is used as a cloak for, or is inextricably associated with, a traditional Russian imperialism.

This is a most complex consideration. Let us first notice that on one level communist ideology runs directly counter to Russian imperialist tendencies. It is quite impossible for any Russian statesman to admit for one moment that Russia is seeking to rule other peoples. It is true that this has proved no barrier to the suppression of the Hungarian people by one of the very bloodiest operations in the recent history of imperialism. Nevertheless, it must be, to put it at its lowest, inconvenient for the Russian leaders to have to pretend that they are somehow helping and liberating the Hungarian workers and peasants by shooting them down. And such inconveniences, merely verbal as they may seem in the first instance, are apt to become serious in the long run. It is credibly reported that of the Russian troops used in Hungary, some of the Ukrainian and other non-Great Russian formations, wavered in several instances, partly at least because of the gnawing doubts and conflicts raised in their minds by the inescapable contradictions between what they have been told all their lives and what they were being ordered to do. After all, other imperialists have simply told their own peoples that the subject races were "lesser breeds without the law". No such relatively straightforward methods are open to the heirs of Lenin. On the other hand, of course, Russian troops on the offensive can be told that they are liberating peoples for communism: and if the said peoples do not, like the Hungarians, actually show that they would rather die than be so liberated, the propaganda may well be convincing enough.

A more important question is the extent to which either the handful of men who rule Russia, or the fairly wide circles the opinions of which these rulers are probably beginning to take into account, continue to believe in a Messianic mission to spread communism through the world. On the one hand, they certainly do not believe, and never have believed, that Russia should set out to conquer the world for communism by sheer military force. They have been taught to believe, on the contrary, that it is the military force of the West, and that alone, which prevents the peoples of the world from spontaneously embracing communism. That is universal communist dogma. To what extent informed Russians still believe it: how unimpaired is their faith by their experiences in Eastern and Western Europe, is unknown and probably unknowable: it may well be that the leading men in Russia hardly know themselves what they really believe till the matter is put to the test. But to the extent that they do still believe in their creed, there is little doubt that they will be willing, if the risk is not thought too great, to give history a helping hand along its way, as it were, by using their own military force. This is natural to the extent that they suppose that if only the enemy's force can be cleared out of the way, the liberated peoples will rally to them. This delusion that the peoples everywhere must "really" be longing for the advent of a communist régime is probably by far the most dangerous element remaining in their ideology. For like other delusions it may lead to terrible miscalculations. But for the rest, there are surely signs, not indeed that the communist faith is being repudiated or even in one sense weakened in Russia—we shall delude ourselves if we suppose that—but that the *temperature* at which that faith is held is slowly but surely dropping. What matters above everything else for the world is that the cooling process should continue for many years.

There is also one further material consideration which militates against Russian imperialism. In one simple respect at least the Russian economy is unsuited to imperialism. Russia is still after all a by no means highly developed country; she would still have immensely advantageous opportunities of internal development under any economic system. It is difficult to see, therefore, how any specifically economic compulsions towards imperialist expansion can arise for her for a long time.

To sum up. Many of the same obstacles as we saw obstructed the growth of American imperialism obstruct *mutatis mutandis* the growth of Russian imperialism also. In her case, also, she faces an intensely nationalistic world, composed both of young and weak undeveloped states, but also of much older and stronger states of the middle rank, for the most part in their post-imperial periods. She faces also in America a rival power-centre of her own magnitude, ready and anxious to support any movements of national resistance to her. And, finally, she herself is in some respects at least, unsuited to the imperial role, both by her ideological tradition and her economic structure. All these obstructing factors cast doubt on the plausibility of the assumption, which is so frequently made, that the world is in acute danger of falling under Russian domination.

Before attempting an assessment of the chances of the peoples of the world avoiding a further imperialist epoch, it is necessary at least to glance at the emergence of a third potentially imperial power—namely, China. The Chinese communists have already, in less than a decade, re-established the unity and power of the vast Chinese nation. This is a world-shaking achievement. The world will never be the same kind of place again now that, after an interregnum of forty years, and after more than a century of decline before that, the more than 600 million Chinese are all again living under one effective government. There can be no doubt that China will now resume her habitual place as one of the very greatest of the nations. By 1959 it was becoming apparent, moreover, that some far more dynamic process than the restoration of China to her traditional place in the world was occurring. It seemed clear that over 600 million human beings were being flung (and not necessarily unwillingly) into a process of industrialisation the momentum of which dwarfed any previous experience of this sort in human history. It was still far too early even to attempt any assessment of the Chinese part in the general, world-wide, process of "the great awakening". But already a tremor can be felt running round the whole world. In the late nineteen-fifties men are becoming aware of an event which may prove to be of a different order of magnitude, even, from the industrialisation of America or Russia. (It is all this which makes the American attempt to pretend that China does not exist so pitiful.)

The question is, will China, as she has sometimes done in previous periods, attempt to dominate the non-Chinese areas of Asia? There is nothing inherently improbable in such a suggestion. Russian experience demonstrates that China's communist social and productive relations provide no assurance that she will not: indeed, it will require great restraint on the part of her rulers to moderate the no doubt intoxicating sense of reborn power which must be expected soon to animate the Chinese people. Whether, however, a bid either to world-wide, or more probably to Asian, empire will be made by China remains to be seen. The biggest single factor in determining the issue will un-doubtedly be the success or failure of Indian development. If a second nation, of the same order of magnitude as China, successfully develops in Asia, then the temptation to empire will be far less. A reasonable balance will tend to establish itself. Fortunately, Indian development, of one kind or another, is virtually certain to go forward fairly rapidly during the remainder of the century. Hence there will probably be no Asian vacuum into which China might be almost compelled to expand. Again, her close communist ally, Russia herself, is not certain to wish to aid and abet Chinese expansion, in all circumstances and in all directions. Thus the nascent nationalisms, which would be absorbed by such expansion, may not lack *points d'appui*, in Russia perhaps, as well as in the Western powers, upon the basis of which to attempt to maintain their independence against a possible Chinese imperialism.

We have now glanced in turn at the prospects of the establishment of major new empires by the two existing super-powers, America and Russia, and the potential super-power, China. The possibility of each, or all three, of them successfully attempting to found mighty new empires by subjugating large parts of the world cannot be dismissed. Nevertheless, we have noted that serious obstacles exist to a sustained and successful imperialist drive in each case. The balance of world forces, the intensity of nationalism, the counter-impulses, economic and psychological, to whole-hearted imperialism within the potentially imperialistic super-states themselves, and finally the rivalry between these states, are all interlocking obstacles to the establishment of a new imperialist epoch. These obstacles are not insuperable, but they are formidable. On balance they make it probable that the coming period will be characterised by an unprecedentedly large number of more or less independent nations rather than by the apparition of new world empires. No doubt the alternative is not clear-cut. It may be that some areas of the world will fall, to a greater or lesser extent, under the domination of one or other of the new super-states. Clearly this has happened to some extent already, *e.g.*, South and Central America under America, Eastern Europe under Russia. But these dominations appear to be becoming less, rather than more, stable; and they may not prove incompatible with an increasing degree of genuine national independence in other regions of the world. I reiterate the conviction that the issue may well turn, more than on any other single factor, upon the success or failure of Indian development under democratic institutions.

CHAPTER XXI

MY BROTHER'S KEEPER?

IN SPITE OF ALL the considerations discussed in the last two chapters, the old lust for domination may yet assert itself as the governing motive of the rulers of America, Russia and, later perhaps, China. Their own domination may be seen as a necessity by each of the contending super-powers, not so much as a method of obtaining private or public gain, but rather as the only way in which they can imagine organising the world. If so, nothing anyone else can do can prevent them from seeking to extend their respective empires over the rest of the world, and then from headlong collision between themselves. For their respective views as to the way in which the world can be organised are flatly incompatible. It is only if they will recognise that they cannot, and need not, impose their wills upon the world that there can be a future for the human race upon our crowded planet. Genuine tolerance of each other's existence for an indefinite period is the alternative to mutual destruction.

No doubt this gospel of abstinence from imperialism may seem to the more fiery spirits amongst the leaders of the colossi the wisdom of the elderly, unsuited to gigantic nations bursting with expansive vigour. Perhaps it is; but it may be wisdom none the less. Senators and Commissars alike, no matter how dynamic, will have to face the fact that the world has become a place in which suicide is the only prize of conquest. No one can stop them throwing hydrogen bombs at each other over the North Pole, if they feel so inclined. But a world desert, not a world empire, will be the result. The twentieth-century world has become, partly as a result of nuclear physics, but also as a result of the awakening of communities which even thirty years ago were almost unselfconscious, inhospitable of new imperialisms. Attempts to create them will be more likely to result in the break-up of our period of civilization than in the founding of new world empires. The sole way forward for mankind lies through toleration, restraint, mutual respect and the sparing and temperate exercise of force.

But is the concept of a predominantly non-imperialist world anything more than a dream? The fact that it is becoming apparent that a world without imperialism is likely to be the only world which will be habitable to man is inconclusive. There are, however, as we have noted, substantial reasons for supposing that the world is now entering a period in which it may be possible for the nations to live without trying to establish empire over each other. That possibility arises from the ever accelerating march of technique. We are unmistakably learning how to command our natural environment (although only a small minority of mankind have begun actually to do so). It is now undeniably possible to secure adequate supplies of food, shelter, and the other requirements of existence by an expenditure of labour which leaves much time for those more complex forms of activity which are indispensable for civilisation. Moreover, we can now, if we like, see to it that our numbers remain suitably adjusted to our environment. This means that civilisation has ceased, for the first time in history, to be dependent upon the enslavement, or even the exploitation, of one man by another.

Civilisation has always hitherto necessarily resembled the human pyramid of a troupe of acrobats. The immense majority of men have had to expend all their strength in upholding a small minority upon their shoulders, who in turn have carried a handful upon theirs, till traditionally the apex of the pyramid was reached in one culminating individual. There was no other way in which any part of the human race could be raised into the light and air in which considerable cultural achievements became possible. Till a revolution in technique had taken place it was not possible to dispense with empire. Interwoven at a thousand points with the exploitation of one class by another within communities, the institution of empire has enabled small groups to raise themselves upon the ill-requited labour of others, to a position of power, ease and culture. Even to suggest that all this is now to stop may seem fanciful in the extreme. Nevertheless, it is a fact that the existence of empire is becoming no longer necessary to civilisation. In the more developed human communities of the mid-twentieth century it is clearly possible to maintain civilisation without any considerable degree of the exploitation of the labour of other men or other nations.

No doubt this does not necessarily mean that men and nations will not in fact continue to exploit each other. While no longer indispensable, such exploitation may still be thought advantageous. Getting other human beings to do the drudgery for one is still a very attractive thing. Moreover, empire, conquest and subjugation are perhaps propensities of human nature as it has had to evolve. It will be prudent to assume that men will tend to perpetuate this deeply established pattern of behaviour even after its economic necessity has largely disappeared.

Nevertheless, when the economic necessity of such an institution as empire has gone out of it, it may be expected to begin to lose its power. After all, there is now an intense resistance to imperialism. The underdog is not only growling but also on occasion biting far more effectively than ever before. And that, too, is in the last resort connected with the dawning consciousness that the existence of underdogs is no longer an objective necessity. Thus, on the one hand, resistance to the exploitation of the labour of one human group by another grows more formidable and more expensive to overcome; on the other, it becomes increasingly possible to live well by reliance upon the new techniques instead of upon other men's underpaid work. We are entitled at least to envisage the breath-taking possibility of the end of the imperialist epoch. That would mark a hardly less momentous stage in history than did the emergence of civilisation itself some six millennia ago.

An end of the imperialist epoch is then both possible and a precondition of our survival. Nevertheless abstention from imperialism will, in itself, by no means solve the world's problems. It was asserted that the contemporary revolution in technique had given men the objective possibility of commanding, fairly satisfactorily, their natural environment. But little attempt to make that possibility actual has yet been made by the immense majority of mankind. And between the possibility and the fact there is an immense gulf.

Socialists in particular should by now be aware that they have here been guilty of a major foreshortening of the historical perspective in this connection. Because the socialist ideal arose in the industrial, or industrialising, nations, and reflected their conditions, the industrial revolution was taken to be something which had already happened: in that sense indeed it was taken for granted. It is only now when the whole world has to be taken into account that the full parochialism of this assumption is revealed. The fact is that the industrial revolution, for the immense majority of mankind, is an event of the future, not of the past. Moreover, the industrial revolution, it is now only too painfully apparent, is not merely a revolution in the technique of production. It has specifically economic aspects which are profoundly important. Before a change in the technique of production can be achieved, a redirection of productive labour at the existing level of technique must be undertaken. And that redirection of productive labour must be away from the satisfaction of immediate wants and towards the satisfaction of future wants. Thus it may initially involve, other things being equal, an actual fall in existing standards of life.

In the peasant countries of the undeveloped world there is, it is true, a vast reservoir of unused or underused labour which, if it could be tapped, might enable the basic work of industrialisation to be done without diverting *usefully employed* labour from producing goods and services for immediate consumption. This is the unused, partially used, or misused labour of the peasant masses, who at their primitive level of agriculture can work, it is often reckoned, no more than 100 days in the year. If somehow or other this less than half used supply of labour could be applied to the tasks of industrialisation immense achievements would become possible. But almost insurmountable tasks of social reorganisation must be faced before anything of this sort can even be attempted. First the system of individual peasant agriculture which has endured for millennia must be destroyed and uprooted. (And this was the task which came so near to proving beyond the power of even the Russian dictatorship that Stalin told Churchill that the worst crisis of the second World War was not so grave as the crisis brought on by collectivisation: this is the task before which every single communist régime in Eastern Europe has now recoiled.) But this is only the first, negative, side of what has to be done. Next a new agricultural system which will produce more food with a far smaller labour force has to be organised, and finally a way of putting the millions of ex-peasants thus released on to the work of building the basis of an industrial system, must be found. Moreover in the under-developed world of to-day all this must be gone through in the midst of an explosive rise in population due to the onset of preventive medicine. Any attempt quickly to put through the profound agricultural revolution necessary to tap this one great source of unused labour in the undeveloped countries is, surely, in practice impossible without resort to a communist dictatorship using totalitarian methods.[1]

But short of this agricultural revolution whence can the labour for the immediately unproductive task of industrialisation come? Even if, as in India, there exists a pool of unemployed town workers, their consumption will have to be raised sharply if and when they are brought into employment. Moreover they must be provided with tools and plant and equipment without which the process cannot begin. But where are the resources, the extra food, clothing and shelter as well as the necessary tools, plant and equipment to come

[1] China in 1959 is in the throes of this revolution, which is being attempted on the most gigantic scale, by ultra-totalitarian methods and at a speed even greater than that imposed by Stalin.

from? Again in default of the methods open to a communist dictatorship, can there be any doubt that they must largely come from outside?
that initially at least they must be supplied in one way or another out
of the resources of the developed world?

A whole economic literature on these hardest of hard facts of the
contemporary world is beginning to appear.[1] In this matter, as in so
many others, it is the first step which is almost insufferably painful.
Once a country has industrialised itself (including, especially, the
development of its agriculture) up to a certain point, the rest is comparatively easy. For, by then, it will be comparatively rich. The output
of its citizens per man year will be, that is to say, markedly above what
is needed to sustain them. There will be nothing very painful in their
diverting a part of their national effort from feeding, clothing and
housing themselves, to making machines, to building harbours, railways, schools, hospitals, roads, dams, factories, steel mills, power grids
and, also (which is in some ways more difficult) to training the men and
women to operate them. As the process of industrialisation goes
forward, the devotion of more and more of our labour to better
satisfying future wants (in terms of money this is called saving—either
public or private saving) becomes easier and easier; it is the first step
which is agonising.

There is thus a profound contrast between the relative ease of
saving, investing, accumulating—call it what you will—it is in essence
the process of adding to the stock of means of production—in the
developed countries and the initial agony of that process in undeveloped countries. It has been reckoned that the highly developed
countries year by year add to their means of production more per head
than the entire production per head of the undeveloped countries.
Therefore, even if the Asians, Africans and other peoples of the undeveloped world could live on air and devote the whole of their
labour to investment they would still be adding to their stock of productive equipment more slowly than we are. In fact, of course, no
undeveloped country can hope to set aside more than between 10%
and 20% (at the very utmost) of its productive power to adding to its
stock of means of production: if it attempts to do so more and more of
its people will drop below subsistence level. But this means that the

[1] See, for example, Professor Arthur Lewis' *Theory of Economic Growth* (Allen and
Unwin, 1954), Professor Gunnar Myrdal's *An International Economy* (1957), and *Economic
Theory and Under-developed Regions* (Duckworth, 1958). Professor Ragnar Nurkse's
Problems of Capital Formation in Under-Developed Countries (Oxford, 1953); and for a
Marxist-Leninist view of the matter *The Political Economy of Growth*, Paul A. Baran
(Monthly Review Press, 1957).

undeveloped countries can only hope, even by the most heroic efforts, to add to their means of production at a relatively modest rate. We, of the developed countries, on the other hand, by the almost painless process of setting aside between 10% and 20% of our effort, can add to our means of production perhaps ten times as fast (per head) as the undeveloped countries can hope to do.[1]

The gap between the standard of life of the peoples of the developed and the undeveloped world, already very wide, will on this reckoning almost inevitably grow wider and wider. It is true that if—and it is an immense if—the efforts of the peoples of the undeveloped world are well directed and successful, and if their self-discipline and capacity for self-denial holds firm, their absolute standard of life will be slowly rising. But ours may well be rising something like ten times as fast! Who can tell what such an ever-widening gap in development would mean? It may be argued that so long as the absolute standard of life of the main body of the human race in the undeveloped countries is slowly rising, it will not matter so much if the standard of life of the small advanced guard of the industrialised nations rises far more rapidly. But even if this doubtful proposition proves true, it assumes complete success on the part of the peoples of the undeveloped countries and their governments. In the far more likely event of some initial failures and setbacks in their plans, we may well face a period in which the standard of life of the undeveloped peoples will actually be falling while ours is rapidly rising. (This according to some estimates is the case to-day.) What would happen then? The world is incomparably more aware of itself than ever before. For the first time in history, the nearly two thousand million peasants of the undeveloped world know of the existence of that other life in the West which seems to them so fabulous. What if they discover no way by which they may share in its benefits? What if they see and hear of atomic power stations, jet air liners and, far more important, schools, hospitals, healing drugs, houses, tractors and, simply, enough food to eat, but find that somehow the ability of man to produce such things is of no use to them? They are not economists. They will scarcely appreciate the fact that an immensely arduous effort on their own part is, in any case, necessary, before these marvels can be introduced to their lands. The first natural reaction of anyone who does not habitually think in

[1] It is necessary to warn the reader that the statisticians who compile such figures as these are the first to warn us of the wide margins of error to which they are subject. They should be regarded as orders of magnitude illustrating general trends, rather than as real estimates. But that is sufficient for our purpose.

economic terms is to suppose that once the technical problem of production has been solved, everything else follows easily enough. Our minds, as much in the developed as in the undeveloped world, tend to skip over the specifically economic aspects of the problem. We tend to ignore, for example, such facts as that the atomic generation of electricity, though it may in the end transform the world, requires a far greater accumulation of capital per unit generated than does any other method of power production: that the production of raw electric power is itself only the next step in a long chain of productive processes, the establishment of each one of which requires a large preliminary accumulation of capital. It needs, that is to say, the diversion of a large number of man-hours of labour on to work which will be, for years on end, unproductive of consumer goods. We seldom allow for the fact that all this has to be successfully accomplished before the invention of atomically generated power can benefit an Asian peasant by a single anna.

What is to be done? We now observe that the question which we are really asking is this: what is to be put in the place of empire? For fully developed capitalist imperialism was a method—of a sort—for transferring capital from the developed to the undeveloped world; and that, clearly, is what has somehow or other to be done. Under imperialism capital was transferred to the undeveloped world by the lure of private profit. When it arrived it imposed one form or other of subjugation and exploitation upon the undeveloped peoples: it was irresponsible, rapacious, blindly acquisitive: it dragged the armed violence of its governments along with it. But to a certain extent, and at a cost which is now prohibitive, it did the job. We now see that we cannot just destroy imperialism and put nothing in its place. There must be *some* relationship between the developed and the undeveloped, the strong and the weak. The great centres of industry, capital and power cannot possibly cut themselves off from the vast undeveloped hinterland which still comprises by far the greater part of the world. A new relationship between these two worlds must be found. This, however, will entail profound changes in their attitude towards each other of both the developed and the undeveloped peoples.

In the first place the undeveloped peoples must learn successfully to protect their own interests in the course of their necessary but difficult intercourse with the industrialised nations. This problem is in many respects analogous to the problem which was discussed in the first volume of this study, namely the problem of the relations, within states, between the directing minority and the mass of wage-earners and farmers or peasants. We saw that the general tendency of capitalism, unless powerfully counteracted, was to suck up the whole national product, over and above a mere subsistence for the wage-earners and independent producers, into the hands of a now relatively small category of property owners and their dependents. What had prevented, in a few favoured nations, this tendency from having long ago gone to lengths which must have wrecked the system was the fact that the mass of the population had been able to use their political power, fairly effectively, to redress this economic balance. It was political democracy, persistently used, which had prevented the innate tendencies of capitalism from taking the major industrial societies to catastrophe. We had learnt, in some few, but highly important, nations, to count the vote of the wage-earner and the farmer as genuinely equal to that of the property-owner. Thus the former had more and more succeeded in using the power of the state for their own benefit. Is it not clear that some analogous process of countervailing power (in Professor Galbraith's phrase) can alone prevent lethal consequences arising from the present extreme disproportions of wealth and power as between nations? We have quoted Professor Myrdal's account of how, on the international scale, also, the "haves" tend in the nature of things to denude the "have-nots" even of what they once had. It was not so much that, we saw, the developed nations directly acted to exploit the under-developed: it was rather that exploitation arose quite naturally and spontaneously out of the "free", uncontrolled, economic intercourse of the strong with the weak. It is indispensable to find some way of counteracting this process. Otherwise out of their economic contacts, indispensable in themselves, with the "have-not" nations, the capital-generating centres must tend to suck up the world's life's blood, and then to fight to the death amongst themselves.

The only force available for such counteraction is some form of democracy applied between nations, in a way analogous to that in which the democratic principle has been applied within (a few) nations. But international democracy is a very difficult thing to practise. The nations of the mid-twentieth century are very far from being equal, either in degree of development, in experience, in social coherence, in capacity for organisation, in wealth or in power. To ask the United States to exercise no more power in the world than Paraguay is to ask the impossible. One nation, one vote, is a far more difficult ideal to apply in practice than one man, one vote. Fortunately, it is no more necessary to achieve this ideal of perfect equality in the international field than it has been to effect perfect political equality in the internal field in order to reverse the process of ever-increasing misery. The political power of a millionaire in America or Britain is still far greater than that of a wage-earner. Nevertheless, the fact that, with his vote and his Union, the wage-earner is not impotent has in actual practice succeeded in ensuring that the will of the wage-earners as a group has sometimes, and in important respects, prevailed over the will of the millionaires. (For there are so many wage-earners and so few millionaires.) In the same way, it may suffice to check and even reverse the overweening strength of the highly developed peoples if the weaker nations retain some power: for there are a great many of them. It is by strengthening the hand of the "have-nots" that apparently impotent institutions such as the United Nations can have an importance. They provide a forum within which the beginnings of an international public opinion can arise. (And this, of course, is why the United Nations and its international institutions are likely to become increasingly unpopular in certain circles in the developed nations.)

But all this will not be enough. It will not be enough by itself to save the world, most probably from total destruction, certainly from totalitarian dictatorship. For there to be any chance at all for the survival of free societies, a basic change of attitude is required of us, the inhabitants of the highly developed nations. For the world cannot depend exclusively upon the strength and influence of the undeveloped countries to put a co-operative relationship in the place of empire. Something more, something from the side of the strong will be needed if intolerable inequality, leading to catastrophes at least as great as those of the imperialist epoch, are to be avoided. And that something more cannot be anything else but deliberate acts, motivated by conscious moral and intellectual convictions, on the part of the developed peoples themselves. It is necessary that the developed countries should deliberately intervene *against* their own interests, or at least against their apparent interests: that they should deliberately refrain from buying as cheap or selling as dear as they might: that they should give, or lend at especially low rates, to the undeveloped world, or should undertake a combination of such measures.

To some extent a precedent for such action may be found in the Marshall Aid programme undertaken by the United States, in the Colombo Plan programme of the British Commonwealth, and in the similar programmes of the last fourteen years. Have not these programmes, it may be said, made some sort of a start at reversing the centripetal forces of the market by means of a centrifugal flow of capital consciously directed by non-economic motives? It is necessary, however, to say two things about these programmes. In the first place, they are quantitatively wholly inadequate to the task which now faces the world. They are inadequate not simply in the sense that they will not do enough: they are inadequate in the sense that they cannot be expected to do anything decisive to save the situation. Second, the one really considerable programme, that of Marshall Aid, was not directed to the movement of capital from the developed to the undeveloped world at all. It was a salvage operation between America and the other war-shattered but developed countries. It may have been—indeed, it was—indispensable: but it did not directly even touch the real problem. Moreover these programmes are constantly and perhaps increasingly under fire. They were originally launched for various motives, but, it must be agreed, above all in order to enable Western Europe to rally sufficiently to withstand communism. Now that that indispensable purpose has been achieved such programmes are widely thought to be unnecessary. The very conception of a sustained effort, on an adequate scale, and made for its own sake, without prospect of profit, to aid in the industrialisation of the undeveloped world is profoundly alien to the mental climate of accumulative societies such as ours.

The difficulty is not, indeed, that the sacrifices demanded of the rich nations would be large. A slight slowing up of the rapid rate of progress which they are in a position to make would be enough. For, as we have seen, it is of the essence of the situation that the disproportion between the national incomes of the internationally rich and the internationally poor is already so great, that a quite marginal gain or loss for the rich may well make a decisive difference for the poor. The developed, post-industrial, world cannot be expected to provide the bulk of the huge quantities of capital which will be needed over the decades to set the feet of the main body of mankind upon the road of development. All that can be done, and all that is necessary, is to provide that relatively small but decisive quantity of capital which will overcome the initial inertia of economies which have been technically static for millennia. What has to be provided is the "assisted take-off", without which the undeveloped world can never under democratic institutions get under way at all. Indeed, it can be argued that the provision of this degree of aid will actually benefit the post-industrial nations themselves as against what would happen in practice if they did not provide it. For, as we have also noted, there is evidence to show that if and when the rich nations push their advantage to the hilt it becomes so great that even they do not really benefit. International exchanges become so disrupted (as in the 'thirties) that more is lost to the rich nations in this way than is gained by them on the terms of trade.

What has to be faced is not, then, an economic but a moral difficulty. Any attempt consciously to replace the imperialist relationship by a new relationship of genuine co-operation necessitates a decision to give away money, or advantage of one kind or another, to the undeveloped world. And there is simply no provision for any such action in the system of ideas which has grown up in association with capitalist relations of production. The mental climate of capitalism still strongly presupposes that there is something unreal, if not positively wrong, in making economic decisions which run counter to the visible pull of profit and the tangible push of loss. Thus proposals for the aid of the undeveloped areas necessarily seem, at best, unbusinesslike and fanciful to dominant opinion. It is not that those who own or control the capital surpluses of the developed world are uncharitable men. On the contrary, as long as a proposal is labelled as charitable they will give away many millions of dollars. The great American foundations, such as the Ford Foundation, habitually do so. But unfortunately this is not what is needed. Such charitable distributions can never be of the order of magnitude necessary. What is needed are, precisely, economic decisions as to the disposal of a small but significant part of the developed nations' main capital surpluses; economic decisions which are based on considerations wider than those of the pull of profit and the push of loss. And it is just this sort of decision which inevitably seems so wrong to men steeped in the ideology of capitalism. It strikes them as a mixed, false sort of decision: a decision which requires them to be false to the very values which they have pursued all their lives. Why, they feel, should capital be poured into Asia or tropical Africa, where it will yield very little or nothing at all, when it could be invested at home, or if not at home in Canada, Australia, Western Europe or South Africa, to yield a handsome profit? Would it not be sloppy sentimentalism to do so? Would it not be a sin against the rules of a free enterprise society, a socialistic interference with the necessary and beneficial workings of the world-wide economic system?

Hitherto this attitude of mind has been overcome—to the relatively minor extent to which it has been overcome—mainly by using the argument that if we do not give or lend to the under-developed world, the communists will inherit it. This is almost certainly true. Nevertheless, to rely on such an argument will not do. Experience shows that aid given from such fear-ridden motives will be reluctant, sparse and conditional: it will have such "strings" attached to it that it will arouse resentment rather than appreciation. Indeed on the level of the direct and immediate self-interest of the rich countries, there *are* no conclusive arguments in favour of generosity. For it may be quite plausibly asserted that we may actually increase the propensity for revolution in the undeveloped world by helping to rouse it from stagnation. Thus if the argument stays on this level the most likely outcome will be that the developed world, while perhaps refraining from embarking upon a new epoch of positive imperialism, will come to regard the undeveloped world with a sort of semi-hostile indifference. (One may sense such a mood in much comment on present-day India, for example.) Am I my brother's keeper? may be the surly response of the rich nations to the struggles and sufferings of the nations undergoing the great awakening. But if we offer the stone of indifference in place of the sword of empire we shall ourselves perish.

The truth is that there is only one conclusive reason why we should help the peoples of the undeveloped world: and that is because it is right for us to do so. It is morally right. It is to-day a moral imperative for the nations of the Western world to use a part of their great resources to aid the peoples who still live and die in destitution. If this is not right, what is? It is not until the argument is taken to this level that we can see that our duty and our interest are one. It is we, the nations of Christendom, who have preached to the world that to do as we would be done by is the supreme moral imperative. Shall we now practise it? If we fail in this neither denunciations of "atheistic communism" nor nuclear weapons will avail us. The sole future for the highly developed countries is in this. They can only expand and grow in and through the development of the rest of the world. The moral and the material factors are inextricably united. Only a generous, expansive climate of opinion can save such mature societies as ours from a progressive sclerosis of both mind and heart; only unself-seeking participation in the vast enterprises of world development can generate such a national morale. Two thousand million hungering, suffering, struggling men and women need the help which we alone can give. The world to-day is a ten thousand times more dynamic place than ever before in its history. We have only to go out into it both to lose and to find ourselves.

PART III

TOWARDS A THEORY OF IMPERIALISM

THE FOLLOWING PAGES discuss the subject matter of this book from a more theoretical point of view. They have been placed at the end since they may or may not interest the reader. I must admit to a sustained interest in the attempts which historians, economists and sociologists have made to discover the nature of such major historical phenomena as the establishment, growth and nature of empires. These attempts have never, it is true, been particularly successful, and perhaps they never will be. Nevertheless, it would be a poor generation which ceased to make them.[1]

In the Preface the term empire was defined very broadly as meaning any successful attempt to conquer and subjugate a people with the intention of ruling them for an indefinite period. No doubt it would be equally permissible to define empire and imperialism more narrowly. For example, some people probably have in mind almost exclusively contemporary capitalist imperialism, as it has existed in the last hundred years when they use the term. But clearly imperialism has a wider meaning than this. Everyone talks of the Roman Empire and Roman imperialism. Therefore so narrow a definition would contradict common usage. Again some people might be inclined to reserve the term for conquests beyond the seas, usually over peoples of another race. But such a definition would exclude such conquests as the Tsarist annexation of the Caucasus, which was, surely, a typically imperialist act. Finally, most people would suppose that imperialism was associated with the exploitation of one people by another.

This last consideration will involve us in the question of how and why the empires of the world originated. For we had to insist, in order to give the term much meaning, that even on the broadest definition imperialism is something distinct from simple war and aggression. We insisted that it involved the attempt to rule a subject people more or less permanently. Inevitably then the question arises of why one people, one nation, society—group of human beings however organised— should wish to subjugate and rule other such groups. Moreover this question of the motivation of imperialism will present itself sharply

[1] See below, p. 341n.

when we notice that if we go back far enough in human history, namely to the epoch of primitive societies, such a motive did not, apparently, exist. For such societies did not attempt to rule each other.

The anthropological record shows that some primitive societies have been pacific, others violent and aggressive. A good many of them waged war often enough, if on the whole in rather a desultory sort of way compared to our own standards. But one thing they did not do: they did not attempt to found empires over each other. This is an undeniable but neglected fact. On the other hand, it is equally a fact that whenever and wherever men have reached a certain stage of social development, which we usually call civilisation, but not before, they have begun, not merely to fight, but also to found empires—to conquer, to subjugate and to enslave each other. Only one explanation has ever been given of the fact that empires do not appear upon the stage of history before this point in social development is reached; but that explanation is simple and satisfactory. Men did not subjugate each other before they were what we call civilised because it would not have paid them to do so.

It would not have paid them because below a certain level of technique a man's labour did not, on the average, yield an appreciable surplus over and above what was indispensable to maintain himself, and spread outwards at a thin density of population over the earth's surface. In such conditions what would have been the point of capturing and enslaving another man? Even if you had successfully enslaved him, you could not have got anything out of his labour; for he had to devote all his time to maintaining himself. If you had tried to take any appreciable part of the fruits of his labour from him for your own use, you would soon have found yourself in the position of the French peasant in the story. The peasant complained, it will be recalled, that no one had such bad luck as himself. Just as he had taught his donkey to live without eating, the wretched creature had died. It was not until men learned to produce more than they had to consume in order to live, that the dazzling possibility of living off other men's labour, of subjugation, slavery and exploitation, and therefore, as we shall notice in a moment, of empire, could appear in history.

We must call that possibility dazzling, as well as dreadful, for two reasons. In the first place, let us face the fact that civilisation could never have developed without some men living off the labour of others, *i.e.*, without exploitation; moreover, it could never have developed without the original and absolute form of that exploitation—namely, slavery. At the level of man's command over nature at which men had only just learnt how to produce a modest surplus over and above their basic needs, but no more, the whole elaborate structure of civilisation could not have been raised on any other basis than that of exploitation by means of enslavement. How else, at that level, could there have been scope for specialisation, for the development, on the basis of a social division of labour, of mental work, of writing, of new techniques of production, as well as for the more equivocal benefits of a leisured class?

In the second place, the discovery of the possibility of living off other men's labour was doubtless dazzling in a simpler and more personal sense also. To live without labour is delicious: or at least it has always seemed so. To be relieved from the curse of Adam must have seemed to those first ruling classes of the first civilisations a most wonderful thing. But at that time it could only be accomplished by means of the direct enslavement of other human beings. At this early stage of development what was at issue was no sophisticated question of the exchange of commodities at unfair ratios of exchange. In those days you could only live without working if you could directly and physically compel other men to grow your food, weave your clothes, and generally minister to your wants, in addition to maintaining themselves: if, in a word, you could command the labour of slaves. It was at this point in human development, when the major, primary inventions, agriculture, the wheel, writing, building in brick and stone, were being made: when the first civilisations of the great river valleys were beginning (and not before) that exploitation, in its original and absolute form of slavery, and consequentially imperialism, made, and had to make, their appearance.

For no sooner did the new kind of civilised societies appear than they became, or attempted to become, empires. Sumer, Assyria, Egypt, the Indus States, the States of the Yellow River, the South and Central American societies—wherever the archaeologist's spade has begun to discover for us the (so far as we know) earliest examples of civilisation, we find empires. We find, that is to say, that men in the act of organising themselves into those larger, more powerful societies called civilisations used their new powers, not only, and perhaps not even principally, to increase further their command over nature, but also and above all to subdue and enslave other men, and so to increase their command over human labour.

In those days a man-hour of human labour was inescapably wealth itself. There was no other practicable way of acquiring wealth than to acquire the command of man-hours of other people's labour. And the simplest way to do it was to enslave those other men. But where were the slaves to come from? Much the best source was obviously the conquest of other peoples. True, the progressive exploitation of the poorest sections of the population of the emergent empire itself, including sometimes their final enslavement, was possible, and was not neglected. But that was a slow and cumbrous method of acquiring the command of other people's labour compared to the conquest and enslavement of whole nations. Wars with neighbouring peoples had been going on since time immemorial; there was nothing new in them. What were new were the invention of settled agriculture in the great river valleys and the techniques of urban life which could be built upon it. It was these techniques which made it pay to take prisoner a conquered people instead of eating, killing or scattering them. The labour of the captives now had value; they had become too useful to kill. Therefore whole nations were, if possible, enslaved by the first successful empires and their labour used to provide the indispensable surpluses. Thus, originally at any rate, exploitation, enslavement, subjugation and empire are indissolubly connected concepts. The establishment of the first empires came about as a result of the attempt to provide an adequate supply of surplus-producing, slave, labour. True, a part of the home population could be itself enslaved, but these internal supplies were evidently inadequate without resort to the subjugation of other peoples. Thus imperialism in its original form could almost be called enslavement applied externally: and the enslavement of a part of the home population could almost be called a sort of internal imperialism.

The above account of the evolution of human society was, of course, first clearly formulated by Marx and Engels. And as in the case of their other major discoveries, all of which were, and still are, profoundly unwelcome to their educated contemporaries, unceasing efforts have ever since been made to ignore it, to deny it, to explain it away and to pooh-pooh it. In particular it was urgently necessary, it was felt, to get rid, somehow or other, of this horrid notion that human civilisation was originally built upon exploitation and enslavement. But when all the angry denials or patronising comments have been made, can anyone doubt that this is one of those big, broad sociological discoveries which, once they have been made, can never be disposed of again? We may think what we will of this or that part of the Marxian vision of historical and social development. But we shall never succeed in effectively denying some of its broad, simple insights, such as this one that the very possibility of the exploitation and subjugation of one set of men by another—including the possibility of empire—is indissolubly associated with the development of technique beyond that critical point at which men, on the average, can produce a surplus over and above their subsistence.

No doubt the idea, once stated, is sufficiently obvious. But the fact remains that no one *did* adequately state it before Marx and Engels, and that it is steadily ignored or resisted.[1] But that very resistance betrays the validity of the concept. For of course it is just *because* civilisation always has been, and to a decreasing but substantial extent still is, founded upon exploitation that we find it so painful to acknowledge the fact. The science of individual psychology as it has developed since Marx and Engels' day makes it easy to recognise all the hallmarks of a typical repression in the resistance which these otherwise almost self-evident concepts of sociology still encounter.

Engels declared in a famous passage that at a primitive stage of human development slavery was unquestionably a progressive institution. The passage occurs in the *Anti-Dühring*, and it may be useful to quote the whole of it both for its intrinsic interest and because it will serve as a summary of the concept just set out. Engels is writing of the critical point in social development at which civilisations appear:

"Production had so far developed that the labour power of a man could now produce more than was necessary for its mere mainten-ance; the means of maintaining additional labour forces existed; likewise the means of employing them; labour power acquired a *value*. But within the community and the association to which it belonged there were no superfluous labour forces available. On the other hand, such forces were provided by war, and war was as old as the simultaneous existence alongside each other of several groups of communities. Up to that time they had not known what to do with prisoners of war, and had therefore simply killed them; at an even earlier period eaten them. But at the stage of the 'economic order' which had now been attained the prisoners acquired a value; their captors therefore let them live and made use of their labour. Thus force, instead of controlling the economic order, was on the

[1] In connection with this question of how we ought to treat Marx and his work, I cannot resist repeating the opinion of Professor Toynbee, expressed in a letter to the writer. Professor Toynbee wrote that we must not regard Marx as on the one hand an infallible prophet or on the other as one nineteenth-century sociologist amongst many, but rather as "just an ordinary man of genius"!

contrary pressed into the service of the economic order. *Slavery* was invented. It soon became the predominant form of production among all peoples who were developing beyond the primitive community, but in the end was also one of the chief causes of the decay of that system. It was slavery that first made possible the division of labour between agriculture and industry on a considerable scale, and along with this the flower of the ancient world, Hellenism. Without slavery, no Greek state, no Greek art and science; without slavery, no Roman Empire. But without Hellenism and the Roman Empire as a basis, also no modern Europe. . . .

"It is very easy to inveigh against slavery and similar things in general terms, and to give vent to high moral indignation at such infamies. Unfortunately all that this conveys is only what everyone knows, namely, that these institutions of antiquity are no longer in accord with our present conditions and our sentiments, which these conditions determine. But it does not tell us one word as to how these institutions arose, why they existed, and what role they have played in history. And when we examine these questions, we are compelled to say—however contradictory and heretical it may sound—that the introduction of slavery under the conditions of that time was a great step forward. For it is a fact that man sprang from the beasts, and had consequently to use barbaric and almost bestial means to extricate himself from barbarism. The ancient communes, where they continued to exist, have for thousands of years formed the basis of the most barbarous form of state, oriental despotism, from India to Russia. It was only where these communities dissolved that the peoples made progress of themselves, and their first economic advance consisted in the increase and development of production by means of slave labour. It is clear that so long as human labour was still so little productive that it provided but a small surplus over and above the necessary means of subsistence, any increase of the productive forces, extension of trade, development of the state and of law, or beginning of art and science, was only possible by means of a greater division of labour. And the necessary basis for this was the great division of labour between the masses discharging simple manual labour and the few privileged persons directing labour, conducting trade and public affairs, and, at a later stage, occupying themselves with art and science. The simplest and most natural form of this division of labour was in fact slavery. In the historical conditions of the ancient world, and particularly of Greece, the advance to a society based on class antagonisms could only be accomplished in the form of slavery. This was an advance even for the slaves; the prisoners of war, from whom the mass of the slaves were recruited, now at least kept their lives, instead of being killed as they had been before, or even roasted, as at a still earlier period" (*Herr Eugen Dühring's Revolution in Science (Anti-Dühring)*, by Frederick Engels; Martin Lawrence, pp. 205-7).

No doubt many nice distinctions could be drawn between enslavement and subjugation on the one hand and empire proper. For example are we to reserve the term empire for the rule of one people by another while leaving them in their original territory, or should we extend it to cover "Babylonian captivities" in which conquered peoples such as the Jews of old or the Negroes of recent centuries have been "imported" as slaves into the territory of the conquerors? On the whole common usage seems to give the term the narrower sense in this respect. But surely it does not much matter. The essential thing is to grasp the concept that empire and imperialism—whatever they may have become in the end—were originally attempts to secure adequate supplies of surplus-producing labour. For my part, I find this the only rational explanation of the undeniable fact that the regular subjugation of one group of men by another, growing into the vast historical phenomenon of empire, appears universally at the dawn of civilisation, and not before.

It follows naturally from the above concept that the first empires were of a particular kind; and in fact they have often been called "the servile empires". This brings us to the question of whether or not it is possible to distinguish different kinds or varieties of empires. Three such varieties have been distinguished, namely (i) the original, servile, empires based upon slave labour, (ii) the mercantile empires based upon the plundering sort of commerce which we have described in some detail in the case of the East India Company's eighteenth-century empire in India, and (iii) the fully developed capitalist empires discussed in later chapters. These distinctions between different kinds of empires seem useful so long as they are not pressed too hard; so long that is to say as it is realised that they are not clear cut, that many empires have been to some extent instances of at least two of these varieties. It may be worth while to say something as to each variety.

First, the servile empires. We must not, of course, conceive of the achievement of civilisation as anywhere happening suddenly or quickly, still less as happening by means of conscious volition. On the contrary, this decisive event, which is the starting-point of recorded human history, was a most complex process. From the economist's standpoint it was an effect of the development of the technique of production beyond the point at which man can produce not only a product but also a *surplus* product. From the sociologist's standpoint it was the evolution of the city and of a *social* division of labour, in which not merely odd individuals but whole classes of citizens could be increasingly withdrawn from directly productive labour, and become engaged professionally in fighting, governing, performing the priestly function, and in writing, calculating and in the plastic arts. This whole wonderful evolution took place over comparatively long periods of time, by fits and starts, with local variations, and not without episodes of failure and regression to simpler conditions. Nevertheless, it marks the first great watershed of human history. I do not think that anyone knows why or how the thing happened. But that it began to happen some six thousand years ago and that it happened probably independently, and certainly repeatedly, in some of the great river valleys of the world, is undoubted. It is also undoubted that this pattern of development into civilisation was in each case similar, at least to the extent that the event was of the peculiarly two-sided kind which we have discussed. It was, that is to say, at one and the same time a vast liberation of new productive forces and an enslavement of whole peoples.

Here, however, a distinction is necessary. The original ancient empires cannot all be regarded as essentially slave hunting societies. Some of them, Assyria, for instance, and to a surprising extent Rome itself in a later period, seem to have remained essentially that. In other instances, however, the original empires, after an initial phase of slave gathering conquests, settled down into long, static periods, in which predatory wars occurred only at intervals. In these periods, so characteristic of the major Asiatic empires, the indispensable process of exploitation, by means of which the surplus product was taken from its producers for the use of a governing class, was not exclusively or even mainly effected by means of direct enslavement. It was done by means of two familiar techniques (very early evolved) by which nominally free, or semi-free, peasants were relieved of the surplus which they produced over and above their own subsistence. It was done by the devices, as old as civilisation itself, of rent and taxes, such rent and taxes being paid either in kind or in money. The main forms of feudalism are from our point of view merely variations on this theme.

In this way many of the early empires became peasant rather than slave empires. And these vast, unchanging peasant empires have endured, in some cases, from the birth of civilisation to our own day. Their emergence marked, no doubt, the next great advance in specifically *social* technique, *i.e.*, the invention of a way in which men could be exploited without the cumbrous and difficult business of directly enslaving them. Moreover it really was an advance: there need be no irony in speaking of it in these terms. For on the one hand, some form of exploitation, of the removal of the surplus produce from its producers, was indispensable to any form of civilisation at that stage of human development. And, on the other hand, it really was preferable to be a peasant, however exploited, than a slave. Moreover, the ruling classes of the peasant empires did give their subjects something in return for the surplus product of which they relieved them. They gave them government, of a kind; law courts of a sort, a law and order which was sometimes (although not always) preferable to mere anarchy; and in some cases they gave them irrigation also.

The peasant empires have differed widely amongst themselves in the degree of return which their governing classes have given to their governed. Ancient China, no doubt, in its great periods, reached the highest point ever attained by this form of human society. There a regular, administrative civil service, to which the sons of peasants themselves had access, was evolved. A humane and intensely cultured imperial government was established. Granted that no further development in man's command over nature could be achieved, nothing higher than the Chinese model could be created. In this case it may be misleading to use the word exploitation at all. True the peasant's surplus product was duly removed from him and he was held at or near subsistence while a land-owning and governing class lived in great luxury on his back. But, again upon the major premise that there could be no further advance in technique, this was the best available arrangement even for the peasants themselves. And that is at bottom why peasants have eternally acquiesced in any government which was even tolerably efficient and effective.

More often, of course, the governments of the peasant empires fell far short of the excellence of the Chinese model at its best. (And China itself periodically fell into periods of tribulation.) The still only half free peasants were (and are) hardly more capable than slaves of correcting by revolt the inevitable excesses of their governing classes. Accordingly, more often than not, the peasant was exploited in the full sense of the word, in that he was relieved of his surplus and given no adequate return for it by way of proper government, justice or administration. Moreover, even when the original slave empires had become, partly, peasant empires they seldom lost their predatory character. The acquisition of slaves by conquest still, in many cases, offered their ruling classes glittering prospects. They attacked not only the more primitive societies surrounding them which had not yet crossed the border of civilisation, but also each other. The repetitious history of what might be called the early generation of empires— Sumer, Babylon, Assyria, Egypt, the Hittite Empire, the Indus States— consists essentially in this double process of their expansion and of their collision. Indeed, this process of expansion and collision is the essence of the history of every kind of empire from the earliest to the latest.

If we now transfer our attention from the early empires we bring into view what might be called the second generation of empires in our part of the world—namely, Athens, Macedonia, Persia, Carthage, Rome. (It is no doubt only ignorance and parochialism which prevent me from cataloguing a similar succession of empires in Asia proper, of Asoka and his successors in India, of the anterior and the posterior Han, and many another, in China; and also a similar succession in Central and South America.) When we thus shift our attention from five or six to only two or three millennia ago, we find an immense increase in our information. We possess relatively ample written accounts of the second generation empires. And the first thing which must strike us about them is that they are still essentially slave empires. This is as true of the exquisite miniature empire of Athens as of the three mastodons which devoured her, and each other, Macedon, Carthage and Rome itself.

The representative empire of this second generation was, of course, Rome, and it may be useful to take Rome as the type of the servile empires. Having become an empire, first by means of conquering the neighbouring Italian peoples and then by means of a series of desperate collisions with Macedon and Carthage, Rome set out upon a course of world expansion which lasted for several centuries. The purpose of that expansion was the enslavement, in one form or another, of the con-quered peoples. In part this was done by means of actually transporting them from their own countries and setting them to work as slaves upon the plantations of Italy. This, the most direct form conceivable of human exploitation, differing in no important respect from the Babylonian Captivity of the Israelites, was still, let it be recalled, the basic process of Italian production for several centuries A.D. Indeed, it is usually considered that it was this process which, by completing the ruin of the Italian free peasantry, in the end destroyed the empire.

But, of course, by no means all of the peoples conquered by Rome were sold into slavery and brought to Italy. The Roman Empire was a much more highly developed organism than the slave empires of the first generation. Less direct but more convenient methods of exploitation than direct slavery had been evolved and were also used. It would have been a dull-witted Roman Governor, or for that matter Roman merchant, money-lender or banker, who did not know how to get command of immense quantities of the labour, or rather of the fruits of the labour, of that majority of the population of the provinces which was left in its own lands. From the simple extraction of tribute to every kind of trading at grossly inequitable "terms of trade", to usurious money-lending, enforced by the power of the Imperial Government, the Roman rich appropriated to themselves most of the surplus production of their subject peoples: and even the Roman poor shared in the spoil in the notorious form of bread and circuses.

Rome came, it is true, to the very verge of establishing distinctively capitalist "relations of production", *i.e.*, the characteristic capitalist forms of economic organisation such as freedom of contract, the organisation of large scale production by means of masses of capital collected in one man's hand, or a few men's hands, the merchant partnership, the money-lending enterprise, the bank, the mortgage, and finally wage labour. Yet Rome cannot be said to have crossed that verge and become a capitalist society in the true sense. That was impossible so long as the decisive part in production was taken by slave instead of wage labour.

Moreover it may well have been, precisely, Roman imperialism which decided the issue of whether or not Rome should ever develop the much higher productive relations of wage-earners and capitalists. No doubt in the case of the original generation of empires the level of technique in the broadest sense of that term, including the techniques of transport and exchange as well as the technique of production, never rose high enough to permit of anything but a servile basis of society. But in the two or three thousand years which separated these original empires from the heyday of Rome (a longer period than separates Rome from ourselves) these techniques had improved, very slowly by our standards, but very fast by the standards of any previous period of history. There is little reason to suppose that by, say, the end of the Roman Republic the level of technique in what was by now

OVER

becoming a Roman world was intrinsically too low to have made possible the development of capitalist relations of production, *i.e.*, capitalist employers and free wage-earners. If Roman society could have evolved out of itself these higher capitalist relations of production instead of the slave-owner and the slave, everything would have been different. But there was no chance, because no need, of this while Rome was conquering and enslaving her world. Thus it may well have been an ample supply of servile labour secured by successful imperialism, which blocked the way to further social and technical progress. The issue is, I am aware, a disputed one, but for myself I can never see any reason to doubt that it was essentially slavery which prevented the emergence of something like capitalist relations of production, and with them the industrial revolution, in, say, the second, instead of the sixteenth, seventeenth, eighteenth and nineteenth centuries A.D. After all, most, although no doubt not all, of the basic mathematical and theoretical work necessary for the technical side of the industrial revolution had been done. Hero of Alexandria had actually produced a working steam engine (on the turbine principle) as a toy. Still more significant, perhaps, a vast unified market had been created. Throughout Europe the means of transport both by sea and land had reached a degree of perfection which they were not to regain until the late eighteenth century. (An Imperial candidate could travel from York to Rome in eight days.) It was, surely, above all the dead weight of slavery itself, fed by imperialism, which made the forward leap represented by industrialisation and capitalist relations of production impossible.

No doubt there was another and simpler reason why Roman social development was aborted. And it, too, was a consequence of Roman imperialism. From the beginning of Roman history to the time of Augustus, war was virtually unceasing. There were few pauses even in the wars of conquest over peoples at lower levels of organised power (although in the case of the Hellenic peoples at a higher level of culture). These wars were not particularly damaging. The collisions with rival empires, such as the collision with the declining Macedonians, and the life-and-death struggle with Carthage, were far more serious. More disastrous still were the civil wars between the social classes into which the free upper strata of the Roman population were divided. Finally there were the servile wars against the great slave revolts of the period of Spartacus (when a slave army actually dominated the whole of Italy for two years). And each and all of these types of wars went on simultaneously and interacted upon each other. Thus Roman society only arrived at a period of stability, torn, bleeding, exhausted, mutilated and with its capacity for further social development beaten out of it, by the perpetual warfare involved in the imperialist process.

We may perhaps here catch a glimpse of what appears to be a repetitive tendency in human history. Empires appear to exhaust their possibilities of development at a certain point. They do not always immediately decline, by any means: they may continue to expand by conquest over their neighbours and they may maintain their military power for several centuries. But they cease to be socially creative. Professor Arnold Toynbee has illustrated this hypothesis with a wealth of examples, including a magnificent account of Roman development. He rejects with indignation the main explanation here advanced, namely that the technical-economic-social base characterised by slave labour was the limiting and conditioning factor which forbade further social creation, and that this base could not be changed without the dissolution of Roman society. But if his historical prime mover is different, and indeed opposite, his account of the process itself is similar.

Moreover, long before Professor Toynbee advanced his generalisations on social evolution, historians had pointed out this unmistakable freezing of Roman society at the point at which it threw up its last great institution, namely Caesarism. Mommsen, writing over 100 years ago, saw this, and in so doing showed, as it seems to me, a grasp of the historical process as a whole superior even to that of his giant contemporaries and immediate successors amongst the nineteenth-century historians, such as Macaulay, Ranke, Acton, Prescott or Motley. In a well-known passage, Mommsen states his sense of the inevitability of the work of his hero, Caesar, resulting in nothing better than the Empire. The passage has a startlingly twentieth-century ring about it. It shows, too, that the great classical historians were by no means afraid of the charge, considered so dreadful to-day, that they held "a theory of history", with which they could at any rate attempt to make sense of their subject matter. Mommsen wrote:

"Fate is mightier than genius: Caesar desired to become the restorer of the Civil Commonwealth, and became the founder of the military monarchy which he abhorred; he overthrew the régime of aristocrats and bankers in the state only to put a military régime in their place, and the commonwealth continued as before to be tyrannised over and worked for profit by a privileged minority.

"And yet it is the privilege of the highest natures thus creatively to err. The brilliant attempts of great men to realise the ideal, although they do not reach their aim, form the best treasure of the nations. It was owing to the work of Caesar that the Roman military state did not become a police state till after the lapse of several centuries."

The whole issue of the role of individual genius at the turning-points of history is raised by Mommsen. And the implied suggestion (with which Mommsen's contemporary Marx would probably have agreed) that the hero, while he cannot alter the broad lines of development can, within limits wide enough to be significant, effect the way in which that development takes place, is surely worthy of consideration. In any case Mommsen agrees that Roman technical, economic, social and political development was frozen at approximately the level reached at the establishment of the empire. I suggest that this was basically because servile society had exhausted its possibilities.

And with that exhaustion came in due course, the inevitable decline. Late Roman history has a sombre fascination for twentieth-century readers, for we see, worked out in the most exhaustive details, the inevitability of ill-fortune for an empire which cannot recast the basic relations of production upon which it rests. Everything is tried: everything happens, and nothing is accomplished or even changed. The best men, as well as the worst, accede to supreme power. At the end of a line of emperors, each far above the average in both ability and enlightenment, Marcus Aurelius, the last Antonine, ascends the Imperial throne. With him the philosopher is at last King—and King of the world at that. And he can do nothing. He is reduced to recording in his *pensée* what is surely the most profoundly, if calmly, pessimistic, remark ever made by a reflective ruler:

"Any man of forty who is endowed with moderate intelligence has seen—in the light of the uniformity of Nature—the entire Past and Future" (*Meditations*, Book IX, Chapter 2, quoted by Professor Toynbee in Volume X, p. 126, of *The Study of History*).

For his own day, Marcus' glacial pessimism was irrefutable. He had the insight to see that for such a society as his the doctrine of the eternal return of all things was fundamentally true. For Rome was irretrievably committed to basing her economy upon servile labour: therefore she could not advance a step beyond those crude techniques which such labour could alone employ. Such techniques could in turn sustain nothing higher than the servile relationship of production. There seemed to be no way out of this closed circle of social cause and effect. Nothing, it seemed, could ever happen, nothing but the meaningless round of the imperial system. But Marcus forgot the other side of the picture. He was right that the emergence of anything good, anything constructive, anything hopeful, was inconceivable for his empire. Nevertheless the human race *could*, and did, emerge from the imperial cul-de-sac. It could emerge by dissolving the imperial society's master institution, slavery. And the institution of slavery began in fact to be dissolved: it began to be dissolved partly because slave labour was ceasing to pay amidst the universal decay, partly because of the Christian revolt against it, and partly because the empire's servile productive system had produced a lack of the will and means to resist the barbarians with their far less advanced, but for that very reason, largely pre-servile, social organism.

Humanity could, and did, emerge from the impasse of the last great servile empire, but only at the cost of shattering civilisation as a whole: at the cost of that "funeral of the world", as a still later Roman, Sidonius Apollinaris, called the events of the fifth century, resulting in the dissolution of the Western Empire. This Gallo-Roman aristocrat made the mistake of almost all members of possessing classes at the end of their tether. He identified his own privileges, and the particular civilisation built upon them, with civilisation itself. The dissolution of Roman society was not the funeral of the world: it was merely the funeral of *his* world. The events which he saw around him with such horror were also the agonising birth-pangs, prolonged over 1,000 years, of that new world in which we live. Moreover the modern world emerged, after the interregnum of the dark ages, not indeed without exploitation and empire, but without, or nearly without, slavery. Apparently 1,000 years of preliminary social regression were the allotted price which humanity had to pay for that advance. During the first few centuries of the Christian era the institution of slavery had become a nightmarish obstacle to the further development of human society. What had originally been, as Engels had the hardihood to point out, not only an inevitable but a relatively progressive institution, compared to what had preceded it, had become a fetter on further advance, which had, even at the cost of the destruction of existing civilisation, to be struck off. The servile empires were at length dissolved and after a long interval a new kind of civilisation, based upon higher techniques came into existence. And with the new social relations built upon these new techniques, there appeared also new kinds of empires.

In the world as a whole there was no interval between the servile empires of antiquity and those mercantile empires of which we chose the empire of the East India Company in Bengal as our example. "The Dark Ages" are largely an optical illusion of Western parochialism. Civilisation did indeed perish in Western Europe when Rome crashed. But to call Rome the last great servile empire is still to think in local terms. Once we think in terms of world history we see that a number of empires of the old kind, servile, peasant or, for the most part, mixed, continued to exist elsewhere. For example, the Eastern Roman Empire itself survived with great success at Byzantium. The Arab Empire of the Bagdad Caliphate not only appeared, but came very near to subjugating Western Europe. Later the Turkish Empire succeeded to the heritage of both of these. And in Asia proper the Gupta Empire persisted for some time in India, while in China a unified empire, under successive dynasties, continued without decisive interruption. However, none of these empires (so far as I know) represented any significant departure from the original type which we have attempted to define. Some may have depended to a greater extent upon the labour of semi-bound, but in any case effectively exploited, peasantry, and to a lesser extent upon the labour of outright slaves, than others. But that and a varying degree of social efficiency and culture was about the extent of the difference between them.

It was in Western Europe, just because the old imperial structures had there been destroyed, that a series of empires, to begin with much smaller and less important, but of a distinguishably different type, began to arise. The first of these empires of a new kind to attract our attention should clearly be Venice. The Venetian empire, while it never grew to any great size, is interesting in several ways. In the first place it almost spans the gap of the dark ages; for it was founded by refugees from the crash of the Italian provinces of Rome. More important for our purposes it was from the outset essentially a *mercantile* empire. The wealth, *i.e.*, the surplus drawn from other men's labour, on which the governing class (and to some extent its population as a whole) lived was drawn, not, as always hitherto, from the labour of more or less unfree peasants or slaves, but from maritime trading and plundering expeditions carried on with neighbouring peoples.[1] And

[1] No doubt this mercantile element was present in the Athenian Empire. Nevertheless, slavery was its real basis.

the subjugation of these neighbouring peoples by the Venetians arose rather from a determination to trade with them on more and more advantageous terms (and to prevent other people from trading with them at all and so competing with the Venetians) than from a determination to enslave them (or reduce them to a readily exploitable peasantry) and live off their directly exploited labour.

This new mercantile, maritime, and relatively indirect form of the exploitation of other men's labour was the characteristic basis of the new group of empires which arose in Europe between the fall of Rome and the rise of capitalism proper—between, say, A.D. 600 and 1800. Naturally the distinction between these new-type empires and the original generation of empires based on servile labour is not clear cut. The Venetians had slaves, chiefly domestic slaves: they had no moral scruples about the matter. But they did not themselves live off slave labour. They did, however, trade in slaves on a great scale. Indeed they made themselves slave procurers for the still flourishing servile empires to the east of them, by handling the traffic in the human cattle of the Slavonic tribes of Central Europe.[1] This intermediate position, in which an empire is not itself based upon slave labour, but in which it trades extensively in slaves, is, as we shall see, typical of this whole third generation of immediately pre-capitalist empires.

Venice was intermediate in another sense also. She was almost wholly mercantile; but she was by no means wholly maritime. She depended heavily, that is to say, upon the overland caravan routes across Asia. Moreover her own maritime commerce was Mediterranean not oceanic, local not world-wide. Nevertheless, she was definitely a mercantile empire. The relations of production on which she basically depended, that is to say, were not those of the slave-owner and the slave, but of the merchant, his suppliers, his customers and his employees. And, sure enough, the political system, the ideas, the art, the "way of life", which grew up (so gorgeously in the Venetian instance) on this basis were very different from anything which did, or could, grow up upon the servile basis. Again the relationship of Venice to the peoples whom she conquered does not seem to have been quite so nakedly exploitative as that of the servile empires. In a

---

[1] The derivation of the word "Slav" from the word "slave" is a terminological point which seems worthy of the attention of twentieth-century statesmen. If for several centuries you treat one of the great races of Europe as a slave-reservoir, to be drawn on for the purposes of the slave trade, and do so to the extent that you simply call them slaves, *tout court*, you must not be surprised if, when that race at length achieves its independence, it proves awkward.

THE END OF EMPIRE

word, we have now moved to a higher level of social development—although still at an early stage. Plundering, warring, exploitative, utterly without scruple as the mercantile empires were, they yet represented a new and higher stage of the development of society.

As a second instance of a mercantile empire we may briefly consider Portugal. As a society Portugal was much less brilliant than Venice. But her empire marked, in some respects, a higher point in development. It was essentially maritime; indeed it was oceanic and world-wide; for her colonies were scattered over three continents, Asia, Africa and South America. Finally, it was the Portuguese who made the technical invention which rendered possible such oceanic and world-wide empires as this: they invented the ocean-going ship. Professor Toynbee has an illuminating passage emphasising the epoch-making importance of the conquest, by Prince Henry the Navigator, and his contemporary Portuguese shipwrights, of the technique of trans-oceanic mobility.

"The Portuguese achievement of learning how to navigate the ocean was, of course, not merely a decisive event in an encounter between the West and the Islamic World; it was an epoch-making event in human history, because it made man master of a medium of communication that was sufficiently conducive, and near enough to being ubiquitous, to knit the entire habitable surface of the planet together into a home for an oecumenical society embracing the whole of mankind. At the time of writing in the first century of a post modern age of Western history, the social unification of the world which had been brought about by the Portuguese invention of an ocean-faring sailing-ship had found new instruments in the aeroplane and the broadcasting station; but however high the latter day conquests of the ether and the air might rank in the honours' list of scientific inventions, it was manifest that they could not compare with the conquest of the Ocean in point of social importance. As means to the social end of knitting the whole of Mankind into a single society, aerial navigation and wireless communication merely served to draw closer a world-encompassing net which Man's conquest of the Ocean had long since flung round the globe. The decisive step in the unification of the world had been the invention of the type of ocean going sailing vessel that came to be known as the ship *par excellence*, and Henry the Navigator and his companions had not only required no successors; they had also no predecessors; for the enduring unification of the whole surface of

the globe, which was the fruit of their work, was a social achievement whose consequences in its own sphere differed in a degree that
virtually amounted to a difference in kind from the effects of the
fitful inter-communication between the civilisations of the old
world that had resulted in earlier ages from the achievements of
Minoan pioneers in the navigation of inland seas and of Nomad
pioneers in the training of horses."

17th cent.

Professor Toynbee is here emphasising the long-range importance
of the invention of the ship in making technically possible a single
world-wide society of all mankind: a possibility which is still by no
means an achievement.[1] But the immediate effect of the invention of
ocean-going ships, equipped with the mariner's compass, full rigged,
decked and fitted with cannon capable of firing a broadside, was more
limited. What it immediately made possible was a series of oceanic,
scattered, trading, plundering empires founded upon mercantile relations of production. Portugal, with her primacy in India and her
conquest of Brazil, the heart of the South American continent, founded
the first of such merchant empires on the oceanic scale. Holland
followed her, over a century afterwards, as soon as she became an
independent society, building an empire of essentially the same type.
But, before the Dutch, and almost contemporary with the rise of the
Portuguese Empire, there had arisen a much greater empire, which
fits but partially into the category of the mercantile empires. The
greatest of this generation of empires, until the British example three
centuries later, was the empire of Spain. And the Spaniards were,
surely, the most unmercantile people that ever lived. They had
employed Columbus, and they had produced the circumnavigators
Magellan and Amerigo. But then they produced the Conquistadors.
Under the military, anti-mercantile leadership of Cortez and Pisarro
the world seemed to be returning, around A.D. 1500, to the ancient

[1] It is interesting to see Professor Toynbee, the great contemporary expositor of
historical idealism, who in principle rejects historical materialism with repugnance, in
practice recognising that the possibility of human solidarity, to which he attaches the
utmost importance (see also his essay in *Civilisation on Trial*), arose out of a technical
invention, that of the ship. Indeed, like many a convert, and especially an unconscious
convert, he seems to me to oversimplify the matter. Like so many other people, including
many Marxists, he leaves out the indispensable intermediate links through which the
technical development in question is associated (partly as cause and partly as effect) with
the general transformation of society. The whole ganglion of Renaissance inventions, of
which the ship was only one, the compass, printing, gunpowder, etc., were indissolubly
connected with the new relations of production, the new social order, the new kind of
state, the new versions of the dominant religion, the new art, and the new ways of
thought. It took all these things, not just the ship, to prepare that unification of the world
which now at length looms before us as an indispensable objective.

pattern of empires of direct conquest and plunder, based upon servile labour. True the Spaniards did not actually revert to the Hellenic model and import millions of American slaves into Spain to dispossess the Spanish peasants and create latifundia for the Hidalgos. But this was only because they set their conquered slaves to work in the mines of the new world. And then they transported the resultant surplus, in the traditional form of actual gold and silver, back to Spain in their treasure fleets. With that surplus they maintained armies of invincible pikemen who nearly aborted the further development of Europe. Finally the Spaniards, when the supply of servile labour proved insufficient, organised a massive slave trade from Africa to their American mines and plantations. (It was, of course, in the remarkable role of high-jackers on these two fabulous Spanish trades, the Eastward movement of treasure and the Westward movement of slaves, that the British first appeared upon the imperial stage.)[1]

Thus there was little enough that was truly commercial or mercantile about the Spanish Empire. But yet this major Spanish exception may serve to illustrate the rule that the empires of the immediately pre-capitalist epoch were, typically at least, mercantile empires/For it is usually conceded that it was precisely the unmercantile character of the Spanish Empire which, in the conditions of the sixteenth and seventeenth centuries, was its, and Spain's undoing. It was the inability of Spain to emerge from the quixotry of semi-feudal relations of production, and a semi-feudal political, social and religious superstructure, in an age which had elsewhere established mercantile relations, and their appropriate superstructures, which made Spain and her empire, almost from first to last, a gigantic anachronism. Spanish society was too anachronistic to be able to absorb the torrent of surplus value which poured in upon it from the subjugations of the Conquistadors. The

---

[1] I am disregarding the vigorous feudal imperialism of mediaeval England in the Hundred Years' War and before. For this was more the personal imperialism of the Plantagenets and their Baronage, who were, after all, as much overlords of Western France as of England: the West European national states were not sufficiently articulated and delimited to launch out on a genuinely nation-based imperialism. It was in the Middle Ages also that England began that long drawn out piece of parochial imperialism, within the British Isles, the subjugation of Ireland. But here again this was an essentially feudal operation by which native chieftains were displaced by English rent-collectors. True, the occupation went on right into the twentieth century and in closing this chapter of imperialism we showed none of that flexibility and statesmanship for which I have made such high claims in respect of the more distant parts of the British Empire. On the contrary the British behaved in Ireland from first to last no better than most of the ordinary run-of-the-mill imperialists of history. Therefore, if some readers think that the real reason why I have not used the British occupation of Ireland as one of my examples of imperialism, has less to do with the feudal parochialism of the matter than with the tragic, dreary, disgraceful folly of British conduct in Ireland over the centuries—well they may be perfectly right.

Spanish ruling class literally did not know what to do with the money, except to terrorise the rest of Europe with it. In the event that part of the tribute which did in the end get used productively (*i.e.*, to afford capital for the next stages of development) was used, in the main, by far more mercantile societies such as England and by Spain's own rebellious Dutch provinces. For these small but up-and-coming societies managed, either by interception or by some more indirect means, to syphon off some of the loot from the sterile, because anti-mercantile, Spaniards.

It is strange that the French, who became in the seventeenth century the best organised, most unified and most populous nation in Europe, and who by no means lacked the commercial spirit, did not succeed in creating an oceanic, world-wide mercantile empire. The stock explanation seems to be the true one. Under the inspiration of Colbert the French at the height of their power in the seventeenth century nearly turned towards the formation of a mercantile empire. But in the end they were too dominated with the older conception of simply conquering their next-door neighbours in Europe. When, by the eighteenth century, they had been beaten back from this path it proved just too late. The French monarchial system was just too exhausted to bring off the acquisition of major trans-oceanic possessions. But it was not for the want of trying. In the case of both India and North America, the two outstanding prizes available to the eighteenth-century imperialists, the French came within an ace of beating the British to it. And in the case of North America, although they lost their own possessions, their ding-dong struggle with Britain resulted in the main prize going to neither, but to the North American colonists, who were thereby enabled to found what was consciously intended to be the first post-imperial society.

As the early chapters of this volume have attempted to describe, at the end of the day it was the British, principally through the agency of the East India Company, who set up the outstanding example of a mercantile empire. Thus it can hardly be doubted that societies using newly accumulating capital resources, essentially for the long distance exchange of goods, rather than for industrialisation (for which the technique did not yet exist), have always hitherto been led into an attempt to impose their rule over the peoples with whom they traded.

Moreover, in the process of attempting to do this they have invariably become involved in bloody collisions with each other. It would be to oversimplify matters quite unrealistically, however, to suggest that the empires of merchant capital were consciously or exclusively established for these purposes. The actual acts of conquest were often undertaken simply because the would-be traders found no other way of trading at all than by establishing their own rule over the primitive, chaotic or decadent societies with which they were determined to do business. Of course they might simply have refrained from trading. But that they would not do, for they had before them the vision of an enrichment such as the world had not known since the fabulous enrichments of the senators and equities of ancient Rome. They did not, usually or particularly, want to conquer, if they could obtain their profits without conquest. But obtain those profits they would, or die in the attempt, as so many of them did. At this stage of development the "auri sacra fames", the fatal ravening for gold (as the embodiment of surplus labour) was certainly the mainspring of aggression.

Finally there have been the empires of fully developed capitalism, the characteristics and dynamics of which we discussed in Chapters V to VIII. We saw that societies of this kind develop, unless extremely vigorous steps are taken to modify them, a distribution of income and other characteristics which leave their directing classes little choice but to attempt the conquest, colonisation and exploitation of as much of the world as they can get hold of. If, however, they can be modified, as some of them have been during the past twenty-five years (Lenin foresaw this as a theoretical possibility, although a practical impossibility, see p. 110, above), they become capable of living, and trading, quite successfully, with countries which they make no attempt to conquer. The proof of this is that highly developed capitalist societies such as Britain have in the last fourteen years relinquished by far the greater part of their empires while at the same time actually raising the standard of life of their populations to a marked degree.

Moreover, we saw that there is mounting evidence of the sheer unprofitableness of empires in present-day conditions. The question inevitably presents itself of whether we may be entering a new stage in the development of advanced societies in which empire will be unnecessary to them. Even if this is so, it gives us no guarantee that they will in fact abstain from their old imperial courses. For conquest and aggression may suit only too well one side at least of human nature as it has had to evolve. But the internal modifications which they are undergoing, if they are carried far enough, may at least enable them to abstain from empire if they will.[1]

[1] I am aware that to suggest there may be something useful to be learnt from history; that history may be more than an unrelated jumble of facts and dates; that there may be connections between events and so some pattern or meaning which it may be worth while to try to grasp, is to incur the full fury of the great majority of professional historians, and in particular of the now dominant "anti-historicist" school of thought.

It may be useful to instance in this connection the views of the father—and in my opinion the best—of the anti-historicists, Professor Karl Popper. In his well known work *The Open Society* (1945), Professor Popper tells us that "the social engineer", of whom he approves, "does not ask any questions about historical tendencies" (op. cit., Vol. I, p. 17). And he goes on to contrast this "engineering" attitude to social institutions to the "historicist" attitude, of which he strongly disapproves. "The historicist", he writes, "is inclined to look upon social institutions mainly from the point of view of their history, *i.e.*, their origins, their development, and their present and future significance" (p. 18). Not so the admirable social engineer who "will not worry much about such things". For an example of a social institution, Professor Popper instances "a police force". The historicists, he continues, would try to determine whether a police force should be described as "an instrument for the protection of freedom and security" or "as an instrument of class rule and oppression". But the social engineer will simply make of the police force what he wants. This attitude is certainly well described by Professor Popper as an "engineering" attitude. It is indeed almost exactly the attitude of that great engineer Mr Henry Ford, when he said that history was bunk. If the "origins, development and present and future significance" of social institutions do not matter, then clearly to study history is a pure waste of time.

Nevertheless, I doubt if even engineers would get on very well if they adopted the anti-historicist position in this extreme form. For example, Professor Popper's engineer, lifting the bonnet of a motor car, might notice a convoluted protuberance from the cylinder head which he knew was called the carburettor. He would conclude that the fact that this protuberance had originated, after many experiments and false starts, as on the whole the best way of vaporising the petrol by passing it through a fine jet, was all historicist nonsense. What he wanted to do was to make the motor car go faster, so why not vastly increase the size of the jets so as to get more petrol into the cylinders? Such an engineer might be unpleasantly surprised to find that the result of his efforts to make the carburettor what he wanted, was to prevent the motor car from going at all.

I am bound to admit that I cling to the old-fashioned view, which Professor Popper and his supporters denounce as "reactionary and mystical", that if you want to change and improve something, it is not a bad idea, first of all, to study how it originated, how it developed and what is its present and future significance—in a word, its history. It is only too true that in the case of social institutions, this is a very difficult thing to do—of a different order of difficulty from the study of natural phenomena. That is why "social engineering" is so much more difficult than engineering.

It is only fair to say that Professor Popper does not dream of following his own preposterous advice. On the contrary, throughout the two volumes of *The Open Society* he uses historical evidence for all it is worth. In fact it is precisely by setting Plato, Aristotle and Hegel in their historical settings that he is able to produce his devastating criticism of their doctrines, and his still more devastating attack upon the failure of subsequent commentators, generation by generation, to criticise them. Of course it is true that the systems of all these oracular gentlemen are now of historical interest only. When Professor Popper comes to Marx, however, he is in a difficulty. In general he treats Marx with admirable fairness and with far greater comprehension than is normal. Nevertheless, he unhesitatingly writes him off as "a historicist" in the derogatory sense of a thinker who *predicts* that a certain development is the fixed destiny of humanity, without anyone having to do anything about it. But is it really possible to say this of a man whose two basic remarks on the issue were: "Hitherto philosophers have interpreted the world in various ways: the thing is to change it", and "men make their own history, but not out of the whole cloth". In other words, Marx had got through to the common-sense view that we can control our own future, but not just as we please: that we are limited by the historical raw material of already established social institutions on which we must work: that it is in fact only in so far as we really grasp the "origins, development and present and future significance" of these institutions that we can successfully mould them to our will. (This is not to say that Marx, and still more his followers, always live up to this attitude. It is quite true that they sometimes degenerate into destiny-mongers. After all Marx, like so many of the rest of us, had to overcome his education.)

Professor Popper is severe, as can be imagined, on contemporary "historicists" such as Professor Arnold Toynbee—though here too he is fair compared at least to the pack of academic historians who yap at Professor Toynbee's heels. And it is true that the earlier volumes of *The Study of History* (which were alone available to Professor Popper) can be read as an essay in despair, mitigated only by the consolations of religion. But now that we have the whole work it is clear that Professor Toynbee is at heart a rather sanguine Englishman who believes that humanity can win through (to some instinctively glimpsed goal) if only it pulls its moral and intellectual socks up. Professor Popper has no difficulty in catching out Professor Toynbee in myth-making. Professor Toynbee has so lush an historical imagination that one feels that he makes ten new myths, theories, historical generalisations, laws of development—call them what you will—every day before breakfast. But after all, what is a myth but an embryo scientific hypothesis? The Homeric Greeks explained the thunder as the voice of Zeus. We have hypotheses which we prefer as more adequately explaining the observed phenomena. But the Homeric hypothesis was a first attempt and a lot better than nothing. Social science is still at a very early stage of development. Why sneer and jeer at the men who are trying to work out some rough hypotheses to explain the apparent chaos of social phenomena?

The fact is that most present-day British professional historians are convinced that no historical studies are legitimate which go beyond tracing the activities of the more obscure place-men of King George III's parliaments. Curiously enough, they have taken as their watchword the opinion of Hegel, the most extreme of all the historicists, that men learn only from history that men learn nothing from history. They assure us that history has no meaning whatever. Very well then, we will shut up their books and never, never open them again.

INDEX

India, Republic of—*cont.*
within the Commonwealth, 253-4
Indirect rule, Russian and Chinese, 302-3
Indo-China: acquired by France, 79; relinquished by France, 141, 142, 193
Indonesia, Dutch imperialism in, 31
Indus States, 328
Industrial technique, subject to fixation, 210
Iraq, 141, 154, 158, 162; its civilisation in mediaeval times, 167; decline of population, 167; revenues and expenditures of the Development Board, 168-9; flood control, 168; lot of the *fellah*, 169-70; problem of land tenure, 170-1; Rashid Ali's revolt, 196
Ireland, Republic of, and the Sterling Area, 181, 270
Israel, 172-4

James II, 14-15
Japan: and the European problem, 71; first acquisition of colonies, 79; increase of power after first World War, 125; war with China over Korea, 127; invades Manchuria, 129; invades China, 129-30; a temporary major empire between two World Wars, 137
Jehan, Shah, 58
Jordan, 154, 175

Kenya, 140; race problem, 255; Mau Mau rebellion, 256
Keynes, Lord, 57, 212*n*. *General Theory*, 99, 103, 104
Kipling, Rudyard, 74
Kirkpatrick, Colonel, 55
Kitchener, Lord, 86
Korea: Sino-Japanese war over, 127
Kuwait, 158, 162, 270

Labour Party: anti-imperialist tradition in, 215; *Industry and Society*, 235

Lancashire, mill-owners' trade with India, 72
Laski, H. J., 113
Latin America: fails to benefit from liberation from Spain, 202; American power predominant in, 282
Lawrence, T. E., 172
Lenin, analysis of imperialism, 99, 102, 103*ff.*, 190; concept of Soviet democracy, 208
Liberal imperialists, 133
Liberal Party, anti-imperialist tradition in, 72-3, 215
Lloyd George, D., 134, 229-30
Lok Sabba. *See* India, Republic of
Luce, Henry, 285

Macartney, Lord, 71
Macedonia, 328-30
Macmillan, Harold, 227
Madagascar, 141, 142
Magellan, 337
Magreb, the, 172
Malaya, 141, and the Sterling Area, 181, 185, 186, 270; communism in, 256
Malta, 255
Malvern, Lord, 301
Manchuria: acquired by China, 129; invaded by Japan, 129
Marcus Aurelius, 332-3
Marshall Plan, 123, 315-16
Marx, Karl, 332; on British India, 48-51, 52, 78; diagram of capitalism, 104; on lack of a fatherland for the proletarian, 287; on evolution of human society, 322-3
Mau Mau rebellion, 256, 258
Menzies, R. G., 262
Military technique, subject to fixation, 210-12
Mill, James, quoted, 43, 72
Mill, John Stuart, 72
Milner, Lord, 74, 81; key figure in the annexation of S. Africa, 91; imports Chinese indentured labourers, 92; vision of empire, 93-6
Mir Jaffier, Nawob of Bengal, 26-8, 29, 33-4, 39

Strachey, Sir John, 55, 59
Strachey, Sir Richard, 55, 56, 57n., 59
Sudan. *See* Nile Valley
Suez Canal Zone, 141; Suez crisis, 173, 174, 205, 226
Sumer, 328
Sun Yat-sen, 127
Surajah Dowlah, 19-21, 24-6, 28, 30, 36, 38n.
Surman, John, 16
Sweden: strength of its army, 227; the welfare ideal in, 230-1
Syria, 154

Taiping revolt, 127
Taj Mahal, 58
Tanganyika, 140
Tientsin, Treaty of, 126
Tito, Marshal, 302
Toynbee, Arnold (the elder), 95
Toynbee, Professor A. J.: on nations being subject to fixation, 205-7, 210; on Roman development, 331; on technique of trans-oceanic mobility, 336-7; Professor Popper's strictures on, 341n.
Trans-oceanic mobility, Portuguese achievement of, 336-7
Transvaal. *See* South Africa
Trotsky, Leon, 218
Tunisia, 141, 142, 213, 300
Turkish Empire, 334

Uganda, 140, 183, 185
Unearned income, 232-6
Uneven development, Lenin's law of, 105
United Kingdom: divestment of colonial possessions since 1945, 140-1; worth of empire, in terms of trade, 146ff.; terms of trade, 149-53; and oil (*see* Oil); and the Sterling Area, 181-5; alleged to be exploiting her former colonies, 195-8; effects of empire upon national psychology, 204-12; danger of fixation upon imperial past, 212-16; in danger of Americanisation, 219; need for adequate

defence, 226-7; relations with the U.S.A., 227-9; and the welfare ideal, 228-30; unearned incomes in, 232-6; anomalies of educational system, 236-8; need for perfection of democratic political institutions, 238-9; inadequate expenditure on education, 240-1; balance of the educational curriculum, 241-3; other national objectives, 243-4; need to help undeveloped world, 244-7
United States: acquires Cuba, Puerto Rico, Philippines, 80; agricultural cartel in, 110; causes of its fitful imperialism, 119-21, 134; former parts of Japanese Empire under her influence, 139; ideal of personal enrichment, 219-26; median family income, 220; expenditure on advertising, 221-2; stinting of public services, 223; defence expenditure, 223-5; possibility of her economic development leading to imperialism, 276-8; disproportionate magnitude of capitalism in, 278-82; anti-imperialist tradition in, 282-3; first phase of imperialism, 283-4; her economy *c.* 1900 not ready for empire, 284; conquest of the homeland, 284; internal development, 284-5; likelihood of cloaked imperialist propaganda, 285-6; obstacles to growth of a major imperialism, 286-91
U.S.S.R. *See* Russia

Venice, and her empire, 334-5

Walker, Patrick Gordon, *Policy for the Commonwealth*, 251-2
Washington Conference (1922), 128
Watson, Admiral, 24, 26
Welfare ideal, 229-31
Wellesley, Marquis, 47
West Africa, 141